Architectures
of Russian
Identity
1500 to the Present

The papers in this volume grew out of a conference sponsored by the Joint Committee on the Soviet Union and Its Successor States of the Social Science Research Council and the American Council of Learned Societies.

Architectures of Russian Identity

1500 to the Present

Edited by

JAMES CRACRAFT
AND DANIEL ROWLAND

Cornell University Press

Ithaca and London

The publisher gratefully acknowledges the assistance
of the Social Science Research Council (SSRC) in the
publication of this book.

First published 2003 by Cornell University Press
First printing, Cornell Paperbacks, 2003

Printed in the United States of America

Library of Congress Cataloging-in-Publication Data

Architectures of Russian identity : 1500 to present / edited by
James Cracraft and Daniel Rowland.
    p. cm.
Includes bibliographical references and index.
    ISBN 0-8014-4106-4 (cloth : alk. paper) — ISBN 0-8014-8828-1 (pbk. :
alk. paper)
    1. Architecture—Russia (Federation) 2. Architecture, Modern.   I.
Carcraft, James.   II. Rowland, Daniel B. (Daniel Bruce), 1941–
NA1184.A73 2003
720'.947—dc21   2002154780

Contents

Preface

Architecture has been called "music in space," a "frozen music, as it were." In organizing this volume and the conference that preceded it, we've liked this metaphor for its suggestion that architecture, too, finds expression in an almost infinite variety of forms. Indeed, both it and the term "Russian" are used rather flexibly in the essays that follow, the latter to evoke first of all the polity known successively as the Muscovite tsardom, the Russian Empire, the Soviet Union, and, since 1991, the Russian Federation. We recognize that liberties are thus being taken but trust that, given our overall program, readers will not be unduly dismayed. In ethno-national terms, certainly, Russia has always included among its subjects or citizens, or as members of its elites, numerous non-Russians; and traditionally, of course, perhaps since the Renaissance, architects and art scholars have denied the status of architecture to constructions that did not clearly meet certain aesthetic or functional criteria. We recognize the relative validity of these claims, but in pursuing our purposes have not felt bound by them. Nor have we limited our construal of identity to static political or national definitions, preferring instead to be responsive to the wide array of group assertions—imperial, national, class, dynastic, religious, regional, ideological— that we've found in our research. The title of this book is meant to suggest a plurality of variations on a simple central theme.

The authors of these essays, scholars from a variety of disciplines working at various stages in their careers, are united by their conviction that architecture broadly understood can serve not only as the principal subject of research but also as an effective means of studying other important aspects of the political, social, cultural, indeed geographic entity known as Russia—still, as it has been since the seventeenth century, by far the largest country in the world. They are in this respect pioneers in the vast field of Russian studies, as the Russian built environment has been the province until very recently of architectural history of the most narrowly traditional kind. Excited by advances in scholarship pertaining to other parts of the world, by Russia's new openness to students, by developments in architecture itself, they are demonstrating in their work new ways of apprehending the multiplicity of collective identities that was and is Russia.

We are very grateful to the Social Science Research Council of New York for sponsoring a conference that brought together twenty-five scholars from the United States, Europe, and Russia, and to the Humanities Institute and the Office of the Vice Chancellor for Academic Affairs at the University of Illinois at Chicago for providing supplementary funding. Fourteen of the papers read and discussed at the conference, variously revised, have been included in this volume, and we are grateful again to the SSRC for a subvention that helped make publication possible. We are also very much indebted, for their critical encouragement, to three scholars who graciously consented to attend the conference and to comment on its proceedings from the perspective of their different geographic areas and more advanced historiographies: Randolph Starn and Thomas Metcalf of the Department of History at the University of California, Berkeley; and Robert Bruegmann of the Department of Art History, UIC. Their comments and advice helped to point our efforts in more salutary directions—to elevate our noise to something more like music.

JAMES CRACRAFT
University of Illinois,
Chicago

DANIEL ROWLAND
University of Kentucky,
Lexington

Architectures

of Russian

Identity

1500 to the Present

Introduction

James Cracraft and Daniel Rowland

In a special issue of *The Journal of Interdisciplinary History* devoted to questions of "art and meaning" in history, Theodore Rabb, a historian, and Jonathan Brown, an art historian, observed cautiously: "It may be that historians and art historians will forever maintain distinct sets of priorities when they examine works of art." The sentiment was forcefully reiterated by the late Francis Haskell, another prominent art historian: "Fruitful cooperation between the historian and the art historian can be based only on a full recognition of the necessary differences between their approaches."[1] These admonitions from on high might usefully be borne in mind at the outset of a volume that proposes, in effect, to ignore them.

In the years since these admonitions were published, specialists of all kinds have continued to blur conventional disciplinary divisions and the audience, appreciative at least in principle of interdisciplinary scholarship, has grown correspondingly. In particular, projects treating buildings and the built environment less as objects of critical analysis and more as forms of historical evidence—projects that attempt to bridge the boundaries between history and architectural history—continue to appear. At the same time, such progress as has been made in this direction seems to have enhanced awareness of the "distinct sets of priorities" and "necessary differences" of approach maintained by historians and architectural historians as they go about their business. Indeed, a heightened appreciation of both risks and benefits now seems to prevail. Historians who ignore the often compelling evidence left by past builders and their patrons—actual physical remains as well as scholarly reconstructions, individual buildings as well as details or ensembles of buildings, contemporary depictions including photographs as well as other graphic evidence, books and treatises on architecture, architectural contracts and codes, correspondence and personal papers, and so on—risk drastically impoverishing their own fields of inquiry; critics can with justice note the missing architectural dimension. Equally, architectural historians who concern themselves largely if not exclusively with matters of style, ignoring larger questions of context and the likely constitutive relations between context and style, run the same danger. The risk in either case seems especially great in view of the ever-improving means for storing, retrieving, and reproducing visual as well as verbal or quantitative data. Yet many working historians, like many working architectural historians, appear to remain wary of the enterprise.

The challenge confronting scholars who would use the built environment as an important source for studying wider political, social, economic, and cultural trends may be essentially linguistic or rhetorical: a better framing of the terms of the enterprise may be needed along with clearer statements of what to expect. Perhaps the main task facing us now is to elicit from existing discourses a common scholarly language, a way to communicate common or transcendent interests and concerns when discussing architecture. Such a language must be readily intelligible to everyone wishing to take part in a mutually if variously beneficial conversation that necessarily respects the often differing starting points and diverse destinations of the participants.

This volume attempts to provide such exchanges in the Russian field. We are not attempting to resolve the disciplinary issues raised earlier; still less do we claim to exhaust the richness of our themes. We do hope that the essays below will demonstrate the remarkable fertility of the theme of architecture, broadly defined, for a variety of disciplines dealing with Russia and its surrounding territories in their various political configurations over some five centuries. We also hope that students of architectural history and related fields who specialize in other cultures and civilizations will find these essays both provocative and useful. Our contributors themselves come from many disciplines, including history and art and architectural history as well as linguistics, literary studies, geography, and political science. And from their essays a number of common themes arise. It is to several of these that we now turn.

Given the power of the Russian state (and the statist historiography that has dominated much of the scholarship about Russia), one such theme is the importance of architecture with its dominance of the visual landscape in expanding and defending the power of the state itself. In the context of a largely illiterate population, Russian rulers have used architecture not only to project state power but also to convey a variety of messages about themselves and the state that they represented. Boris Godunov's fortresses, in Daniel Rowland's account, projected the power of his state into the farthest reaches of the realm, simultaneously providing protection for trade and agriculture. At the same time, his religious architecture conveyed, according to the sophistication of the viewer, either the simple message of the tsar's piety or a more complex analogy of Moscow and Jerusalem. This analogy had already been richly elaborated on the royal pew of Ivan the Terrible, as carefully interpreted for us by Michael Flier.

Much later, the emperors Alexander III and Nicholas II chose church architecture to proclaim a new image of the dynasty, one connected to imagined roots in the Russian past, to a renewed connection with Jerusalem rather than Rome. Their churches represented a calculated "act of repentance for Western culture," as Richard Wortman writes. For Ivan IV and Godunov as well as the last two Romanovs, claims about an imagined religious past made chiefly through church architecture and furnishings were used to inspire national cohesion and to justify political control in the present and future.

The Romanov (like the Godunov) churches were built in various locations around the Empire to assert political and religious domination. This domination was expressed both by the height of the new buildings and by the commanding locations chosen for them. For the Romanovs, this form of architecture was particularly favored in the western border regions to express unmistakably the Russian (rather than Western European) dominance of these regions. Yet, in the preceding decades, the same Russian state used specifically classical, rather than traditional Russian, architectural forms to express its colonial control over Tashkent, signaling a civilizing mission based on all-European values. The "Russo-Byzantine" Cathedral of the Transfiguration in Tashkent, completed in 1888, stressed by contrast traditional Russian culture and Orthodoxy, a message clearly manifested in an annual procession with icons, crosses, and liturgical banners which began at the cathedral and crossed over into Old Tashkent.

James Cracraft's chapter reminds us of a startling example of how the government used architecture not merely to project an image of state power, but to define and legitimize that power. The amazing eighteenth-century feat of building new towns and reconstructing old ones started by Peter the Great surely did more to define the new European face of Russia for the overwhelmingly illiterate inhabitants of the Empire than any other act of government. For the literate, the massive importation of foreign architectural terms and the translation of architectural treatises had a revolutionary effect on the way Russians wrote and thought about architecture.

Similarly, after 1917 the Soviet state developed a new architectural vocabulary to define and legitimize its power, one based on industrial efficiency, abstract geometric forms, and avoidance of ornament. These forms celebrated Soviet values of industrialization, mechanization, and communal life, while serving as a slap in the face of accepted pre-Revolutionary aesthetics. Yet, as Greg Castillo shows, constructivist architectural forms served the goals of social control that were held in common by Soviet commissars and American business moguls. Thus the links between architecture and state power were if anything strengthened after 1917. The Soviet state achieved an unprecedented monopoly over architectural and other artistic forms. So complete was this monopoly that, after the fall of the Soviet Union, anti-Stalinist members of Memorial found themselves constrained, through lack of access to alternatives, to use the official cultural language of the Soviet state, socialist realism, in order to unmask the crimes of that state. Kathleen Smith explains how this impoverished artistic language, as well as conflicting ideologies, made decisions about a monument to Stalin's victims so difficult for members of Memorial.

Even this brief list, however, indicates that matters were more complex than the state speaking and the people listening. The Memorial example already shows how opposition groups can appropriate the artistic program promulgated by the government for purposes quite opposite to the ones for which that program was intended. Within the context of Christian culture, St. Paul's idea that pride could vitiate the most worthy deeds was used by almost all of Godunov's contemporaries to dismiss his architectural achievements. The nationalistic architectural language favored by the court in the decades before the 1917 revolution was not the result of a real, "organic" relationship to the past, as alleged, but was a concoction thrown together by contemporary architects desperately seeking a style pleasing to their imperial masters. Lauren O'Connell demonstrates in fascinating detail how *le style Russe* was the result of complex negotiations between the French architectural historian and theorist Viollet-le-Duc and his Russian publisher. Robert Crews argues that the state's architectural program ultimately failed in Tashkent. The Europeanizing and civilizing symbolism of Tashkent's neoclassical new town called forth a new appreciation of the existing native quarter and the values it represented. Inhabitants resisted the social programs of many of the constructivist buildings that were built, while the reality in most industrial sites remained a very far cry from the utopian dreams of the state planners.

What emerges from the chapters dealing with the state as architectural patron, then, is the complex nature of the negotiations by which an appropriate architectural language was chosen. Equally complex was the process whereby this language was received, modified, or opposed by a variety of publics, each with its own agenda. In spite of the high cost of architecture and the resulting near-monopoly of patronage by the state, the state was entirely unable to maintain a monopoly of meaning. The meaning intended by the government at the time could be subverted by contemporaries in many ways and its accepted meaning could change over time. As the remarkable history of the Church of Christ the Savior in Moscow shows, even the wrecker's ball could not always write *finis* to an architectural act by the state; once that state collapsed, the church was rebuilt. What seemed a straightforward exercise of state power in Tashkent provoked actions and reactions that doubtless continue down to the present. Blair Ruble's chapter illustrates the complex reactions that contemporary inhabitants of Yaroslavl have to the church building and town planning that took place in their town many centuries earlier.

This point brings us to architecture as an expression of the identity of some group other than the state. Priscilla Roosevelt's chapter on the architecture of the aristocratic country house is the most obvious example of this theme. Here again we discover the central place of architecture in the minds of patrons and audience as a means for constructing and living out a particular identity. In this case, the main architectural cues came from the ruler. Indeed, the Catherinian aristocrat consciously used the architectural language of the court to establish a dominant position in the local community by depicting himself as a kind of stylistic mirror of the ruler. His ability to reflect the taste and grandeur of the center insured dominance at the periphery. Thus local power was envisioned not as a rival to the power of the state, but as a reflection of that power. Yet the particular tastes and personality of the patron also played a role; he was free to display his own architectural talents or to indulge a hobby. This freedom emphasizes the enormous power exercised by a nobleman over his miniature "kingdom."

By the late twentieth century, the politics of architectural identity had become vastly more complex. The certainties provided by Orthodox culture or Catherinian ideas of enlightenment have disappeared, to be replaced by what Blair Ruble dubs "a frantic search for appropriate architectural antecedents that can impose order on the bewildering turmoil surrounding the meaning of 'Russian-ness.'" The tensions inherent in this search doomed to failure the effort to create a public monument to Stalin's victims. Kathleen Smith's fascinating reading of these tensions reveals the diversity of opinion about almost every aspect of such a monument, from questions of artistic style to the projected image of the victims to religious orientation. Her discussion also illustrates the importance attached to memorials by people from all levels of society, and the role of such memorials in constructing religious, political, and national identities. In Yaroslavl, at a time when urban forms are and will be determined by private actors, the city serves as a concrete illustration of the many forces at play in post-Soviet society. Ruble documents the numerous architectural conflicts currently under way in Yaroslavl, and surveys public opinion there. Although many disputes are still unresolved, the heat of the debates leaves no doubt about the importance of architecture in the minds of *Yaroslavtsy*. Indeed, any American preserva-

tionist would be jealous of the importance assigned to historic preservation by contemporary residents of Yaroslavl.

Blair Ruble's investigations in Yaroslavl illustrate the invented and contested nature of the "Russian architectural tradition" at the end of the twentieth century. The chapters by Lauren O'Connell and Richard Wortman show that the same held true a hundred years earlier. Students of the recent (and not so recent) literature on nationalism will scarcely be surprised by this discovery: nationalism is commonly described in academic contexts as a cultural construct, and nations themselves as "imagined communities," to use Benedict Anderson's phrase.[2] This book illustrates with particular clarity how Russians constructed an imagined architectural past, and how astonishingly important that imagined past was and is in actual politics.

The gulf between academic and lay ideas on Russian architecture in contemporary Russia is illustrated by a story told by one of our contributors, Dimitri Shvidkovsky. On a plane returning to Moscow several years ago, he met a team of American architects going to present a proposal for a major new project in Moscow. Several days later, the American architects called him early in the morning with an urgent question. They had been prepared to answer the usual queries about structural stability, parking, and so on, but had been asked none of these. Instead, they had been repeatedly challenged to describe how their project was related to "the Russian style of architecture." Afraid that the success of their proposal would hinge on their answer, they begged Professor Shvidkovsky, a world authority on the subject, for his help. The visiting Americans were thus implicated, unwittingly, in the continuing task of inventing the Russian tradition in architecture.

If real-life politics has continuously intruded on Russian architectural life, the chapters in this volume also document a seemingly contrary impulse, the utopian one. Recent scholarship has uncovered the strong utopian strains in Soviet and pre-Revolutionary Russian culture, and several of the essays here demonstrate the strength of utopian idealism throughout the half-millennium of architectural development under discussion. For the Muscovite period, the image of Jerusalem functioned as a utopian vision, since it recalled at once the Old Testament "chosen people" with their temple, the Holy Land with its sacred sites, and the New Jerusalem of the Apocalypse. The image acted powerfully on the Muscovite imagination in both the sixteenth and the seventeenth centuries as a model of a sacred and godly state for the Russians to imitate. The image of Jerusalem was central both to the pew of Ivan IV and to many aspects of architecture under Boris Godunov, particularly his plan for a new "Holy of Holies" in the Moscow Kremlin.

The utopian strain in architecture became even stronger in the eighteenth century. Dimitri Shvidkovsky shows us how Catherine used the landscapes in and around Tsarskoe Selo to create an allegory of good governance, an actualized version of her famous *Instruction to the Legislative Commission* of 1767. From her palace, she could conveniently see an ideal town with neoclassical architecture and even streetlights, an ideal noble estate, and so on, laid out in real space as a working version of her ideals of government and society. Priscilla Roosevelt shows us the remarkable efforts of at least some noblemen to turn their estates into paradigms of order and prosperity based on the ideals and estate designs of their empress. A handful of Russian travel writers in the first half of the nineteenth century saw in monasteries and their surrounding landscapes paradigms of Russian piety and national character in general, as Christopher Ely shows. A half-century later, the architects of Russian Tashkent conceived of their new town as a "metonym of order, progress, legality, and a superior European civilization," in sharp contrast to the perceived chaos, squalor, and unsanitary conditions of the native town (similar observations were made by European visitors to pre-Petrine Russia). Even the newly invented "Russian" styles of architecture and decoration in the second half of the nineteenth century were seen in some ways as utopian retreats from "the world of politics emerging at

the beginning of the twentieth century," as Richard Wortman puts it.

That world had plenty of utopian impulses of its own. At first they were oriented toward the future rather than the past. Greg Castillo describes the use of constructivist utopian urban planning and architecture for the purposes of social control and repression. The idyllic rural landscapes that formed the background of many socialist realist paintings, as Mark Bassin tells us, functioned as a means to sanctify the "eternal order utopia" of Stalinism by associating the various tasks of social construction with the timeless utopia of the Russian landscape. During and after World War II, depictions of pylons and tractors disappeared entirely, leaving the pastoral landscape on its own to convey messages of family peace and harmony with nature. The planners who dreamed of rebuilding Stalingrad after the war, as Andrew Day tells us, had more obviously utopian plans for both massive monuments and improved housing. Our two chapters on the post-Soviet period provide less evidence of this utopian theme, and seem to signal a retreat from the social and religious dreaming that has characterized so much of Russian architectural history.

The final theme that we will mention here is the importance of the Russian landscape in creating identity and even legitimacy for a variety of rulers and thinkers over half a millennium. The imagination of a figure like Boris Godunov obviously remains opaque to us, but his desire to imagine and thereby rule his vast new domain is attested by his interest in maps and by the ability of his bureaucrats to site his fortresses and churches in positions that dominated the open Russian landscape. The ability simultaneously to imagine these very remote locations and to organize the construction of fortresses and churches there is one of the most remarkable achievements of his administration. Valerie Kivelson has argued that legal maps reveal an almost pastoral regard for the beauties of the Russian countryside as early as the seventeenth century.[3] The preoccupation with the landscape as a site for the display of enlightened rule is a central theme in the chapters by Dimitri

Shvidkovsky, James Cracraft, and Priscilla Roosevelt. Shvidkovsky shows how Catherine made the landscape around her palace in Tsarskoe Selo a metonym for order, prosperity, and good governance. Catherine's noble courtiers, as Roosevelt argues, followed her example at a local level, turning their estates into landscapes that illustrated both these general themes and the individual personalities and inclinations of each particular landowner. Cracraft's chapter treats architectural change in a larger context, showing how the reign of Peter revolutionized not only architectural practice but the very language with which Russians discussed and understood architecture. Peter's revolution took place with the self-conscious aim of creating a new identity for Russia and her ruler alike.

In the first half of the nineteenth century, the landscape began to be perceived romantically as the place where Russians could find sources of their Russianness. Christopher Ely describes this process of national self-discovery as it was worked out in travel literature at a period roughly contemporaneous with the appearance of the Slavophile movement. For these writers, the monastery in its landscape setting constituted a kind of epitome of Russian identity, one to be set off against the Western European landscapes encountered on the grand tours usually taken by educated Russians.

Mark Bassin describes how the nineteenth-century reverence for the natural landscape returned under Stalin to overcome the abstract, antinature approach characteristic of the early Soviet years. In one of the ironies so typical of Stalinist culture, depictions of the Russian landscape served as a very effective tool for socialist realist painters. These depictions associated the construction of socialism with the eternal harmony and peace of the Russian rural landscape, obscuring in the process the disastrous effect industrialization was actually having on the countryside. In so doing, they brought out the alleged "beauty of Soviet life" and enabled the Stalinist triumph to be depicted as eternal, as existing outside of time. Most important for the effectiveness of socialist realist art as communication with its intended audience, these depictions of typical visions of the Russian landscape seem to have struck a deep chord in Soviet viewers, a response absent in the cases of modernist art and depictions of urban scenes. Bassin thus demonstrates the success of the project, begun by Ely's travel writers, of connecting the Russian landscape with Russian identity.

We trust that readers will find other themes informing the essays which follow, and invite them to join our interdisciplinary conversation, in spite of the caveats cited at the beginning of this introduction. Mindful of "the differing starting points and destinations" characterizing the various disciplines represented here, we nevertheless hope that these essays will advance the individual agendas of our separate disciplines while enriching our common understanding of many of the main themes in Russian culture.

1 Peter the Great and the Problem of Periodization

James Cracraft

Periodization is a problem that bedevils all historical inquiry, and Russian architectural history certainly is no exception. Customarily the field as a whole is divided, implicitly if not always explicitly, into two main periods, an "Old Russian" (*drevnerusskii*) and a "modern" (*novyi*), with the reign of Peter I "the Great" (1689–1725) marking the break (*perelom*) between the two. But this division suffers from having been initially determined by a preestablished view of the general course of Russian history rather than by architectural criteria as such, a view that itself has been seriously challenged by succeeding generations of historians since it was first fully elaborated, by S. M. Solov'ëv, nearly a century and a half ago. It also suffers from the fact that the nature of the Petrine break in Russian architectural development has still to be generally agreed upon. My essay attempts to clarify if not resolve this basic historiographical problem, and thus to provide readers with some rough chronological and thematic scaffolding for the very diverse essays which follow it.

As expounded around 1860 by Solov'ëv, who has been termed "probably the greatest Russian historian of all time,"[1] the various reforms or "transformations" (*preoobrazovaniia*) of Muscovite state and society instated by Peter I constituted nothing less than a "revolution" (*perevorot*, sometimes *revoliutsiia*), one which wrested Old Russia from her medieval clannishness, emotionality, and eastward drift and decisively oriented her westward, thence to take, or retake, her place in Europe and thereby gain entry into the "new" or modern age (*novaia epokha*). In Solov'ëv's highly influential, heavily documented account, Peter carried out "his duty to raise his weak, poor, virtually unknown nation from its sad state by means of civilization," the civilization of "the West." But Russians were also to understand that the "Petrine revolution" was at the same time a national revolution—*nasha revoliutsiia*—and only an episode, albeit uniquely heroic, in the "organic" unfolding of Russian history, itself to be seen as an inseparable if long deviant part of general European history.[2] Solov'ëv never reconciled his organic-nationalist conception of the general course of Russian history with his characterization of the Petrine era as a revolutionary one. Nor did his many followers, including, most notably, V. O. Kliuchevskii (1841–1911), perhaps the second most influential historian of Russia. In his famous *Course of Russian History*, which originated as lectures at Moscow University and which has been frequently reprinted, Kliuchevskii too adopted an organic-nationalist approach to his subject and went on to depict the whole Petrine project of reform (*reforma Petra*), defined as the "central point of our history," in these terms:

> Modest and limited in its original design, directed to a restructuring of the armed forces and a broadening of the state's financial resources, the reform gradually turned

Words printed in **bold** later in this chapter indicate technical loanwords naturalized in Russian under Peter, typically by means of translation from European treatises and manuals. By contrast, obvious borrowings printed in simple italics—e.g., *regula* or *modeliony*—did not survive in Russian.

into a stubborn internal struggle, stirring up the stagnant mold of Russian life and agitating all classes of society. Initiated and led by the supreme power, by the customary leader and director of the nation, it took on the character and methods of a forced upheaval [*nasil'stvennogo perevorota*], of a kind of revolution [*svoego roda revoliutsii*].

It was a revolution, Kliuchevskii explained, not by reason of its intentions or results, which neither envisaged nor produced fundamental economic or social change, but because of its coercive methods and the "impact it had on the minds and nerves of contemporaries," inflicting a great "shock" on Russian society that was the "unforeseen consequence of the reform but not its intended aim." The Petrine revolution, on this account, was essentially psychological in nature and a much more mixed blessing for Russia than Solov'ëv had maintained.[3]

Kliuchevskii, like Solov'ëv, did not indicate how architecture fit into the grand historical scheme. That task was left to the pioneers of Russian architectural history and notably Igor' Grabar', who, in a four-volume work compiled by himself and others and published in 1910–1912, accepted the now-standard periodization of Russian history and made it apply to the development of building. In their account, an analogously "organic" transition took place in Peter's time from an indigenous "Moscow baroque" of the later seventeenth century, which represented the crowning achievement of "Old-Russian" architecture, to the largely imported "St. Petersburg baroque" of the earlier eighteenth century, which marked the debut of the "new" or modern architecture in Russia, which thenceforth swam in the European mainstream.[4] But this view of things, as we can also readily see, was no more successful in harmonizing Petrine developments with an organic conception of the relevant history than was the larger scheme, elaborated by Solov'ëv, Kliuchevskii, and others, on which it obviously depended. Nor could it plausibly account for the huge stylistic and other major differences to be observed between pre-Petrine building in Russia and the contemporaneous architecture in Europe with which it was allegedly linked.

The standard periodization of the general course of Russian history was soon greatly problematized and then rejected by historians working in the Soviet era, who devised a putatively Marxian or "Marxist-Leninist" program to replace it. In its purest form, as represented by the historiography of the Pokrovskii school, Russian history was segmented into feudal, capitalist, and socialist periods, with the reign of Peter, like that of every other ruler, submerged in an ineluctable progression of economic and related social developments. But no such scheme was devised for architectural history to replace, or fill out, the supposedly organic evolution of styles adumbrated by Grabar' and his colleagues in 1910–12. This situation left the overall Old Russian–modern Russian division at least implicitly in place while permitting specialists to subdivide the field without much regard for the whole. Geographical, political, simple chronological, or, rarely, architectural criteria, or some combination thereof, were employed by scholars both Russian and foreign to periodize Russian architectural history, the resultant constructions varying from one scholarly study to the next. Nor was the nature of the Petrine break in Russian architecture adequately documented and explained: Was it spontaneous or planned? Indigenous in its sources or exogenous? Episodic in its significance or epochal? Certain extraneous considerations, now Marxist as well as nationalist in origin, had worked to confuse the matter in Russia itself while the few interested Western specialists tended to follow uncritically the standard Soviet authorities.[5]

To a considerable extent, the persistent lack of a clear and consistent, architecturally configured periodization of Russian architectural history may be attributed to the subject itself. From its provincial Byzantine beginnings in the tenth century of the Christian era until late in the seventeenth century, surviving Russian architecture exhibits, by comparison with contemporaneous building in Europe (or "the West"), a certain homogeneity of style as well as continuity of technique. Development in Russian architecture in these centuries was mainly a matter of multiplying conventional forms in both structure and ornament, of what could be called stylistic agglomeration and the additive method in the organization of space. Technical breakthroughs were relatively few; wood remained the dominant building material; the growth of towns was spontaneous rather than planned. Pre-Petrine Russian architecture was a largely autarkic phenomenon, in other words; stray external influences—Byzantine, Turkish, or Persian arriving from the south and east; Romanesque, Gothic, Renaissance, or baroque emanating from the west—were thoroughly localized or, better, rusticalized.[6] With Moscow's rise to dominance over the Russian plain, it is true, regional variation in building gradually gave way to a quasi-national Muscovite architecture, one whose fantastical forms would later inspire architectural revivalists in Russia (compare the neo-Gothic in Western Europe) and even came to symbolize Russia itself (the church of Basil the Blessed on Red Square). But from its beginnings right up to the reign of Peter I, and particularly by comparison with western European architectural development over the same span of time, building in Russia underwent few major changes in either technique or style.

Historians of Russian architecture have been reluctant on the whole to fully acknowledge this fact, however, a reluctance that has clouded their assessments of the Petrine break in Russian architectural development as much as it has bedeviled their attempts to periodize its history. Yet it seems incontestable, when all of the relevant evidence has been assembled and read,[7] that architectural developments in Russia during Peter's time constituted not just a break but a very sharp break with what had gone before. They constituted, in fact, a revolution, one which set the stage for the whole subsequent course of Russian architectural history. Now by "revolution" here I refer not just to abrupt innovations in architectural style—compare, for instance,

the "revolutionary classicism" of Ledoux and others in later eighteenth-century France invoked by the art historian Thomas DaCosta Kaufman[8]—but to changes of much greater import. They included changes in scale as well as in decoration, in building techniques and the use of materials, in town planning and architectural training, in the kinds of structures to be designed and erected (hospitals and academic buildings, now, as well as churches and palaces), and in the very language of architectural discourse. Architecture in the European Renaissance tradition, together with contemporary European practices in fortification and shipbuilding, were implanted in Russia by Peter's regime following a massive injection of European expertise, a feat that in due course transformed the entire Russian built world. It has been estimated, no doubt conservatively, that during Peter's reign more than a thousand European masters were engaged just in the building of St. Petersburg, a figure that contrasts strikingly with the thirty European builders known to have worked in Russia during the entire previous century.[9] This invasion, for which historical analogues, though much smaller in scale, can be found in Europe north of the Alps after 1500 or so and in the European colonial world, was entirely unprecedented in Russia. And it was part and parcel of that wider "Petrine revolution" first posited by Solov'ëv but then submerged by him and virtually all his successors in their organic nationalist or Marxist (or Marxist-nationalist) accounts of the general course of Russian history.

The Petrine architectural revolution, it is also clear in retrospect, went through several distinct yet interrelated stages. A crisis was precipitated in late Muscovite architecture by the haphazard encroachment on patrons and builders of the new architectural norms emanating from Europe, norms that arrived chiefly via the work of immigrant Belorussian craftsmen in Russia and the use made by native masters of details to be found in the European architectural prints and illustrated manuals which happened to come their way. The result, not surprisingly, was an agglomerative complexity and asymmetry of composition together with an overloading of ornament and a fragmentation or degeneration of form which even sympathetic students of late Muscovite architecture, still mainly church architecture, have observed (fig. 1.1). (One may compare this development to the florid "degeneration of style" which followed the introduction of Italian Renaissance forms in sixteenth-century Holland.)[10]

Muscovite builders, practitioners of a craft based on age-old custom, on simple rules of thumb learned on the job, were manifestly unprepared to accommodate their patrons' budding taste for the new. The crisis was unfolding even as Peter assumed power, and was accelerated by the wholesale conversion of members of the topmost Russian elite (including the young tsar himself) to building in the new style. An unprecedented flurry of such building ensued in Russia, most notably in and around St. Petersburg, the new capital city built entirely in the new style. This style, which can be considered a variant of the northern European baroque, became known as the St. Petersburg baroque (fig. 1.2); it owed nothing, later scholars have demonstrated, to the so-called Moscow baroque identified by Grabar' and others with reference to certain monuments of late Muscovite architecture, proof though the latter are of encroaching European influence (fig. 1.3). The architectural revolution that St. Petersburg embodied was then institutionalized by various means, most conspicuously by the foundation (1757) of the St. Petersburg Academy of Fine Arts under Peter's daughter Empress Elizabeth, who consciously followed paternal precedents. Catherine II endowed her revered predecessors' Academy with a magnificent home, still standing (fig. 1.4), which was jointly designed in the current neoclassical style by an imported French architect, J.-B. M. Vallin de la Mothe, and a native Russian master, Alexander Kokorinov. In the course of training it offered, in its publications, exhibitions, and prizes, in the innumerable buildings its graduates designed, the St. Petersburg Academy conclusively certified Russia's place in the European architectural mainstream (fig. 1.5).

Crisis, conversion, institutionalization: actions by Peter I and his associates at first exacerbated the crisis looming in late Muscovite architecture, by favoring the new over the old, and then resolved it, by institutionalizing in Russia their wholehearted conversion to contemporary European building practices and norms. These were radically different from traditional Muscovite architectural ways, which were considered "medieval" in technique by the standards of the former and in style, "coarse and deformed to the utmost degree." This judgment was pronounced by the famous Bernard Fontenelle in his eulogy of Peter I delivered to the Paris Academy of Sciences in 1725, in which he went on to declare that the recently dead tsar-emperor had "caused architecture to be born in his country."[11] It was only the most dramatic expression of an assessment that was common among Europeans familiar with the Russian scene and one that had come to be shared by Russia's own elite. The Petrine revolution in Russian architecture was thus a top-down, Europeanizing "revolution by decree" but a revolution nonetheless: a process, relatively brief in duration but lasting in its consequences, both consciously intended and recognized as such by contemporaries, whereby the values and techniques of contemporary European architecture were deliberately transplanted to Russia. Ordinary urban and suburban housing, warehouses and wharves, churches and palaces all came within the revolution's purview, as did country estates, official buildings of every kind, and warships, fortresses, and other military structures. (Naval and military together with "civil" construction were still regarded as coeval branches of architecture, although considerable specialization had already set in). The Petrine architectural revolution was responsible for bringing to Russia everything from large-scale and detailed town planning and the landscaped park or garden to the art of applying plaster and alabaster modeling in the interior decoration of buildings. Scarcely any building or ensemble of buildings of any social importance would ever again be the same.

Fig. 1.1 Church of the Trinity at Ostankino, Moscow, 1678–83. Courtesy Hoover Institution, Stanford, Calif. (Voyce Collection).

Nor was it only a matter of cities and towns, or of architecture at the upper levels of society. In due course Peter's revolution reached into the villages of the vast Russian hinterland, where succeeding Imperial regimes, pursuant to his decree of August 1722, required that houses be built in standard sizes following new-style designs and face forward in a straight line flush with a would-be street (fig. 1.6), thus supplanting the semi-submerged huts and random "circular plan" of the traditional Russian settlement. Initially a matter of necessity with respect to fortification and shipbuilding but essentially one of taste with regard to civil construction, Peter's revolution affected every

aspect of the building art in Russia as well as every element of the built environment, sooner or later imbuing it with a more or less European or "modern" appearance. After Peter, every major advance in European architecture was promptly reflected in Russia, where fully realized variants of the successive international styles—baroque, neoclassical, empire, romantic, eclectic, modernist—were produced and related technical innovations readily absorbed.[12]

The verbal aspect of Peter's architectural revolution offers additional evidence, hitherto neglected, of the larger process at work. A case in point is the Russian reception of a famous Italian work on architecture, the *Regola*

it was the first textbook to demonstrate a simple method or "rule" for proportioning each of the five architectural orders devised in antiquity and revived in the Renaissance—the Tuscan, Doric, Ionic, Corinthian, and Composite—in all of their component parts (column, capital, entablature) and various applications (building facade, doorway, fireplace, tomb, and so on).[13] Russian editions of the Vignola, *Pravilo o piati chinekh Arkhitektury*, were printed at Moscow in 1709, 1712, and 1722, the first such book ever to appear in Russia, where it remained the single best-known work on architecture for nearly a century.[14] It thus played a critical part in the diffusion of Renaissance architectural principles to and within Russia. But it could have done so only after Peter and his collaborators had struggled to make it comprehensible to its intended readers: initially, the Russian students and assistants of the European and especially Italian (or Swiss-Italian) architects—G. M. Fontana, Gaetano Chiaveri, Niccolo Michetti, above all Domenico Trezzini (fig. 1.2)—who had been recruited to build St. Petersburg.[15]

In January 1709 Peter ordered the Vignola to be printed and sent to him for review, and in September of that year he duly advised an official in charge of the project that

Fig. 1.2 Church of Sts. Peter and Paul, Peter-Paul Fortress, St. Petersburg, 1712–32. Domenico Trezzini, architect. Author's collection. Structure in the foreground erected later in the eighteenth century, under Catherine II, to house the "granddad of the Russian navy," that is, the boat in which Peter I learned to sail.

> we have looked over the little architectural book [*knishku* **arkhitekturnuiu**] sent by you, and in certain places it is incorrect, about which we send herewith a list of notes. Following this list order architect Fantanna [**arkhitekturu** *Fantanne* = G. M. Fontana] to correct [the mistakes] together with some Russian who might know architecture, however little [*s kem-nibud' ruskim, kotoroi by khotia nemnogo znal* **arkhitekturu**]. And after correcting [it], order a hundred copies to be printed, and send us five or ten as soon as possible.

delli cinque ordini d'architettura by Giacomo Barozzi da Vignola (1507–73). Vignola's *Rule of the Five Architectural Orders*, a concise illustrated treatise first published in Rome in 1562, enjoyed an immense popular and academic success all over Europe, having gone through scores of editions in all of the main European languages over the next century and a half. This success was owed to the economy with which it encapsulated in drawings and words the architectural revolution inaugurated in Renaissance Italy. More precisely,

The attached list of mistakes needing correction indicated that the captions to various of the figures were misplaced and in "many places" were "unclear."[16] Fontana and his still unidentified Russian assistant endeavored to revise the Vignola in compliance with the

Fig. 1.3 Church of the Intercession of the Mother of God at Fili, Moscow, 1690–93. From M. I. Rzianin, *Pamiatniki russkogo zodchestva* (Moscow, 1950). Courtesy of Regenstein Library, University of Chicago.

Fig. 1.4 Academy of Fine Arts, St. Petersburg, 1764–88. J.-B. M. Vallin de la Mothe and A. F. Kokorinov, architects. Author's collection.

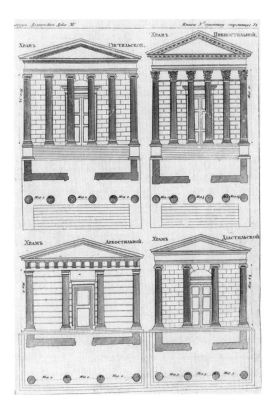
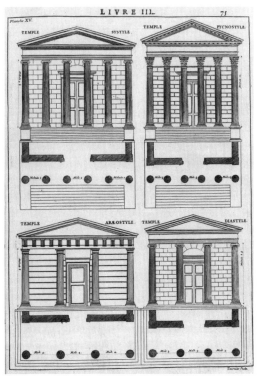

Fig. 1.5 Extracts from (left) the Russian edition of Vitruvius's *Ten Books on Architecture* published 1790–97 by the St. Petersburg Academy of Fine Arts, and (right) the 1694 French edition of same from which the text of the Russian edition was translated and its illustrations copied. The Russian translation "with further explanatory notes for the benefit of architectural students" was done by Vasilii Bazhenov, member of the St. Petersburg Academy of Fine Arts and a leading Russian proponent of neoclassicism in architecture. Courtesy of the British Library, London.

tsar's order, as the subsequent Russian editions show, while adding an Italian-"Slavonic" glossary of technical terms: a *Perevod Gospodina Arkhitektura Fantanna Obretaiushchikhsia vo* **arkhitekturnoi** *knige italianskikh rechenii na slovenskoe rechenie* ("Translation by Mr. Fontana the Architect of Italian words found in [this] architectural book into Slavonic words"), which was printed in parallel columns. The glossary is remarkable for its mix of straight transliterations printed in the drastically simplified Cyrillic or "civil" type that Peter was now introducing—the basis of the standard Russian alphabet used to this day—with roughly equivalent extant terms and attempted literal or semantic calques. Thus *Modeliony* in the "Italian" column is simply *Modeliony* in the "Slavonic," **Arkhitrave** becomes *Arkhidrat,* *Plinto* becomes **Plintus,** *Regula* is *Sposob*

mery, the phrase **Kolonna ili paliastr** is rendered *Stolby,* and so forth. The same sort of mix occurs in the lists of architectural terms accompanying various diagrams in the book, in the captions to its hundred or so illustrations (reengraved in Moscow by artists working under the Dutch master Pieter Picart), and in its longer descriptive or instructional passages. These passages begin on the first page, where it is explained that the book's purpose is

To treat of the five orders of columns, that is, the Tuscan, Doric, Ionic, Corinthian, Composite, wherefore it is fitting first to show figures of each separately, which will [then] be discussed, even though their rule is still unknown [is not yet explained here]. For only then are they ready for an explanation of the general rule. After that what

Fig. 1.6 A Russian village ca. 1790 as drawn and etched by J. A. Atkinson. One of a series of drawings done by Atkinson in Russia in the 1780s and 1790s, this one is captioned by him: "The villages of Russia are generally composed of one street with houses on each side; their length, in consequence of this plan of building, is sometimes very considerable; nor is the uniform shape of their houses less remarkable, all of them having the same roofs and facade." Courtesy of Houghton Library, Harvard University.

is peculiar from one part to another will be clear. [*Traktovat' o piati ordinakh kolonov, to est', O toskane, Doriko, Ionika, Korinto, Kompozito. Pokazalosia za dostoino, da by v nachale pokazat' figury vsiakuiu osobno, o kotorykh traktovat' budet, khotia eshche mery ikh neizvestny. Ibo tokmo zdes' onye polozheny sut' dlia ob"iavleniia generalnoi reguly. A posle sobstvenno ot onoi chasti k drugoi ob"iastemo budet.*]

Later in the book it is explained that the five orders are divided into "a certain number of modules [*moduli*]": in the *ordona dorika*, for example, the base under the column (*baza pod kolumnoiu*) and the surmounting capital (*kapitel'*) are each one module high and the column itself, fourteen modules. The precise number and ratio of the modules one to the other, the explanation continues, established the strength, proportions (*proportsii*), and

regularity (*reguliarnost'*) for which ancient Roman architecture was justly praised. And so the book proceeds, through each of the architectural orders, its component parts and various applications, the whole exercise copiously illustrated.[17]

There can be little doubt that the detailed illustrations provided in the Russian editions of Vignola's treatise mightily assisted the transmission from Italy to Russia of the technical vocabulary and verbalized concepts of architecture in the Renaissance tradition and the subsequent diffusion of these terms and concepts within Russia. But we might also notice that the very act of translating Vignola's verbal building instructions and architectural descriptions simultaneously facilitated the emergence of the modern Russian language, or the transition from the heavily Slavonicized literary Russian (or Russified Church Slavonic) that Peter had inherited, where such discourses were virtually unknown, to a newer, simpler, more vernacular "civil" language capable of articulating this as well as the other arts and sciences of contemporary Europe. The phenomenon is repeatedly encountered in Petrine architectural sources. They thus document in their prosaic way the enactment in Russia not just of Peter's architectural revolution but of his larger cultural revolution as well, a revolution that was driven by his determination to achieve a place for his kingdom (*tsarstvo*), now empire (*imperiia*), in the European state system.[18]

It therefore seems imperative, to revert to our main theme, to retain the customary overall division of Russian architectural history into Old Russian and new or modern periods, with the era of Peter I—the Petrine revolution—marking the decisive break between the two ("modern" as used here is of course a general historical term, and should not be confused with "modernist," which refers to a particular architectural style or family of styles). The conventional periodization of Russian architectural history now makes sense, and we are left with the task of subdividing these two great periods in ways that similarly respect historical reality. I propose that the first be segmented into an early Old Russian or East Slavic phase, lasting from the tenth to the fourteenth centuries and consisting of variants of provincial Byzantine architecture; a middle Old Russian or early Muscovite phase, occurring in the fifteenth and sixteenth centuries and corresponding with the consolidation of the Russian polity under Moscow; and a late Old Russian or late Muscovite phase, extending through the seventeenth century, when population aggregates, accumulations of wealth, and the concentration of political power in the tsar's offices had all reached levels sufficient to support a boom in building on a truly national scale. It should be obvious that this subdivision of Old Russian architectural history into three successive phases, the latter two marked by significant expansion as well as variation of the architectural legacy inherited from the first or Byzantine phase, is meant to register the largely autarkic as well as relatively indeterminate nature of pre-Petrine Russian architectural development, especially when it is placed in an all-European context—precisely the context in which its students have always sought to place it. At the same time, periodizing pre-Petrine or Old-Russian architecture in this way leaves ample room, within the larger framework, for locating the regional variations in structure and ornament and the successive developments in mass or style to which Russian architectural scholars have devoted so much detailed attention.[19]

The post-Petrine or modern period in the history of building in Russia, by contrast, may be subdivided into baroque, neoclassical, empire, romantic (historicist, or neo-Muscovite), eclectic, and modernist phases—taking the story up to Soviet times and confining ourselves, here as throughout this essay, mainly to high-style, elite, or public masonry building (archaic styles and techniques of domestic building in wood, to take the most obvious instance, certainly persisted in peasant Russia well into the twentieth century). These proposed subdivisions of the modern period are essentially stylistic, as are their counterparts in European (or Western) architectural historiography. As such, they are meant to emphasize that the Europeanization (Westernization, modernization) of Russian architecture, a process decisively set in motion under Peter I, is the preeminent feature of the Imperial era, the era of the Russian Empire (1721–1917). It was then, and not until then in Russia, that fully realized variants of the successive international styles were produced and related technical innovations readily absorbed. Thereafter, with the onset of the Soviet era and the rise of Stalin, a partial reversion to architectural autarky took place amid a new fluorescence of hybridized styles. Yet even in the Soviet era a heady interlude of architectural experimentation took place (in the 1920s), paralleling that which occurred elsewhere; and under Stalin and his successors (1930–1970s) classicism and rigorous town planning made a decisive comeback, with echoes here and there of the modernism that had triumphed in the West. Moreover developments since the demise of the Soviet Union (1991) would seem to have brought Russia back into the European or Western, now the global, architectural mainstream. The legacy of Peter the Great, Russia's first architect in the modern sense of the term (as designer and builder as well as patron), was never extinguished in his homeland, and the modern period in Russian architectural history proceeds apace.

I hope that this capsulized account of the Petrine revolution and related discussion of the problem of periodization will help readers locate in time—in the long view of history—the variously specialized contributions which together make up the substance of this volume.

They are grouped for the sake of convenience under four general headings: those pertaining to Muscovite Russia, to Imperial Russia, to Soviet Russia, and to Post-Soviet Russia. Taken together, they represent the most diverse expressions of Russianness in architecture very broadly, indeed heuristically understood. Nor can these many architectures, our contributors say as well, be contained within the parameters of a narrow Russian nationalism: no more than can their meanings be interpreted in the terms of a single scholarly discipline. But that, and much else besides, readers will discover for themselves.

Part 1

Muscovite Russia

2 The Throne of Monomakh

Ivan the Terrible and the Architectonics of Destiny

Michael S. Flier

Yet have I set my king upon my holy hill of Zion.

Psalms 2:6

The architectural structure of the Throne of Monomakh, one of the most prominent cultural artifacts of the reign of Ivan the Terrible, provides the basis for the present investigation into architecture and the expression of group identity. A throne, by virtue of who sits in it, establishes an immediate relationship with the edifice housing it, asserting its significance, reconfiguring its division of space, defining lines of semiotic tension with its occupants, and inviting comparison with other thrones in other sites in which the ruler is presented to an elite subset of the ruled with a particular message or messages to communicate. To the extent that the identity of the group ruled may be clarified by the architectural presentation of the ruler, we do well to pay attention to the throne as an important symbol of governmental policy, an instrument that establishes simultaneously the function of the ruler and his subjects.

By the middle of the sixteenth century, during the reign of Ivan IV, the Terrible, Moscow had three royal thrones in buildings facing Cathedral Square, the primary locus of major ceremonies and processions involving the heads of church and state. Like the altar of a church, the tsar's throne in each case was located at the eastern end of the room containing it, near the southeastern corner. The throne in the Golden Hall presented the tsar seated face-to-face in audience with his own nobility and with foreign dignitaries. Here petitioners proposed and the tsar

disposed, an active agent whose seat of honor was the iconographic as well as the political focus of attention, surrounded as he was by images of military power, royal authority, and the divine wisdom of God. In the adjacent Faceted Hall, the enthroned tsar presided over sumptuous banquets, personally overseeing the flow of courses, toasts, and entertainments for those invited to partake of his generosity.

It is perhaps perversely appropriate that the most famous throne in medieval Rus'—the Throne of Monomakh—is not really a throne in the conventional sense and did not belong to Grand Prince Vladimir Monomakh. According to the scanty evidence available to us, the Throne was actually a tsar's pew (*tsarskoe mesto*), an architectural enclosure that demarcated the tsar's space in the main church of Moscow, the Cathedral of the Dormition, in the heart of the Kremlin (fig. 2.1). It was apparently dedicated in the fifth year of Ivan IV's reign as tsar, on September 1, 1551, the first day of the Orthodox new year.

Here in Muscovy's cathedral church, the Throne (or Tsar's Pew) inverted the major features of those thrones associated with the throne room and banquet hall sketched above. Although located in the southeast end of the nave, it faced away from those present, placing the tsar in the very front line of worshippers, whose attention and thoughts were directed not to him but to the message of the iconostasis, with its revelation of the Incarnation and

Fig. 2.1 Tsar's Pew (Monomakh Throne). Cathedral of the Dormition, Moscow Kremlin, (1551).

the Metropolitan in his ceremonial robes, wearing his little cap and carrying the staff or *posokh*, upon which he leaned. . . . [The Grand Prince Vasilii III] stood by the [south] door through which he enters the church, his back against the wall and leaning upon his staff.[2]

Standing is customary during Orthodox services and thus we find nothing particularly striking about the scene just described except for the placement of the head of state. In East Slavic cathedrals from the days of Saint Volodimer in the late tenth century, the grand prince stood during services in a gallery *above* the main floor of the nave, his dominant position in society directly demonstrated by his location above the congregation. Indeed, in 1472 architects Krivtsov and Myshkin included upper galleries in their plans for Moscow's new, enlarged Cathedral of the Dormition.[3] When the Italian architect Aristotele Fioravanti was invited by Ivan III to redesign their collapsed cathedral, however, he was allowed to place aesthetic form over sociopolitical requirements by opening up the nave to the requirements of Renaissance space.[4] The typical U-shaped upper gallery was eliminated, thus creating a voluminous space broken only by slender columns and the high iconostasis separating central nave and sanctuary, and simultaneously presenting the practitioners of protocol and dramatic effect with a dilemma: where to put the grand prince? The answer was prescribed by longstanding tradition.

From various foreign and domestic sources, Ivan III was certainly aware that the emperor's throne in Constantinople's Hagia Sophia was located in a space near the southeast corner of the south aisle, apparently behind a screen.[5] In Moscow's Dormition, the southeastern corner of the nave was a fortuitous choice in all respects for locating the grand prince, because it is the adjacent south door that leads directly onto Cathedral Square and serves as the regular and clearly more dramatic entrance and exit, used as such by the ruler in processions. We must note, however, that whereas the Byzantine

the ultimate apocalyptic promise of the Last Judgment and eternal salvation. It provided an environment for standing, not sitting, during church services.[1] In this context, the tsar was a passive participant rather than an active agent, set apart nonetheless as the leader of a people come into the presence of God to pray for redemption. An approach to understanding the function of the Monomakh Throne must begin with some basic information.

In his commentary on Muscovy, Sigmund von Herberstein mentioned two occasions, in 1517 and 1526, on which he was able to attend church services in Moscow's Cathedral of the Dormition, during the feast of the Dormition of the Mother of God on August 15:

In the midst of [the cathedral] was a platform raised upon two steps and here stood

emperor *sat* on a throne in Hagia Sophia, the Muscovite grand prince *stood* without a throne near the south door of the Dormition.[6]

The reconstructed Dormition was dedicated in 1479. In the front of the nave, built into the inner column on the south side, there was a Metropolitan's Pew, or Throne (*mitropolich'e mesto*). The Metropolitan's Pew can be understood originally as a re-creation in the nave of the so-called Cathedra (Bishop's Chair or High Seat [*gornee mesto*]) located in the main apse of the sanctuary in the midst of a curved row of seats (*synthronon*) against the back wall. The Cathedra is the seat of the highest ranking ecclesiastical figure and a symbol of his authority. The entire structure was traditionally intended for the bishop and his presbyters, the ecclesiastical representatives of Christ and his disciples (figs. 2.2, 2.3). We have no precise date for the introduction of the Metropolitan's Pew: some scholars are inclined to assign it to the date of the cathedral's completion, 1479; there are no grounds, however, for this conclusion.[7] The Pew may in fact be better associated with the completion of the iconostasis by Dionisii and his workshop, probably by the mid-1480s. Although the iconostasis contained only the Deësis, Festival, and Prophet tiers, it is likely that High Seat in the altar disappeared from view, thus apparently prompting the need for an analogous seat in plain view.

The Metropolitan's Pew might at first have looked like the High Seat, a flat surface carved into the column. Snegirev infers that it was during the early patriarchate in the late sixteenth century that the current structure with baldachin was built around it.[8] It is possible, however, that the stone seat of the prelate described in sixteenth-century documents refers to the current structure. The Metropolitan's Pew was a place of honor that demarcated the space of the high prelate during parts of the ceremony in which he played a passive rather than active role, displayed as it were before the entire congregation as the head of the church.

The very presence of the Metropolitan's Pew in the Cathedral of the Dormition served

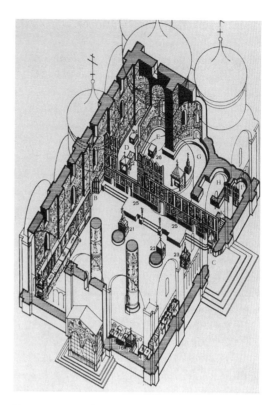

Fig. 2.2 Aristotele Fioravanti, Cathedral of the Dormition, Moscow Kremlin, 1475–79. Isometric projection from Irina Rodimzeva, Nikolai Rachmanov, and Alfons Raimann, *The Kremlin and Its Treasures* (New York, 1986), p. 83. Reproduced with permission.

to define a space before the iconostasis that regulated the placement of the chief prelate of the Russian church and, under special circumstances, the highest echelon of Muscovite royalty. That space had been used for temporary seats in the coronation ceremonies of Crown Prince Dmitrii in 1498, and Tsar Ivan IV in 1547 (fig. 2.4).[9] The delimitation of such a hierarchically superior space in the nave was a necessary semiotic prerequisite for the permanent Tsar's Pew introduced by Ivan IV in mid-century once he had been officially crowned as tsar.

In the historical context of reform following Ivan IV's coronation in 1547—the redecoration of the Golden Hall Throne Room (1547–53), the writing of a new Code of Laws (*Sudebnik*) in 1550, the Manual of Church Governance (*Stoglav*) in 1551, all involving the close collaboration of tsar and

Fig. 2.3 The Metropolitan's Pew (1479? 1480s?, now Patriarch's Pew) and the Tsar's Pew (1551, Monomakh Throne) in the Cathedral of the Dormition, Kremlin, Moscow. Photograph from Irina Polynina and Nicolai Rakhmanov, *The Regalia of the Russian Empire* (Moscow, 1994), p. 29. Reproduced with permission.

metropolitan and their advisers—the Tsar's Pew was presumably conceived and built. We do not know the identity of the builder or the specific motivation of the design. Oddly, there is no written mention of it in the major records of the period, including the sixteenth-century *Tsarstvennaia kniga* and the *Nikon Chronicle*, but schematic versions of the Pew are reproduced in miniatures in the *Illustrated Chronicle Compilation* (f. 532) and in the *Tsarstvennaia kniga* (f. 285). The *Piskarev Chronicle*, a compilation of late sixteenth- and early seventeenth-century texts, places the date sometime in 1552.[10]

Otherwise, the primary evidence of the date is contained in a manuscript from a collection of sixteenth-century letters.[11] The manuscript, labeled "Fragment on the Coronation of the Tsar of All Rus'" (hereafter "Fragment"), reproduces the entire carved inscription around the cornice of the Pew

and on the two doors in front, but adds a lengthy statement about the historical circumstances of its creation, perhaps a text carved elsewhere and subsequently lost.[12] The text refers directly to the God-ordained coronation of Ivan IV as tsar in the Cathedral of the Dormition and his anointing by Metropolitan Makarii on January 20, 7055 (1547) and then describes the Pew: "This Tsar's Pew, which is a throne, was constructed in the year 7060 (1551) on September 1 in the fifth year of his reign as tsar and sovereign."[13]

The basic form of the Pew is that of a low cubicle surmounted by a baldachin or tower-shaped canopy resting on four slender colonnettes (fig. 2.1). The cubicle itself rests on the backs of four crouching animals with twisted torsos.

The baldachin (fig. 2.5) consists of an eight-sided tent-tower topped by a small cupola and

Fig. 2.4 Ivan IV and Metropolitan Makarii seated on temporary thrones during the coronation ceremony in the Cathedral of the Dormition, Moscow, *Tsarstvennaia kniga*.

shape, twelve chalices in all—four over the corners and eight over the pointed tops of the ogival kokoshniki in row one.

The four crouching animals supporting the Pew are variously named in "Fragment": the first (southeast corner) is said to have three names, *liutoi*, "fierce, the fierce one"; *lev*, "lion"; and *skiment*, "lion cub" (cf. Greek skúmnos, "lion cub").[14] The second (southwest corner) is called *uena*, "hyena" (cf. Greek húaina, "hyena"); the third and fourth (northeast and northwest corners) are both identified as *oskrogan*, a name not yet deciphered. The word *orel*, "eagle," although listed in the manuscript along with the words for the crouching animals beneath the Pew, apparently refers to the double-headed eagle at the top of the baldachin. No explanation has yet been offered to explain the choice of beasts that support the Pew, nor their particular placement.[15] The entire Pew is made of walnut and was originally painted gold, except for scattered silver highlights, the blue of the recessed background, and the crimson of the throne's architectural lineaments.[16]

Each of the external northern, western, and southern sides of the cubicle holds four panels in bas-relief with carved inscriptions describing each panel (see fig. 2.6). The panels follow a narrative sequence depicting Grand Prince Vladimir Monomakh's military victory over the Byzantines in Thrace and the translation of the Byzantine regalia to him: top left-to-right, bottom left-to-right.[17]

Northern Panels

1. The devout Grand Prince Vladimir Monomakh meets with his princes and boyars in Kiev, telling them of the courage of their ancestors, how they used to exact tribute from Constantinople.[18]

2. The devout Grand Prince Vladimir Monomakh gathers his skilled and judicious commanders and establishes the ranks of officers: the thousand-man, hundred-man, fifty-man battalion leaders, however many military expertise might require.[19]

3. The troops of Grand Prince Vladimir Monomakh head for the lands of Thrace.[20]

a two-headed eagle. The base of the baldachin is framed by thirty-six rounded kokoshniki, nine on each side. Three rows of variously shaped large kokoshniki rise in increasing height toward the center of the tower. Row one consists of eight ogival kokoshniki; row two, of eight trefoil kokoshniki; and row three, of eight triangular kokoshniki. Large rosettes occupy the spaces between the kokoshniki of row one. Intricate patterns of leaves, vines, flowers, and clusters of grapes are carved in the large kokoshniki of the first row, whereas somewhat geometrical, moresque vines are to be found in those of the second row and around the base of the spire. The valances beneath the cornice have carvings of leaves and flowers with different birds at each end. The small, rounded kokoshniki at the base each have a multi-branched geometrical plant painted in gold against a dark background. Perhaps the most remarkable features of the baldachin are what appear to be chalices bearing spherical forms stacked in a pyramidal

Fig. 2.5 Tsar's Pew (Monomakh Throne). Detail of a baldachin.

Fig. 2.6 Tsar's Pew (Monomakh Throne). Detail of the four western panels.

4. The military commanders of Grand Prince Vladimir Monomakh stormed a Thracian town.[21]

Western Panels

5. The military commanders of Grand Prince Vladimir Monomakh captured Thracian villages . . . [22]

6. . . . . and returned with many riches.[23]

7. The pious Emperor Constantine Monomachus was in Constantinople then, also involved at that time in a war with the Persians and the Latins.[24]

8. The devout Emperor Constantine Monomachus convenes his wise and imperial council and dispatches his emissaries to the Grand Prince Vladimir Vsevolodich in Kiev: Neophyte, metropolitan of Ephesus in Asia, along with two bishops, from Miletus and Mitylene; as well as the military commander of Antioch; Eustathius, the hegumen of Jerusalem; and others of his people.[25]

Southern Panels

9. The devout Emperor Constantine gives worthy gifts to Metropolitan Neophyte and the bishops and the emissaries and dispatched them from Constantinople to Kiev for Grand Prince Vladimir Vsevolodich.[26]

10. And having been dispatched, Metropolitan Neophyte and the bishops and the aforementioned emissaries from Constantinople boarded the ship sailing for Kiev.[27]

11. The emissaries from Constantinople arrived in the city of Kiev and appeared before Grand Prince Vladimir, and they brought to him the worthy imperial gifts and many others and sued for peace with him.[28]

12. The Holy Metropolitan Neophyte crowned the devout Grand Prince Vladimir Vsevolodovich as Monomakh.[29]

The general narrative sequence is thus articulated by three main themes: (1) Rusian ambition (northern panels), (2) Byzantine capitulation (western panels), (3) and transference of authority (southern panels). The current placement of the Pew immediately

adjacent to the south wall is surely inaccurate, because the view of the thematically most important southern panels is blocked; undoubtedly the Pew was originally located closer to the central nave. This conjecture is supported by the schematic drawing of the coronation service for Mikhail Fedorovich from the *Book of the Election of Tsar Mikhail Fedorovich* (fig. 2.7).[30]

The front of the Pew is bifurcated by two doors, each door bearing two circular insets with inscriptions that relate the historic events between Rus' and the Byzantine Empire, some of which are depicted on the panels. The text is taken from the sixteenth-century *Tale of the Princes of Vladimir*, which traces Rusian genealogy back to Caesar Augustus.[31] The inscription on the right door (as one faces the Pew) ends with a direct statement by Metropolitan Neophyte to Vladimir Monomakh, telling him to accept the royal regalia from Emperor Constantine Monomachus:

> . . . and from this time forward you are to be called Emperor crowned by God. Crowned by the hand of the most holy metropolitan prelate Neophyte and the bishops with this imperial crown, from that very time on Prince Vladimir Vsevolodich would be called Monomakh and tsar of Great Russia, and thereafter he remained in peaceful and loving relations with Emperor Constantine and to this day the princes of Vladimir are crowned with that very same imperial crown.[32]

That Constantine Monomachus (d. Jan. 1055) had died fifty-eight years before Vladimir Monomakh became grand prince (April 1113) was information conveniently ignored. What was undoubtedly not missed, however, was the symbolism of corporate participation in the highest affairs of state. Both rulers depicted on the panels—Byzantine emperor and Rusian grand prince—carry out their solemn, God-ordained responsibilities in full consultation with their noble and military elites. In the case of Muscovy, the Pew thus served not only to underscore the

Fig. 2.7 The coronation ceremony of Mikhail Fedorovich as tsar inside the Cathedral of the Dormition, Moscow Kremlin, as illustrated in *Kniga o izbranii . . . tsaria . . . Mikhaila Fedorovicha*, 1672.

tsar's impeccable pedigree but to confirm that government at the highest level, with its strict hierarchy and centripetally oriented vectors, included a place for the active participation of the boyar elites and their clans. Through such architectural symbolism, the Pew gave expression to images of the very group whose support was vital for effective government and military operations, the same group alluded to in the larger contextual network of images in the major churches and reception halls of the Kremlin. Like these more grandiose architectural monuments, the Pew contributed to a sense of order and stability in the realm.[33]

The prominence of the Monomakh panels prompted early nineteenth-century critics to call the Pew the Throne of Monomakh and to view it as yet another expression of the notion "Moscow—Third Rome."[34] At a time when Ivan IV was in fact the most powerful ruler in the Orthodox world, there is little doubt that

he valued lineage that could be traced through Vladimir Monomakh back to Caesar Augustus himself. The large wall murals in the Golden Hall throne room opposite the throne illustrated the very translation of the Byzantine regalia as depicted on the Pew. But the eschatological aspirations of Moscow rose above the material splendor and power of ancient Rome, as did the allegorical and eschatological images of the vaults and ceiling of the throne room over the historical scenes below. In fact, Jerusalem played a far more significant role in cultural imagery than Rome or Constantinople during the reign of Ivan IV.

In the original and striking icon "Blessed is the Host of the Heavenly Tsar," assumed to be painted around the time of the defeat of Kazan' in 1552 and, if an early seventeenth-century inventory is accurate,[35] hung on the Dormition south wall adjacent to the Tsar's Pew, a larger-than-life Vladimir Monomakh, mounted on a steed, makes his way in procession with three victorious columns of Rusian and Muscovite soldiers from a city in flames to a city on a hill guarded by the Mother of God and Christ. These cities are usually interpreted as the historical Kazan' and Moscow, but allegorically as Sodom and Jerusalem, respectively.

The Palm Sunday Ritual, one of the most solemn and impressive ceremonies involving the tsar and the metropolitan, recreated Christ's triumphant entry into Jerusalem every year. By 1561 the Ritual procession extended beyond the Kremlin walls to the newly completed Church of the Intercession on the Moat, which memorialized the victory over Kazan'. Later known as Saint Basil's Cathedral, this microcosmic Jerusalem with its ramparts and onion-domed towers at the edge of Red Square provided one of the major stations for the procession, the Chapel of the Entry into Jerusalem. A raised circular dais just to the north was called *Lobnoe mesto,* "the place of the skull," that is, Golgotha.

On January 6 of each year, a hole dug in the ice of the Moscow River served as the site of the important Epiphany Ritual, which included the tsar and the metropolitan. The water thus rendered accessible for the ceremony was called *Iordan'*, "the Jordan." The Tsar's Pew is thus best understood as an integral piece of a network of semiotic connections with Jerusalem. The decision to surmount the Tsar's Pew with a towerlike baldachin provided a clear opportunity to exploit its attendant symbolism with the personal destiny of Ivan IV.

The pyramidal eight-sided tent-tower and the kokoshniki of the Tsar's Pew replicate in the nave of the cathedral church the Church of the Ascension in the royal compound at Kolomenskoe, built in 1530 by Vasilii III to celebrate the birth of his son Ivan IV (fig. 2.8). It was this church that provided important structural and stylistic inspiration for the design of the Church of the Intercession on the Moat. The towerlike baldachin thus serves as a personal architectonic stamp that unites the church memorializing Ivan's birth, the church commemorating his greatest military and Christian victory, and the ark that

Fig. 2.8 Church of the Ascension, royal compound at Kolomenskoe, 1530–32.

houses him in prayer in the cathedral church of the Moscow Kremlin.

For a medieval artifact of some significance, the Tsar's Pew has received remarkably little attention in the scholarly literature.[36] The uniqueness of the Tsar's Pew raises questions about possible sources. Bocharov refers to a number of Western European bishop's thrones as general models, especially the eleventh- and twelfth-century Italian episcopal thrones studied by Grabar, some of which rest on the backs of animals.[37] He also refers to the prototype par excellence of most Christian thrones, the throne of Solomon:[38]

Moreover, the king made a great throne of ivory, and overlaid it with the best gold. The throne had six steps, and the top of the throne was round behind, and there were stays on either side of the place of the seat, and two lions stood by the stays. And twelve lions stood there on one side and on the other upon the six steps; there was not the like made in any kingdom. (1 Kings 10:18–20)

This particular description seems to characterize the Ivory Throne of Ivan IV, a sixteenth-century imported West European throne in the conventional sense, more than it does the Tsar's Pew. It is thus Shchepkin who properly saw the primary influence of the Pew in the ciborium or baldachin, especially that found in Byzantine and Western European altars.[39] In a Christian context the use of the ancient ciborium was soon extended to sacred relics and artifacts of various kinds, and finally to the seats, pews, and other accoutrements of high prelates and important secular figures as well.[40] It is beyond the scope of this paper to go into these matters here, but it is useful to keep in mind that the Throne of Monomakh is truly a pew, and not a throne. Therefore we might anticipate structures other than thrones playing important roles in influencing the Pew's ultimate architectural shape. Shchepkin's intuitions about ciboria seem a more productive line to pursue.

In the confines of an Orthodox church, it is first and foremost the altar that is covered with a baldachin, which itself refers to the canopy-like configuration—the *aedicula*—over the Tomb of Christ in the Church of the Holy Sepulcher in Jerusalem. The altar in the Dormition has a pyramidal hipped-roof baldachin, actually similar in shape to the baldachin of the Metropolitan's Pew. For the Tsar's Pew, part of the inspiration for the architectural form must have come from the Dormition's Small Zion, with its three rows of rounded kokoshniki on the baldachin and an inscription surrounding the base (fig. 2.9).[41] Dated 1486, this type of liturgical vessel—a Jerusalem (*ierusalim*)—represented the Church of the Holy Sepulcher and accordingly was probably used to hold the bread prepared for the celebration of the Eucharist. When greater complexity was introduced in the proskomide in the twelfth century, a flat

Fig. 2.9 Small Zion of the Cathedral of the Dormition, Moscow, 1486. Electroplated copy of now lost original. Photograph from *Gosudarstvennaia Oruzheinaia palata*, ed. I. A. Bobrovnitskaia, et al. (Moscow, 1988), p. 57. Reproduced with permission.

diskos was used instead, but Jerusalems continued to be carried symbolically during the Great Entrance. According to written testimony the Jerusalem seemed to have represented in larger perspective a composite of Jerusalem holy sites, including Solomon's Temple and the Holy of Holies with the Ark of the Covenant.[42] This conflation of distinct reference may explain why Jerusalems came to be called Zions (*siony*) from the seventeenth century on. Zion refers to the mount adjacent to the site of Solomon's temple—God's house—*not* the site of the Church of the Holy Sepulcher, built near Golgotha, outside the walls.

In the case of the Tsar's Pew, the allusion to Solomon's Temple is made more plausible if we take into account a curious fact previously ignored in the literature: the Throne of Monomakh is *completely* lacking in the common symbols of Christianity one might have expected to see on the royal pew of this most powerful Orthodox Christian emperor. There are no crosses, no images of saints or the Mother of God or Christ anywhere on it. Rather it employs animal and vegetal imagery and makes symbolic and textual reference to the Old Testament and its Russian parallels. By contrast, the Tsar's Pew in Novgorod, constructed nearly twenty years later, has numerous images of saints and features an image of the New Testament Trinity on the ceiling inside.[43]

Accordingly, if the lower, cubical portion of the Pew is devoted to successful serial developments in the history of Rus' that legitimize Muscovy's claim to secular and religious authority in the Orthodox world of the present, then the upper, pyramidal portion is dedicated to specific themes of the Old Testament relevant for Ivan IV's destiny as tsar and for Muscovy's eschatological pretensions as a nation of the Chosen People, the New Israel, a broader group reference that literally rests on a base of hierarchical but corporate government authority.

The clue to the baldachin and the larger meaning of the Tsar's Pew comes from the inscription on the cornice, identified by Zabelin in 1850 and by all subsequent commentators as simply "words from biblical text":

The Lord said, "I chose you as tsar, I took you by the right hand and arranged for you to rule my people all the days of your life. If you follow my commandments and do my will, I will give you an understanding heart and wisdom, and you will be as no other king before or after you, and if you pass judgment and render justice over the land and hear the groans and tears of those in grief, and govern them I shall immediately multiply the years of your life and grant you dominion against your enemies and I will let you multiply your earthly fruits and secure your seed and establish your kingdom and throne unto the ages and will be like a father to you and you like a son to me. Moreover, I will give you what you did not ask for, glory and riches, and nations will yield to you. If your iniquity appears, I will chasten you, [but] I will not take my mercy away from you."[44]

Presented in direct address from God to the ruler himself, this inscription is not actually a simple citation from the Bible, but rather a composite of statements by God to King David and King Solomon, with some phraseology borrowed from the ideas of Agapetus articulated in the coronation ceremony itself. The opening lines seem to combine some of the Agapetus-based text of the coronation ceremony:[45] "For the Lord God says to the prophets, I have raised thee up as king with righteousness and have taken thee by the hand and have strengthened thee."[46] and the biblical description of the prophet Nathan instructing David to lead his chosen people:

Now therefore so shalt thou say unto my servant David, Thus saith the Lord of hosts, I took thee from the sheepcote from following the sheep to be ruler over my people, over Israel (2 Samuel 7:8). And when thy days be fulfilled, and thou shalt sleep with thy fathers, I will set up thy seed after thee, which shall proceed out of thy bowels, and I will establish his kingdom. He shall build a house for my name, and I will establish the throne of his kingdom for ever. I will be his father and he shall be my son. If he commit iniquity, I will chasten him with the rod of men, and with the stripes of the children of men: But my mercy shall not depart away from him, as I took it from Saul, whom I put away before thee. And thine house and thy kingdom shall be established for ever before thee:

thy throne shall be established for ever. (2 Samuel 7:12–16)

Later statements from God are heard by Solomon in a dream:

Behold, I have done according to thy words: lo, I have give thee a wise and an understanding heart; so that there was none like thee before thee, neither after thee shall any arise like unto thee. And I have also given thee that which thou hast not asked, both riches and honor: so that there shall not be any among the kings like unto thee all thy days. And if thou wilt walk in my ways, to keep my statutes and my commandments, as thy father David did walk, then I will lengthen thy days. (1 Kings 3:12–14)

The allusion to God's interaction with David and Solomon echoes the direct mention of God's anointing of David in Ivan's coronation ceremony: "Lord, our God, King of King and Lord of Lords, who having chosen his servant David through Samuel the prophet indeed anointed him as king over his people, the people of Israel."[47] The theme of God's wisdom as found in the words of Solomon inspires Ivan's Golden Hall mural decoration, contemporaneous with the Tsar's Pew and with the addition of the Prophet Tier and the Forefather Tier to the iconostasis of the Cathedral of the Annunciation, the palace church. The central images of the Prophet tier are the Mother of God with the Christ child on her knee: to the left stands David holding the Ark of the Covenant and to the right, Solomon, holding the Temple.[48]

The lack of traditional Christian symbols on the Tsar's Pew and the abundance of images and carvings of plants, flowers, fruit, and birds on the baldachin indicates the representation of a heavenly paradise in the model of a cosmic house.[49] The effect of this world of peace and harmony beyond time is continued inside the Tsar's Pew itself. On the ceiling the octagonal divisions produced by the first row of kokoshniki are painted deep blue with depictions of flowering vines in gold. Above them, in the recesses between kokoshniki, the deep blue of the heavens is studded with four-pointed and eight-pointed stars. The center of the ceiling, enclosed in a large circular wooden frame, is divided into twelve sections by wooden ribbing. Each section contains geometric intertwined vines with large ochre leaves and small red flowers. The presentation of the ruler under such a cosmic canopy has a long pedigree, traceable through the Byzantine Greeks and the Romans back to the ancient Near East, Persia, and China.[50]

The stylized heavenly garden paradise in the upper zone of the Pew just above the inscription about rulership must color any interpretation of individual elements on the Pew, including the striking and highly unusual chalices mentioned earlier (fig. 2.7). To read them as nothing more than charming decorative accents—chalices crowned by "pineapple goblet" tops—that lighten the mass of the baldachin[51] is to underestimate their numerical and thematic resonance with other elements of the Pew based on multiples of 3 and 4. Furthermore, their rather awkward positioning, balanced on the very points of the first row of kokoshniki or straddling the four corners, calls attention to them and suggests a larger role within the context presented by the baldachin.

Their positioning reveals once again an analogy with the Small Zion. Similar pyramidal structures are placed at the top of each round kokoshnik on the baldachin of the Small Zion, nine on a side, thirty-six in all (fig. 2.10). None of the existing literature on the Small Zion comments on them, yet they clearly distinguish the nine individual kokoshniki (three rows of three angels each) depicted on each side of the baldachin, that is, heavenly powers above as opposed to earthly saints below. And like the bowls of the chalices on the Pew, they rest on a broad triangular base at the very top of the kokoshniki. In profile, they appear to replicate the general shape of the large cupola of the Zion, although the staggered rows of scales on the latter are countered with even rows of spherical balls on the former.

The chalices on the Pew, although similarly positioned, apparently serve a different pur-

Fig. 2.10 Small Zion of the Cathedral of the Dormition, Moscow, 1486. Electroplated copy of now lost original. Detail.

pose. They demarcate the first row of kokoshniki with carvings of leafy vines and clusters of grapes, ancient symbols of fertility, plenty, and life itself. The chalices seem to contain neatly stacked objects rising to form a capped pyramid. Against the background of a New Jerusalem paradise and the pointed references to King Solomon in the cornice inscription ("and I will let you multiply your earthly fruits and secure your seed and establish your kingdom and throne unto the ages and will be like a father to you and you like a son to me"), the chalices may refer to the symbolic fruit associated with Solomon's Temple, as described in the Bible (e.g., 1 Kings 7:18,20,42). The pillars are linked by networks and lilywork and topped with hundreds of decorative pomegranates, symbols of fertility, resurrection, and eternal life. The stylized form and presentation of the pomegranates, stacked in stepped rows on a footed dish, would be appropriate for the Pew, in which all vegetable imagery tends toward the schematic and geometric.[52]

Such an interpretation is purely speculative, but it seems appropriate for the early 1550s, when the issue of royal succession was very much on the mind of Ivan and his wife, Anastasia, after they experienced three childbirths and three deaths. Dynastic continuity apparently played a role in the naming and placement of some of the chapels in Saint Basil's Cathedral on Red Square.[53] It is possi-

ble, even likely, that the tsar would not let the opportunity pass to bestow upon himself the symbolic blessings of fertility and continuity enjoyed by Solomon and his progeny.

An alternative interpretation of the chalices sees them in the context of the sacralization of the tsar as vessels containing myrrh, used in the anointing of the tsar, a ritual introduced in the coronation ceremony for Ivan IV.[54] This is an attractive hypothesis since it alludes to one of the unique aspects of the 1547 royal ritual, but we have no evidence that the oil used for the official anointing was kept in such vessels. In the coronation ceremony itself, the myrrh is simply described as being brought in a golden plate (*na zlatom bliude*)[55] and, indeed, the 1672 illustration of the moment of Tsar Mikhail's anointing in the *Election Book* shows the sacred oil in a golden plate held by three (arch)bishops.[56]

The introduction of the Tsar's Pew into the space before the Dormition iconostasis seems part of a general plan to sacralize this first Russian ruler crowned as tsar, placing him in an environment linked unequivocally with the representation of the most sacred of God's houses in Jerusalem, Solomon's Temple and the Church of the Holy Sepulcher, at the altar where the Eucharistic gifts are sanctified. Recall that the Church Slavonic word *prestol* means "throne" as well as "altar." This brief survey has suggested a number of different levels—historical, iconographical, eschatological—on which the Tsar's Pew might be interpreted in Muscovite Rus'. In its avoidance of Christian symbolism, the Pew states even more strongly than the Golden Hall the vital nature of the Muscovite tsar as God-chosen, the leader of the latter-day Israelites, the bearer of secular authority in the Muscovite realm, an emperor and his line sustained by God in his house for perpetuity. In the space before the iconostasis, it communicates in a very direct way that it is the tsar in concert with the boyar elites who will lead Muscovy to its political and spiritual destiny.

3 Architecture and Dynasty

Boris Godunov's Uses of Architecture, 1584–1605

Daniel Rowland

The political and geographic environment in pre-Petrine Rus' favored architecture as a major but little-investigated arena for symbolic action by the ruler. Although conditions obviously varied from time to time and place to place, there were four overlapping characteristics of all of the various states of Rus' before Peter that made architecture particularly useful as a tool of state-building: territories that were very large by European standards, the presence of multiple political and cultural units within those territories, relatively weak governmental structures, and almost entirely illiterate populations. Under these conditions, rulers from St. Vladimir to Peter the Great used architecture both to demonstrate their power and to define their image. Texts could be read only by a tiny minority; the largest pictures could be seen by but a few. Buildings, on the other hand, were large and tangible; they were visible from a distance over the consistently open Russian landscape, and, though they may have communicated a sophisticated meaning to the learned observer, they required little or no special knowledge to understand at a basic level. They could mark various points distributed over the whole territory of a state, and thus create in real space visual symbols of the unity of that state.

This was so at least from the conversion to Christianity, for Vladimir, Yaroslav, and their successors effectively used architecture, in the form of new Christian churches, to create the image of a single Christian people and state in place of the fragmented tribal territories that existed on the ground. Architecture was working in harmony with the other arts in this case: chronicles, saints' lives, sermons, and monumental painting were all making the same point. For most of this period, it is difficult to document the people's reaction to architecture, but we do know that architectural construction, whether of churches, fortifications, or palaces, was avidly noted in chronicles from the Primary Chronicle to the Nikon Chronicle and beyond.

Rulers or elites who were rich enough to afford it used architecture to define and justify their rule as well as to demonstrate their wealth and power: Saint Vladimir and Yaroslav the Wise, Andrei Bogoliubskii, the merchants of Novgorod, and Ivan III, to say nothing of Peter and Catherine, Stalin, and our contemporary, Mayor Luzhkov of Moscow—all expended great personal effort, considerable bureaucratic resources, and a lot of money on buildings. Scholars, especially historians, have yet to match their effort: at least in the pre-Petrine period, architecture finds too little place in discussions of political history, and is too often sequestered (and in a way trivialized) in chapters (or books) dealing with "the arts."

A brief discussion of the ways that Boris Godunov used architecture will make a useful case study of this issue for several reasons.

After this essay was substantially complete, Andrei Batalov was kind enough to send me a copy of his excellent *Moskovskoe kamennoe zodchestvo kontsa XVI veka: problemy khodozhestvennogo myshleniia epokhi* (Moscow, 1996). Although his book arrived too late to be incorporated in this essay, my footnotes reveal the extent of my debt to Andrei Batalov. His is one of the best books on Russian architecture to appear since World War II, and I recommend it warmly to all readers of this essay.

First, although the architectural efforts of Ivan III (in the Kremlin) and Ivan IV (in the construction of St. Basil's) have received due attention from historians, Boris's architectural activities have not been widely discussed, particularly in relation to his other activities as a ruler or to the symbolism of political power in Muscovy. Second, we have a small but tantalizing amount of evidence about Boris's own intentions, plus the comments of a number of contemporaries, native and foreign, on his architectural enterprises. These latter materials allow us access to some perceptions of Boris's architectural efforts, and thus enable us to gauge how successful those efforts were. To this information may be added excellent studies, particularly of church architecture, by Russian architectural historians who have studied not only the buildings as they currently exist, but such documentary evidence of their past states as can be found. They have also examined the results of "above-ground archeology," the study of a building's history as revealed in its surviving fabric, a study that is often carried out in the process of restoration work and reported in restoration reports. Finally, to complement the chapters in this volume that deal with architecture as a tool of government and state building (those of Flier, Shvidkovsky, and Wortman), a brief survey of all of the uses of architecture made by one ruler serves as a starting point.

When, after a good deal of maneuvering, Boris Godunov finally managed to arrange his own coronation in 1598, he faced the enormous problem of establishing his own legitimacy as tsar and the legitimacy of the Godunov clan as the new ruling dynasty. This problem was unprecedented. In the past there had been disputed successions and rulers too young to really rule, but past difficulties had centered around too many heirs rather than too few. The dynasty, even in the form of a powerless young boy such as the young Ivan IV, was the slender thread that kept the political system from sliding into chaos. The accession of Ivan's son, the mentally handicapped Fedor Ivanovich in 1584 (under whom Boris as royal brother-in-law exerted the real power)[1] still left room to hope for a new heir, but the death of Fedor in 1598 snapped the thread and ended the dynasty.

The selection of a new ruling dynasty was thus the most pressing political problem that Muscovy faced at the end of the sixteenth century, and it had two obvious components. First, a political consensus at court had to be found (or forged) around a new ruler and his clan. Here Boris faced a major difficulty because his own clan was less prestigious in terms of origins and service than its main rivals, the Romanovs and the Shuiskies. Second, since the political culture of Muscovy was built around the idea that God alone chose the tsar, this political process had to be concealed under a myth of divine choice. Given his weak genealogical position at court, Boris needed especially to rely on the public propagation of his and his family's image as embodying accepted ideals of Christian rulership and thus demonstrating God's choice of them. This symbolic side of his actions has received much less attention than his political efforts.

The sheer amount of building that Godunov either planned or carried out, the remarkable amount of obviously scarce resources that he devoted to his various architectural projects, and the comments of native and foreign observers at the time all testify to the emphasis that Boris placed on architecture as a means to establish his legitimacy and that of his clan. His choice is hardly surprising. Ivan III had expended great effort and money in his campaign to rebuild the Moscow Kremlin, carried on largely through the efforts of his Italian architects and engineers. Vasilii III had commissioned the dramatic, tent-roofed Church of the Ascension at Kolomenskoe to commemorate the birth of his young son. That son, Ivan IV, in turn built the Church of the Intercession on the Moat, popularly known as St. Basil's, to commemorate not only his conquest of Kazan', but also, as Michael Flier has recently shown, his success in producing a male heir.[2] The connections of architecture with both dynasty and military victory in sixteenth-century Muscovy were thus established as a subset of the relationship, common in virtually all states, between architecture and state power. From Boris's point of view, architecture had the advantage over painting or texts. Here architecture operated in tandem with the growing reach of the governmental apparatus. In earlier years, when he stood looking at a church or fortification, the Russian peasant was probably having a rare direct encounter with the government under which he lived. Now the very bureaucratic forces that enabled Boris to carry out his comprehensive architectural program also brought his government into closer contact with his subjects on a wide variety of social levels. These contacts reflected several areas of governmental concern, particularly the collection of taxes, the performance of military service, and the apparatus of justice.

Historians of Muscovite Russia might well be alarmed by my promiscuous use of the word "people" in connection with Boris's ambition to become and remain tsar. Surely, they might say, it was the boyars who made and unmade tsars. The answer to this question reveals an important reason why architecture was so important to Boris. It was in the Boyar Duma that Boris had the most enemies, or so the traditional scholarship tells us;[3] during his campaign to become tsar, he successfully used the Assembly of the Land and the Sacred Council to bolster his position in the Duma. His strenuous staging of rituals of popular acclaim demonstrate his desire to appeal to an audience wider than the Boyar Duma.[4]

Architecture, as we have seen, had a better ability to communicate with people geographically and socially outside the elite than any other weapon in the cultural arsenal of Muscovite rulership. And indeed the presumed audience for Boris's projects was remarkably wide. The elite, both secular and ecclesiastic, would have been powerfully impressed by his planned transformation of Cathedral Square in the Kremlin. His fortified trading towns like Astrakhan' and Archangel were of great benefit to merchants; his towns to the south and east provided protection and land to members of the middle and lower service classes, and new military positions for an expanding service elite. His building projects, whether on frontiers or in the central regions, provided employment. The great visibility of many projects made them accessible to anyone who passed through the wide Russian landscape. Finally, traditional Christian ideals of rulership stressed the tsar's obligations to the Christian people as a whole, not just to the elite. Architecture, of all the arts, allowed Boris to be perceived as fulfilling these obligations.

From a practical point of view, surely the most important of Boris's architectural activities was his construction or renovation of fortresses. The scale of Boris's fortress building in virtually every section of the country is staggering. It required the mobilization of enormous resources, human and material, and was probably not equaled again until the building campaigns of Peter the Great. (When we consider that Boris mounted this effort after the many disruptions of the latter part of Ivan the Terrible's reign, his achievement becomes even more remarkable.) The most recent scholar of his work has estimated that the state built or rebuilt over fifty fortresses during the twenty-one years (1584–1605) that he ruled either directly or indirectly.[5] In the south, Boris extended and strengthened the "abatis lines" (*zasechnye cherty*), which consisted of natural features (rivers, forests, and so on) joined by either wooden walls or, more usually, rows of felled trees, linking fortified towns that were the administrative as well as the military centers of their regions. These towns were built according to detailed instructions containing maps and drawings (*chertezhi*), worked out on the basis of continuing exchanges between local agents and the central bureaucratic apparatus in Moscow, in this case usually the Military Chancellery (the Razriadnyi prikaz).[6] Towns founded in the south by Boris included Voronezh and Livny (1585–86), Novyi Elets (1592), Belgorod, Kromy, Valuiki, and Staryi Oskol (1596), and Kursk (1597), as well as Tsarev-Borisov (1597) and Borisov Gorodok (1600), whose names reflect Boris's desire to connect these construction projects with himself and his dynasty. Boris was similarly active on the western frontier, where his greatest achievement was the construction of 6.5 kilometers of massive stone fortifications around Smolensk, built under Boris's personal supervision by Fedor Kon'. These fortifications enabled its defenders to resist for many months an intense Polish siege before their final defeat in June 1611, and turned its defenders into national heroes, celebrated in numerous patriotic circular letters in 1610 and 1611. He also repaired (or continued repairing) fortifications in Ladoga, Orekhov, and Pskov (1584–85), and improved the defenses around several strategically placed monasteries, finishing the new masonry walls of the Cyril–White Lake Monastery (1580–90) and building stone fortifications around the Ipat'ev Monastery (1586).

In the east, Boris established defensive points all along the crucial Volga trade route, beginning with the replacement of the wooden fortifications in Astrakhan' with new masonry walls between 7 and 11 meters tall. Between Kazan' and Astrakhan', Boris founded three major fortress-towns, Samara, Tsaritsyn, and Saratov, and, in addition, built smaller intermediate forts between these major points. He thus created a defensive line along the middle and lower reaches of the Volga, effectively protecting the crucial trade route between Muscovy and the great markets of the Middle East.[7] On the middle Volga, on the territory of the old Khanate of Kazan', Boris built a series of fortified towns, one after the other: Kokshaisk (1585), Sanchursk (1586), Tsivil'sk (1590), Iaransk (1591), and Urzhum (1595), not to mention his continued work on the fortifications of Kazan' itself. Slightly further east, Ufa was established in Bashkiria. Further east still, in Siberia, the list of towns established during the period under consideration is equally impressive: Tiumen' (1586), Tobol'sk (1586), Surgut (1594), Tara (1594), Verkhotur'e (1598); along the Ob, Berezov (1593), Obdorsk (1595), and Narym (1596); Mangazeia on the Enesiey River (1601) and, further south, Tomsk (1604). While the earliest town

foundations may have been carried out by the Stroganovs and their cossacks with little direction from Moscow, soon Boris's *prikazy* were bringing their formidable organizational and design skills to the task.[8]

In the north he improved fortifications along the White Sea, establishing in 1584 an *ostrog* or wooden fortress at Archangel, complete with musketeers, and soon furnished with many new buildings for trade. By the late 1580s, the government was reaping rich financial rewards from the taxes collected from the Archangel trade. Major fortifications were built around the Solovetskii Monastery and a smaller fort was constructed in Kem'. In Moscow itself, Boris built nine kilometers of massive new masonry walls around Belgorod and completed an oak wall around all of Moscow in less than two years (1591–2) (aptly named *skorodom* or *skorodum* ["quickly built"]), with fifty-seven towers and twelve gates, an astonishing 16 kilometers in length.[9]

As the above brief (and probably incomplete) account indicates, there were several motives, practical as well as symbolic, for the building of these fortresses. The expansion of the state and the defense of newly conquered territories depended on these structures, as did the growing (and increasingly profitable) trade through Archangel, down the Volga, in Siberia, and elsewhere. In these newly conquered territories, fortress towns, usually constructed on a bluff or high point near a river, established a visual dominance (see fig. 3.1) over the surrounding countryside that was the counterpart and visual reinforcer of the military dominance exercised by the fortress and its garrison. In many of these territories, trade was constantly threatened by bands of Nogais, Crimeans, Cossacks, or other raiders; in the south, raiders regularly carried off massive numbers of Slavic slaves. In this context, Boris's fortresses can be seen as potent visual symbols of government strength: under their walls trade could flourish and the military servicemen could cultivate their small estates.

Astrakhan' can serve as an example.[10] Refounded in 1558, two years after its conquest,

Fig. 3.1 Early eighteenth-century view of Astrakhan' by Cornelius de Bruyn, from the private collection of James Cracraft. Used with permission.

at an elevated site downstream and on the other side of the Volga from the Old Tatar town, the original wooden fortress was rebuilt in masonry in the 1580s. The result was impressive: the solid walls ranged in height (depending on the topography) from 7 to 11.3 meters, and were marked by 8 towers. The site made the fortress the dominating feature of the landscape. The fortifications themselves were similar in style to two later fortresses built under Boris (Smolensk and Belyi Gorod in Moscow). These similarities indicate more than a possible similarity of building personnel; by 1605, they created a visual link among major fortresses on the western and southern frontiers and the Moscow center. From a distance, the center of the town composition was the new stone Dormition Cathedral, built around 1600. The original church was pulled down and rebuilt at the end of the seventeenth century, but we may guess that the five-cupola design of the original church linked it with two pentacupolar Kremlin churches that had become canonic. The first of these was the Dormition Cathedral which served as a model for many churches in the provinces during the sixteenth century in such towns as Rostov, the Sergius Holy Trinity Monastery, Vologda, and Kazan', usually under government sponsorship.[11] A stronger visual connection was made with the Archangel Michael Cathedral, which was an important model, as we shall

see, for other Godunovian churches as well as for other sixteenth-century churches in general. Like Astrakhan's fortress, then, its main cathedral was linked to other similar structures in widely scattered parts of the country and was further identified stylistically with the Godunov clan.

The commanding position of the Dormition Cathedral over the Astrakhan' landscape can be seen to symbolize, like the Dormition Cathedral in Sviiazhsk (near Kazan', built under Ivan the Terrible), Christian Moscow's conquest and domination of a Muslim people. The theme of Moscow's troops as a sacred army conquering the infidel was an important theme in Muscovite political culture.[12] This chauvinistic theme did not interfere, however, with Boris's well-known desire to promote trade, in this case multiethnic trade. In the 1590s, two covered markets (the Bukhara and Persian markets) were built near the Astrakhan' kremlin, and in the seventeenth century an Indian market, an Armenian *dvor*, and a Tatar bazaar were set up. Mosques and Armenian churches soon followed. This pattern is consistent with Boris Godunov's encouragement of the German Settlement (Nemetskaia sloboda) in Moscow, and his promotion of foreign trade through Archangel.[13]

Beyond these particular considerations, common sense would dictate that fortress architecture, by its bulk and obvious expense, served as a symbol of the wealth and power of a state, quite apart from the military or economic advantages it conveyed. A large scholarly literature on fortresses in Russia as well as in Western Europe confirms this view.[14] A revealing piece of evidence on this point is that, soon after the completion of the impressive (and expensive) walls surrounding Moscow's Belyi Gorod, Boris Godunov rerouted the standard path followed by foreign ambassadors and their retainers so that diplomatic processions would pass by these walls.[15] Within Muscovite political culture, the image of the tsar as the figurative leader of the army in its struggle with foreign enemies occupied a central place. Literary sources and such visual monuments as the "Church Militant" icon and the murals in the Golden Palace throne room repeatedly emphasized the importance of the military strength of the monarch. Boris's victory over the Tatars in 1598 was an important factor in persuading the Boyar Duma to support his candidacy for tsar. His use in the 1598 campaign of a *guliai gorod*, a kind of collapsible wooden fort on wheels, was remarked on by many Russian contemporaries. The *Piskarev Chronicle*, a semi-official chronicle apparently sponsored by the Printing Office (Pechatnyi dvor), enthusiastically listed Boris's military and ecclesiastical building projects for those who had not noticed them. Boris's military architecture, therefore, fit a well-defined cultural niche.

Although by European standards Russia's wooden forts seemed primitive, and even the massive Smolensk fortress conservative, in the Russian context these structures were impressive, as chronicle accounts make clear. They were major improvements on what had existed earlier, and were a tangible and valuable sign of the growing power of the state, symbolizing both its geographical reach and, especially for the masonry fortifications, its physical strength and ability to marshal considerable resources. (The Smolensk fortress required some 100 million bricks and enormous quantities of other resources. Foreshadowing the measures of Peter the Great, Boris's government prohibited on pain of death non-state masonry construction while work on

Smolensk proceeded.) As technology changed in succeeding centuries, the semiotic place of fortress architecture was taken in large part by military parades, but the need for the state to express its military might through symbols remained a major feature of Russian culture.

Boris may also have had a more mundane (and more modern-sounding) motive for his vigorous program of military building. Contemporary opinion, according to Ivan Zabelin,[16] held that Boris's projects, particularly the construction of the *skorodom* in Moscow (1592), were aimed in part at providing work for the poorer people of Moscow, and thus securing their political support for him. This motive would be consistent with his later coronation promise that he would abolish poverty and divide his last cloak with his subjects.[17] Events in the very near future were to demonstrate the political power of the people of Moscow.

Was this strategy successful? As usual, there is a frustrating lack of source testimony to help us answer this question. The behavior of the inhabitants of some of Boris's new fortress towns during the Time of Troubles, however, may provide a clue. It turns out that many of these men deserted Boris at the first opportunity. Oskol, Valuiki, Tsarev-Borisov, Voronezh, and Belgorod all acknowledged the First False Dmitrii in January and February of 1605 (well before Boris's sudden death in April 13 [old style] of that year), followed shortly thereafter by Elets and Livny.[18]

Before leaving the subject of Godunov's military architecture, we should at least mention in passing a complementary achievement of his government that was crucial to his remarkable record of town-building. I refer to the making of maps. We have already discussed the use of maps in the creation of these new towns. The personnel of the Military Chancellery (Razriadnyi prikaz) would prepare maps with instructions on the basis of preliminary investigations of the site. The local *voevoda* and his staff could alter the plan if they saw fit, but otherwise (and this seems usually to have been the case) the town was constructed according to plans drawn up in Moscow. The planning, provisioning, construction, and staffing of a very large number of towns and fortresses spread over a space gigantic by European standards, from Smolensk in the west to Mangazeia in the east, must have required the ability to imagine fairly accurately the geography of Muscovy. It is not surprising, therefore, that the first map (or more likely collection of maps) that Russians ever made of their country, the famous Bol'shoi chertezh or Great Map, seems to have been made in the reign of Boris Godunov. The map or maps themselves have perished, but we have the accompanying text in a copy dating from the 1620s. Scholars are agreed that the original, whatever its form, dates to Boris's time. In addition, an early and startlingly accurate map of Russia accompanied by an equally impressive map of Moscow (the so-called Petrovskii chertez (see fig. 3.2) was also drawn up, surely by a foreigner, during Godunov's reign. We will have occasion to consider the Moscow map in another context, but for now we need only note that a very early version, published in Holland by Hessel Gerritsz in 1613 and provided to Gerritsz by Isaac Massa, is ascribed by Massa to Boris's son, Fedor Borisovich.[19] These maps formed an important complement to Boris's architectural projects. Just as those projects were designed to make the government and the Godunov family visible to the countryside, so Boris's various maps made the countryside visible to the government. Indeed, the process of making the maps brought about over time sharp changes in the countryside being mapped. Empty spaces were filled with forts, armies, agriculture, and trade, first on paper and then, when circumstances permitted, in fact.[20] This double accomplishment was remarkable at any time, but has received only scant attention from historians of Boris's reign.

The construction of churches and other religious buildings represents the other main arena of Boris's architectural efforts. Here again, architecture answered requirements that were essential parts of the Muscovite ideology of rulership, in this case two closely connected requirements that were universally clear both in written texts and in painting. First, the tsar had to protect and support the Orthodox Church, an obligation that church construction obviously helped to fulfill. Second, and more important, the tsar had to be seen as being personally pious. As his piety alone insured that his will would reflect God's will, it was essential to the validation of the whole political system.[21] The piety of the tsar, a private virtue, was not easy to demonstrate to the general public, but architecture offered an important means of doing this. The tsar's piety was a constant theme in official history writing, in Kremlin art (especially in the halls of state), and even in royal titulature. The wider public in Moscow was shown royal piety during public rituals (Palm Sunday, Epiphany); pilgrimages, which by Ivan IV's reign used up a great deal of the ruler's time and put a considerable strain on the royal family, especially on the tsaritsa, accomplished the same goal in some central and northern districts.[22] Church-building, though it was less personally linked to the ruler than pilgrimages or other ceremonies, was more visible, lasted much longer, and was capable of projecting an image of the ruler's piety into distant regions. Boris had his name inscribed in a very conspicuous religious place: in the gold letters that still surround the golden dome of the Ivan the Great Bell Tower (see fig. 3.3). This tower, due to Boris's addition of two extra stories, was to dominate the Kremlin and even the Moscow skyline down to the twentieth century.[23] Foreign visitors to Moscow in the seventeenth century frequently mentioned the bell tower and its visibility from great distances over the countryside.

This example of *superbia* was roundly condemned by contemporaries such as Isaac Massa and Ivan Timofeev. Timofeev, following the model of Paul's interpretation of the story of Cain and Abel, used this example of Boris's pride to dismiss all of Boris's church building activities as praiseworthy acts that were vitiated by the motive (pride) that lay behind them.[24] This reaction shows how slippery were the slopes of Muscovite ideology. Since, following Christian tenets, contemporary writers focussed on the motive as well as

Fig. 3.2 Plan of Moscow engraved before 1646 by Matthaus Merian (in his *Newe archontologia cosmica* [Frankfurt/Main, 1646]), based on the Petrov plan made in or before 1605 by order of Boris Godunov. Courtesy of the Harvard College Library.

the act, even virtuous acts could be undermined in the public view if the motives for performing it were judged to be bad. This approach, which made the estimation of a ruler turn entirely on motives that could be only guessed at, allowed most commentators, especially those writing after the death of Boris, to condemn Boris's architectural achievements as vainglorious. Even these accusations, however, testify to the central place that church building occupied among the duties of a tsar: building churches was seen as a great good even if Boris's motives were suspect in this case.

Architectural historians in Russia, particularly A.L. Batalov, have investigated the churches built under Godunov with great care. In a short essay there is regrettably no space to go into much detail, but there seems to be a consensus about several features of

Godunovian church architecture. First, in spite of the use of several church types ("columnless" churches with a single dome, five-dome churches, tent-roof churches), Godunov-era churches share more features than do churches built either under Ivan IV or in the first part of the seventeenth century. This sense of consistency has led E. G. Shcheboleva to suggest the existence of a "Godunov school" of architecture, including two major builders (or artels) that used common building techniques as well as common design features. She singles out a small group of churches closely connected with Boris Godunov and probably supervised by the Masonry Chancellery as being especially consistent. Though varying in type, they are characterized by compact massing of the central block, high pyramidal roofs with prominent rows of *kokoshniki*, and the careful use

Fig. 3.3 The Ivan the Great Bell Tower in the Moscow Kremlin. Photo by Elizabeth English, 1995. Used with permission.

of Italian-inspired architectural "orders," based directly or indirectly on the Archangel Michael Cathedral in the Moscow Kremlin. The idea of a Godunov school of architecture and the governmental control implied by this research suggests that Boris chose to identify himself and his dynasty with a particular set of architectural characteristics.[25]

What was the message that this architectural language conveyed to Boris's contemporaries? Like almost all aspects of Orthodox Christian culture, church design was confined within narrow stylistic boundaries. Many viewers were likely sensitive to relatively small stylistic variations. One fairly obvious point is that the changes wrought by the "Godunov School" were quite conservative compared to those inspired by Ivan III or Ivan IV. No basic new forms were introduced, and the stylistic "signature," while recognizable, seems to have been aimed at conveying the message that Boris's churches were securely anchored in traditional Russian architecture. In this context, the use of surface detailing based on Italian architectural orders, what Russian architectural historians refer to as "Italianisms," is meant to convey not an affinity with Italy or with foreign design principles, but a self-conscious, even archaizing, reference to one of the most influential buildings in the Kremlin, the Archangel Michael Cathedral, the burial place of Russian tsars.[26] Given Boris's desire to establish a new dynasty, his choice of this building, with its explicit dynastic connections, can hardly have been accidental. The pyramidal massing, created by more rows of higher *kokoshniki*, and, in pentacupolar churches, by the increasing height of the domes and their drums, and the placement of the four subsidiary domes closer to the central dome, is harder to decipher. If we take the single-domed Cathedral of the Don (fig. 3.4) as typical, we can see a striking similarity between its pyramidal massing and "Zions," liturgical vessels that were meant to reflect the Church of the Holy Sepulcher in Jerusalem.[27]

For those less able to appreciate architectural subtlety, Boris turned to that staple of architectural self-assertion, tall buildings. We have already briefly mentioned his additions to the Ivan the Great Bell Tower (fig. 3.3). This building was 81 meters tall and its golden dome (with its prominent mention of Boris and his son) was the first building in Moscow to be seen as a visitor approached the city. Equally impressive was the Church of Sts. Boris and Gleb in Borisov Gorodok (fig. 3.5), a personal estate that Boris built near Mozhiask. Some 74 meters tall without the cross, this was the highest church built in Russia up to that time. Set high on a river bank, it could hardly have been better suited to proclaim the arrival of a new and powerful dynasty.

Can we discern an iconographical theme behind Boris's works? One theme that powerfully linked Boris's desire to portray himself

Fig. 3.4 The Old Cathedral of the Don, taken from I. E. Grabar, W. N. Lazarew, and W. S. Kemenow, *Geschichte der Russischen Kunst*, vol. 3 (Dresden, 1959), plate 256, p. 337.

both as a pious God-chosen ruler and the founder of a new dynasty was the idea of Moscow as a New Jerusalem. This idea had already taken form just outside the Kremlin in the Cathedral of the Intercession on the Moat (now usually referred to as St. Basil's), which contemporaries routinely called "Jerusalem." Architectural historians have asserted that two images of Jerusalem were read into that building: its design was believed to have been modeled on the Church of the Holy Sepulcher in contemporary Jerusalem, a church that figured prominently in pilgrims' accounts. At the same time it was apparently seen as a reflection of the Heavenly or New Jerusalem of the Apocalypse (Revelation 21: 18–21; Isaiah 54: 11–14), a golden city with walls in the form of a square, walls encrusted with precious stones and containing twelve gates, three on each side. According to the testimony of both native sources and foreign witnesses, Boris Godunov intended to de-

velop this idea further by building a new church in the Kremlin that would eclipse all others in richness of decoration as well as in size. This church was to have been based simultaneously on Solomon's Temple in ancient Jerusalem (Boris referred to the projected church as "the Holy of Holies") and on the church of the Holy Sepulcher in contemporary Jerusalem. According to Elias Herckman, Boris asked his assistants to search for evidence of this "Holy of Holies" both in scripture and in the works of Joseph Flavius on Jewish history. On the other hand, Timofeev tells us that Boris was equally intent on making an exact copy (*meroiu i podobiem*) of Jesus' tomb or coffin (*grob*) in Jerusalem, which many historians have taken as a reference to the Church of the Holy Sepulcher there. A. L. Batalov, however, has persuasively argued that Timofeev and other contemporary authors referred to "the Lord's coffin" (*grob Gospoden'*), a piece of liturgical

Fig. 3.5 The Church of Boris and Gleb and the fortress in Borisov Gorodok, near Mozhaisk. View from the second half of the eighteenth century. Taken from *Gradostroitel'stvo Moskovskogo Gosudarstva*, ed. N. F. Gulianitskii (Moscow, 1994).

furniture used in the Orthodox liturgy especially during Friday and Saturday of Holy Week.[28] Boris's opulent version was cast in gold and encrusted with precious stones, and that impressed Timofeev deeply. The image of Moscow as the New Jerusalem is suggested by the design of the oak wall (*skorodom*) with which Boris surrounded Moscow. In a map of Moscow (the so-called Petrovskii chertezh) based, as we have seen, on a copy of a map drawn up under Boris, the wall is represented as a square with rounded corners, with twelve gates, three on each side.[29]

There is a revealing piece of evidence about Boris's architectural intentions that has been overlooked by historians. It is found in the murals in the throne room of the Palace of Facets, decorated under Tsar Fedor Ivanovich, but with the obvious participation of Boris, who had himself depicted as Fedor's chief boyar on the south wall, directly next to the tsar's throne. (The entire north wall and one third of the east wall are devoted to the story of the Old Testament hero Joseph, a figure Boris clearly saw as a symbol for himself.) On this same south wall, in addition to Fedor, Boris, and the boyars, are a series of rulers meant to convey the message that divinely inspired leadership originated in the Old Testament and passed to Rus', leading

directly to the living tsar, Fedor Ivanovich, and his advisor Boris. The series begins with Moses (who is shown before the Ark of the Covenant) and includes David (also shown worshipping before the Ark after repenting his sin with Bathsheba), Solomon, Vladimir Monomakh, and, finally, Fedor and his court. Solomon is shown before the Ark of the Covenant inside the temple, specifically called in the inscription "the Holy of Holies," near which is a columnar cloud. Priests stand near Solomon, and the people of Israel stand behind Solomon. The inscription, carefully copied by Simon Ushakov and his assistant in 1672 and therefore probably an accurate version of the original, is worth quoting in full:

And when Solomon finished [building] the Holy of Holies, the priests left the building, and a cloud filled the temple of the Lord, and the priests could not stand and serve before the face of the cloud, since the temple was full of the glory of God. Solomon, having come to the stairs, worshiped to the Lord, as did all the sons of Israel, who saw the cloud, fell down on the ground, and praised the Lord.[30]

The interpretation of this wall and its relation to Boris's position seem clear. In each of the Old Testament scenes, the presence and protection of God, the covenant between God and His people, is symbolized by the Ark of the Covenant. In each case the leader of Israel (including "Tsar" David and "Tsar" Solomon) affirms the covenant by his religious act. Moses places the ten commandments in the Ark; David worships God before the Ark after being punished for his sin by the death of his son; Solomon brings the Old Testament series to a climax by building a temple (the Holy of Holies) for the ark; in so doing, he earns God's favor, a favor not extended to the priests, and, through Solomon's architectural efforts, the people of Israel are brought to worship God.

These three scenes epitomize the link between religious and political leadership by illustrating three types of religious performance by the ruler: Moses gives the sacred law, David repents and then displays his personal piety by worshiping before the Ark, and Solomon builds the temple.[31] No Ark of the Covenant is present in the last two, Rus'ian scenes, those depicting the courts of Vladimir Monomakh and Fedor Ivanovich. Its absence prompts the viewer to wonder where the Rus' version of the Ark is, and what the religious *podvigi* of Vladimir Monomakh and Fedor are. As the *Tale of the Vladimir Princes*, illustrated on the adjoining east wall, explains, Monomakh received charismatic regalia from Byzantium. What of Fedor and Boris? Boris's scheme to build a new and sumptuous "Holy of Holies" based on scriptural descriptions of Solomon's temple would seem to supply both an ark (in the form of the Lord's tomb) and a *podvig*. Thus, by building a new version of the Temple in Moscow, Boris casts himself as a new Solomon, reaffirming the covenant between God and His people through the architectural act of church construction. Note that in the scriptural description of the building of the temple (1 Kings 6:11–13), Solomon's building project was described as a sign of the continuing covenant between God and Solomon and between God and the people of Israel. Michael Flier's chapter in this volume shows the Muscovite use of this idea in the 1550s, when a new prophet tier was added to

the iconostasis in the Annunciation Cathedral. In the center of that tier was an image of the Mother of God with Christ on her knee, flanked on the left by David holding the Ark of the Covenant and on the right by Solomon holding his temple. For Tsar Boris as for Tsar Ivan IV, the analogy with Solomon symbolized both divinely inspired kingship and the all-important dynastic theme, "the fertility and continuity enjoyed by Solomon and his progeny," as Flier puts it.

This evidence about a project that would have transformed the very sacred center of the Muscovite state indicates how strong was the identity of Moscow and Jerusalem in the mind of Boris Godunov and how important were the twin images of God's houses in Jerusalem, Solomon's temple and the Church of the Holy Sepulchre. To this evidence may be added the already-observed similarity in form between "Godunov-school" churches and "Zions," liturgical implements that contemporaries believed reflected the design of the Jerusalem Church of the Holy Sepulcher, a similarity that takes on added meaning in this context.

This conflation of Jerusalem's two churches reminds us of Boris's apparent confusion of three Jerusalems, Solomon's Jerusalem in the Old Testament, present-day (that is, sixteenth-century) Jerusalem, and the New Jerusalem of the Apocalypse, a conflation that has puzzled many commentators. I think that we see here an example of a typological sense of time that was characteristic of Orthodox culture generally.[32] It bears a striking resemblance in particular to the sense of time in the so-called "Church Militant" icon, in which an army is represented simultaneously as the Old Testament army of Israel, the present army of Muscovy under Ivan IV, and the army of the righteous led by Christ at the Apocalypse. Certainly, the theme of Russia as a New Israel was central in Russian culture of the time, and was richly represented both in the various tales about the Time of Troubles and, as we have seen, in such visual monuments as the mural cycle in the Palace of Facets.[33]

One last important (but less exalted) piece of evidence on Boris's uses of architecture remains to be considered in our investigation: the *Piskarev Chronicle*. The section of this compiled chronicle dealing with the reign of Ivan IV has been crucial to the interpretation of that period, but the section describing the reigns of Fedor and Boris has received less attention. This section, which Tikhomirov believed was written by an employee of the Printing Office, is unique in the history of Russian chronicle writing for the proportion of space it devotes to architectural projects, mills and bridges as well as fortresses and churches.[34] In several sections, the chronicle is nothing more than a listing of these projects, one after the other. Not surprisingly, the *Piskarev Chronicle* has been a basic source for the architectural history of the period. What interests us here, however, is the motive for compiling such a text. If Tikhomirov is right about the identity of the author, this section of the chronicle may have been a sketch compiled in the Printing Office for an official chronicle of Boris's and Fedor's reigns, the completion (and dissemination) of which was cut short by Boris's sudden death. If so, this text shows the extraordinary importance attached to architecture by Godunov's official publicists. Even if it was written under other circumstances, it indicates at the least what an important place Boris's architectural projects occupied in one person's recollections of his reign.

Our brief investigation suggests several conclusions. First, Boris Godunov was an extremely active patron of architecture; his decision to devote so many scarce resources to buildings of various sorts, I would argue, was closely connected to his own insecure position at court and his need to accomplish the virtually unprecedented task of establishing a new dynasty. His attention to architecture in this context testifies to the confidence Boris had in this particular kind of symbolic action. Second, this survey of the scope of Boris's architectural undertakings illustrates the extraordinary competence of his government in carrying out many large-scale projects in widely separated geographical regions. Third, the uses that Boris made of

architecture showed him (or his helpers) to have been remarkably skillful in elaborating and manipulating the accepted political culture of the time, a culture that stressed the protective military abilities and the personal piety of the ruler. Fourth, the work that Russian architectural historians have done to establish both the generally high degree of similarity among churches of Boris's time and, more particularly, the existence of a "Godunov school" closely connected with Boris himself, may at least suggest that Boris imagined the idea of a kind of signature set of features that that would visually connect buildings that embodied them with Boris himself and with the Godunov dynasty. Fifth, a good deal of evidence indicates that Boris intended to rebuild Cathedral Square, the sacred center of the Muscovite state, to develop further the inherited idea of Moscow as a new Jerusalem, a component of the notion of Muscovy as a new Israel that seems to have been popular among many different groups at the end of the sixteenth century. All that survives of this grandiose scheme is the rebuilt Ivan the Great Bell Tower. Had Boris survived to complete his scheme, his impact on Russian architecture would now be considered almost equal to that of Ivan III. Finally, the murals in the Palace of Facets explain why Boris devoted so much energy to architecture, particularly church architecture. He felt that building was a sacred task of rulership, closely connected through Old Testament models to the establishment of a God-chosen dynasty.

Was Boris's remarkable architectural campaign successful? His sudden and unexplained death in 1605 makes that question hard to answer. The ensuing Time of Troubles makes it difficult to see Boris's reign in any light other than a tragic one. Yet Boris's obvious skills in almost every sphere of government lead one to suspect that, had he survived, he might well have established a new and successful dynasty. At the same time, both domestic and foreign contemporaries wrote that Boris's architectural projects, as admirable and impressive as they were, merely served to illustrate the measure of his pride. Although this judgment was usually made after Godunov's death rather than during his reign, it illustrates how subjective the criteria for rulership were in Muscovy and in Europe, since the tsar's (presumably unknowable) internal righteousness was the fundamental quality without which even the most praiseworthy deeds were useless or even harmful. Thus the interpretations of Boris's architectural efforts by his contemporaries show how difficult, perhaps impossible, was his image-building task. As modern historians and Boris's own contemporaries look back on Boris's building campaign through the prism of the intervening Time of Troubles, what might have been regarded as one of his major accomplishments has been seen instead as evidence of his sinful nature.

Part 2

Imperial Russia

4 Catherine the Great's Field of Dreams

Architecture and Landscape in the Russian Enlightenment

Dimitri Shvidkovsky

The development of Russian architecture during the eighteenth century was determined to a large extent by state policy in the field of construction. In the beginning of the last century, scholars like I. Grabar thought that architectural style in eighteenth-century Russia was influenced, first of all, by the personality of the monarch. This idea was not popular during the Soviet period for obvious reasons. Nevertheless, one can see differences in eighteenth-century Russian architecture that correspond with the reigns of Peter the Great, Anna I, Elizabeth I, and Catherine the Great; one can even see some changes in architecture linked to the brief reigns of Peter II or Peter III. The power of the emperor to choose the architectural image of every new building and to shape the formal plan for every town in Russia was confirmed in a series of special laws. The mechanism to fulfill these laws through Senate, Synod, governors and police captains worked well.

As soon as Catherine the Great came to the throne she changed the country's style of architecture to what could be called classicism in the Age of Enlightenment. These efforts were not merely her caprice; she wanted to finish the process of transforming Russian architecture into a branch of European architecture, of putting Russian architecture on a footing fully equal to that found in the most developed states of Europe. For Catherine, architectural policy was at the same time a means of creating an image or model of her political ideals (architecture as allegory) and as a tool for implementing these ideals of enlightened rulership (architecture as policy). To achieve these ends Catherine the Great

boldly deployed a wide variety of architectural styles, European and non-European, to convey a series of carefully constructed messages.

Catherine began her reign by using architectural styles fashionable in Europe, rococo and chinoiserie, to build her urban palaces. Later, she used other styles to express her political will: town planning was done primarily using French-inspired classicism to create well-organized urban centers for the benefit of the Russians; the Turkish wars unleashed nationalist elements expressed in the medieval Russian neo-Gothic style. By the 1780s, Catherine was more and more drawn to a Palladian-inspired classicism that combined the purity of French classicism with a sensual appreciation for ancient, particularly Roman, forms. Charles Cameron's works best expressed this last style, a style that transformed her summer palace at Tsarskoe Selo and adjacent rural estates. At the same time English landscape gardening on a grand scale was used to bring these various elements together by combining ideal examples of towns, memorial gardens, and rural estates into Catherine's vision of Enlightenment Russia—the *Gartenreich* or garden kingdom that strove to reflect her ideals of governing.

Catherine implemented her grand design at her rural estate of Tsarskoe Selo. At the estate's center were Cameron's classical baths, and the gallery from which Catherine saw her vision become reality. From within the gallery she could see the Temple of Memories, created to commemorate Russian victories over

Edited by Daniel Rowland and Kelly Vickery.

the Turkish sultan; she could see the town of Sophia, created especially to be viewed from the gallery as the model of an ideal town in enlightenment Russia; she could see her son's estate, Pavlovsk, created as the model private estate of a perfect gentleman; and she could see the Alexandrova dacha and, later, the enormous palace of Pella, estates of her grandson Alexander, from whom she expected the greatness achieved by his ancient Greek namesake. Each of these specific areas was created in a different style; each style was carefully chosen by Catherine to mold Russia metaphorically and actually into the enlightened state of which she dreamed.

The startling control exercised by the monarch over architecture, a power unusual for Europe during the Enlightenment, was in the spirit of eighteenth-century Russian history. Only the power of the monarch could accomplish the required transformations in the field of construction. Absolutist power had compressed into a comparatively short time the evolution of architecture from a late medieval style, which had a very distinctive national character, to the rather typical European building style found at the beginning of the nineteenth century. This development, which lasted in western countries for at least three centuries, was accomplished by Russian architecture in one hundred years—much faster than anywhere else. The English garden writer J. C. Loudon, who visited St. Petersburg and Moscow in 1812–13, wrote of it: "Nothing can be more extraordinary . . . than these well-known facts, that a century ago there was scarcely such a thing, in any part of Russia, as a garden; and, for the last fifty years, there have been more pine-apples grown in the neighbourhood of Petersburg than in all the other countries of the continent put together."[1]

For this acceleration, the wide use of architectural experience from different states in Europe was needed. At the same time the new architecture of Russia had no single Western model. The influences and patterns from many countries served as "letters" in a new architectural "alphabet," which was used by Russians to express their ideas. And one can

say that the "grammar" of this language was determined by the mentality of the Russian Enlightenment, sometimes similar to, sometimes very different from the Western one.

Russian architecture in the first thirty years of the eighteenth century had many stylistic trends connected with the different stages of European architectural development. Several kinds of baroque can be found in the buildings of St. Petersburg and Moscow constructed during this period, buildings in which one can trace late medieval, Renaissance and classicist influences. The variety of architectural styles during the reign of Peter the Great was the result of the interaction of foreign masters, who came from Prussia, Saxony, Italy, France, Holland, Poland, and Ukraine. Peter the Great even wanted to get a Chinese architect, but did not succeed in doing so.

The individual styles of the various European architects did not survive later than 1740. The "polyphony" of stylistic trends characteristic of Peter's reign was largely changed by the indivisible style of the Russian baroque developed during the reign of the Empress Elizabeth I. The works by B. Rastrelli, S. Chevakinskii, and D. Ukhtomskii in St. Petersburg, Moscow and Kiev showed the force of this single style. But the architecture of Elizabeth's baroque came to an end at the very moment of its full flourishing, when it gave no sign of tiredness or weakness. Why? Because it was stopped by the taste of the new sovereign.

As soon as Catherine the Great came to the throne in 1762, she changed the style of architecture in the country to what could be called classicism in the Age of Enlightenment. Using architecture, landscape architecture, and town planning, she dreamed of establishing a civilization in Russia equal to that found in the most developed states in Europe.

Architecture allowed Catherine to declare her Enlightenment ideals of rulership and to mold a civilization in Russia to rival that in Europe; she worked out a special mechanism to do this, based on the simultaneous use of several architectural experiences in the field of construction. The mechanism exposed the ideas of French, English, Italian, and German architectural Enlightenments to each other under Catherine's active patronage to produce a new Enlightenment style. Of course the architecture produced by this mechanism was not strictly planned; the empress did not always intend the same meaning in her architectural desires as was actually produced by her architects, whether Russian or foreign. Nevertheless, in the second half of the eighteenth century several "ideological trends" in Russian architecture connected with different European traditions to form a single distinct style.

The most difficult time to determine what was specifically Russian in Russian architecture is the second half of the eighteenth century. It certainly was the period when the new architecture of St. Petersburg and Moscow was strongly linked with the international development of style. But for Catherine the Great and her contemporaries there was no general European style. They saw the distinctive differences in the national architectural schools found in different countries, and they were especially interested in what was most new or striking or vivid in each of them. Carefully and skillfully, with the help of a system of artistic spying, the empress and her circle were selecting models to create the architectural taste of a new enlightened Russian architecture.

The first "architectural trend" of the Russian Enlightenment was one of exotic dreams. The primary models of the architectural environment for Catherine were the palaces and gardens in Potsdam, created for the King of Prussia in whose troops her father, prince of Anhalt-Zerbst, was the field marshal. She forced an Italian, Antonio Rinaldi, the pupil of Luigi Vanvitelli, to turn to rococo in the taste of von Knobbelsdorff. In this manner, the so-called Private Estate of Catherine the Great in Oranienbaum was built in the 1760s.

It is interesting that at the Russian court rococo soon began to loose its classicist spirit, being forced out by classicism itself and appearing more often in the form of the exotic architecture of the "jardin anglo-chinois" in its French or German version. A vast ensemble in Chinese taste was created at Tsarskoe Selo from the end of the 1760s to the 1770s. Antonio Rinaldi, Georg Velten (an architect of German origin), and later Charles Cameron (who came from London) participated in the creation of this next architectural trend. We must underline that the architects at Tsarskoe Selo, instead of using Dutch and German examples as had been done in the middle of the eighteenth century, turned to the English pattern books in Chinese taste by Chambers (and by authors like W. and J. Halfpenny,[2] who popularized Chambers's ideas) or to French publications—especially the volumes of Le Rouge.[3]

This first ideological trend of the Russian architectural Enlightenment connected with rococo and chinoiserie addressed itself first to the senses and only secondarily to reason. The Enlightenment began in Russia with a game—the creation of an exciting and curious environment.

In the same playful rococo context, the first examples of neo-Gothic buildings came to Russia from Britain in the beginning of the 1770s. The chivalrous game of pavilions in medieval taste erected in landscape gardens began near St. Petersburg in the early 1770s—Chesmenskii palace, the Hermitage kitchen, and the Admiralty in Tsarskoe Selo. Then it came to Moscow during the festival devoted to the victory over the Turks in 1774, where the neo-Gothic provoked an interest in the national Muscovite architecture of the Middle Ages. In the environs of the ancient capital of Russia, the language of Russian neo-Gothic was spoken with an eighteenth-century British accent: classical and oriental, but with a mostly Russian, medieval, seventeenth-century Muscovite motif. The spirit of this strange mixture resembled the eccentricity of baroque theater. But one can find in the architecture of Vasilii Bazhenov in Tsaritsino, an enormous neo-Gothic ensemble near Moscow, an attempt to work out a new language of "architecture parlante," not in the spirit of Ledoux, but based on different stylistic and national sources; not on the alphabet of spatial forms, but more on decorative ones.

Rococo, chinoiserie and neo-Gothic were

developing in palace and estate architecture together with landscape gardening, while in the construction of towns, classicism dominated. True, building during the two first decades of Catherine the Great's reign, up to 1780, had a firm French orientation. Jean-Baptiste Vallin de la Mothe was invited to St. Petersburg to construct the building used to house the Academy of Arts, which was to become a stylistic manifesto for urban architecture. The function of the building itself made it the model on which the new classical style was to be founded.

The most talented young Russian architects, Vasilii Bazhenov and then Ivan Starov, were sent to Paris where they studied under Charles de Wailly. It is important that their teacher belonged to the younger generation of French architects of the 1750s and 1760s—those with the most modern ideas. In St. Petersburg and Moscow, French architectural editions were used as textbooks,[4] a choice that greatly influenced the other leading architects—Matvei Kazakov, Ivan Nikitin, and others. In the last quarter of the eighteenth century the French architect Nicolas Legrand worked in Moscow and played an important role in directing classicism in the old capital of Russia toward French patterns.

At the same time, the ideas of classicism were used in Russian town planning on an enormous scale. They are considered to be of French origin, but it seems extraordinary that it is so very difficult to find the direct sources of Russian city plans from the time of Catherine the Great in France itself. The urban legislative environments in Russia and France at that time were very different, and attitudes toward the towns, property, and land, as well as the organization of life on them, were not comparable between the two countries. This explains the reason for the absence of direct analogues between Russian city plans and those in France of the 1750s through the 1770s. But we must also consider the town planning practiced by French military engineers outside the metropole. Even the ideas of L'Enfant for Washington or the structure of New Orleans of that time can easily be compared with the results of town planners in the

Russia of Catherine the Great. The example of Paris itself was of some importance to Moscow: one must think about the project of Vasilii Bazhenov to change the Kremlin into a neoclassical ensemble, or the planning of circular boulevards on old ramparts proposed by Nicolas Legrand—the author of the first design master plan for Moscow, in 1774–75.

All these facts show that during the first two decades of her reign, Catherine the Great was moving from the German-oriented rococo to the influence of French classicist architectural authorities. In her mind the image of civilized towns, strictly classical in the mid-eighteenth-century French sense, had to be the expression of enlightened and rational prosperity for her country; this was combined with the image of exotic rural residences, where the senses could add their charms to reason.

In the middle 1770s, and especially on the eve of the 1780s, the architectural policy of Catherine the Great changed. She was "poisoned" with "plantomania," as she wrote herself, which "inhabited her heart with passions for things like curved alleys, lawns, picturesque groups of trees—all the symbols of 'jardins a l'anglaise.' "[5] She became interested in the natural countryside. Her model of the image of enlightened Russia was widened. Now to the massive use of French ideas in town architecture, the English attitude toward rural landscape was added; the widened image contained a landscape garden decorated by estate buildings, handsome post offices on the roads, and ideal villages with nice huts. This again was an exaggeration. Catherine the Great and her assistants often began to think about planning huge territories, if not whole provinces, in the manner which the English (William Shenstone, for example) used for their comparatively small private estates and their gardens.

To some extent Catherine the Great received her taste for ideal territorial planning from Germany. She was always in contact with her second cousin, Prince and Duke Franz II of Anhalt-Dessau, who was at that time remaking his tiny but independent state

(30 x 8 km. in size) into a Garden Kingdom, a "Gartenreich."[6] He followed closely the advice of Voltaire, their common friend and correspondent, "to cultivate the garden of one's life." The example of Franz's landscaping in Worlitz, Luisium, Stiglitz, and territories between these gardens was especially recommended to Catherine by her Belgian confidant Prince Charles de Ligne in his letters. It was in this small state in Germany, so close to the heart of Catherine, where the enlightened life of the landscape garden was put into state practice. This model was used by the Russian empress on a bigger scale.

The manor houses to be placed in the landscape were mostly designed in a classical style. But the classicism was different from that of the 1760s and 1770s. Changes in Catherine's ideal of antiquity came simultaneously with her increased interest in landscape gardening.

In 1778 Catherine wrote to Baron Grimm that she would like to have two Italians, because "we have here those French, who know too much, and build bad houses, only because they know too much."[7] It seems strange that the enlightened empress would accuse someone of knowing too much. This needs an explanation from other sources. Catherine the Great was tired of "normal" classicism with its laws and science. She wanted to turn once more from the mental, rational, French model of classicism to the sensual revival of antiquity, more in the English or Italian taste. "I want to build a Greco-Roman rhapsody in my gardens in Tsarskoe Selo," she wrote.[8] A program to be fulfilled by architects was distributed in Europe. She said in it that the Empress of all the Russias asks the artists "to seek in Antiquity for a house with all the furniture . . . to create the epitome of the epoch of Caesar, Augustus, Cicero . . . where one could place all them together."[9]

The French were the first to give an answer. Charles de Wailly sent the design of the Pavilion of Minerva. This was a building where all the laws of "normal" French classicism were fulfilled, but there was no sensual revival of antiquity, which was what she was looking for. She turned to Rome, and addressed the French in Rome. Charles-Louis Clerisseau tried to answer her task exactly. He had found the type of building where famous Romans were often together and where the way of life could be easily recreated. He sent to St. Petersburg his design of the Roman Baths in Tsarskoe Selo, made on the model and scale of the Baths of Diocletian.

Catherine liked the idea, but the dimensions of the building were impossible, as was the amount of money Clerisseau wanted for his work. At this moment Catherine thought of Italians, but Italians of a very special kind. We can trace the personalities of the architects invited. The name of these "Italians" were Giacomo Quarenghi, Giacomo Trombara, and, strangely, Charles Cameron.

Giacomo Quarenghi, born in Bergamo, was educated in the traditions of "natural" Palladianism of Northern Italy,[10] and represented in Russia this trend of Italian classicism. It was important for Russian architecture that his buildings had a neo-Renaissance feeling. Of course Catherine did not think about this, but she certainly intended that the great Italian classical traditions were to be introduced into Russian architecture.

Charles Cameron was for the Empress a special kind of Italian, an Italian Scotsman. She wrote that he was a "Jacobite by birth, brought up in Rome at the court of the pretender to the English throne."[11] So, in addition to the Italians, Catherine invited a Scottish specialist who was studying antiquity in Rome. She was not mistaken; nevertheless she received false information about the biography of Charles Cameron.[12] He did have personal connections with representatives of the Scottish Enlightenment, and he was in Rome where he was inflamed by passion for the sensual revival of antiquity. In reality he was brought up in London, not in Rome. In London, Charles Cameron became closely connected with the ideas of the second generation of the Palladian patterns in the Burlingtonian manner, with a devotion to the "archeological" classicism of Adams. This combination was the essence of his influence on Russian architecture. He built the famous Cameron Gallery in Tsarskoe Selo for Catherine the

Fig. 4.1 The Cold Baths of Tsarskoe Selo. Drawing of the 1780s. From Dimitri Shvidkovsky, *The Empress and the Architect* (New Haven, 1996), fig. 44, p. 51. Used with permission.

Great as a "working model" of the baths of the Romans (see fig. 4.1). In the palace of Pavlovsk Cameron decorated a Palladian manor house with images of real antiquity. Later this was done by Ivan Starov in the Tauride palace in St. Petersburg, built for Prince Potemkin, and on a large scale in the palace of Pella near St. Petersburg. There Starov tried to recreate the birthplace of Alexander the Great as the residence of the Empress's grandson, Alexander.

The Palladian classicism of Anglo-Italian orientation became the dominant style of rural residences in Russia in the second half of 1780s and the beginning of 1790s, as Priscilla Roosevelt points out elsewhere in this volume. The Imperial estates were the stylistic models for the majority of private ones. Town planning still remained under French influence, and the buildings in towns were being constructed largely according to French classicism, and more rarely in Italian Palladian taste when Giacomo Quarenghi or Giacomo Trombara were involved. This situation existed up to the death of Catherine the

Great in 1796. Her son Paul I, with his eccentric views, changed the nature of Western influences on classicism in Russian architecture at the very end of the eighteenth century. But already his reign did not belong to the period of the Enlightenment. He was certainly a romantic or proto-romantic emperor, with a special love for castles, like the castle of St. Michael in St. Petersburg, Prioratskii Castle in Gatchina, or Fortress Bip in Pavlovsk. He destroyed a lot of monuments created in the architectural spirit of his hated mother and her architects. And the "child of Catherine's heart," Alexander I, did not return to the construction habits of his grandmother.

Nevertheless, the ideal country of the Enlightenment, as Catherine the Great saw it, was created in reality and even survived the two centuries of rebuilding, destruction, and restoration. Certainly, Tsarskoe Selo is her ideal country of the Enlightenment, her "Gartenreich," her Garden Kingdom, every bit as interesting as the one around her Anhalt cousin's Worlitz. And, as in Worlitz, Tsarskoe

Selo was an attempt to adapt the planning system of the English landscape garden to very large territories and to fill them with architectural features with precise meanings, which, as a whole, could form a kind of ideological system determined by the empress.

Tsarskoe Selo was a whole constellation of artistic "worlds" brought to life by the different nuances of aesthetic thought in the Enlightenment. Its territory included not only gardens and palaces but also model villages, ideal towns, well-cultivated fields, forests, and lakes, each of which comprised its own special world. Here there was a massive chinoiserie complex, a striking country of an exotic eastern game. Alongside these appeared a world of political dreams where historical plans were reflected. This was a space densely packed with allegories, where ideological symbols were combined with geographical associations. In addition, there was created an illusory but existing world of "enlightened well-being" with idealized pictures of the park, the town, agricultural lands, villages, and estates. And in the center was the nucleus of the ensemble, the ancient ideal brought to fruition in Charles Cameron's pavilions, inspired by a strong feeling for the classical revival. The territories where these ideas were carried out adjoined one another; thus Tsarskoe Selo was an artistically planned reality that united these worlds in the space of several landscape parks.

The location did not favor the construction of picturesque parks. Around Tsarskoe Selo stretched a smooth gloomy plain covered by stunted forest, and there was insufficient water, but this did not stop the architects and gardeners. Powerful hydraulic structures were begun much earlier, in the time of Peter the Great, and were finished only in the late 1770s. Canals, which in some places ran underground through vaulted galleries, were miracles of technology for their time and brought water from twenty miles away. Numerous lakes were dug out, linking the channels. With the help of a waterfall they were connected to the Great Pond, whose banks were constructed so as to have headlands and bays. Artificial hills were created. Finally, attractive groups of trees were planted.

It must be realized that this first Russian attempt at landscape style was a long way from the parks that would be created in the environs of St. Petersburg by Charles Cameron and later by Pietro Gonzago. This first garden was something of a plaything. It did not show the passionate, unbounded admiration for living nature that is experienced in the works of Kent and Brown. Thus far the Russian garden communicated only the desire not to be left behind the rest of Europe. Moreover, the pavilions were constructed in accordance with particular models. The Siberian Bridge crossing one of the channels was an exact copy of the Palladian bridge at Wilton built by Roger Morris in 1737. The admiralty and the kitchen attached to the Hermitage Pavilion and built by the Neelovs, local Tsarskoe Selo architects, carried traces of English neo-Gothic in the style of Kent. Similarly, they erected a pyramid in the form of the one existing at Kew, meant to recall the pyramidal tomb of Sestius in Rome.[13]

The Tsarskoe Selo pyramid was dedicated to sentimental memories. Behind it were buried three of Catherine the Great's favorite English greyhounds, and on the tombstone was engraved an inscription by the French ambassador, Count de Segur: "Here lies Zemira and the mourning graces ought to throw flowers on her grave. Like Tom, her forefather, and Lady, her mother, she was constant in her loyalties and had only one failing, she was a little short-tempered . . . The gods, witnesses of her faithfulness, should have rewarded her for her loyalty with immortality."[14]

The empress wanted to secure the immortality of everything and everybody she loved by filling the gardens of Tsarskoe Selo with architectural monuments devoted to them. The most noble and gentle of Catherine's favorites, Alexander Lanskoi, was honored by such a monument. He died young and suddenly, and his monument was included in the empress's "world of immortal feelings" together with her dogs; all of them were famous for never betraying her.

Part of the park was laid out to represent the world of political fancy, a model of Catherine's political dreams on the international front. This was the time of the Russo-Turkish wars in which the Russian army achieved brilliant victories. "While this war continues," the empress wrote, "my garden at Tsarskoe Selo becomes like a toy: after each glorious military action a suitable monument is erected in it. The Battle of Kagul . . . resulted in an obelisk with an inscription. . . . the Sea Battle of Chesma produced a Rostral Column in the Great Pond . . . moreover, I have had the idea of having a Temple of Memory built in the little forest, the approach to which would be through Triumphal Gates where all the previous actions in this current war will be represented on medallions."[15]

Thus a developed system of allegories grew up in symbolic panoramas, buildings recalling this or that historical event, and monuments. The landscape was dotted with columns and obelisks on pedestals bearing edifying inscriptions, like that on the Rumiantsev Monument: "In memory of the victory on the River Kagul in Moldavia, 21 July 1770, under the leadership of General Count Rumiantsev, [when] 17,000 Russian troops made the Turkish Vizier, Hamil-Bey, flee along the Danube with his force of 150,000 men."[16] Such structures gave a feeling of serenity and celebration. This was straight classicism without breaking the canons and with a traditional treatment of order.

In the year 1771, as Catherine's letter describes, Antonio Rinaldi created designs for Triumphal Gates and a Rostral Column in the center of the Great Pond to commemorate the sea victory of Russian sailors led by Alexei Orlov, the brother of Catherine's first favorite, and Captain Greig, a native of the small Scottish town of Inverkeithing, who had entered Russian service to fight against the Turkish fleet.

All these structures were erected on sites selected quite deliberately. However, it is not easy to elucidate the precise significance of the eighteenth-century park allegories, and it is quite impossible without the key that un-locks the content of any given composition. In this case, fortunately, the notes of Khrapovitskii, Catherine's private secretary, are of great assistance in reconstructing the empress's intentions. He recorded his conversation with Catherine when awaiting the arrival of Potemkin, her former favorite. It must be remembered that all this happened in the context of constantly erupting wars with Turkey.

In 1791 Catherine the Great lamented the fact that to honor many military leaders she had ordered the construction of "Triumphal Gates" but had completely forgotten Prince Grigorii Alexandrovich Potemkin-Tavricheskii. "Your Majesty," said Khrapovitskii, "you know him so well that you have not honored him." "Yes; that is true. However, he is also a man and perhaps he would also like some honor," replied the empress. Then Khrapovitskii continued, "So it was ordered that in Tsarskoe Selo the Triumphal Gates should be illuminated and decorated with naval and army armaments and a banner should be inscribed with verses selected from Petrov's Ode to Ochakov: 'You enter with splashing waves into Sophia's Temple.'"[17]

The last line was the literary key to the allegory that the views of the Tsarskoe Selo park represented and which was begun as early as the 1770s. The significant phrase was: "You enter with splashing waves into Sophia's Temple." Sophia's temple, of course, was Hagia Sophia, the famous symbol of the city of Constantinople. In the course of the Turkish wars, the idea of sending troops by sea to the capital of the Ottoman Empire to occupy it had been frequently proposed. It was supported by, for instance, General Suvorov and Admiral Ushakov. Catherine the Great was attracted by this idea or at least she wanted to give that impression. The banner fixed to the Triumphal Gates also hinted at such a military-political perspective, and that was revealed further in a whole set of park views.

The initial inscription on the Triumphal Gates was as follows: "Orlov has saved Moscow from the plague," in reference to Orlov's having set off for Moscow when he learned that a bad epidemic of the plague had broken out there and that there had been a popular revolt brought about by panic. However, Orlov soon ceased to be the empress's favorite and the inscription on the gates was changed accordingly. Immediately after passing through the Triumphal Gates the visitor was met by Georg Velten's Ruined Tower, built in honor of the Russian capture of the Turkish Ochakov fortress. This event was memorialized in quite a different way. The tower took the form of part of a gigantic ruin buried under the earth. The capital of a Doric column and an arch reared up in front of the viewer, who was struck by the cyclopean form. Up on the square created by the colossal abacus was a summerhouse with arched embrasures, made in a conventional Turkish style. The allegory of the mighty power of Greece with its ancient past slumbering under Ottoman rule was conveyed by the grotesque and hyperbolic architectural form. Further on, by the bank of a stream, the visitor could see the Turkish Pavilion, a copy of a building standing on the banks of the Bosporus. In order to ensure the copy was precise, a ship had been sent to scrutinize the model in Constantinople.[18] The same stream was adorned by the Red or Turkish Cascade, with a little tower on each side of it reminiscent of the Orient. The construction of this is attributed to Cameron.

These structures were intended to attune the visitor to a Turkish mood. Beyond them began that part of the park that provided an allegory of political dreams. In front of the viewer stood a long Ionic colonnade, raised on a small base and decorated by numerous statues and bas-reliefs. Attached to this was another Triumphal Arch.[19] Cameron's famous design for the Triumphal Arch shows an arch embellished with round medallions showing battle scenes.[20] These are those very medallions representing "all the previous actions in this current war" of which Catherine had written.

There can be no doubt that Cameron was precisely following the empress's intention here in erecting a Temple of Memory which was indeed the apotheosis of the theme of victory in the Russo-Turkish war. (Unfortu-nately, in 1797 the building was demolished on Paul I's command). As it stood in a raised position in the park, above the lake, it was probably from this very place that it was possible to see, through the broadly spaced colonnade, the allegorical panorama.

On the lake stood Rinaldi's Rostral Column and across the water, in the distance, could be seen the dome of a cathedral. This provided the most interesting part of the composition. The cathedral was built to the south of the Tsarskoe Selo park, beyond the Great Pond, and bore the name of Saint Sophia (see fig. 4.2). It was constructed by Cameron, and it was generally believed that the architect had built a copy of Hagia Sophia in Constantinople.[21] In fact this building had little in common with its famous namesake. Here it suffices to stress that the unusual dome of Cameron's cathedral was indeed considered a symbol of the church in Constantinople. The symbol of sea victories was combined with the symbol of re-establishing Orthodox Byzantium, and the lake became a portrayal of the Black Sea, which opened the way to the capital of the Turkish Empire.

The Triumphal Path through the park did not end at the Temple of Memory. This stood two hundred meters from the baths along the axis of the *pente douce* (a gently inclined ramp) of the Cameron gallery, and on leaving the Temple it was possible to see the formal sculpture on the *pente douce*. Approaching it, a ceremonial procession could ascend into the splendid world of ancient harmony that Cameron had created as a reward for victories and martial feats, entering those "mansions which it is only proper for the gods to create." The contemporary heroics of the war acquired immortality because of this association with the eternal antique ideal, whose visible image had been created by Cameron in his baths and gallery (fig. 4.1). Bringing antiquity to life here took on a concrete meaning. The whole concept of the park and the composition of its elements formed a triumphal procession toward this aim. Soon the poets put this idea into verse, as here in the words of Ivan Bogdanovich:

Fig. 4.2 Giacomo Quarenghi, *The Central Square in the Town of Sophia*, from the 1790s. From Shvidkovsky, *The Empress and the Architect*, fig. 119, p. 107. Used with permission.

Monuments of famous Russian deeds have
  appeared.
There in their glory antiquity
Has raised a temple for herself.[22]

In the extensive legacy of poetry devoted to the Tsarskoe Selo park, the glory of the ancient ideal is consistently fused with the glory of Russian deeds in this way.

There was something special in the fascination of the gallery and the baths that caused them always to be singled out among all the magnificent Tsarskoe Selo buildings. To contemporaries of Cameron it seemed that in these works an ancient Olympian and divine beauty had been reborn. The great Russian eighteenth-century poet Gavril Derzhavin called Cameron's gallery "the temple where the graces dance to the sound of the harp."[23] Another famous poet, Ivan Bogdanovich, declared that "it is only possible for the Gods to have created" such halls. Alexander Pushkin also gave this structure its due, calling it "the temple of the Minerva of Rus'."

There are few buildings in Russia that have been considered worthy haunts for the muses or Minerva by a whole constellation of classicist poets. Something greater stands behind these poetic images than the familiar use of mythological subjects. In his construction Cameron succeeded in achieving something

that can still be felt today, something that is striking in the sensuality of its classicism. He managed to animate ancient images in those visual forms that still dominate our conceptions of ideal ancient beauty. The power of the relatively small building of the baths consisted above all in the emotional impact of the composition. It had neither the blinding splendor of the cool and brilliant works of the eighteenth-century French architects, nor the balanced rationalism of the quiet Palladians such as Quarenghi. And yet the baths at Tsarskoe Selo represent the very flesh of classicism: they are the realization of the deepest, intimate, personal belief of Cameron in the ancient ideal. This is what struck the viewer then, as it does now.

It is difficult to imagine a more classicist building. The architect did not only use exact forms verified by scholarship for the design of his gallery, but he created a real working model of the buildings of antiquity. He tried to organize in it the most sensual revival of Roman life. As the author of the gorgeous volume devoted to the Baths of the Romans (1772),[24] he could do this on the basis of very detailed research, which revealed to him what Roman baths looked like and how one was to bathe inside them in the Roman style. This revival of the ancient way of life was symbolic:

the place where the empress was present—Tsarskoe Selo—was turned into the incarnation of the ideal of antiquity.

If the baths were designed to help the court live an ancient life, then the gallery served to create the emotional mood necessary to aspire to the ancient ideal. Under the colonnade one felt distanced from the present moment, from the hurly-burly of ordinary life. Everything predisposed one to contemplation and recalled the calm promenading of ancient philosophers in the gardens of the Academy in Athens or under the porticoes of Roman villas. The gallery, which was erected in 1787, struck its contemporaries by its magnificent silence.

The architecture of the Cameron Gallery used ideas established during the first stage of the development of the baths complex. The ground floor again served as an unintentionally archaizing foundation for the first floor, which was light and refined. Above, Cameron used the same Ionic order, with capitals derived from the Erechtheon. All this strengthened the integral connection between the two structures.

From the park could be seen the dark dense mass of the ground floor and above it the white colonnade with two porticoes projecting forward. If one stood right beside the façade, it seemed as if the first floor was flying upwards. It was outlined against the sky like part of an ideal celestial world. Pushkin had good reason to refer to the gallery as "a mansion rushing to the clouds." The poet, however, was also impressed by the lower part of the building, with its heavy power and tense monumental strength. The viewer's glance took in the bold and coarse rustication covering the wall of the ground floor. Pilasters projected from this highly plastic mass and between them were arches with deliberately coarse keystones. At the cornice the coarseness of the covering disappeared, as if the passing of the centuries had smoothed the stones to leave a smooth wall above. The simple capitals of the columns here provided a gentle transition from the severity of the ground floor to the sparkling elegance of the first floor.

The end wall of the gallery recalled an ancient temple. The oval ceremonial staircase gave the composition a sense of ascent from the earth up into a world of perfect ancient harmony that seemed by some miracle to have survived the centuries. As soon as a visitor approached the steps, enclosed by pedestals with gigantic statues of Hercules and Flora, he was protected by them from the surrounding park. The staircase seemed to embrace him in its flight and to lead him upwards. Ascending, he would see in different perspectives the pediment, the columns, the capitals, all of whose strict lines created a refinement of great simplicity.

At last, on the first floor the visitor found himself between unusually widely spaced columns that gave an unaccustomed sense of spaciousness. The entire park could be seen from here: the lake on which there was an island, the greenery overhanging the water, the neo-Gothic admiralty, with its towers recalling a small castle, the Rostral Column in the distance and nearby a grotto from Rastrelli's time, turquoise with gilded details. There were boats, swans, and the light ripple of waves disturbing the smoothness of the water, as well as ladies and their escorts in beautiful court dress. It was truly a charmed island in the world of the eighteenth century, a place where ancient heroes could have lived. Of this scene the poet Derzhavin wrote:

> Here idols were preserved,
> And altars smoked with sacrifices.[25]

The town of Sophia (fig. 4.2), built by Charles Cameron, is among the least known of the architectural ensembles created in Russia during the age of Enlightenment. It has hardly been studied at all. Founded next to Tsarskoe Selo in 1780,[26] the town existed for only twenty-eight years. By 1808 it had been abolished as a community and most of its houses had been demolished for their bricks.[27] At the end of the eighteenth century, however, it had an important role to play as a district center, built to replace the old settlement attached to the Tsarskoe Selo imperial palace.[28] But its significance was not limited to this. It was proposed that Sophia should become one of the centers of the St. Petersburg guberniia, or region,[29] and to this end a marketplace and factories were built there, operated by a specially assembled population of merchants and workmen.[30]

All this was done to create an idealized facsimile of urban life, where townsmen would act as model subjects under the eyes of the court. As a result, Sophia became a model of a town rather than a real settlement. From the Cameron Gallery foreigners were shown, as one of the sights, what the Belgian nobleman the Prince de Ligne called "the view of the little town"[31] which ran in a semicircle around the Tsarskoe Selo park. It is curious that there was street lighting in the town (unprecedented in Russia in the 1780s), but the lamps were lit only when Catherine was in residence at Tsarskoe Selo. The Scottish craftsmen invited to Sophia by Cameron even wrote about this lighting in their letters home.

Anyone who traveled from the capital along the road to Moscow, according to the first guidebook of this route published in 1802, was met by the line of "huge Sophia houses," the outstanding cathedral built in the image of the Constantinople Sophia, the many vast state buildings for the Post Office, the Office Buildings, the Arcade, and the residential houses.[32] All these buildings were constructed by Charles Cameron, who had arranged them in an unusual fashion.

Overall, a unifying system of stylistic and symbolic relationships had been created between the different parts of the Tsarskoe Selo ensemble, to which Cameron gave a classical precision. The baths, the Cameron Gallery, the *pente douce,* and the Temple of Memory formed a powerful antique nucleus for the ensemble, providing its main organizing element. On the right was the grandiose and fantastic Chinese ensemble with its own integrated spatial structure. Between this Chinese ensemble on the right and the classical nucleus on the left, beside the avenue that led from the Triumphal Gates to the baths, was the section of the ensemble devoted to the victory theme.

Further, beyond the park's trees, which were not then very tall, was a sight still more surprising: the entire town of Sophia, which had been specially constructed to embellish the view from the park.

Sophia's purpose—to provide a pleasant view within a landscape—was unambiguously stressed in the order for the founding of the settlement signed by Catherine the Great: "to dispose the streets corresponding to the paths of the neighboring garden so that they should create a view."[33] With its fan-shaped plan, the town embraced the whole south side of the park. Seven longitudinal streets led toward the side of the park. Had they continued beyond its boundary they would have converged at a point in the area of Cameron's baths. This is reminiscent of Versailles, but the irregular form of these paths made the plan more picturesque and gave each quarter of the town a unique shape.

That part of Sophia that faced the imperial residence was intended to be particularly lavish. Documents show that Cameron made sketches not only for individual buildings but also for entire street frontages.[34] In effect he created a design to frame the Tsarskoe Selo park architecturally. This was achieved with model houses, which provided a strip of elegant three-story façades.

All this was highly unusual for a landscape garden. In conventional theory, the boundary of such a park should lose itself amid the splendor of nature. Here, by contrast, it was proposed that a park be surrounded by architecture. The imitation of nature—winding streams and paths, lakes, picturesque clumps of trees—took on a specific and theatrical character in these conditions, which seemed to underline the fact that they had all been created by man. The theater of the landscape park was united with the theater of architecture.

It is significant that the panorama from the Cameron Gallery was not limited to views of the park and the town. Catherine the Great wrote to Voltaire: "Sitting in the colonnade I can see in front of me Pella [one of the imperial palaces], although it is at least 35 versts from here and, besides Pella, I can see for about 100 versts around me."[35] There is doubtless some exaggeration in her words,

Fig. 4.3 Plan of Pavlovsk end of the 1780s. From Shvidkovsky, *The Empress and the Architect*, fig. 148, p. 134. Used with permission.

but they do show with great clarity the scale of the spatial relationships here. The claim to such distant visibility is explained in part by a drawing of the Cameron Gallery (now in the Hermitage) where a courtier stands in the colonnade looking at the surroundings through a telescope.[36]

The telescope on the Cameron Gallery or this exaggerated distance in the letter of the empress are symbols of the attitude found in the suburbs of St. Petersburg toward the whole "ideal country" of the Russian Enlightenment. This long-distance view existed in the mind of the empress more than in reality. She saw in her political dreams the development of these territories as an allegory of the future development of Russia. The word she used in the letter to Voltaire—Pella, the name of the capital of Macedonia—indicates that Alexander the Great is the key to the idea which she wanted to transmit to Voltaire in allegorical form. The image of Pella comes from her dreams concerning her beloved grandson Alexander I. But we have to move topographically from "the capital of Russian Enlightenment"—Tsarskoe Selo—to what comes next on the landscape.

The Pavlovsk estate of Grand Duke Paul Petrovich, the heir to the throne (fig. 4.3), adjoined the territory of Sophia.[37] Thus all three ensembles to which Charles Cameron contributed—Tsarskoe Selo, Sophia, and Pavlovsk—fused into one spatial entity. In this system Pavlovsk played a very special role. We must underline that in this context one must think of the early Pavlovsk of the 1780s, the residence of the Grand Duke, not the later residence of the Emperor Paul I. At the time, when he was still the heir to the throne, Pavlovsk was a modest but most elegant estate with a Palladian house built by Charles Cameron, and the landscape park was where the British architect changed the features of the "jardin anglo-chinois à la francaise" into an original British landscape garden in the taste of the famous Capability Brown. This impression was a strong one for contemporaries, and even such an important garden writer as John Loudon confirmed it when he visited Pavlovsk.[38]

Pavlovsk, in the Gartenreich of Catherine the Great, served the role of model private estate of the perfect gentleman, only very loosely linked to the court. This relationship mirrored that between the empress and her son and heir, whom she did not want as the future sovereign. The early Pavlovsk was filled with the sense of natural life, of elegant nature becoming more beautiful and ideal—decorated with pavilions in the taste of mixed

Greco-Roman antiquity and huge numbers of statues, among which the ones of Apollo and the muses were the most numerous and meaningful.

The house in Pavlovsk was not originally an imperial palace: it was not big enough and later had to be seriously enlarged. It was created by Charles Cameron as an estate house with all the necessary facilities. It was inhabited not only by the owner but, as in Catherine the Great's residence, by the memory and the personages of antiquity. Charles Cameron used original ancient sculptures and architectural fragments inside the house. The center of the palace was a kind of full-scale model of a Roman hall, around which were situated the "normal" eighteenth-century rooms.

All those images were the ideal ones, meant to exist in the present day, when Paul was grand duke, not emperor, a situation that Catherine the Great preferred to be permanent. Near to Pavlovsk was constructed an ensemble totally devoted to the future.

It was called Alexandrova dacha (fig. 4.4)—a small estate not far from both Tsarskoe Selo and Pavlovsk, built as an educational complex for the grand duke Alexander Pavlovich, the future Alexander I. There was a landscape garden organized around a lake, curved alleys, and a rather strange-looking house, displaying a mixture of Palladian and chinoiserie features. The most interesting point about the Alexandrova dacha is that it was built, according to a scenario written by Catherine herself, in the form of a fairy tale.[39] The main hero of the tale was named Tsarevich Khlor. Khlor had to overcome certain obstacles and to acquire special virtues which enabled him to find at the end the "rose without thorns, which doesn't prick." A huge system of allegories was put into the complex to serve the sentimental education of a perfect man and good sovereign. This ensemble was linked to an enormous *ferme ornee* where the grandsons of the empress could, at the same time, study and practice agriculture under the tutelage of their professor of religion, who was also a well-known agronomist, Father A. A. Samborskii.[40]

From these practical efforts to form the future of the royal family and the empire according to the ideas of Catherine the Great we turn to her efforts to construct the image of this future, the architectural symbol of the next reign. It is well known that Catherine the Great wanted to make her grandson Alexander I, not her son Paul I, the emperor after her death. In view of this, we return to the creation of the complex of Pella already mentioned.

In 1784, when the main works in Tsarskoe Selo and the construction of the house in Pavlovsk were already finished, Catherine decided to begin building a new and enormous palace. What is extraordinary is the choice of style for the new ensemble and the selection of the architect. Having been devoted to Palladian classicism of the British and Italian models, she suddenly changed her mind. Now she invited Ivan Starov, a Russian architect trained in France, and ordered him to build a palace in the spirit of the gigantic designs that French architects had proposed at the time of the competition for the Prix de Rome.[41] Among those French designs that survive are many features common to both the work of Starov and his French colleagues.

The Russian architect proposed a highly rational structure, consisting of a dozen palaces put into a rigid rectangular frame of long, open colonnades. It was more the image of a town of antiquity than the image of one building. This was not strange. The name given to the place by the empress—Pella—was enough to make clear that the imagined capital of ancient Macedonia would be the prototype for this complex.

There is additional evidence for the interpretation of Pella on the banks of the Neva as an image linked to Alexander the Great. At this time, Catherine ordered a series of pictures from the life of Alexander the Great to decorate the rooms of her grandson.

There is one more moment that is important. The nearest analogue of Starov's complex in Pella is not found among the works of the young French architects, but in the designs of a very experienced master. Many features of Starov's design were taken from a design for the rebuilding of Versailles made by E.-L. Boulée in 1784, the very year when

Fig. 4.4 View of the Alexandrova Dacha, which was built by Grand Duke Alexander by order of Catherine the Great. Engraving of the 1780s, printed in 1810. From Shvidkovsky, *The Empress and the Architect*, fig. 260, p. 228. Used with permission.

work on Pella was begun.[42] It is quite possible that the Russian empress's system of artistic spying yielded a copy of Boulée's famous design.

So when Catherine wrote to Voltaire that she could see Pella while seated in the Cameron gallery in Tsarskoe Selo, she meant that she was dreaming about the image of the new reign of her dear grandson. In the architectural form of ancient Pella, this dream was of a capital of the country from which Alexander the Great could emerge to conquer the world. She could imagine her grandson's Pella as the improved, enlarged, and embellished Versailles—a new antique Versailles for the Russia of the century of "Alexandre du Nord," as Alexander I was called in the dedication to him by C. N. Ledoux in his famous book.[43]

Thus was the ideal country, the Gartenreich, of the Russian Enlightenment, built according to the orders of Catherine the Great. One can see that it was developing not only in space, covering more and more territories, but in time as well, when dreams and images extended from Greek and Roman antiquity, to ancient China, and on to modern Russia and the Russian empire of the next century. As always the models and ideas were collected everywhere in all countries and epochs, but they were unified and organized by the political will of the great empress.

5 Russian Estate Architecture and Noble Identity

Priscilla Roosevelt

Elegant estate architecture helped to create group identity for Russia's elite, particularly during the golden age, 1762–1830, when most great estates were built. Prior to the Emancipation edict of 1861, ownership of an estate with a serf population was restricted by law to the hereditary nobility, and thus estate ownership in itself conveyed membership in a privileged group. Estate architecture was one method of signaling one's position within this group. Even after the Emancipation edict, which democratized the social composition of Russia's estate owners, estate ownership and architecture continued to offer a remarkably consistent source of group identity for the Russian elite.

From the reign of Peter the Great, membership in the upper ranks of the nobility had rested on a number of foundations: lineage, titles and imperial honors, rank in service, wealth (measured in land and serfs), and adoption of Western cultural norms. Shortly after mid-century, a series of imperial decrees changed the framework for noble identity. Of these the most significant in terms of its impact on estate life was probably the decree of Peter III in 1762 freeing nobles from compulsory service to the state. For the first time, estate owners could choose to spend most of their time on their domains. Yet it is paradigmatic of noble attitudes that the vast majority continued to regard state service as at least a moral obligation, and to prize the ranks and imperial honors it brought as symbols of status. In 1775 Catherine the Great's banner legislation reorganized provincial Russia, creating a host of official positions in the provinces. In 1785 her charter to the nobility

awarded Russia's elite a certain amount of corporate self-rule. These two legislative initiatives brought nobles new provincial responsibilities, and, to the upper echelons of the nobility, new means for assessing their standing within its porous ranks.

It is therefore not surprising that 1762 marked the beginning of the estate's golden age: a period in which estate architecture and estate building contributed to a more visible identification of certain landowners as part of an elite group of nobles. The noble landowner's public identity still derived mainly from his or her relationship to the state, but also from ownership of, and sole control over, a personal kingdom. In relation to his peasants the estate owner was both the agent of the state and a ruler in his own right, responsible for "his" people's physical and spiritual welfare. The noble landowner's identity as a local autocrat often mandated planning and supervising the construction of a model kingdom. Many estate owners had resident architects at hand to plan not only the palace for this kingdom, but whatever other structures the kingdom required, whether utilitarian outbuildings or garden caprices. Thus estate architecture of this period encapsulated an owner's desire to establish his identity in two opposite directions: upward, by reaffirming his links to the sovereign; and downward, by creating an estate physically reflecting the owner's hierarchical dominance over a local society.

I would like to express my gratitude to the editors of this volume, whose comments were immensely helpful in the final shaping of this article.

It should be noted that whereas urban architecture in this period was regulated by imperial decree, estate architecture was not. Yet the fact that the architecture of manor houses located in far-flung corners of European Russia, not to mention the architecture of the monuments in estate parks, was more similar than dissimilar leads to the hypothesis that the group identity of the landowning elite involved the use of a specific architectural vocabulary. As will be seen, by and large, throughout the imperial period, this favored vocabulary was that which was promoted by the crown. The imitative aspect of estate architecture supports the thesis advanced by Richard Wortman in his *Scenarios of Power*: that in the Russian tradition, power could not be acquired through competition with the ruler; rather, it devolved upon the highest ranks of courtiers through proximity to the tsar. In other words, the courtier could only acquire power as the byproduct of positioning himself within the aura radiating from the crown. Architectural imitation offered an ideal vehicle for moving into this aura. It emphasized one's identification with the crown: estate architecture advertised the owner's proximity to the source of all power in Russia, and his or her assimilation of the ideals behind the architecture. Although changes in the architectural vocabulary used on the estate offer evidence of the evolution over time of the elite's group identity, they also tend to confirm the leading role of the autocrat as the ultimate arbiter of taste.

The evidence I will present for the above statements is far from conclusive. The laborious spadework in this fertile field has yet to be done, and as will be seen, there are many exceptions to the rule. My own database is highly selective. First, I have looked at surviving architectural monuments—houses and park structures or selective reconstructions of estates by scholars. I have also examined paintings and pre-Revolutionary photographs of structures now vanished. Second, I have relied on the few statements of intent or ideological motivation I have come across in letters, memoirs, and secondary literature. It remains to be seen whether the Russian archives contain a wealth of material disproving or confirming my now tentative hypothesis. My focus here is on what material culture can tell us of the social and cultural identity of those who create or use certain artifacts (in this instance, architectural evidence in the broad sense). Of necessity, my methodology has been eclectic, and my hunch is that the subject will never be quantifiable in any meaningful sense. That is, I doubt that the data exist for a clear statistical subdivision of group identity along class or educational/intellectual lines (that is, distinct subgroupings within the nobility as a whole), though these divisions certainly existed, as some of my examples will indicate.

In architectural matters, builders of estates were slaves to imperial taste, though they undoubtedly would have been reluctant to admit this. Even the architecture of pre-Catherinian estates owed much to imperial example. The design of the Griboedovs' Khmelita (begun 1754), the only baroque country mansion in Russia today, for example, seems to have been lifted directly from St. Petersburg. There, private mansions in the Italian baroque style synonymous with the name of Bartolomeo Rastrelli and characteristic of the city's great imperial palaces had been in vogue for several decades. Indeed, the mansion of Khmelita is so similar to the Stroganov Palace in St. Petersburg that there is good reason for the belief of Khmelita's restorer, Viktor Kulakov, that Griboedov commissioned the design for Khmelita from Rastrelli.

In the reign of Catherine, who initiated a flood of public and private building, imperial imitation was overtly encouraged. Catherine openly acknowledged her passion for construction in an oft-cited letter to Baron Grimm: "The fury to build is a diabolical thing. It devours money; and the more one builds, the more one wants to build. It is as intoxicating as drink."[1] Catherine purposefully transformed the face of her empire on a scale few other rulers in history have attempted. Not only were imperial palaces remodeled and new ones built; she embarked on large-scale town planning, producing a network of over two hundred new provincial towns (and an equal number of redesigned urban centers) with uniform neoclassical centers, connected to each other by new highways. The large public spaces, broad boulevards, and imposing official buildings of these towns were visual symbols of a new, enlightened era.

The same impulse led Catherine to erect a model for her courtiers at Tsarskoe Selo.[2] This twenty-square-mile area was devoted to architectural experimentation, as Dimitri Shvidkovsky explains elsewhere in this volume, designed to enlighten all her subjects but preeminently her courtiers. For my purposes, the most important of her commissions here was Pavlovsk. Not only was the central palace designed as a model estate house for Catherine's son, the future Emperor Paul I; it was at the center of a model landowner's kingdom complete with a *ferme ornee* and a vast, poetic English garden. Catherine also erected a model of economic management: the village of Sophia (which housed Charles Cameron's workers) with its various cottage industries. The gardens of Tsarskoe Selo were studded with allegorical structures documenting her enlightened outlook and expansionist ambitions. If imitation is indeed the most sincere form of flattery, Catherine's courtiers seem to have expended much effort in flattering her own sense of taste and style, for all the examples at Tsarskoe Selo found imitation on grand private estates. The models the elite created on their estates in turn influenced provincial neighbors of lesser status.

Since pre-Petrine Russia provided few examples of large-scale country residences, it is small wonder that eighteenth-century Russians turned to European models. In the first half of the century, Dutch and Italian models were favored. But very early in her reign Catherine expressed a preference for Palladian architecture. It was more refined in style, more balanced, and more consonant with Enlightenment ideals. Perhaps the fact that the absence of highly decorated facades and rooftop statuary kept the cost down was an additional attraction for an empress afflicted with buildomania. As early as the mid-1760s, writing from St. Petersburg, the eminent engraver Mikhail Makhaev recommended "the now fashionable Italian style, which our all-merciful sovereign deigns to favor," to his godson Nikolai Tishinin, for his estate Tikhvinskoe near Rybinsk overlooking the Volga. By Italian Makhaev meant, of course, not the highly ornamented baroque style earlier in vogue, but the restrained Palladianism Catherine favored.[3]

Many aristocrats commissioned country mansions from experienced, often foreign-born architects simultaneously working on court commissions, although the actual authorship is often murky: in many instances the original drawings for well-known estate houses are missing. To cite only one example, Baturin, the Razumovsky estate in Chernigov guberniia, has been attributed to Charles Cameron by many authorities over the years. More recent evidence indicated that his compatriot Adam Menelaws, whom Cameron originally brought to Russia as a bricklayer but who achieved fame there as an architect, actually designed it.[4] In the absence of hard evidence Russian architectural historians have used general design principles, or occasionally specific features, of a manor house to deduce probable authorship. This uncertain methodology has probably led to a great deal of misattribution, especially where Kazakov, Bazhenov, Starov, and Quarenghi are concerned.

We are on firmer ground looking at the houses themselves. In most cases, the grand estate house of the late eighteenth or early nineteenth century was planned as an imposing but balanced and restrained edifice. A triumphal arch, and then a pillared or pilastered ceremonial entrance into the house from the courtyard, a grand staircase leading to the piano nobile above a rusticated basement, and a vestibule announcing the stylistic theme of the house, were all common, though a great deal of variation in the specific design of these features is evident (fig. 5.1). In at least one instance, an estate owner named Durasov commissioned a house conforming to this pattern, but designed to imitate the imperial order of St. Anna, which he had just received (fig. 5.2). Decor within the house, while uti-

Fig. 5.1 Znamenskoe-Raek (Tver guberniia), an eighteenth-century Palladian house designed by Nikolai Lvov. A grand open colonnade encircles the entire courtyard. Photo from collection of the author.

lizing neoclassical motifs such as scenes from mythology and Pompeiian color schemes, also incorporated numerous references to imperial power and service achievements by family members.[5] At the Apraksins' Olgovo (Moscow guberniia) in the late eighteenth century the great hall was adorned with semicircular plaques above the windows which contained fanciful depictions of heroic Apraksin ancestors in high relief on a red background, with the words "killed," "died from wounds," and other such inscriptions testifying to bravery and sacrifice in the line of duty. At Count Pyotr Sheremetev's Kuskovo, the ceiling painting in the ballroom is surrounded by a decorative border into which were worked artistic renditions of all the imperial orders the count had been awarded. Imperial and family portraits hanging in close proximity, artistic renditions of imperial awards won by members of the family, and the "state" bedroom all emphasized the noble's role as courtier.

Other elements of house design seem likely to have been borrowed from imperial models (though they might also have derived directly from Palladio's villas, well known to Russian architects). For example, the oval hall of Arkhangelskoe, encircled by massive pillars, is similar to the one at Pavlovsk. The oval hall of Ostafievo may represent a more modest variant of the same impulse. Colonnades similar to the sweeping ones at Pavlovsk, attached to the main house, are to be found at Arkhangelskoe, Ostankino, and Valuevo. The division of a house into male and female halves, with differing decors for the master and mistress, was evident at Pavlovsk (and later, Elagin Island). This style was not ubiquitous and its origins are unclear, but it might also be attributable to imperial example. Two to four wings balanced the main house, completing the central part of the estate; they might be used to house servants, as the kitchens and office, or as guest quarters.

Some owners, however, while crediting a Quarenghi, Cameron, or Starov with a hand in the design of their estate, emphasized their

Fig. 5.2 Lyublino, a fanciful neoclassical house designed in the early nineteenth century in the shape of the Order of St. Anna, whose statue crowns the cupola (*Stolitsa i usad'ba*, no. 29).

own contributions. Alexander Kurakin, for example, boasted that "all three facades" of his Nadezhdino, in Saratov province, had been constructed according to his own design.[6] Although a drawing by Starov of Ostafievo exists, family legend credits the overall design to Prince Andrei Viazemskii. Certainly, nobles like Kurakin and Viazemskii were imitating Catherine in their passion for building, and in the style they favored. Thus such statements might best be taken as a loyal subject's pride in having mastered the architectural lessons of the crown, rather than as assertions of independence.

The landscaping of Russia's large estates likewise paid homage to the ruler, although even before Catherine declared herself an Anglomaniac in gardening, some nobles had become converts and designed "English" or irregular gardens, then very much in vogue throughout Europe, for their estates. Here, one aristocrat even took the lead. In a letter to his friend M. L. Vorontsov, Ivan Shuvalov raved about the new style in landscape archi-

tecture. "The gardens are beautiful, in a taste completely different from others; . . . the whole art consists of making it conform to nature."[7] Shuvalov even offered to assist in designing the gardens of Vorontsov's estate Kimora, Tver guberniia. Catherine announced her conversion to Anglomania in a letter to Voltaire of 1772, denouncing French formalism in no uncertain terms. "I profoundly despise straight lines. I hate fountains that torture water in order to make it take a course contrary to its nature; in a word, Anglomania dominates my plantomania."[8] In the last few decades of the eighteenth century Anglomania swept the Russian aristocracy, transforming the estate landscape as thoroughly as rural England had been altered in the preceding half-century to correspond to a new Enlightenment sensitivity to nature.

Sukhanovo, the Volkonsky estate south of Moscow, illustrates the customary division of the eighteenth-century park into four discrete theoretical areas—that is, spaces promoting different emotions and activities—appropriate for the Enlightenment garden. Dimitri Shvid-kovsky believes that the landscape park of Oranienbaum provided a highly influential model for the aristocracy in this regard. In such parks, the first part of the landscape enshrined "modern memories" through monuments such as temples or obelisks commemorating the visits of members of the imperial family to an estate. The temple sheltering a bust of Catherine the Great at Arkhangelskoe and the commemorative obelisks in the park of the Chernyshevs' Yaropolets, the Potockis' Sofievka, and the Sheremetevs' Kuskovo document this impulse to enshrine the noble's role as courtier.

The second part of the park alluded to the economic function of the estate and to the important role of the landowner as enlightened agriculturalist, promoter of the economic health of his kingdom. Here too the estate owner paid subtle homage to the ruler, as enlightened economic stewardship coincided precisely with Catherine's neoclassical view of the noble's place in society. In the garden one might find either a complete *ferme ornée* with a decorative dairy in which the mistress offered guests fresh milk, or on its periphery one or more highly ornamental buildings for livestock. The Golitsyn estates Rozhdestveno, Kuz'minki, and Trostianets, the Volkonskys' Sukhanovo, the Baryshnikovs' Aleksino, and the Trubetskois' Znamenskoe-Sadki are only a few of the many estates that featured decorative farm buildings.

The third section of the park comprised an allegorical park of "ancient memories" in which there might be family tombs or a mausoleum, as well as monuments on neoclassical themes. Imposing mausoleums are still to be found at Sukhanovo, Arkhangelskoe, and V. G. Orlov's Otrada. Like the interior adornment of the house with ancestral portraits and imperial awards to family members, such mausoleums and tombs celebrated a family's local longevity and ancestral feats in a fashion popular among the Russian elite well before the Petrine era. The fact that the mausoleums and monuments erected were typically in the latest neoclassical style served further to emphasize the education and taste of the owners.

Last, the typical park included a pleasure garden with modern amusements such as the Russian form of lawn bowling, and the occasional "Russian hills" or roller coaster, a smaller version of the famous one at Oranienbaum. Kuskovo's pleasure garden had, in addition to a bowling lawn, a labyrinth, a carousel, and a "fire-eating dragon." For a wealthy, pleasure-loving aristocrat of the early nineteenth century like I. I. Bariatynskii, this was the most important part of the park. He wrote his architect in 1818, "I want various games, swings, carousels and so forth to be placed in the park not very far from the house, and in such a manner as to be visible from the living-room."[9] It is hard to decode Bariatynskii's intent in having the amusements he specified placed within ready view. Perhaps he merely wanted to make sure that no one overlooked these symbols of his public beneficence, for we know that public entertaining in the park was very much part of the noble's self-definition. Here again the noble was imitating the sovereign's behavior in opening suburban palace grounds to the public, or in staging elaborate amusements in the park for the populace. Large country estates often served as regional amusement parks; wealthy nobles considered it their duty to offer substantial and frequent entertainments, particularly if they were marshals of the nobility, whether on the district or provincial level (fig. 5.3). (So important a part of the latter's duties was lavish entertaining that, in fact, only nobles of a certain means could afford to assume the position of marshal.)

We know from paintings and archival photographs that the Russian estate owner reveled in various Oriental structures, architectural borrowings from both the Near and Far East, for the garden. I know of none that have survived to the present. Their purposes were multiple. Like all garden structures, they reaffirmed the owner's personal good taste, for enlivening the garden with exotic touches was very much in vogue. Near Eastern structures reminded viewers of Russia's longstanding ambition to take Constantinople, a goal writ large in the structures of the "political garden" at Tsarskoe Selo. For this part of the

Fig. 5.3 1770s sketch of Armino's costume for Mozart's *The Magic Flute*, performed in the Kuskovo theater by Count Sheremetev's talented serf troupe. Courtesy of Kyra Cheremeteff.

park Catherine commissioned Turkish cascades, a mosque, and a minaret (fig. 5.4). Such structures might also recall a family member's exploits in the Russo-Turkish campaigns of the eighteenth century. Both impulses may have prompted the building of the mosque and minaret that once graced the garden of the Chernyshevs' Yaropolets.

After William Chambers's treatise on Chinese gardens appeared in Russian in 1771, chinoiserie became the rage. In aristocratic gardens we see not only direct imitation of stylish gardens in Western Europe, but also of Catherine's projects. Tsarskoe Selo featured an entire Chinese village designed by Vasily

Neelov at Catherine's behest; to the best of my knowledge, this feat was not duplicated on a private estate. But Chinese bridges, pagodas, and even teahouses such as the one at Sofievka were plentiful.

There can be no doubt about the fact that once Catherine the Great endorsed Palladian architecture, her aristocrats followed suit in designing their estate houses. Far more difficult to determine is the degree to which the latter were *as* immersed as was their empress in identification with the rediscovered neoclassical world—the world of rational elegance, harmony, and "pastoral" simplicity, and what the creation of such a world on an estate contributed to the owner's identity. Like the Hermitage Catherine designed as a rebuke to the ostentation of Elizabeth's Winter Palace, the vast majority of grand estate houses conformed to the restrained design and decor consonant with Enlightenment ideals. Some were specifically designed to emphasize these ideals.

Nikolai Lvov, self-taught architect and brother-in-law of Garvrila Derzhavin, Catherine's poet laureate, was a man of great erudition and a devoted follower of Palladio. It was, in fact, Lvov who translated Palladio's famous *Quatri Libri della Architectura* into Russian. Lvov designed two very similar estate houses that resonate with Enlightenment ideas: Zvanka, for Derzhavin's family in Novgorod guberniia, and Nikolskoe-Cherenchitsy for his own in Tver guberniia. In these houses, while dining room and parlor satisfied the need for ample entertaining space, the master's study—the throne room of his domain—was situated in a place of honor, near the main entrance to the house.

In most other grand estate houses of the eighteenth century, by contrast, one striking feature is the vast proportion of public interior space, designed for entertaining on as regal a scale as the owner's means permitted.[10] The enfilade (a French design principle), a suite of grand reception rooms crowned by the "great hall" (zal) or ballroom, usually took up the entire piano nobile. Family rooms were typically on another floor; they were far smaller and were haphaz-

Fig. 5.4 The Turkish towers framing a cascade at Tsarskoe Selo. Collection of the author.

ardly decorated and furnished. It is worth noting Prince Alexander Kurakin's remark, upon his exile to Nadezhdino in Saratov Province, that he remembered "how they lived in ancient Rome: never in demeaning idleness, always either in active service to the fatherland or in complete, far-removed solitude, in service to themselves, providing the spirit with new forces, the mind with new ideas and abilities."[11] Nadezhdino was designed as a huge neoclassical palace, however. And Kurakin not only surrounded himself with a mock court composed of servants, each of whom had court titles, but staged endless entertainments for his neighbors. Thus life at Nadezhdino, far from demonstrating any real commitment by Kurakin to the Enlightenment ideal of spiritual renewal in a pastoral arcadia, replicated the court life he had known.

By the late eighteenth century the "enlightened" noble's sense of identity certainly included a feeling of noblesse oblige toward the serf population of his estate. How dues were apportioned, whether proper housing, health care, and educational facilities were provided, and whether famine and old age support were forthcoming were all measures of an enlight-

ened approach to one's domain. In 1786 General A. V. Suvorov, upon inspecting the conditions of his peasants at Konchanskoe, Novgorod guberniia, ordered his estate manager to "differentiate between the wealthy, upstanding peasants and the indigent peasants and have the former alleviate the taxes and labors of the indigent. Pay particular attention to those of the poor who have many children."[12] Some decades later the far wealthier Ivan I. Bariatynskii, thinking about his plans for Mar'ino in Kursk guberniia, wrote: "what calling could be better for the wealthy man, who employs his means for the enlightenment of his kingdom, improving agriculture, introducing art and industry, bringing contentment and happiness to society, and who civilizes his native land by his example?"[13] Bariatynskii expressed concern that his numerous building projects were "burdensome and even ruinous for my peasants," and built a dispensary hospital, a home for poor families, and a school and church for them. Letters of Count Nikolai Sheremetev to his accountant in St. Petersburg around the same time similarly reflected patriarchal concern for his peasants at Kuskovo.

Such enlightened sentiments clearly

prompted architectural activity on estates. Most estate school and infirmary buildings, none of which survive today, were undoubtedly utilitarian. But a number of aristocratic estates had ornamental villages near the manor house, designed for house serfs and artisans. In other instances, owners even paid attention to the architecture of more remote villages on the estate. Alexei B. Kurakin's architect, V. A. Bakarev, reports in his memoirs that in 1823 he was ordered to Kurakin's village of Mokretsy, Orel province, to renovate sixty peasant houses on the post road. They were rebuilt with unusual facades, featuring porticos, birch columns, and stuccoed exteriors.[14] Kurakin's idea of "gluing on" neoclassical features to peasant houses must have been exceptional, for it robbed columns and porticos of even the remotest relationship to noble status.

This relationship of neoclassical architecture to status was widely acknowledged. In his memoirs, for instance, the aristocrat Buturlin sneers at the fact that lesser landowners customarily aped the neoclassical exterior of the provincial palace. "Onto the more ingenious of [their houses] four columns with a triangular pediment above them were glued, so to speak, to a gay background. Among the better-off, these columns were plastered and smeared with whitewash; with the less wealthy landowners the columns were made of skinny pine logs without any capitals."[15]

Village architecture on an estate had its own code. Landowners themselves identified "better" serf owners as those whose village cottages had chimneys and were well maintained. In the 1780s Nikolai Novikov, an exceptionally enlightened individual, designed model houses for the two hundred peasants on his modest estate of Tikhvinskoe south of Moscow. (A number of these houses have survived to the present, and are still occupied by local peasants, as is the main house.) Clearly more practical in design than those of Kurakin's village, the identical brick houses had chimneys, each held four families, and they were built, as was customary, on both sides of the village street near the modest manor house.

In other instances attractive housing, mainly for house serfs and artisans, was dictated by the general decorative scheme for the estate. At the Golitsyns' Kuz'minki, for instance, to this day there exists, to the left of the main entrance gates, a well-preserved *slobodka*: a string of relatively large, decorative houses with Palladian windows and elegant facades, lower in the back, that provided lodgings (possibly dormitory-style) for servants. Beyond them is a decorative neo-Gothic cattle courtyard, with housing for the cattle-keepers. Clearly these buildings, like the surviving twin baroque buildings for servants in front of the main house at Aleksino (Smolensk guberniia) or this estate's "Fyodorev Fortress" (a decorative folly, complete with tower and bastions, concealing cattle barns) were intended to be ornamental features of the estate ensemble.

In a few instances, Catherine's zeal for city planning and features of her model town, Sophia, at Tsarskoe Selo appear to have been emulated on the estate. The Wilmot sisters talk of Princess Dashkova building new villages at Troitskoe, though they do not describe them. They also mention that near the manor house there was a "whole town" for estate artisans.[16] The estate of Bogoroditsk (Tula guberniia), whose mansion was designed by Starov with landscaping by A. T. Bolotov, included a new town visible from the mansion and gardens. Watercolors of the Kurakin estate Stepanovskoe, in Tver province, likewise suggest a very unusual, geometrically laid out "city" imitative of a district town as part of the decorative landscape. From the front portals of the estate house, one looks past two large obelisks marking the entrance to the main street of brick buildings, which housed guests or contained shops. A theatrical gothic fortress (which was actually the estate theater) marks the end of the street, behind which is a *sloboda* of houses of uniform architecture for the domestic servants. There could hardly be a clearer expression in architecture of the estate as miniature kingdom.

On the estate one's role as master of a large kingdom of dependents was inseparable from one's personal identity. Whereas B. A. Kurakin's self-image evidently inclined him toward theatrical and showy extravagance, other wealthy landowners like I. I. Bariatynskii, viewing themselves as enlightened and therefore benevolent princes, were more likely to expend time and resources on their peasants' material well-being. The lord of the manor was also protector of the faith on his lands. He was responsible for his peasants' religious instruction and for their life as members of the Orthodox polity. For these reasons, considerable attention was paid to estate church construction. On larger estates, the church close to the house was reserved for the owner's family and house serfs; separate village churches (wooden, not brick) were built for the rest of the serf population. While most newly built estate churches were neoclassical in style, there are at least two examples of stylistic deviation that deserve attention: the Dolgoruky church at Podmoklovo (Tula guberniia), dating from the 1750s, and the Muromtsovs' estate church at Balovnevo (Riazan guberniia), built in the early nineteenth century.[17] Both are Italianate churches, and both have statues of saints—at Podmoklovo life-sized—which are a break with Orthodox tradition. The Balovnevo church also had a basin for holy water and an elevated, separate place of worship for the Muromtsov family. In general, Russian Orthodoxy with its rituals and feast days provided a powerful bond between the estate owner and the peasant, a reminder that for all their differences they shared a common culture that stretched from throne to peasant hut. But in the two cases cited above, the nontraditional, semiheretical elements of church architecture seem to suggest an insistence on the all-powerful role of the estate owner, even in matters of religion.

On more than one estate, design was strongly influenced by the personalities and interests of the owners. At the Golitsyns' Kuzminki, the prominent positioning of the decorative stable *dvor*, with an elegant music pavilion at the main entrance, directly across the lake from the main house reflected this family's substantial investment in horse breeding as well as entertaining (fig. 5.5). Nikolai Krivtsov's house and gardens at Lyubichi (Tambov guberniia)—complete with an English watchtower—reflected his Anglomania. The significance of the unusual planned village at Stepanovskoe is harder to unravel. Boris Alexeevich Kurakin, who commissioned it, inherited Stepanovskoe from his uncle Alexander and appears to have shared the passion for architecture so pronounced in his father and two uncles. His son Alexei's watercolors have survived, documenting the appearance of the village, but researchers have apparently found nothing enabling them to decode the vision that inspired the village's creator.[18]

The frequency of neo-Gothic elements in estate design such as the "fortress" in this village was assuredly no accident. Neo-Gothic walls and outbuildings contrasting with a neoclassical house were not uncommon, particularly in the Moscow area. Prominent examples are the neo-Gothic gates, walls, and pavilion of the Goncharovs' Yaropolets, the *ferme ornée* at the Trubetskois' Znamenskoe-Sadki, the decorative and profitable paper factory of the Goncharovs at Polotniany zavod, Kaluga guberniia, and the servants' quarters at Sukhanovo. Entirely neo-Gothic estates, which the design of Tsaritsino or Petrovskoe might have inspired, are relatively rare. I know of only two from the golden age of estate building: Marinka (where only the stable has survived); and Marfino, remodeled in this style in the late 1830s (save for the church). Shvidkovsky has hypothesized that subsidiary elements of an eighteenth-century estate complex executed in neo-Gothic style were a signal that the owner belonged to a Masonic lodge. Since virtually the entire Catherinian elite belonged at one time or another to some lodge, this might account for the profusion of such structures. If so, one might view neo-Gothic elements as an architectural expression of a private and somewhat dangerous allegiance. On the other hand, neo-Gothic buildings or walls might merely have been fashionable, eye-catching elements, quite in keeping with loyalty to the ruler and, in fact, just as imitative of imperial taste.

Fig. 5.5 The stable courtyard, with music pavilion at its center, viewed from across the great lake at Kuz'minki. Lithograph by F. Benois, from an album of drawings by J. Rauch, 1841. Courtesy of the State Historical Museum, Moscow.

An apparent shift in cultural identity signaled in estate architecture appears in the reign of Nicholas I. Prior to this time there were precious few Russian architectural elements in the grandee's estate complex. Indeed, grandees appear to have been consciously—and a bit defensively—measuring their houses against those of Europe. Prince Bezborodko, for example, spoke of his suburban Moscow mansion, completed at the very end of the eighteenth century, as proof that "in this country, in this century, taste was known."[19] Catherine's favorite, Count Peter Zavadovsky, proudly invited Count Semen Vorontsov, then Russia's ambassador to England, to compare his newly built estate house at Lyalichi with the best houses England had to offer, citing Lyalichi's exceptional beautifully proportioned facades.[20] The rule of distancing oneself from old Russia was broken when an occasional seventeenth-century estate church was retained alongside a new neoclassical estate house, as at Ostankino and Arkhangelskoe. Generally speaking, however, estate churches for the most part were "modernized" along with the house.

Other consciously Russian elements in the estate complex arrived relatively late. Although we know that Catherine erected an izba made of birch logs in the Gatchina park, and that Maria Fedorovna had a similar birch cottage at Pavlovsk, wooden park structures have not survived to the present, and I have found no mention of such rustic izbas in private parks in memoirs. But in the reign of Nicholas I the elite began searching for a more consciously Russian idiom, following the example of Nicholas's neo-Gothic "Cottage" at Tsarskoe Selo, which the imperial family preferred to its more magnificent palaces. On his trip of 1839 the Marquis de Custine mentioned visiting several grandiose log cabins built by nobles (with very grandly decorated and furnished interiors): "this is the sole dwelling which might be termed national in style," he proclaimed.[21] The rebuilding of Spasskoe-Lutovinovo after a fire in 1836 as a traditional wooden (though not log) house with a gingerbread trim might have

Fig. 5.6 The "round court" or coliseum, housing a serf circus, built at Trostianets in the 1840s (*Stolitsa i us-ad'ba*, no. 54).

been a conscious stylistic choice reflecting the change in taste. At the same time, Countess Panina was remodeling Marfino in what has been termed "Russo-Byzantine" style. At Trostianets to the south circa 1840, the Golitsyns built a "round court" or coliseum, which housed their serf circus (both performers and animals) in medieval Russian style (fig. 5.6) Estate architecture in the Crimea, to judge from the examples of the Vorontsovs' palace at Alupka or Countess S.V. Panina's *dom ot-dykha* at Gaspra, was even more fanciful, combining Near Eastern motifs with the neo-Gothic style of the "Cottage."

Interest in developing an identifiably Russian architectural style intensified as the nineteenth century progressed, leaving its mark on estate design. By the 1870s and 1880s certain members of the Russian elite, notably Savva Mamontov, a railway magnate, and Princess Tenisheva, of old lineage but modern ideas, were using their estates for architectural experiments on old Russian themes. At Mamontov's Abramtsevo the bathhouse and studio were designed as log cabins with folk art decor, and a new church erected in 1880 utilized old Novgorodian architectural themes. At Tenisheva's Talashkino there remains an unusual church, designed as a stylized dragon with tail lifted to the sky, so obviously pagan in inspiration that it was, in fact, never consecrated by the local clergy. The facade of the nearby *teremok*, Princess Tenisheva's studio, similarly incorporates pagan folk art motifs that her avant-garde artist friends reinterpreted to serve as ornamentation for this structure.

I view the Russophile or historicist trend in estate architecture of the late nineteenth century as proof that the Russian elite was just as intent as Russia's rulers were to lay claim to an identity linked with Europe, but also to a uniquely Russian cultural identity. A brief tour of two estates, Kargashino and Kiritsy, built in Ryazan guberniia in this period illustrates the point. They are both striking, late-nineteenth-century attempts to recreate, albeit in updated fashion, Bazhenov's eighteenth-century homage to old Muscovy in his tour de force, Tsaritsino.[22] It should be noted that the unknown designer of Baron von der Launitz's pseudo-Gothic stud farm at Kargashino, and Fedor Shekhtel, the author of the project for S.P. Dervis's estate house at Kiritsy, in fact had a local model for the updated pseudo-Gothic vocabulary they employed: an elaborate pseudo-Gothic, eighteenth-century cattle courtyard at A.P. Ermolov's neighboring estate, Krasnoe. According to local experts, this structure, still extant, is so redolent of "Bazhenov romanticism" as to trumpet his authorship.

Fig. 5.7 The "little house in the woods" at Gremiach, late nineteenth century (*Stolitsa i usad'ba*, no. 50).

As these examples suggest, by the turn of the century a fascination with folk culture, with medieval Russian history, and with Russian architectural and decorative motifs seems to have gripped the entire nation, from conservative court circles to wealthy industrialists and the artistic avant-garde. Grand ducal palaces featured pre-Petrine decor similar in its lavishness to the sets designed for Mussorgsky's operas on similarly pre-Petrine historical themes. On the estate as in the palace, command either of the Palladian architectural vocabulary that had dominated the golden age of estate building, or experimentation with the more native architectural idiom Bazhenov had invented for Catherine, were now equally acceptable proofs of status, subscribed to by both the old and the new elite. *Stolitsa i usad'ba* (The Capital and the Estate), the glossy, large-format magazine that sprang into existence in 1914 and ended its run in August 1917, endorsed this ten-

dency toward an eclectic fusion of architectural motifs from different periods of Russia's past. In a 1916 issue, a lengthy article was devoted to the Golitsyns' Gremiach, in Chernigov guberniia. At this "Russian Versailles," the author noted, the long, one-story house was "very old," but the park surrounding it had been filled with symbolic structures of more recent vintage. In one photograph, Princess Golitsyna is shown milking a prize cow in her *ferme ornee*, dressed in the native costume of the Gremiach area. Another photo shows a rustic and thoroughly Russian cottage in the park, with two costumed servants on its steps (fig. 5.7).

The Palladian estate house retained its symbolic power to the end of the old regime. The pages of *Stolitsa i usad'ba* also feature some of the last-built houses of pre-Revolutionary Russia, commissioned by wealthy merchants, that—in contrast to the railway magnate Derviz's Kiritsy—seem to have sprung full-fledged from the Catherinian model. The new mercantile elite was clearly modeling its architecture on old traditions. While it seems to have been equally at home appropriating either old architectural style for brand new estate houses, Palladianism offered a more resonant vocabulary, recalling as it did the glory days of estate life. The emotional pull of this style is writ large in Borisov-Musatov's nostalgic paintings of neoclassical manor houses and their inhabitants, often viewed at twilight, and sometimes vanishing like phantoms into the dusk.

At the same time, the estate was coming into its own as an object of serious study. *Starye gody* (Bygone Years), a scholarly cultural journal of the period, devoted an entire issue in 1910 to what now was termed "estate culture," examining the warp and woof of the entire world created on these often remote properties scattered throughout central Russia over the course of two centuries. The authors were right to claim that this world was precious as a uniquely Russian phenomenon, and to bemoan the already crumbling or defaced walls of numerous once-grand manor houses. They were perhaps less appropriate in their attacks on the nouveau-riche purchasers of the countryside's white elephants, for this new elite was no less proud to honor the traditional architectural markers of nobility than the old elite had been to create them. I have pointed to the many ways in which most of provincial Russia's grand estates, privately commissioned architectural masterpieces arising seemingly out of nowhere deep in the provinces, owed much to their owners' obeisance to court fashion throughout the imperial period. Close to its end, in a countryside where old notions of privilege were beginning to be democratized by the arrival of a new aristocracy of wealth, estate architecture showed few signs of breaking from this tradition.

6 The Picturesque and the Holy

Visions of Touristic Space in Russia, 1820–1850

Christopher Ely

As the most public of art objects, architectural structures indiscriminately offer themselves up to unanticipated uses and unforeseen interpretations. Simply the way buildings occupy space—with their interiors and exteriors, their massive and minute scales, their encapsulating proximities and unobtrusive distant views—ensures that their function and the interpretations of observers will regularly proliferate beyond the original builder's intentions. Thus the spatial context of a given structure always helps determine its significance. To put it another way, as the central focus of attention an architectural object says one thing, as part of a group of buildings it says another, and as part of a larger natural environment it says something else again. The altered context changes the interpretive possibilities. What do architectural structures tell us when they are situated in the landscape as part of a distant view? The following discussion concerns the perception of Russian architecture in the nineteenth century from one such distant vantage point: that of the tourist.

Twentieth-century distaste for tourism had long tended to discourage its serious study as an academic subject. In recent years, however, scholarly explorations of leisure travel have rewarded researchers with new insights in such areas as aesthetics, the experience of empire, transnational studies, and national identity formation.[1] Russian studies, too, has benefited from renewed interest in travel writing.[2] But tourism proper, defined as travel for recreational or educational purposes, has seldom received the attention of specialists in the Russian field. This lack of interest has a logical basis in Russian history. In comparison to the practice of tourism in Western Europe, the idea of domestic leisure travel developed slowly and rather awkwardly in Imperial Russia.[3]

Yet even though domestic tourism was generally held in low repute among educated Russian elites, travel writing played an important, if sometimes little-noted, role in Russian literature. Radishchev's *Journey from St. Petersburg to Moscow* (1790) and Karamzin's *Letters of a Russian Traveler* (1791–1801) are arguably the two most important prose works of the eighteenth century. A short list of nineteenth-century literature that borrowed from the genre of travel writing includes Pushkin's "Onegin's Journey" (1832), Gogol's *Dead Souls* (1842), Sollogub's *The Tarantas* (1845), and Turgenev's *Hunter's Sketches* (1852). Each of these works uses the device of a traveling protagonist to comment on the people and sights of the tsarist empire, particularly with respect to provincial European Russia. The prominence of travel themes in the literature of the first half of the century was not merely incidental; it provided an excellent forum for writers to explore the question of Russian national identity, a prime subject which absorbed the attention of intellectuals and artists in pre-Emancipation Russia.

Travel writing initially forces the writer to confront a set of deceptively simple questions: why travel, where to, and to see what? For Russians journeying through European Russia during the nineteenth century, answers to these questions did not come easily. "It is in foreign countries that people travel," wrote

Sollogub in *The Tarantas*, a novel about traveling in provincial Russia.[4] Sollogub's assertion reflected the widespread public opinion that there was no reason to undertake leisure travel in Russia because, especially by comparison to Western Europe, Russia contained nothing terribly worth looking at. This sentiment echoed throughout the literature of Imperial Russia. Dostoevsky asked in *Winter Notes on Summer Impressions*: "Does there exist a Russian . . . who doesn't know Europe twice as well as Russia?"[5] In the 1840s a travel writer named D. I. Matskevich remarked that tourism "as it is understood and undertaken in Western Europe, still does not exist here. . . . Here travel is not an end but a means. That is perhaps the reason we know so little of Russia."[6]

To offer an extreme contrast, the British gentleman on the Grand Tour of Europe knew precisely why he traveled. He was confident which countries merited a visit, and he carried along with him the knowledge of what he ought to see and do upon arrival.[7] Without a reason to see new things, or to see things anew, travel would mean simply moving from one destination to another. Hence Sollogub's rejection of Russian travel: "What kind of travelers are we? Just two gentlemen riding home to the country."[8]

Sollogub played on the uncomfortable position Russians found themselves in during the first half of the nineteenth century with respect to traveling in their own land. This discomfort originated in part from the expanding European interest in, and practice of, leisure travel. While from the seventeenth century onward, the Grand Tour had encouraged European travel abroad, especially for a refined elite able to afford it, the practice of domestic tourism in Europe did not begin to flourish until it found its own *raison d'être*. That new incentive made its appearance in the early nineteenth century and significantly broadened the social base of European tourism. It was a conception of the touristic landscape capable of emphasizing and encouraging domestic travel: the invention of picturesque landscape aesthetics. Picturesque tourism offered its adherents a collection of techniques and aesthetic values that made it possible to appreciate a much wider variety of landscape than that (typically Italian) foreordained as superior by the Grand Tourist. The vogue for picturesque scenery generated a new way of seeing one's surroundings, a new set of travel maps, and a new collection of sights worthy of attention.[9] It thereby opened up new terrain as potential scenery, including rustic countryside, woods, and hilly regions in various parts of Western Europe.

Interest in picturesque tourism had first developed in England during the latter half of the eighteenth century. It later caught on in France and Germany (and even the young United States) after the Napoleonic Wars. At the same time, the rapid growth of nationalism turned eyes toward local landscapes and national points of interest. Russians did not lag behind in their concern for national identity, but in contrast to developments in Europe, images of the Russian countryside remained contested and problematic. The critic Nestor Kukolnik complained in 1837 that books of picturesque sights were published "in France, England and even in Switzerland; but we . . . translate and reprint the old [European] ones, so that we only respect foreigners and are all the more convinced we have nothing good of our own."[10]

Geography itself contributed to the discrepancy between Western European and Russian domestic tourism. The vast, level plains of European Russia contrasted with the hillier, warmer, and more thickly settled landscapes of Western Europe. Impassable roads and miserable accommodations, moreover, made traveling in Russia a sardonic joke to those Russians who spent time on the road.[11] Under these conditions, while Kukolnik was calling for the institution of a Russian picturesque, other more persuasive approaches to the Russian landscape tended to condemn picturesque scenery as an artificial construction of the countryside. In the published fragment "Onegin's Journey," for example, Pushkin expressed a new sympathy for the simple and mundane landscape of the Russian village by comparison to the dramatic and overly romanticized landscapes of the Caucasus and the Crimea. Sergei Aksakov in his *Notes of an Angler* (1847) characterized "the love of landscape" as antithetical to "the love of nature," the former being false and superficial, the latter profound and sincere.[12] And a famous passage in *Dead Souls* attested to Gogol's struggle to define his "unfathomable" attraction to Russia in a landscape he understood to be outwardly desolate and unappealing.[13] In short, Russian space had begun to be celebrated in literature as expressly anti-picturesque.

This approach to Russia's natural landscape as outwardly impoverished but inwardly reflective of a hidden, almost mystical, beauty was elaborated on later in the century in literature and painting. Indeed, it eventually became the dominant and familiar image of Russian terrain. It was not, however, the only way of appreciating provincial Russia. Another group of writers, all nearly unknown today, devised a different approach to their native landscape. These were the travel writers proper, those who toured the provinces and published impressions of their journeys.[14] These writers developed a uniquely Russian model of picturesque scenery by appealing to the most common sight in the countryside to break the horizontal plane of Russia's level landscape: Orthodox churches and monasteries. Attuning their eyes to the built environment, these travel writers answered the implicit challenge of European scenic tourism—to envision a picturesque Russia—by making provincial architecture the central focus of their travels. By such means they devised a new way of seeing the landscape and a new model for touring the Russian countryside.

There was no prototypical picturesque terrain in Russia. Russia had no Alps, no Roman campagna, no Lake District, no Rhine River, and no Forest of Fontainebleau. Russian travel writers had to devise their own new image of scenic landscape, and for this purpose the monastery possessed several advantages. It was open to the public; it was aesthetically pleasing; and it was distinctly Russian, an immediately recognizable form, filled with symbolic potential. Early Russian travel writers attempted to make the monastery accessible, mapping patterns by which their readers (presumably future travelers) could journey through Russia and admire sacred architecture as an expression of Russian history and Orthodox spirituality. In this context, churches and monasteries were recognized not as the expression of a certain style or builder, but as markers of Russianness, as stops on a tour which, taken as a whole, provided the potential reader/traveler with a panoramic and historical vision of the native land. Monasteries, then, facilitated travel writers' attempts to assign significance to Russian space. Three of the most important and characteristic of the early Russian travel writers to adopt this approach were Pavel Svin'in in the 1820s, Andrei Murav'ev in the 1830s, and Stepan Shevyrev in the 1840s. Each writer devised his own distinctive approach to Russian picturesque travel, yet each enlisted the monastery to serve as the fundamental form of a new picturesque Russia.

SCENERY OF THE FATHERLAND

Svin'in founded the first incarnation of the journal *Notes of the Fatherland* (1818–30). He may be best known today as the butt of Pushkin's humorous epigrams or as a possible model for Gogol's *Inspector General*, but in spite of the ridicule he (sometimes justly) endured, Svin'in was a remarkably accomplished man.[15] He had a degree from the Imperial Academy of Arts, wrote verse and prose, spoke several languages, and traveled throughout Europe and the United States in diplomatic service. During his time abroad he absorbed the European fascination for touristic travel. In the United States he demonstrated his aptitude for the travelogue genre, writing and illustrating both a picturesque journey through the American countryside in Russian and an account of Moscow and Petersburg in English.[16]

In these works Svin'in had focused on the appearance and beauty of the natural landscape, which was standard practice in the picturesque travelogues of his day. Although he proved adept at writing inspired descriptions of American wilderness or English gardens near Petersburg, natural scenery never played a significant role in Svin'in's accounts of provincial Russia.[17] He conceived of his native land in a different way. The approach he would take to Russian travel was evident as early as 1820 in the inscription to *Notes of the Fatherland*: "God and Nature command we love our country / But to know it is an honor, a virtue, and a duty."[18] *Notes of the Fatherland* became Svin'in's means of fulfilling this debt to Russia. He wrote and edited its pages in the spirit of national patriotism, offering up the journal as a lesson in Russian history, geography, architecture, and archaeology. *Notes of the Fatherland* gave its readers an uncritical education in Russianness.

Svin'in believed he could inspire a renewed feeling of national self-worth among his compatriots by promoting a form of domestic tourism to the historically significant sights around Russia. Announcing the 1826 edition of the journal he wrote:

As soon as he knows his Fatherland, the Russian can feel his own dignity to its fullest extent, becoming convinced by experience that his blessed Fatherland abounds with all the treasures of the world. . . . Just having realized all this, I repeat, it is possible to be cured of the blind partiality to foreigners and finally to travel through wide Russia for pleasure and gain.[19]

The most important influence on Svin'in's conception of travel was Nikolai Karamzin. In 1803 Karamzin had written a short travel piece about the outskirts of Moscow in which he called the famous Trinity–St. Sergius Monastery, "holy not only to devout hearts but also to zealous lovers of native glory."[20] The medieval monastery, Karamzin argued in a proto-Slavophile vein, retained some of the essence of Russianness that had been lost after the reforms of Peter the Great. Karamzin had followed his search for Russian identity mainly into the study of history, and he was partly responsible for the upsurge of interest in the Russian past which had

gripped the public by the 1820s.[21] Svin'in developed Karamzin's model of national study in touristic travel and extended it much further. Taken together, his travel sketches in *Notes of the Fatherland*, beginning in 1818, form a rough guidebook to provincial Russia.

Yet Svin'in did not rely exclusively on the public's interest in history, nor did he entirely abandon the model of picturesque travel he had imbibed in the West. Despite his rejection of picturesque *natural* scenery as a subject suitable for the scrutiny of the Russian public, pictorial travel impressions did constitute a sizable part of the contents of *Notes of the Fatherland*. In his effort to portray the Russian countryside as a scenic space, he introduced the monastery and the provincial church as the most visible and important feature of the Russian landscape. Svin'in tended to refrain from close, detailed descriptions of these structures, preferring to invoke what might be called the "tourist's view" of Russian architecture. Readers were asked to appreciate the aesthetic qualities of monasteries and churches from a removed perspective. A word that continually arises in Svin'in's descriptive vocabulary is *"mestopolozhenie,"* perhaps best translated as the "situation" in the landscape of a building or city. His evocation of the Khutynskii Monastery outside Novgorod provides a characteristic example of his enthusiastic but economical descriptive technique: "One could not pick out a more pleasant and beautiful monastery. Standing atop the highest place in its surroundings it can be seen from anywhere. Its open spaces are covered with gardens and stone walls."[22] For all his interest in the picturesque, Svin'in never developed a particularly enthralling aesthetic imagery. His reader must rest satisfied with simple and superficial, though numerous, images of provincial sights.

In publishing his travel sketches, Svin'in clearly intended to establish a pattern of tourism in Russia. He commented that he had written one of his travel pieces, "in the hope that it can be put to use by many travelers like me—rich in curiosity but poor in free time."[23] Still, Svin'in had a special kind of tourism in mind. His vision of Russian travel did not express the familiar element of escape from urban into rural life so characteristic of the European picturesque journey. His conception of tourism was less an escape from the present than an engagement with the past. That past contained within itself an essential knowledge of the "national character" that would bolster Russian pride and dignity. The scenic beauty of provincial church architecture would act as the hinge that opened a door into a deeper sympathy for the native land.

Traveling vicariously through Russia with Svin'in as a guide, the reader of *Notes of the Fatherland* encountered a wide array of well-situated monasteries and churches. Once the picturesque view of a given building had been established, Svin'in typically moved straight into his primary object, to describe the site as a historical point of interest. His spare aesthetic imagery notwithstanding, in the dozens of travel sketches that appeared over the course of more than a decade, *Notes of the Fatherland* built up an elaborate panorama of Russian space. In one of its functions, the journal presented itself as a sort of map to the important sites and sights encountered while touring provincial Russia. By emphasizing the appearance and historical importance of the church and monastery, the journal set a pattern that would be followed by future travel writers. Most important, *Notes of the Fatherland* worked to show that provincial Russia could not be considered an empty wilderness. It was crowded with points of interest that deserved to be studied and appreciated by all educated Russians.

THE SACRED VIEW

A new model for Russian travel appeared in 1836. In the early 1830s Andrei Murav'ev had visited the Holy Land. A group of monks in Jerusalem had asked him about the Trinity–St. Sergius Monastery. Although he had been raised in Moscow, he had to confess that he was unfamiliar with the site.[24] Inspired to know more, Murav'ev began a tour of Russian religious monuments that took him to most of the important monasteries in Russia

and Ukraine. Based on this tour, he published a book of travel descriptions under the title *Journey Through the Holy Places of Russia*. The work became quite popular and would be reissued four times over the next ten years.[25]

Murav'ev's *Journey* built on and transformed a variety of travel that had deep roots in Orthodox Russia. He developed his particular vision of Russian tourism on the basis of the pre-existing institution of the Russian Orthodox pilgrimage. Not only did he treat Russian monasteries with religious veneration, but he also benefited from the special meals and lodging prepared by the monks for the use of pilgrims. Yet as respectful as he was of the pilgrimage tradition, Murav'ev's aims as a travel writer lay elsewhere. In comparing the modern traveler to pilgrims of past centuries, he pointed out that his contemporaries were less interested in "great feats of travel" than in "descriptions of sacred places."[26] In this sense Murav'ev's reasons for writing resembled those of Svin'in. "At the least," he wrote, "I wanted to direct the attention of passers-by to the most important objects and familiarize them with the ancient, holy places of our Fatherland."[27] Murav'ev's *Journey*, then, clearly offered an early model of Russian tourism. Like Svin'in, Murav'ev sought to instill in the public an admiration for Russia by attracting interest to the notable places in the provincial landscape.

It is interesting to note that Murav'ev's vision of provincial Russia differed from Svin'in's by the measure of the difference between their original examples of touristic travel. Whereas Svin'in sought to portray Russian space as picturesque countryside, in Murav'ev's work Russia appears to be nothing so much as an Orthodox holy land. His travel descriptions cleverly transformed the vast distances he covered—from northern Russia to southern Ukraine—into a unified location of Orthodox sites. He achieved this effect by almost entirely ignoring the landscapes and objects between the monasteries. The monastic spaces he describes are sacred locations. By portraying them in magnificent and spiritually untainted isolation he emphasizes their purity and tranquility. With scant reference to nonsacred subjects and locations, while lavishing attention on monasteries across a vast extent of territory in Russia and Ukraine, Murav'ev's *Journey* seems to enfold the entire countryside into its inspired vision of Russia as a sacred, Orthodox space.

Murav'ev attained this effect through the creation of a new descriptive method. Separate sections of the *Journey* typically begin with the entrance into view of the monastery as it is seen from the road. Most chapters open as Murav'ev travels through some unremarkable stretch of countryside. He reaches a promontory and suddenly the splendid domes and spires of a given monastery arrest his attention and call forth a rapturous description of the beauty of the sacred place. He then enters the monastic setting, and there follows a description of its daily life, its history, its gardens, its architecture, and the noteworthy objects it contains. These descriptions, even those of the art and architecture, rarely depict their subjects in secular terms. Everything is a reflection of the spirituality of the place, which in turn represents the spiritual character of Russia as a whole. By narrowing the focus of his travels, Murav'ev found a way to make the Russian landscape interesting and attractive—not as a secular world of scenery and history, but as a hallowed and resplendent Orthodox land.[28]

HOLY LAND TO HOLY *LAND*

Murav'ev enjoyed some literary success with this format, but the *Journey* ultimately failed to inspire any widespread interest in Russian travel. That failure may have resulted from what Murav'ev omitted—namely, everything in between the monasteries. In the meantime, new approaches to the Russian countryside were being pioneered by Slavophiles and others who located the fundamental seat of Russian identity in the practices and beliefs of the Russian people. This shift of interest helped arouse concern among the educated for the culture of non-elites, particularly the peasantry. It also inspired a new attitude toward the provincial environment.[29]

By the 1840s a new conception of Russian nationality had entered into discussions of Russian travel. Gogol, for example, in *Selected Passages from Correspondence with Friends*, implored his countrymen to travel in Russia. He did not have historical sites or picturesque scenery in mind. His was a different sort of touristic goal. "Coming into the first district or province, try to find out about its points of interest," he suggested, "they aren't in architectural structures or antiquities, but in the people."[30]

In the 1840s the influence of such new approaches to Russian identity began to be felt in travel writing. By this time a sort of superficial ethnography had appeared in the language of most Russian travel writers, and the ordinary countryside began to assert its presence in scenic descriptions.[31] Stepan Shevyrev's *Journey to the Kirillo-Belozersk Monastery*, about a trip in the summer of 1847, is a prime example of this new approach. Shevyrev's *Journey* followed in the footsteps of Murav'ev and Svin'in. It used the monastery as the basis of a picturesque journey through provincial Russia intended to arouse appreciation for the history and spirituality of the nation. As with Murav'ev's travelogue, Shevyrev's *Journey* took him from one monastery to another, but in this work more than half the descriptive material concerns the people and places *between* the monasteries. Whereas Murav'ev had made the Russian countryside interesting by narrowing his vision to the monastery alone, Shevyrev interested his readers in monasteries by immersing them within the texture of the surrounding countryside. He reports his conversations with carriage drivers, describes the vast openness of Russia's plains as the special "picturesque quality" of the Russian landscape, and always depicts the monasteries he visits within the context of their natural environment.

Shevyrev was a professor of literature at Moscow University. He had been one of the most ardent admirers of *Dead Souls* when it appeared in the early 1840s. In his review of the book, Shevyrev seconded Gogol's special appreciation for the Russian landscape, but he did not sympathize with what he perceived as the novel's denial of Russia's scenic character. He chose to supplement Gogol's "one-sided" description of the landscape with his own enhanced visual imagery. The review contains a lengthy supplement to Gogol's landscape description, in which Shevyrev emphasizes the spaciousness of the fields, the colorful vegetation of the marshes, the long-suffering yet picturesque peasants, and the beauty of Russian church architecture.[32] This compilation of landscape elements would also serve as the basis of Shevyrev's travel writing.

In *Dead Souls* Gogol had complained of the absence from Russia of those architectural structures deemed picturesque in Europe, such as ruins, castles, and "ivy-covered cottages." Shevyrev countered in his *Journey* that monasteries provided Russia's own native form of scenic architectural beauty: "From our own ancient period have remained monuments of another sort, the meaning of which has been defined by the religious character of our life. Our castles are monasteries."[33] For Shevyrev the entire Russian countryside presented a subject of interest and a picturesque spectacle equal to anything Europe had to offer.

Shevyrev was perhaps the first Russian travel writer to argue that the natural landscape of central Russia (presented in a reasonably naturalistic manner) could stand on its own as scenic space. In this respect he contended that Russian nature possessed a unique beauty: "Italy and Switzerland, the Appenine and the Alps have greatly indulged me with their views, but I submit there is a moment of nature in our diverse Fatherland, which does not yield to the beauty of the Appenine or the Alps, although it has an entirely different character."[34] From Shevyrev's perspective this natural landscape did not supersede or supplant the architectural landscape. They harmonized to create Russia's unique environment. In trying to arouse a spiritual appreciation for the monasteries he visited, Shevyrev portrayed them as an integral part of the surrounding scenery. "The light and playful architecture," he wrote,

"agreed with the merry impression of its natural surroundings. . . . How beautiful is nature in these holy places. God's blessing and [nature's] pure beauty unite in the mind of the viewer."[35] The natural landscape supported God's affirmation of the Russian land, fusing both nature and the monastery into an almost Edenic amalgamation of Russian space.

The penultimate paragraph of Shevyrev's travelogue summarizes his construction of the Russian landscape in the form of a vision inspired by his travels:

I cannot pass over one impression I experienced two nights before returning to Moscow. We were traveling from Uglich to Kaliazin. The level, flat steppe spread out all around beneath us, reminding me of the endlessly flat steppes of the south. It seemed we were racing along in just the same spot, and the steppe would never end. Little by little the moon rose in the sky; at first it only lit up the edge of the horizon and fields, but then it brightened the whole sky and steppe. Tired out from travel, I lay down in a kind of half sleep. Around me on all sides and high into the sky arose a wonderful white cathedral temple with its gold domes. Above us a gigantic bell tower grew right into the heavens. I'd only just closed my eyes when I was struck by this magnificence, and no matter where I turned, on all sides there appeared a cathedral full of prayer. It shook my soul with its gigantic form, as if all our endless Russia had united its temples, which from the ground to the peak of the sky had formed together into a singular infinity.[36]

It is appropriate that this inspired vision, which combines an evocation of the wider landscape with the image of Russia as an Orthodox holy land, presents itself as a dream. In this period the idea of "Holy Russia," the sense of the land as an essentially Orthodox space, was already being eclipsed by a new sanctification of Russia as the home of the *narod* (the Russian folk). Two such distinct ways of idealizing one place could not long exist side by side, and the presence of the monastery would fade from Russian travel writing for several years to come.

THE MONASTERY AS A RUSSIAN SYMBOL

Shevyrev was an Orthodox conservative and an important supporter of Official Nationality. For these affiliations he was despised by some of Gogol's more progressive admirers like Vissarion Belinskii. On reading a new volume of Murav'ev's travels in the late 1850s, the radical critic Nikolai Dobroliubov reinterpreted the author he had admired in his youth as an immature and outdated hack because his book displayed no empathy toward the laboring poor who inhabited the rural world through which he traveled.[37] Without question all three of these writers, Svin'in, Murav'ev, and Shevyrev, were aligned on the conservative side of the political spectrum in Nikolaevan Russia. They would pay for it with complete loss of respect as Russia liberalized in the late 1850s. They also failed to generate any recognizable increase in tourism in the mid-nineteenth century.[38]

But in communicating their impressions of the Russian countryside, they were part of a trend that, in certain ways, was wider than the disputes of liberals, conservatives, and radicals, or Westerners and Slavophiles. They were engaged in a project to establish a generally accepted vision of the national landscape, and in that effort their contribution provided one important foundation for the articulation of a Russian national identity. Although mostly absent from the travel literature of the early reform era, the monastery returned as an important part of the image of Russian space that was produced in the landscape painting of the Wanderers beginning in the 1870s. Monasteries and churches also emerged as an important scenic site for tourists in the practical, Baedeker-style guidebooks that began to be published in the 1880s and 1890s.

In attempting to envision provincial Russia as a space for tourism, these writers of Russian travel guides seized on the image of monasteries and churches in the landscape to help them portray the countryside as picturesque space while at the same time emphasizing the historical and spiritual identity of the nation as a whole. Svin'in established the basic model, and Murav'ev and Shevyrev significantly extended its expressive possibilities. For each of them in different ways, the monastery was more of a means to an end than an end in itself. Because their subject was rarely the building as a discrete object, one might argue that architecture only makes its presence felt incidentally in these writings. Yet although these writers used the monastery in ways that were removed from its original purpose and conception, that does not necessarily diminish the significance of this previously unsuspected use. The landscape view, the building in the distance, is another way in which architectural structures register meaning and organize cultural practices.

If we examine the travel writing of the early nineteenth century as a whole, what can it tell us about Russia's search for a distinctive national identity in this period? It is worth noting that all three of these writers had spent a significant amount of time abroad. In many ways their work reflects the influence of the Western travel account. That influence is apparent both in the initial impulse to produce a comparable Russian travel literature and in the very style of their travel descriptions. Although each conceived of his task differently, the attempt to create a form of Russian touristic travel provides the main backdrop for one of the essential issues they confronted: how was Russia to become understandable and accessible as a space for tourism?

This was a pivotal period in Russian cultural and intellectual history. In the aftermath of Napoleon's invasion and Russia's resistance, educated Russia became engrossed in the search for national identity. But what that identity consisted of was mired in deep dispute. As all of the aforementioned travel writers noted, Russia deserved to be described and appreciated just as Europe already had been. Still, it remained unclear precisely what native features merited attention. Svin'in, Murav'ev, and Shevyrev proposed different possible constructions of the countryside, yet all maintained the monastery as its principal sight. Because interest in picturesque scenery dominated European tourism at this time, the first task these writers confronted was the need to devise an aesthetic approach to their own countryside. They sought to make the landscape attractive to the touristic gaze, to the gaze of Russians who had read Karamzin's *Letters of a Russian Traveler* or any of a number of foreign and Russian descriptions of Europe.

In essence, the practice of picturesque tourism meant searching out images in the landscape that resembled landscape painting, or would look appropriate as a picture. Thus apparati such as the Claude glass enabled the tourist to tint and frame any view he or she happened upon, rendering it more akin to a landscape by the greatly admired Claude Lorrain. Karamzin, for example, had scanned the European countryside in search of "a landscape worthy of the brush of a Salvator Rosa or Poussin."[39] He also stated without a hint of irony that "spring would not be so beautiful had not Thomson and Kleist described for me all its beauties."[40] In other words, the picturesque was a tautological aesthetic sensibility. Picturesque travel defined landscape beauty according to what had already been construed in landscape painting or literary descriptions as beautiful. Thus picturesque scenery by definition referred to certain kinds of European scenery.

With respect to the visual appreciation of Russian church architecture, it is important to keep in mind that the pilgrimage continued among all social classes in Russia. Monasteries themselves, unlike ruins and castles in Europe, as much as they presented a striking spectacle, did not elicit an *essentially* aesthetic response from Russian viewers. Like Roman or medieval ruins, the monastery might provoke a nostalgic romanticization of the Muscovite past, but it also remained closely connected to Russia's present and future identity. Monasteries contained within their walls an active spiritual life; they were living structures whose history progressed toward and included contemporary concerns. As such, even

when deployed in the travel writer's text as a way to arouse visual or recreational interest, the monastery inevitably wound up embedded in questions about the character and meaning of Russia. In these travelogues, the monastery functioned as a picturesque subject to attract the traveler's eye, but in contrast to European models of scenic travel, it was not set among a group of other interesting or beautiful objects as part of an escapist, aesthetic journey. These travel writers saw it as the basis of a more serious examination of the history, spirituality, and cultural significance of Russia. In spite of some of their stated intentions to promote the leisured enjoyment of provincial Russia, they all converted this touristic approach into a deeper engagement with their native land.

Having designated the monastery as the principal attraction of Russian tourism, Svin'in, Murav'ev, and Shevyrev together helped to establish a new conceptual map of the provincial landscape. The project they undertook can be compared to another attempt to surmount the influence of picturesque scenery as it had been developed in Western Europe. In the United States during the first half of the nineteenth century, Americans were working to reconceptualize their own landscape as an aesthetically appealing and nationally distinctive terrain. American visions similarly departed from established European norms.[41] Over the course of several decades, the dangerous and untamed American wilds came to be seen as the spectacular and pristine wilderness, a sacred space in its own right. Although it was a very different aesthetic conception, the American landscape presented a spectacle as holy as Murav'ev's or Shevyrev's Orthodox image of Russia.

While European forms of picturesque scenery tended to call for a blending of the built and the natural environments into some form of rustic or pastoral whole, the American wilderness came to be exalted precisely for its freedom from human habitation. In the American context, the absence of humanity suggested all the more the presence of divinity. With their emphasis on architectural structures, Russian travel writers adopted the opposite approach. Orthodox monuments exalted Russian history, spirituality and the national character. Their beauty, as well as their sheer quantity across the face of the land, marked out the national terrain as the home of an exceptional, even potentially superior, people, just as the untrammeled wilderness identified the United States as an exceptional land of grandeur and proximity to God.

The question we are left with then is why travel writing on provincial Russia ultimately took such a different path from that of European travel writing. We must first take into account that, particularly in the nineteenth century, the image of the countryside followed a very different trajectory in Russia than it did in the West. Russian writers intentionally produced touristic texts, but their work was embedded in a different set of concerns than those of European guides to tourism. In the rapidly urbanizing and industrializing countries of Western Europe, the countryside had already begun to acquire a nostalgic hue as a place of escape from everyday reality. Studies of Rousseau, Constable, Byron, and the Barbizon landscape painters, to give just a few examples, emphasize emerging conceptions of the countryside as a pastoral or inspiring retreat constructed in opposition to the development of an increasingly normative and encompassing urban life.[42] Leisured elites in Russia, on the other hand, those for whom travel writing was intended, often maintained close ties to the provinces in the form of country estates. For much of the Russian reading public in the early nineteenth century, everyday life still contained some measure of rural isolation. The Russian idealization of the countryside was thoroughly intertwined with life as it was lived on the gentry estate.[43] The rhythms and concerns of the urban world had not yet come to dominate Russian culture to a degree that they now reigned over everyday life in many parts of Western Europe.[44]

During this same period, moreover, those parts of the Russian countryside unaffiliated with the gentry estate were being transformed into a crucial marker of national identity. Dmitri Likhachev speaks of "the distinctly Russian form of Rousseauism that evolved in the nineteenth century: in the *narodnik* movement and in Tolstoyan views on the 'natural man'—the peasant—as opposed to the 'educated class' or intelligentsia."[45] One might say that with the Russian idealization of the *narod*, the Rousseauian concept of "natural man" had been displaced onto peasant culture as a whole. In this sense, to an even greater degree than in Western Europe, the essential nature of Russian national culture came to be associated with images of, and ideas about, rural life. Already during the first half of the century the countryside was coming to represent Russia as the defining locus of the entire national entity. For these reasons too, the growth of "scenery for scenery's sake" was inhibited in Russia. Travel writers could not engage in the casual, lighthearted aesthetic approach to the countryside characteristic of the confident and removed urban voice of the Western European travel writer.

Russian travel writers were caught in an implicit conflict between the search for Russian identity and the European model of travel writing and touristic practice. Church architecture helped them negotiate the two horns of the dilemma. On the one hand, it allowed them to interpret Russia as a unique scenic space in its own right. On the other hand, it offered an expression of Russian national exceptionalism by evoking the mystical presence of "Holy Russia" within the imagined space of a sacred landscape adorned with the architectural splendors of the Orthodox church. "A countless multitude of churches and monasteries with their cupolas, domes and crosses, is scattered all over holy, pious Russia," wrote Nikolai Gogol in 1842.[46] If the form of tourism advocated by early nineteenth-century travel writers has been all but consigned to oblivion, their vision of a sacred Russian landscape continues to make its presence felt in the literary and visual imagery they helped to inspire.

7 Constructing the Russian Other

Viollet-le-Duc and the Politics of an Asiatic Past

Lauren M. O'Connell

The notion that there existed an identifiable "Russian Art" gained currency in France and in Russia in the late 1870s, in large measure through the efforts of three individuals: a French architect of international reputation, a well-traveled French economist with a penchant for the arts, and a Russian museum director with government connections. Their remarkable collaboration gave rise to an educational institution, displays at numerous exhibitions, and several lavish publications, all crafted to promote a particular vision of the origins, nature, and future of this newly defined artistic entity. The mastermind of the venture was Viktor Butovsky, director of the Museum of Industrial Art in Moscow. He instigated the campaign to introduce Russians to their forgotten artistic past, and to promote that past abroad. The economist Natalis Rondot was the intermediary; he cofounded Butovsky's museum and sponsored the publication of Butovsky's writings on Russian art in Paris by Morel and Company, the prestigious publisher of illustrated art books.

The central figure of the effort was Eugène Emmanuel Viollet-le-Duc, whose writings had by this time earned him an international reputation, and the confidence to cross any new historical frontier armed with a well-honed "scientific" method of analysis. Viollet-le-Duc would lend his imprimatur to the movement by writing a comprehensive French history of Russian architecture, isolating for the purpose its distinctly "Russian" qualities. His was not the first French foray into the subject; a decade earlier the noted poet and critic Théophile Gautier had penned episodic travel reports in preparation for a magnum opus on Russia's architectural treasures.[1] But while Gautier's project foundered, Viollet-le-Duc's *L'Art russe: Ses origines, ses éléments constitutifs, son apogée, son avenir* (1877) made an enormous critical splash in Russia and generated significant ripples in France.[2] The vigor with which it was defended and criticized in both countries testifies to the sensitivity and moment of the issues it raised about the past, present, and future course of Russian art and architecture.[3]

The story of this unlikely and productive collaboration, to be retold here through correspondence among the players and in the published texts they generated, has broad implications for our understanding of the perceived political force of the arts and their history in the late nineteenth century. Its unraveling will support Hobsbawm's thesis that histories legitimate nations, and that national histories are by definition inventions.[4] Analysis of this situation will extend that thesis to the art historical case, showing how the

I would like to thank Mme. Geneviève Viollet-le-Duc for graciously allowing me access to her ancestor's correspondence, and Ithaca College for Summer Research Grants that supported this research. An Ailsa Mellon Bruce Visiting Senior Fellowship at the National Gallery of Art's Center for Advanced Study in the Visual Arts provided context and support for additional study. I am grateful to Christian Otto and William Brumfield for commenting on early versions of the manuscript, and to James Cracraft, Daniel Rowland, Susan Bronson, Deborah Marrow, and the members of the SSRC "Architecture and the Expression of Group Identity in Russia" Seminar, whose suggestions contributed to the final version.

invention of an architectural tradition, describable in words and images but also buildable in the present day, could be seized upon as an unusually potent tool for the inculcation of the desired national identity. As well, it will dramatize the taste-making role of books about buildings in the late nineteenth century, which often outweighed that of the buildings themselves. In their portability and, especially, in their exportability, architectural books could prove more potent proselytizers than the immovable objects they described.

Finally, study of the Butovsky-Rondot-Viollet project offers a unique opportunity for cross-cultural analysis, engaging us with defining cultural struggles at both ends of the geographical divide that separated the players. From the Russian side in particular, the study of these undertakings will focus our attention on one of the central tropes of Russian history—the Gordian complexity of Russia's self-image vis-à-vis Europe and Asia. The theories promulgated by this international team will suggest certain parallels with the phenomenon of European Orientalism—the invocation in literature and the arts of what was perceived as exotic subject matter, whether actually Asian, or Middle Eastern, North African, or otherwise foreign and "other." Theoreticians of European Orientalism, following Edward Said's lead, have argued that the Oriental "other" depicted in nineteenth-century French painting, for example, becomes the repository for the European self's fears, desires, and displaced anxieties.[5] Application of this framework to the complicated geopolitical circumstances that framed nineteenth-century Russian architecture will modify these assumptions in significant ways.

The three-man team of Butovsky, Rondot, and Viollet-le-Duc began as a two-person consultancy. On the strength of his authorship of a published report advocating the founding of a Museum of Art and Industry in Lyon that would showcase the artistic products of manufacturing processes, Rondot was invited to Russia in 1862 by Viktor Butovsky to found a similar institution there.[6] Natalis Rondot (1821–1900) was an economist by profession, having arrived at that field by way of the manufacturing trades, which he learned as a young wool-dying apprentice and later practiced as a government expert on the wool and silk industries.[7] The museum he proposed for Lyon, heart of the French silk industry, would seek to improve the quality of domestic products by displaying exemplary historical and contemporary artistic models—in the form of original works of art and plaster cast reproductions. While the direct impetus for such a project came from the specter of improving foreign products that loomed over the international expositions of the 1850s, the strategy was not a new one.[8] The same didactic, patriotic, and economic impulses had motivated France's urge to collect and display her treasures in the wake of the Revolution's depredations in the previous century.[9] Rondot's report struck a chord in Moscow with Viktor Butovsky (1815–80?),[10] who had hopes of similarly stimulating Russian industry to produce artfully national products. Butovsky was director of the Stroganovskoe tsentral'noe uchilishche tekhnicheskago risovaniia (Stroganov School of Industrial Design), which he established in 1860 as a successor to an earlier school founded in 1825 by Count Sergei Stroganov, of the art-patron Stroganov family.[11]

After five years of planning and negotiation, the museum became a reality in Moscow in 1867, housed on Miasnitskaia Street in an annex to the Stroganov School.[12] The museum's pedagogical and economic mission betrayed its French roots. The materials gathered there were to serve as inspirational models to future industrial designers. In underwriting the museum's expenses the Department of Commerce and Manufacture (conveniently headed by Butovsky's brother Alexander) clearly regarded it as a potential stimulant to the export side of the trade equation. The sponsors of the Moscow museum had broad consciousness-raising aspirations as well; the sight of "excellent" models of Russia's artistic traditions would, they hoped, "elevate public taste."[13]

Among the first joint ventures of the museum and school was the publication of a lithographic facsimile of an early Russian icon-painting manual. The manuscript chosen for reproduction, the *Stroganovskii ikonopisnyi litsevoi podlinnik* (Stroganov Iconographic Figurative Patternbook),[14] was itself a representation of earlier material. Compiled in the early seventeenth century by numerous hands and retouched in subsequent centuries, the Podlinnik manuscript drew upon earlier icon calendars to instruct the icon painter in the proper cast and costume for each episode in the liturgical year. Significantly for Butovsky, to publish the Podlinnik manuscript was to celebrate a triumphant episode in the history of the Russian icon (as well as the clan of the institution's namesake). Images associated with the so-called Stroganov School of icon painting of the seventeenth century, which were made in accordance with the Podlinnik's prescriptions, featured a rich warm palette and densely populated compositions, and represented one of the last distinctive phases in Russian icon painting before the appropriation of European modes of representation. And the Podlinnik manuscript itself had been produced in a spirit of nationalistic retrenchment. It was one of a number of manuals compiled in the wake of the 1551 Stoglav (Council of the Hundred Chapters), which had been convened by Ivan IV to address church reform issues, among them the baleful influence of Western innovations on hallowed Orthodox types. Butovsky's resurrection of the Podlinnik in 1869 aimed similarly to instill in Russian audiences an appreciation for the distinctiveness of national traditions by familiarizing them with a particular facet of their past. The national art identified by the museum would simultaneously be brought to an international audience—the renewed Podlinnik was exhibited in Paris at the Exposition Universelle of 1878, along with original objects from the museum's collection, manuscript facsimiles, and drawings by the Stroganov School students.[15]

The museum's icon-painting manual, with its focus on a seemingly "native" phase in the history of Russian image-making, raises an issue that would occupy the eventual threesome through their various endeavors. How

should Russia's national art be defined, given that the territorial boundaries and ethnic identities of the Russian nation were neither fixed nor agreed upon? Eric Hobsbawm has documented, for modern Europe, the overlapping and conflicting ways in which "nationhood" has been constructed, and the resulting instability of any particular definition.[16] The late-nineteenth-century Russian case was no different. In the midst of a two-century expansion drive that had drawn the Baltics, Poland, Siberia, and the southern borderlands into the imperial fold, the limits of "Russia" were shifting from one year to the next. Furthermore, there was no stable historical entity on which to pin national identity. Russia's national history could only be said to have begun in the fifteenth century, when Muscovite princes began to unify disparate provinces after two centuries of Mongol occupation; her Kievan prehistory, and the prior legacy of pre-Kievan peoples, constituted an unwieldy, geographically fragmented, and ethnically heterogeneous amalgam resistant to categorization, much less characterization.[17]

A description of the Moscow museum written by Rondot for the respected *Gazette des beaux arts* broached the national identity issue with an art-historical taxonomy that would be honed in the group's later presentations. The first step was to disentangle a "national" sensibility from Western-inspired trends: "Russian ornamental motifs are derived from two opposing sources," he wrote, "those in the Western—French or German—taste on the one hand, and those in the national taste on the other."[18] In drawing this particular distinction Rondot echoed prevailing sentiment in other fields—the problem of Russia's overweening cultural debt to Europe since the Petrine westward turn is commonly read as a defining motif in nineteenth-century Russian intellectual life. But as Rondot's dissection of the "national" component will suggest, the reality of Russia's cultural patrimony was far too complicated to be accommodated by the binary pre- and post-Petrine model. On the "national" side, Rondot writes, some works "resemble the Byzantine style, others have an Asiatic flavor, and yet others have a specifically Russian character."[19] "National" was not, then, coextensive with "Russian," but forged of Byzantine, Asian, and Russian elements.

The problem of how to quantify—and to account for—the Asian component in particular would emerge as a central preoccupation of the group, and the "Slavic-Asiatic" theory that they eventually fashioned would become the most controversial of their propositions. For Russia's relationship to Asia loomed as large, then as now, in her identity search as did that with Europe. European Orientalist theory has amply demonstrated that Asianness, or "Orientalist" subject matter, had become by this time a well-established trope for the primitive, the primal, and the politically subjected. In this light, the trio's wager that Russians would warm to an Asiatic theory of their own origins and destiny would appear misguided, at best. But the phenomenon of Orientalism was initially defined in Western terms, to characterize European appropriations of non-European cultures, and fits ill with the Russian reality.[20] Implicit in French Orientalist paintings of the North African harem, for instance, or British photographs of a seraglio in Constantinople, as initially theorized after Said, was the geographical, cultural, and political gulf that separates the depictor from the depicted. One speaks of Europe and its Other, or, in postcolonial theory, of metropole and colony.[21] But because of its dual or divided continental status— Russia is a Eurasian continent—Russia's European Self is not distinct from her Asiatic Other.[22]

Indeed, it is precisely Russia's dual, or divided, "Eurasian" continental status that has historically plagued all attempts to define her nature. Mark Bassin has shown that in the absence of clear natural boundaries, the demarcation of the line between the Asian and European continental masses has always followed an ideological rather than geophysical logic, to which her ethnic diversity and protean political history lend no clarification.[23] He argues, however, that Russia's double/split nature only became a matter of acute concern in the eighteenth century, when Petrine philoso-

phy introduced the notion of European superiority, which translated into a Russian image of herself as a European power with colonized Asian edges.[24] In the nineteenth century this view would itself be challenged by competing conceptions; with Russia's hubristic rejection of her own cultural colonization by Europeans came Nicholas I's politics of "official nationality" and the intelligentsia's cultivation of the folkloric as an uncontaminated wellspring. In this climate it became possible to view the embrace of Asianness as a way of breaking out of the European orbit.[25] Thus by the nineteenth century, to invoke the Russian image of its Asiatic self/neighbor in literature or in art was to tap into a roiling well, combining chauvinistic pride with xenophobic fear and loathing. As analyzed by Katya Hokanson, for example, Pushkin's selection of a Caucasian theme for the 1822 narrative poem "Captive of the Caucasus" played to both the attraction and the disdain that the subject might be expected to hold for readers. Written in the wake of the annexation of Georgia in 1801, and in the midst of an intense Russification program in the region, the poem presented its Russian reader with "the literary equivalent of colonization."[26] It offered metropolitan Russia a literary opportunity to revel in her own imperial achievements by surveying, like Napoleon in Egypt, the landscape of her new territories. At the same time, the sense of superiority that the reading of the poem conferred was mixed with an awed fascination with the "exotic" aspects of the colonized culture. Like the North African harem in the hands of French Orientalist painters, the Caucasus depicted reflected back on the depictor's fears and desires.[27]

The relevance of this Asia-Europe paradox to the invention of a Russian art becomes even more apparent in the next joint venture embarked upon by Rondot and Butovsky— the publication of Butovsky's *Histoire de l'ornement russe* in Paris in 1870.[28] According to Rondot, Butovsky's history of Russian ornament would revise French opinion by revealing the "beauty," "originality," and "unity" of an admittedly "strange" art that took shape "at a time when Russia seemed to us not to have a history."[29] Crucial to the project's success would be the author's skill at performing the delicate operation of separating, as though surgically, the various bits of foreign matter that had accreted onto the Russian national body over time. But not all intrusions were equally invasive; according to Rondot, Butovsky's book would bring to the fore neglected works of "incomparable richness" and "rare nobility" that had developed under "Asiatic" or "Greek" influence.[30] The book was published in French, and in France, by the esteemed Paris publishing house of Morel and Company, which would follow with Viollet-le-Duc's *L'Art russe* seven years later. Founded in 1857 and specializing in books on the arts and their history around the world, Morel had quickly established itself as a leader in lithographic and chromolithographic illustration; the house was honored at the 1878 Exposition in Paris as the premier arts publisher in the international community.[31] In placing their manuscripts with Morel the team assured itself wide readership; more important, they decreased the likelihood that their subject would be dismissed, as in the past, as exotic and peripheral.

Butovsky's two-volume history of Russian manuscript illumination contrasted strictly derivative twelfth-century motifs, produced under the tutelage of Byzantine masters, with fourteenth-century "Russian" fragments bearing such telltale "Asiatic" traces as the presence of fantastical opposed animals bound in complex tangles of interlaced strands. Butovsky made a key assertion in his brief introductory text: that the country's two-century occupation by the Mongol Tatars left a pronounced Asiatic mark. Rondot's earlier hint at the Asiatic contribution is thus further developed, and historicized. Ironically, though, in locating the origins of this influence in the Mongol occupation, Butovsky ran afoul of prevailing antagonisms, for late nineteenth-century imperial ideology, bent on east and southeasterly expansion, cultivated a resentment toward Central Asian peoples, whose source could handily be located precisely in the Mongol subjugation.[32]

The team's next book project, Viollet-le-Duc's *L'Art russe*, attempted to defuse this volatile aspect of the theory while applying it to the medium of architecture, which had not been featured in either of Butovsky's publications. Viollet-le-Duc was first drawn into the collaboration in March of 1872, when Rondot (with whom he had corresponded on a few other occasions over a twenty-year period) wrote volunteering to present Viollet-le-Duc with a complimentary copy of Butovsky's *Histoire de l'ornement russe*, judging that Viollet might find it useful in his work.[33] It was, no doubt, the "national" content of Butovsky's project that seemed relevant to Viollet-le-Duc's studies, for by this time, at the end of his career, Viollet was well identified with the quest for national expression in architecture.[34] Viollet wrote back quickly for information on Butovsky's museum and the Stroganov School, and produced without delay a flattering review of Butovsky's book for the French *Encyclopédie d'architecture*, also a Morel title.[35] The circle of acquaintance was completed when Rondot forwarded this encomium to Butovsky, who soon entered enthusiastically into correspondence with his French admirer.

Three years after the review appeared, Viollet was recruited to follow Butovsky's publication with one of broader scope and wider reach. The idea for *L'Art russe* appears to have begun with a contract with Morel to produce a sequel to Butovsky's volumes,[36] but as the project took shape it emerged as a full-blown history of architecture (and art, peripherally), quite unlike Butovsky's essentially graphic compendium. The book was produced collaboratively; a letter from Rondot to Viollet details a surprising history-making protocol, according to which Butovsky would send the Frenchman information he judged relevant to the project, and Viollet-le-Duc would hazard an interpretive framework with which to give that information meaning. Viollet would then send drafts of his manuscript-in-progress to Butovsky, who would check the theory against the larger field of "facts" at his command (that is, recent archeological findings), and alert his French partner to the need to modify or rethink accordingly.[37] The result would be an internationally negotiated identity, grafting European theoretical preconceptions (and misconceptions) onto a selective and narrowly partisan Russian reading of historical data.

The book seeks to recover the Muscovite architectural heritage, extracting its organizing principles for application in the present. Analysis of the complex geometries of the picturesque sixteenth-century Cathedral of the Intercession on the Moat, popularly known as the church of St. Basil the Blessed, for example, yields the distinguishing structural principle of the overlapping corbelled arch, which is used in turn to generate a peculiarly Russian nineteenth-century architecture (figs. 7.1–7.4). Viollet went one step further than Butovsky on the Asian hypothesis, arguing that even the Byzantine elements in Russian art were, at bottom, Asian, because Byzantium itself had Asiatic roots.[38] His elaboration of Butovsky's construct suggests that Viollet was researching the question on his own, and a letter of January 7, 1876, confirms that his "Slavic-Asiatic" theory was not entirely dependent on the materials sent from Russia: "I have some information of the utmost interest on the arts of the Far East," he writes, "thanks to the collection of Mr. Cernuschi, who was kind enough to make it available to me, and I found solutions there that are, I believe, incontestable."[39] He was wrong about the incontestability of his "solutions," for Butovsky and Rondot would both challenge him on their fit with the facts.

The Cernuschi collection, which consisted largely of Chinese and Japanese bronzes gathered by the banker Henri Cernuschi and the art critic Théodore Duret during their travels in 1871–72 and exhibited in Paris in 1873, did modify the Asian theory in important ways. Most significantly, it drew Viollet's gaze farther eastward, inspiring his mention of a possible "Far Eastern" contribution to Russian art.[40] This played perfectly to Butovsky's wish to steer a palatable course between two undesirables: the influence of Western Europe on the one hand, and of the problematic Asiatic Mongol Tatars on the other. Rondot had warned Viollet that Bu-

Fig. 7.1 "Eglise de Vassili Blajennoi, à Moscou, tour octogone sur arcs encorbellés" (Church of St. Basil the Blessed in Moscow, octagonal tower on corbelled arches). Sixteenth-century Muscovite prototype, from which a nineteenth-century architecture will be derived. Viollet-le-Duc, *L'Art russe: Ses origines, ses éléments constitutifs, son apogée, son avenir,* (1877) plate 12.

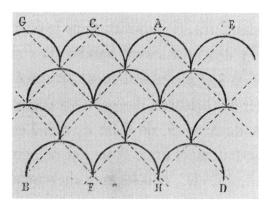

Fig. 7.2 "Système d'arcs chevauchés" (System of overlapping arches). Extraction of the underlying structural principle that will be used to generate a modern, but historically inspired, architecture. Viollet-le-Duc, *L'Art russe*, p. 164, fig. 63.

tovsky had grown concerned about these pitfalls, which had been "exaggerated" in German and Polish scholarship on Russian art, and in the work of influential Russian historians like Karamzin, who followed their lead.[41] Reporting that Butovsky believed too much importance was being accorded by Viollet to Tatar elements, Rondot explained that "this theory, he says, has been definitively condemned. Finnish and Tatar elements are only found in a few parts of Russia; one doesn't find them at all in the heart of Russia proper. . . ."[42] Butovsky himself communicated the sentiment directly to Viollet in a letter that arrived two days later, in which he refers specifically to the relevance of the "Far East" to the developing picture. Again castigating German scholars for depriving Russia of an independent tradition by over-emphasizing its debt to Finns and Tatars, Butovsky seizes upon the Far Eastern alternative: "When you say that 'the foundations of Russian art are clearly based on the earliest arts of the Far East,' these are words of gold."[43] We may not have proof of that, he adds, but Arabic writings tell us that in the ninth century Russians crossed the Caspian Sea and traded by camel with the Far East: "That is why one can also presume that in her early days Russia must have experienced a great deal of artistic influence from the Far East due to the trade she carried out there."[44] In the letter Butovsky

underscores the importance of selecting just the right mix of "influences," and, in particular, the acceptable Asia:

> One cannot dispute the influence of the Far East: but one must stop short of saying that there could have been influence from the Tatars, the Finns, or any other savage race, for that would be to support mistaken German opinions, dictated more by politics than by a fair and true study of art.[45]

The political dimensions of the project are fully explicit here—this history of art would correct distortions wrought by Germans wishing to primitivize Russia by Orientalizing her. The convolutions of Russian *vostokovedenie* (Orientalism), and its slippage with the European paradigm, are equally apparent: to be called Tatar, at that historical moment, was to be likened to the rapacious "hordes" that squelched the brilliant Kievan civilization that Russia claimed as her patrimony; to be allied with the Far East was to draw upon a little understood but apparently "civilized" Asiatic culture untainted by the familiarity that bred contempt. For while Russia had maintained trade and diplomatic ties with China since before the time of Peter, access to, and therefore knowledge of, her own Far Eastern neighbor remained limited until the construction of the Trans-Siberian railroad in the 1890s. A flurry of interest in China had accompanied Russia's attempt to settle the Amur River in the 1860s, but the difficulties of overland communication between the capital and that remote outpost produced meager results compared to Russia's far more intense involvement with her acquisitions in the Caucasus and Central Asia.[46] In fact, Viollet's and Butovsky's turn to the Far East anticipates by several years an upsurge of interest in China and Japan that would emerge in the 1880s in the writings of the *vostochniki*, an influential group of intellectuals-cum-political advisors. They would take a far dimmer view of their Eastern neighbor than Viollet and Butovsky; alarmed at China's apparent designs in Korea and elsewhere, the most extreme among them would warn of a "yellow peril" lurking over the Sino-Russian border. Significantly, Viol-

Fig. 7.3 "Vue perspective intérieure d'une coupole.—Système d'arcs chevauchés" (Interior perspective view of a dome—system of overlapping arches). Proposal for a nineteenth-century architecture based on the analysis of "national" paradigms, which used distinctive overlapping arches to make the transition from square base to polygonal tower. Viollet-le-Duc, *L'Art russe*, plate 25.

let-le-Duc's suggestion that Russia had Far Eastern roots was made before the rhetoric of the *vostochniki*, with its references to "semibarbarous" peoples, would make such a theory just as politically delicate as the Central Asian hypothesis.[47]

In all, several ancient Asias were deemed acceptable by Butovsky:

> If one writes that Russian art is a Greco-Roman-Asiatic art, in which the *Asiatic* element dominates, one might also be in the right, but it must be made very clear that the word Asiatic applies to the ancient peoples of Asia, such as: Persia, Babylon, ancient Armenia, [illegible], India, etc.; civilized peoples, and not to the Tatars or the Finns, who arrived from Central Asia with

no art and contributed only a few Asiatic forms.[48]

Butovsky's emphasis on antiquity in this passage is also revealing. By embracing "ancient" Asiatic sources he conforms to a pattern David Lowenthal has noted in European contexts. For a fledgling or beleaguered national group looking to legitimize itself with reference to an illustrious past, the more hoary the tradition the better, as it is more likely to be free of compromising association with messy conflicts of the recent, remembered past.[49]

The result of this protracted exchange can be read in the book, where Viollet emphasizes, somewhat unexpectedly, the Indian contribution to Russian art. It was India, on

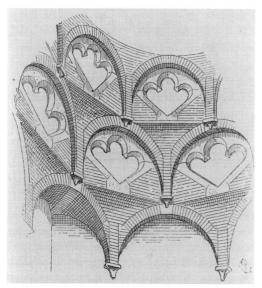

Fig. 7.4 Proposal for an octagonal tower with window lights, based on the overlapping corbelled arch principle. Viollet-le-Duc, *L'Art russe*, p. 166, fig. 65.

Fig. 7.5 Portico of a Russian palace, with "thick bulbous columns, strange in appearance and somewhat reminiscent of Hindu forms." Viollet-le-Duc, *L'Art russe*, p. 183, fig. 72.

Butovsky's approved list, rather than Cernuschi's China and Japan, that seemed to Viollet to offer the most compelling Far Eastern source material. His rendition of a typically Russian palace portico emphasizes vaults supported on "bulbous" brick columns, "strange" to the Western eye, and vaguely "Hindu" in shape (fig. 7.5). Likewise, juxtaposing the bell tower of the seventeenth century Church of St. John Chrysostom in Yaroslavl with a similarly fenestrated contemporary temple at Bhopal (fig. 7.6), he traces both back to ancient "Hindu" types that might have been transmitted to Russia during the period of Mongol occupation. The comparison, incidentally, betrays the tentative state of contemporary knowledge about India's architectural past; Viollet's "Hindu" tower is decidedly Indo-Islamic, or "Indo-Saracenic," to use the British terminology of the time, in character. Typical of the architecture produced under colonial rule in the late nineteenth century (and published in the European architectural press), it conflates Hindu and Islamic elements to yield a hybridized simulacrum of "national" traditions.

At the same time, Viollet-le-Duc attempted to preempt defensive reactions to the Slavic-Asiatic theory by confronting and then dis-

missing Orientalist prejudice: "In telling Russians that they are Asiatic, this epithet has absolutely no significance . . . for what people of Europe is not a composite of various races?"[50] Further on, invoking his theory of the rationality of national expression in architecture, he argues for the moral and aesthetic equivalency of legitimately national traditions:

> It would be as ridiculous to fault the Chinese man, whose architectonic structure is based on the use of rammed earth and bamboo, for not constructing the Parthenon, as it would be unheard of to reproach the Hellenic, who built in stone and marble, for not having erected a pagoda in the manner of the Buddhist structures of Peking.[51]

Judging from Russian reactions to the book, Butovsky was right to signal the delicacy of assigning Russian art an Asiatic pedigree, and Viollet-le-Duc's diplomatic arguments were ineffectual. An 1879 letter from Rondot briefing the French author on the book's reception in Russia alludes to a critical firestorm it ignited around the issue of *Asiatchina*: "No one wants to admit the influence of Asian art, as if Asia represented bar-

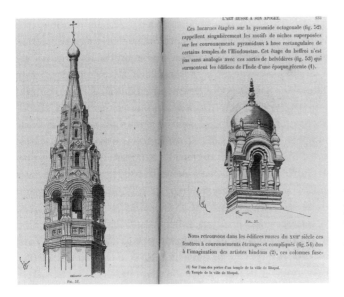

Fig. 7.6 "Campanile, Eglise de Saint-Jean-Chrysostome de Jaroslaw" (bell tower, Church of St. John Chrysostom Yaroslavl) (left); and "Belvedere, temple récent, à Bhopal" (pavilion, contemporary temple in Bhopal) (right). Viollet-le-Duc, *L'Art russe*, pp. 132–33, figs. 52 and 53.

barism!"[52] Butovsky reported the same; critic Fedor Buslaev, a linguist and medieval manuscript specialist, was purportedly beside himself at the suggestion that Russian art was essentially Asiatic in origin and character: "At the mere mention that there might have been some influence from the Far East, he feared that Russia might be pushed back into Asia."[53] The notion of a Central Asian contribution distressed that reviewer no less. On Viollet-le-Duc's suggestion that a fourteenth-century manuscript appeared Romanesque in style only because Romanesque art, too, was derived from Central Asian sources, Butovsky wrote: "he cries, he rants, he's ready to tear his hair out . . . one could die laughing at how he understand this example."[54]

Critics' rejection of the Far Eastern and Central Asian hypotheses alike suggests that the team was unsuccessful in their attempt to invent an acceptable Asiatic past—to construct, through a process of international negotiation and via the printed page, a Russian identity in architectural form. And this despite the fact that in addition to engineering the content of Viollet-le-Duc's book, Butovsky had tried to preordain its favorable reception by clearing its risky propositions ahead of time with the most prominent and vocal scholars—among them Buslaev, quoted above, Ivan Zabelin, the noted archeologist and specialist in early Russian architecture,

and redoubtable critic Vladimir Stasov, ardent promoter of a national style in music and painting.[55] In a final effort at damage control Butovsky penned an elaborate rebuttal to the book's critics, and when a respected journal (*Kriticheskie Obozrenie*) refused to print it, Butovsky resolved to publish the piece himself, as an introduction to the Russian translation of *L'Art russe*.[56] Only the sage intervention of Natalis Rondot, who convinced Butovsky to publish the apologia as a separate volume, spared the book from appearing in Russian with that strident prolegomena.[57] This check to Butovsky's zeal may have assured that Viollet-le-Duc's book, and the other products of the team's collaboration, would attain their catalyzing goal. "You have instigated a movement in Russia that is only beginning," Rondot assured his compatriot, "people are undertaking research, and new studies, and your book is the point of departure for their work."[58]

Ironically, the book's most palpable impact would be felt under the repressive rule of Alexander III, who seized upon the syncretistic Muscovite style it proposed to express the imperial nostalgia of a backward-looking and anti-democratic regime. Viollet-le-Duc died in 1879, the year that Butovsky's museum published *Russkoe iskusstvo*, the Russian translation of his book.[59] Had he lived to see the Viollet-le-Dolcian curiosities that sprang up in the early 1880s under Alexander's patronage, as documented by Richard Wortman in this volume, he would surely have been dismayed at the perversion of his own democratic principles; perhaps his most singular contribution to the historiography of Gothic architecture in France had been the notion that the Gothic cathedral was not the expression of a royal or ecclesiastical elite, but of the popular talent and taste of the medieval commune. He would no doubt have disapproved as well of the very literal way in which the ornamental details of Muscovite architecture were grafted onto modern structure in the new buildings; in *L'Art russe*, and throughout his career, Viollet had argued for emulation, rather than strict imitation, as the key to a productive relationship with the past.

These misappropriations of architectural message, this slippage between theory and practice, tell a cautionary tale about the calculated marriage of architectural form to political agenda. While clearly capable of proclaiming desired messages in enduring, conspicuous, and monumental form, architecture is also a volatile and infinitely manipulable expressive vehicle, whose meanings are exceedingly difficult to control across time and space. The same is true for architecture's texts: in the case of *L'Art russe*, the ambiguities of Russia's Eurasian status may have guaranteed that those offended by the Oriental suggestion would be counterbalanced by those who saw Asianness as the key to Russia's independence from the West. The author's brief, intercrossed with the conflicting agendas of his sponsors and readers, produced meanings that none could fix or predict.

8 The "Russian Style" in Church Architecture as Imperial Symbol after 1881

Richard Wortman

Several chapters in this book (those by Michael Flier, Dan Rowland, Dimitry Shvidkovsky, and James Cracraft) have made clear the declaratory role of architecture in the representation of Russian monarchy. The style and magnificence of thrones, buildings, and parks were meant not only to awe the population and foreign dignitaries but to give each reign its own characteristic aspect, to set each ruler apart as a distinctive ruling presence embodying specific transcendent attributes of power. Ivan the Terrible, Boris Godunov, Peter the Great, and Catherine the Great sought to create their own landscapes, which provided settings for the presentation of their political personae, what I have called their scenarios of power. From 1881, church architecture in "the Russian style" became an important means to display a new national identity of Russian monarchy that set it apart from the goals and methods of the previous reign.

A national style in church architecture first appeared during the reign of Nicholas I (1825–55) as an expression of Nicholas's doctrine of "official nationality." "Official nationality" located national distinctiveness in the Russian people's devotion to their rulers, to the Westernized absolutism that ruled since Peter the Great. Nicholas sought an architecture that would set Russia apart from the contemporary West, which he believed had fallen prey to constitutionalism and revolution. He wished to show the Russian people's piety and loyalty, but without denying the universalistic, Western character of Russian absolutism. He found the answer in a Byzantine cultural tradition that glorified Russia as the highest realization of the principle of absolute monarchy. Architectural design, the Russian art historian E. A. Borisova has pointed out, now became a narrative medium, displaying motifs that recalled particular themes of Russia's historical development.

The architect who divined the emperor's intentions and found the appropriate architectural idiom was Constantine Thon. Thon's project for the St. Catherine's Church in Petersburg in (1830) presented a five-cupola design whose exterior recalled the Moscow-Byzantine style of the Dormition Cathedrals of Vladimir (1158–61) and Moscow (1475–79). Thon's design, grafting the five-cupola form onto a nineteenth-century neoclassical structure, typified the eclectic spirit of Nicholas's official-nationality doctrine, which, while claiming national distinctiveness, sought to defend the Petrine cultural and institutional heritage.[1] Its most prominent example was the immense Cathedral of Christ the Redeemer in Moscow (1837–82), which has recently been reconstructed in Moscow (fig. 8.1).[2] While the proportions, the arcades, and the structure of the cupolas of the cathedral were typically neoclassical, the exterior decorative elements asserted the building's Russian character. The five-cupola silhouette, like the tracery and icons on the facade, identified a Russian church.[3] The Redeemer Cathedral set the pattern for similar churches that would pro-

This article is partially drawn from sections and materials in my book *Scenarios of Power: Myth and Ceremony in Russian Monarchy*, vol. 2, *From Alexander II to the Abdication of Nicholas I* (Princeton, 2000).

Fig. 8.1 The Cathedral of Christ the Redeemer. Constantine Thon, architect. Drawing from *Vsemirnaia Illiustratsiia*, 1879.

vide specific visual references both to the national past of autocracy and to the universalistic context of empire derived from Byzantium. Published explanations of the buildings spelled out these references, disclosing the meaning of Russia's architectural heritage to all. Nicholas made "the Thon style" official. A decree of March 25, 1841, ordained that "the taste of ancient Byzantine architecture should be preserved, by preference and as far as is possible" in the construction of Orthodox churches. "The drawings of Professor Constantine Thon composed for the construction of Orthodox churches may prove useful in this regard."[4]

The national myth introduced by Alexander III in 1881 revealed images of the nature and past of Russian autocracy that were quite different from those of official nationality.[5] The national myth evoked a religious and ethnic bond between the tsar and the Russian people, who had presumably survived the processes of Westernization and

provided the foundations of Russian monarchy and state. The Russian tsar strove to embody not the existing state, contaminated by Westernized accretions, the reformed courts, and zemstva, but the ancient traditions persisting after the Petrine reforms in the people and the Orthodox Church. The Orthodox Church preserved the faith of the Russian people that permitted a union of tsar and people. The buildings erected in this period were meant to be concrete expressions of this union, which evoked, not Byzantine architecture, but an idealized seventeenth century that would replace the reign of Peter the Great as the mythical founding period of the Russian state. Churches would be monuments to the historical past, which showed the persistence of the culture of seventeenth-century Rus'. Church construction intensified, and architects were expected to build churches like those of early Russia: they were to recreate Muscovite scenes in Russia, and particularly in Petersburg, to resurrect the national past by designing artifacts attesting to its persistence.[6]

The church architecture of Alexander III's reign sought to capture a culture rooted in the people which reflected a national spirit, rather than to display the Byzantine roots of Russian culture. For this purpose, it drew on the architectural theories of the 1860s and 1870s, which advocated a democratic national style in opposition to both neoclassicism and the Thon churches. Champions of a popular national Russian architecture such as Lev Dahl, Victor Butovsky, Ivan Zabelin, and Vladimir Shervud sought an architecture that would organically unite form and function in ways that reflected indigenous traditions and climatic conditions. Like A. W. N. Pugin in England and Viollet-le-Duc in France, they used the "realist" principle in architecture to interpret popular forms as structures that answered the practical needs of the people. The peasant hut, pre-Petrine wooden churches, and churches that reflected popular tendencies of innovation and ornamentation provided possible sources for a Russian national style.[7] In the 1870s and the 1880s, the national style gained popularity, particularly among Russian merchants, who favored old Russian motifs in the design of their churches.[8]

Butovsky and others sharing his views succeeded in convincing Viollet-le-Duc to write a study of Russian art. Viollet's book, *L'Art russe*, expressed many of the principles of the national school in terms of his own general theories of architectural development. The author, who had never visited Russia, marveled over the corbelled vaults and tent roofs of sixteenth- and seventeenth-century Russian churches, which he thought were structurally well adapted to lavish ornamentation reflecting popular tastes. As Lauren O'Connell has shown, Viollet's notion of Asiatic influence and his sometimes fanciful explanations of the structure of old Russian buildings prompted angry recriminations from many Russian art critics. But the book gave the confirmation of a renowned authority to the belief that the sixteenth and seventeenth centuries were the true period of national creativity in Russian architecture.[9] Russians, Viollet asserted, had to restore the link with this time broken by Peter the Great and "to repossess the national art dominated for so long by Western arts!" The "reinstallation of Russian art in Russia . . . would be met with favor by the immense majority of the nation and would become the corollary of the emancipation of the serfs."[10] The monarchy appropriated this cultural idiom and invested it with specific political meaning. It utilized revival architecture, as it had been conceived in nineteenth-century Europe, as a means to shape attitudes. Visual imagery could restore a lost purity, change attitudes and reshape society.[11] After 1881, this type of thinking encouraged a kind of inverted archaeology: monuments were constructed to resurrect an invisible national past, particularly in regions deemed to need admonition and edification.

The building announcing the new official national style was the Resurrection Cathedral erected on the site of Alexander II's assassination—in popular parlance, "the Savior on the Blood."[12] The initiative for the church belonged to the St. Petersburg City Duma, which opened a public subscription for the structure. But the decision on the plans was quickly taken over by the tsar, and most of the cost was assumed by the treasury. Again the architect was chosen for his ability to conform with the image in the mind of the emperor, an image that Alexander III, like Nicholas I, did not make clear.

The first competition, completed in April of 1882, yielded projects in the Thon style decreed by Nicholas I in his Construction Statute, which continued to regulate the building of Orthodox churches. But the emperor found none to his taste. A report in *Moskovskie Vedomosti* on April 9, 1882, stated that Alexander III believed that the best eight projects in the competition did not suit the taste of "Russian church architecture." He indicated to various individuals that he wanted the church to be in "Russian style," and "in the style of the time of the Muscovite tsars of the seventeenth century."[13] The journal *Nedelia stroitelia* reported that he announced that he wished a "purely Russian style of the seventeenth century." A comment added that models of these were to be found "in Iaroslavl'."[14]

Architects groped for designs in the new style. The submissions for the second competition, completed only five weeks after the first, incorporated a great variety of pre-Petrine church motifs, none of which seem to have pleased Alexander. He preferred a submission not from a distinguished architect, but from a person close to the court. The hegumen of the Trinity-Sergius Hermitage near Peterhof, Arkhimandrite Ignatii Makarov, contributed a project at the request of the tsar's cousin, Grand Duchess Ekaterina Mikhailovna. Makarov had drawn the sketch of a church, he claimed, "almost automatically," on the day of Annunciation. After considerable reworking by the architect, Alfred Parland, the project, submitted after the deadline of the competition, received the emperor's approval. The final form of the cathedral, Michael Flier has shown, was a composite of the plans of the many architects who were struggling to find a seventeenth-century national style that suited the emperor's taste.[15]

At first sight, Parland's cathedral recalls the kaleidoscopic forms of Vasilii the Blessed, on Moscow's Red Square. Parland himself noted the resemblance (fig. 8.2). The flamboyant decorations, the tent roof, the onion cupolas became signatures distinguishing the building from the Thon model. But as B. M. Kirikov has convincingly argued, the resemblance is deceptive. The new church's five-cupola cruciform structure, with a large central basilica-like hall, has little in common with the intricate warren of Vasilii the Blessed. The external devices—the tracery, kokoshniki, and shirinki—borrow from a great number of seventeenth-century churches in the Moscow-Iaroslavl style.[16] Although the cathedral was not consecrated until 1907, its amalgam of the five-cupola form with pre-Petrine ornamentation became the dominant model for church design in the official Russian style from 1881 to 1905. The new national churches provided a backdrop for the "union of tsar and people" extolled in official state-

Fig. 8.2 Cathedral of the Resurrection (Christ on the Blood), St. Petersburg. Alfred Parland, architect. From A. A. Parland, *Khram Voskresenie Khristova* (St. Petersburg, 1909) Slavic and Baltic Division, New York Public Library. Astor, Lenox, and Tilden Foundations.

ments after March 1. The monarchy, claiming popular national roots, now took up the same undisciplined and flamboyant decorative forms that had been condemned by Nikon and other members of the seventeenth-century church hierarchy.

The "Savior on the Blood" was one of five Resurrection churches erected after 1881 in St. Petersburg, and Flier has given a close analysis of its iconology of Resurrection. The theme of Resurrection is elaborated on the exterior mosaics, which represent Christ's carrying the cross, the Crucifixion, the Deposition, the Descent into Hell, and, on the southern pediment, the Resurrection itself. "Resurrection" referred not only to the Savior; it signified the rebirth of a political and religious heritage long moribund and the repudiation of the symbolic traditions of the previous reigns. The central theme of the church's interior, Michael Flier has shown, displaced the mythological point of origin from Rome to Jerusalem. The model for the layout of the cathedral was the Church of the Holy Sepulcher in Jerusalem, also named for the Resurrection.[17] The interior presents Russia's beginnings not in the Roman Empire—as in the legends of Andrew the First-Called—or at Byzantium, as claimed in the legend of Monomakh. Rather, the origins are set at Golgotha itself, now transposed to Russia, with national and messianic implications. The symbolism has a negative thrust—one of rejecting, of clearing away the previous historical narrative, of removing Rome and even Byzantium as forerunners of Russia. The cathedral expresses the determination to do away with foreign mediation of the divine, to overcome the derivative character of Russian religious doctrine and to identify Russia with the source of Christianity itself. The true Russian spirituality could be manifested only after Russia had thrown off some of its Byzantine trappings but before it had fallen under the domination of Western culture in the eighteenth century—as the national school, echoed by Viollet, had suggested.

The references to Jerusalem, like the popular Resurrection motifs on the exterior, were signs of a new state mythology that conveyed a powerful admonition regarding the evils supposedly besetting Russia. The building of the cathedral was to be seen as an act of expiation to atone for the assassination of Alexander II, the shame of which branded the entire people.[18] Thus Parland placed "the prayer of Vasilii the Blessed" beneath the central cupola. The prayer begged God to forgive the people for their sins. The many icons of Saints Boris and Gleb, the Kievan princes who had died passively to expiate the sins of the Russian land, recalled others whose deaths had expiated Russian sins.[19] But the sins comprised more than the mere act of as-

sassination; they included the weakness, the tolerance, and the laxity presumably responsible for the murder. The cathedral was an act of repentance for Western culture, and the mosaic icons on the exterior were meant to remind Petersburg of its shame. The final lines of Fet's "March 1, 1881," pronounced the transformation of the blood into a shrine.[20]

Nicholas I's 1841 decree encouraging Byzantine-style churches remained on the books, and such churches continued to be built, mainly in non-Russian regions.[21] But most official churches erected after 1881 incorporated the national motifs of the Savior on the Blood, seeking to evoke the spirit of the seventeenth century.[22] The abundance of bulbous onion domes and floral kokoshniki, girki, and shirinki particularly distinguished new churches based on the Moscow-Iaroslavl' style. These included the Petersburg church named after its miracle icon, *The Mother-of-God the Joy of All the Grieving* (*Radosti vsekh skorbiashchikh materi*), designed by Alexander Gogen and A. V. Ivanov and erected in 1894–98, and M. Preobrazhenskii's Alexander Nevskii Cathedral in Reval (fig. 8.3).[23] Viollet had emphasized that the type of corbelled vaulting of seventeenth-century Russian churches lent them to elaborate decoration of the kokoshnik type; he especially admired the famous Moscow church at Putynki with its profusion of tent and kokoshnik forms.[24]

The architect Nicholas Sultanov, the translator of *L'Art russe* and an exponent of the new official style, declared Moscow-Iaroslavl' churches to be exemplary of seventeenth-century church architecture as a whole. He singled out the Church of the Icon of the Georgian Mother of God in Moscow and the Church of the Trinity in nearby Ostankino as the highest achievements of the type and based his submission for the second competition for the Resurrection Church on them. Sultanov also did considerable archaeological work on the Trinity Church and assisted in its restoration.[25] His Peter-Paul Cathedral at Peterhof, completed in the late 1890s, brought the images of the Resurrection Cathedral to

ПРАВОСЛАВНЫЙ СОБОРЪ
ВЪ Г РЕВЕЛЬ

ЗАПАДНЫЙ ФАСАДЪ.

CATHEDRALE ORTHODOXE
A RÉVAL

FAÇADE OCCIDENTALE.

Proj. et exec. par M Préobragensky.

Fig. 8.3 Alexander Nevskii Cathedral, Revel (Tallin). M. Preobrazhenskii, architect. M. Preobrazhenskii, *Revel'skii Pravoslavnyi Aleksandro-Nevskii Sobor* (St. Petersburg, 1902). Slavic and Baltic Division, New York Public Library. Astor, Lenox, and Tilden Foundations.

the playground of the court. Set on a pond, it reproduced the tent forms and kokoshniki of the seventeenth century in brick, which Sultanov considered the building material most suitable for Russian churches. It provided a stark contrast to the Rococo elegance of the palaces of Peterhof.

The new churches were acts of visual provocation—flagrant repudiations of the esthetic premises of Russian autocracy before 1881, and by implication, of its political and spiritual premises as well. The organic motifs of these churches, springing mushroomlike from their surface, defy the order and restraint of neoclassicism and even the eclecticism that had succeeded it, the entwining designs verging on the lushness of art nouveau.[26] The profusion of decoration exemplifies what Randolph Starn and Loren Partridge have identified as the use of redundancy to enhance the totality and expressiveness of monumental architecture: excess as a prerogative of absolute power.[27] The excess was made conspicuous at prominent places so as to admonish the population. Expressing the autocrat's growing dissatisfaction with the western imperial capital, these churches administered an open rebuke to the city itself, constituting an effort to Muscovitize St. Petersburg.[28]

The Resurrection Cathedral built on the site of Alexander II's assassination on Catherine Canal is easily visible from Nevskii Prospect. There is nothing understated in its appearance; it is a declaration of contempt for the order and symmetry of the capital, producing what Louis Réau, the noted French student of Russian art history, described as "a troubling dissonance." A prominent building in Moscow style set in the middle of classical Petersburg was meant to express this rejection. It was, Flier writes, "old Muscovy plunged into the heart of European Petersburg."[29] More than twenty official Russian-style churches went up in St. Petersburg from 1881–1914. (At least eighteen of these were demolished or transformed beyond recognition after the revolution.) Constantine Pobedonostev reported that eight such churches were consecrated in the years 1893–95 alone.[30] The Assumption Cathedral of the St. Petersburg branch of the Kiev Monastery of the Caves (1895–1900) looks out over the Neva from the Nikolaevskii embankment, a five-cupola church with elaborate seventeenth-century decoration. The Resurrection Cathedral on the Obvodnyi Canal (1904–8) within view of the Warsaw Railroad Station combines a Byzantine central basilica with kokoshniki and a tent belfry.[31]

By bringing forth a forgotten national past, the new Russian style churches of the late Imperial period sought to exert an edifying influence on the masses. Since the 1870s, the Orthodox Church had been engaged in a campaign to broaden its moral influence by adopting Protestant and Catholic practices of addressing the people through sermons, lectures, and literature.[32] Churches were built to accommodate large numbers of worshipers

and to provide amenities needed to attract a contemporary population. The celebratory literature about the churches dwelled on their size, convenience, and comfort. The Savior on the Blood held 1,600 people. Parland boasted that he used modern technology to light and heat his cathedral. Large stained glass windows, white at the bottom and rising to light blue at the top, allowed natural light to bring out the colors of the mosaics. His design thus was remote from the appearance of early Russian Orthodox churches, whose thick walls with few and small windows kept out the light and turned the interior into a sanctum separate from the outside world. In the evening, the great expanse of Parland's church was lit by 1,589 electric lights, creating a magical effect. He wrote, "Whatever the weather, whatever the color of the sky, cloudy or threatening, it seems blue in the cathedral, clear, bright, harmonizing with the mood of prayer." The light from the chandeliers flooded the walls "as if bringing to life the severe physiognomies of the saints, as if filling the air of the cathedral to its top." The cathedral was also equipped with steam heat.[33] The attempt to return to the spirit of early Russia had resulted in splendor and show: in Réau's words, it "surpasses all the churches of Petersburg in its sumptuousness." The Resurrection Church on Obvodnyi Canal could hold 4,000 worshippers under its large central dome of reinforced concrete.[34]

Combining function and amenities with beauty was presented as a confirmation of the principle of "realism" in Russian national architecture. Nicholas Sultanov lauded the comfort and convenience of his Peter-Paul Cathedral in Peterhof, which had room for 800 worshipers. He observed that many members of the propertied classes avoided parish churches and prayed at home because they had to wear coats indoors, or because the churches became crowded and overheated. His church, on the contrary, was spacious, and provided good ventilation, cloakrooms, and seats for the old and infirm. A gallery outside was to protect processions of the cross from inclement weather. The official Slavic-revival churches were monumental

Fig. 8.4 Church and Bell Tower at Borki (*Niva*, 1894).

buildings full of light and comfort that had little in common with the smaller, darker, and colder churches of early Russia.[35]

Like the Savior on the Blood, other churches were placed at sites for demonstrations of spiritual purification and contrition.[36] A fanciful single-domed Church of the Savior, covered with kokoshniki and other decorations and accompanied by a tent-shaped bell tower, went up at Borki near Kharkov, the site of the wreck of the emperor's train in 1888, as a sign of miraculous salvation (fig. 8.4).[37] Churches built near factories promoted efforts by the government and church to awaken the religious faith of industrial workers. At the beginning of the 1890s, Leontii Benois designed a church for 2,000 people near the textile factory of the Hofmeister, N. K. Nechaev-Maltsov, in the town of Gusev, near Vladimir (fig. 8.5). This massive edifice was surmounted by a great tent roof and bell tower at one end, and by cupolas and kokoshniki in the Iaroslavl' style at the other. The image of St. George, the pa-

tron saint of Moscow, placed over the portal was probably the work of Victor Vasnetsov, who executed the paintings on the interior walls. From 1901 to 1907, a two-story church erected at the Putilov Factory in St. Petersburg was funded by workers' "contributions" as a memorial to the plant's founder, N. I. Putilov. A drawing of this church, which has since been destroyed, recalls the tent and cupola forms of Vasilii the Blessed. Fedor Shekhtel's large Church of the Savior in the textile center at Ivanovo-Voznesensk, completed in 1898, was built in neo-Byzantine style.[38]

Officials and noblemen close to the court built Russian-style churches on their estates. In the 1880s, Sultanov designed a Moscow-Iaroslavl' church with a brick exterior for I. I. Vorontsov-Dashkov's estate at Novotomnikov in Tambov guberniia. Vorontsov-Dashkov helped shape the national myth and governmental policy at the beginning of Alexander's reign and served as the head of his palace guard and Minister of the Court.[39] Leonid

Fig. 8.5 Church for 2,000 people at Gusev. Leontii Benois, architect. (*Zodchii*, 1893)

Benois's church on the estate of A.D. Sheremet'ev, the prominent choral director and composer, in Smolensk guberniia, was also in Moscow-Iaroslavl' style with a tent bell tower. A flamboyant Moscow-Iaroslavl' church with four altars was built from 1886 to 1892 on Sheremet'ev's tract near Peterhof.[40]

The specific means by which the new style was suggested or imposed by the Imperial government are difficult to determine from the available sources. But it seems evident that the procedures for state approval of official projects ultimately required the consent of those close to the emperor, or of the emperor himself, creating a disposition to conform with their tastes. The construction of Orthodox churches, for instance, required the permission of either the Holy Synod or the local diocese. In St. Petersburg, initiatives from monasteries, religious societies, or even institutions of the government were submitted to the Synod, which was of course dominated by its chief-procurator, Constantine Pobedonostev. Many churches were dedicated to events in the lives of members of the Imperial family, an act that required the emperor's approval and won his favor. The church built to house the icon *The Mother-of-God the Joy of All the Grieving* at the Imperial St. Petersburg Glass Factory commemorated the tenth anniversary of the emperor's survival of the Borki disaster. The proposal came to the Synod from the Minister of the Interior. The 1904 church built on the Obvodnyi Canal was sponsored by the St. Petersburg Temperance Brotherhood to commemorate the birth of an heir to Nicholas II. The Brotherhood's proposal, submitted by the St. Petersburg Metropolitan, received the approval of the Synod and the emperor.[41]

Churches built in the national style symbolized Russian domination of regions that retained elements of religious and political autonomy.[42] In the Baltic provinces and Poland, new churches and cathedrals ensured that the inhabitants would not forget who ruled their land. Cathedrals in Riga and Warsaw carried the name of Alexander Nevskii, Alexander III's namesake, and the traditional defender of Russia against Western Christendom. Publications celebrated their construction, providing explicit statements of domination. A large Orthodox cathedral in Russian-Byzantine style had been built in the center of Riga from 1876–84. In 1888, the Imperial government commemorated the Borki disaster in Riga with an elaborate Russian-style votive chapel of marble shaped in tent form, its surface covered with innumerable icons and mosaics, placed on the square before the city's railway station.[43]

Church construction in Estland guberniia was actively promoted by its governor, S. V. Shakhovskoi, an ally of Pobedonostev and ac-

tive supporter of Russification. Shakhovskoi won central government support for the spread of Russian Orthodox religion and education among the population.[44] His pride was the massive Alexander Nevskii Cathedral (1894–1900) designed in Moscow-Iaroslavl' style, which its architect M. Preobrazhenskii described as "the most characteristic of Russian church architecture" (fig. 8.3). It was placed, Preobrazhenskii wrote in the dedicatory volume, at the "best site," which allowed the cathedral on its commanding heights "to dominate the city." This was Reval's most prominent square, the Domberg, called by Toivo Raun "the traditional bastion of the Baltic German elite."[45]

The acquisition of the property adjacent to the cathedral involved the confiscation of private lands and required considerable pressure from Petersburg authorities and from the emperor himself. A recommendation by a committee chaired by the deputy Minister of the Interior, Viacheslav Plehve, prompted a lengthy interministerial correspondence. The Minister of Justice, Nicholas Manasein, considered the legal grounds for seizure weak, but he concluded that the alternative—building the church at another, lower site, where it would stand beneath Lutheran churches—was inadmissable. Laws, however troublesome, could not deter the symbolic solution: "an Orthodox cathedral, rising above numerous Lutheran churches, will occupy a beautiful, dominating location that is suitable for an Orthodox shrine in a Russian state."[46]

Parish churches constructed between 1887 and 1889 in Estland displayed the motifs of Muscovite architecture. They fit a standard plan: a tent-form belfry beneath an onion cupola was attached by a passageway to the main cubiform church corpus, itself surmounted by a central onion cupola and with four small cupolas at the corners. Kokoshniki decorated the bases of the central cupola, and, in several churches, the tent roofs themselves (fig. 8.6). A luxury album containing photographs of seven of the churches celebrated the achievement. The album was issued by the commission supervising the construction, which was chaired by a member of

Fig. 8.6 Parish church, Estland. *Al'bom vidov tserkvei.* Slavic and Baltic Division, New York Public Library. Astor, Lenox, and Tilden Foundations.

the Provincial Bureau (Gubernskoe pravlenie), A. A. Shirinskii-Shikhmatov, and consisted of Russian officials and priests.[47]

The use of ecclesiastical architecture as a statement of symbolic conquest was most apparent in Warsaw, where almost twenty Russian-style Orthodox churches were built in the 1890s. In Warsaw, as in Riga, the Moscow-Byzantine style remained prevalent, signifying imperial domination. But the principal cathedral, Leontii Benois's immense Alexander Nevskii Cathedral (1894–1912), combined the classical Moscow-Byzantine form with abundant kokoshniki covering the roof, affirming the national character of imperial rule. Its seventy-meter bell tower made known the Russian presence by dwarfing surrounding buildings. It became "the most conspicuous accent of the city skyline," prompting lewd comparisons from the city's residents.[48] Initiative belonged to the Governor-General, I. V. Gurko, who solicited contributions from Russian donors. The chancellery of the Governor-General appealed to residents of Moscow: "By its very presence . . . the Russian Church declares to the world . . . that in the western terrains along the Vistula, mighty Orthodox rule has taken root . . . The appearance of a new . . . church in Warsaw as a boundary and pillar of Orthodox Russia will animate the hopes of the Orthodox Slavs for unification under the Orthodox cross." The journal of the Warsaw Eparchy boasted in 1912, "Under the dome of this magic temple, we find ourselves as if on Russian soil."[49]

Imposing Orthodox churches also announced imperial rule over Central Asia. The Cathedral of the Transfiguration, a large neo-Byzantine church completed in 1888, towered over the governor's house on the principal square of Tashkent. It was the most prominent building in the center of the new Russian city, which Robert Crews has analyzed as an expression of the imperialist and colonial mentality of late nineteenth-century Russian expansion. The Teachers' Seminary, on the other hand, was designed in the 1880s in Muscovite style. In 1898 a tall five-cupola tent-style brick church designed by A. L. Benois was built into the walls of the seminary compound, signifying the particular national and ethnic character of the Russian presence in Tashkent.[50] A similar tent-style church went up in Baku in the 1880s.[51] Russian missionaries and officials in the Caucasus pointed out the symbolic role of Orthodox churches in the religious guidance of mountain peoples. The Viceroy of the Caucasus, Prince Alexander Dondukov-Korsakov, wrote that the "external" aspects of the faith were most important for "Eastern peoples."[52]

Russian-style churches carried the image of Orthodox autocracy abroad.[53] Construction of a Russian cathedral, designed by Alexander Gogen, in Port Arthur was begun in 1902. Its character, announcing Russian ambitions in the Far East was to be "purely Muscovite, without admixture of Byzantine or other style." The architect gave the cathedral the form of a ship, appropriate for a naval base, with seven gilded cupolas and a high tent-shape bell tower. He placed it high above the city so that the cupolas would impress those viewing from the sea (fig. 8.7).[54] Similar churches were built in Carlsbad, Vienna, and Copenhagen.[55] The spiritual significance of the new national myth was announced by the Church of Maria Magdalena, which Alexander III commissioned in 1883, set prominently on the Mount of Olives at the Orthodox Gethsemane. The kokoshnik decoration and tent-shaped bell tower are visible from afar, identifying old Russian imagery and Orthodoxy for all to see across Jerusalem.

The new official style of church architecture repeated the pattern of earlier reigns, using buildings as imposing declarations of visions of change contemplated by the emperor and his entourage. The symbolic break with the past, however, was now sharper and more thoroughgoing, repudiating the Western cultural tradition that had elevated monarchs since Peter the Great and giving the autocracy a specific ethnic identity. It was an architecture alien to compromise, stating the absolute truth of the new myth. The flamboyance of the buildings, their redundancy of forms, their siting, and the proud and self-congratulatory texts that accompanied many of them indicated that the style was a celebration of power, showing the efficacy of the state in shaping the spiritual and cultural life of the nation. The writings that surrounded the design and construction of the churches set them in an ongoing narrative of power. They demonstrated the reality of the myth, the government's capacity to embody the spirit of the nation as enshrined in a particular architectural design.

The buildings themselves announced the resurrection of purportedly forgotten traditions. Manasein's description of the Reval Alexander Nevskii Cathedral as "an Orthodox shrine in a Russian state" characterizes the thinking of the officials sponsoring the new national-style churches. Architecture could resurrect the past and shape attitudes. A shrine, sviatynia, a sacred object, designated not a revelatory religious event or person, but an immanent national identity, made into a dominating visual presence. The sym-

Fig. 8.7 Orthodox church at Port Arthur. Alexander Gogen, architect. (*Stroitel'*, 1902).

bols of Muscovy would command the belief in state and Orthodoxy that officials believed would make Estland part of a Russian state.

The appeal to nationality in architecture represented a reaffirmation of the preeminence of state and empire. To be sure, the new official style responded to the search for native artistic expression of the democratically inspired revival architecture of the 1860s and 1870s. But this style was an official construction, a created architecture—the attempt of an imperial regime to find a grounding in the ruled population by claiming their history. In this respect, it resembles the British colonial administration's creation of a national revival style in India, the Indo-Saracenic style. Like the Russian official national style, introduced after the terrorists' assassination of a tsar, the "Indo-Saracenic" style was invented after a traumatic revolutionary event—the Sepoy mutiny of 1857–which had thrown the premises of imperial rule into doubt.[56] In both cases, the ruling elites claimed the spirit of the nation by using architecture to assert mastery of its past.

The Russian emperor was asserting a claim to an ethnic Russian past, one that previous monarchs had avoided. He was evoking a solidarity between rulers and ruled in the Russian provinces and claiming a national mission in non-Russian territories. In this respect, the new official style enjoyed somewhat greater popular appeal than did the Indo-Saracenic in India—which was ignored by the native population. "Society," and particularly conservative officials, noblemen, and merchants, liked the elaborate decorations on old Russian churches. But with the revolution of 1905, critical voices, especially among the architects themselves, pointed out the flaws and anomalies in the style. Writing in 1905, V. Kurbatov lamented the transformation of churches into "a kind of architectural museum." "In the construction of nearly all contemporary churches, the Russian style has become the unavoidable requirement. One cannot say, though, that this requirement has been successfully fulfilled anywhere." It was based on the erroneous notion that before Peter a single style had prevailed, "all the forms of which could be realized within a single building."[57]

Andrei Aplaksin, an architect attached to the St. Petersburg eparchy, deplored the triteness of national church architecture in a speech delivered to the Fourth Congress of Russian Architects in January 1911. The imperative to follow the prescribed style, Aplaksin declared, cost the architect his professional integrity. "The role of the architect, being reduced to a minimum, amounts to composing a rough draft in the process of planning." He blamed this situation on government restrictions and public taste, but above all on the architects themselves, whom he called upon to go beyond the "crude tastes of the crowd" to study the architecture of the past and struggle against the ignorance of the clergy. Aplaksin observed that some architects had already begun to work creatively with historical forms and to allow more play to their imagination. This "neo-Russian" style, which Aplaksin himself practiced, resulted in innovation and imaginative and tasteful use of the national forms, some of them in churches beyond the jurisdiction of official Orthodoxy.[58]

Many of these churches continued to promote the national mission of Russia in the borderlands. Aleksei Shchusev's striking Trinity Cathedral at the Pochaev Monastery in

Kremenets in the Ukraine followed the prototype of the twelfth century Iu'rev monastery, with its spare white walls, prominent lesenes that articulate the internal structure of the church, and a central dome with a helmet cupola. The Pochaev Monastery was an outpost of Orthodoxy and empire in Volynia province, about five miles from the Austrian border. It was known both for the Pochaev Miracle Icon, which attracted many pilgrims, and the anti-Duma, anti-Semitic weekly *Pochaevskii listok*, edited there by the monk Iliodor. The Trinity Cathedral was an aesthetic national riposte to the eighteenth-century baroque Dormition Cathedral in the monastery.[59]

The seventeenth century remained a model for churches associated with autocracy, especially in and around St. Petersburg. Stepan Krichinskii's Tercentenary Church was built to mark the 1913 celebration of the three-hundredth anniversary of the beginning of the Romanov dynasty (fig. 8.8). The initiative had been taken by the Feodorovskii Gorodetskii Monastery in Nizhegorodskii guberniia. The monastery's hegumen, the Arkhimandrite Aleksii, had worked actively to turn the monastery's small chapel in the Nikolaevskii (Moscow) railroad station into a church. He succeeded in gaining the patronage of Grand Duke Michael Aleksandrovich and secured funds from a national subscription, the St. Petersburg City Duma, church and governmental institutions, and from the emperor himself.[60]

The Tercentenary Church was an exact copy of Rostov wall churches of the seventeenth century, which, Krichinskii asserted, exemplified the true Russian style. But it was considerably more elaborate—built in reinforced concrete—larger, nearly as high as Kazan Cathedral, and accommodated over 4,000 worshipers. It cost, when completed in 1914, one million rubles, several times the original estimate. The north wall had a large majolica icon of the Fedorov Mother of God, based on Iaroslavl' frescoes, and a genealogical tree of the Romanov house. The church bells were cast with reliefs of members of the ruling family and their patron saints. A krem-

Fig. 8.8 Tercentenary church. Stepan Krichinskii, architect. Gosudarstvennyi Arkhiv Rossiiskoi Federatsii, fond 601.

lin was to be built around the church. "The idea was to create an entire corner of the seventeenth century," Krichinskii wrote. It would transplant a bit of Muscovy to St. Petersburg where many, like the art critic George Lukomskii, believed it did not belong.[61]

Krichinskii's design answered the needs of an era when religion retreated from public view to sequestered spaces in the walls of monasteries, to provide a model of the spiritual life. The purpose of the new buildings was exemplary rather than admonitory, showing the persistence and revival of old-Russian piety among those foreswearing the contestation and distraction of contemporary society. Among these were the emperor and empress, who created their own replica of seventeenth-century spirituality at the Feodorov village at Tsarskoe Selo, which was built for the tsar's Convoy and His Majesty's Rifles. The village was to provide a spiritual model shaped by the tsar of a reborn autocratic nation. Krichinskii designed a kremlin wall of elaborately decorated white Staritskii limestone to surround the village.[62] The centerpiece was the Feodorov Cathedral (1908–12), dedicated to the protectress of the dynasty, the Feodorov Mother-of-God. The architect Vladimir Pokrovskii took the model of the fifteenth-century Annunciation Cathedral in the

Moscow Kremlin, which had served as the private chapel for the tsar's family before Peter the Great, but he added seventeenth-century elements—tent-shaped roofs over the main entrance and covered vestibules. He also drew on Novgorod motifs for the bell tower.[63]

The cathedral was intended as a museum of early-Russian religious art that would attest to the rebirth of a national religious aesthetic, and held numerous icons and other religious treasures.[64] For Alexandra, Pokrovskii's assistant, Vladimir Maksimov, constructed a "cave church" in honor of Serafim Sarov below the cathedral, where the imperial family could worship before communion.[65] The walls were painted with motifs from the terems, the chambers where women had been kept sequestered in old Russia. The vestibules were decorated with scenes of Hell and Paradise and above, the fortress of heaven. The chapel held a pitcher of water from the stream at Sarov, in which the imperial family had bathed, an icon of Serafim, a box with a relic, and a copy of the "Tenderness" icon, which Serafim had kept in his cell, and his pectoral cross.[66] The cathedral thus incorporated the symbols of popular charismatic religion into the artistic motifs of early Russia.

The town was to represent a spiritual model of a reborn nation taken from Russia's distant past. The officers and soldiers of the convoy and sharpshooter regiment worshiped in the church and lived in the old-Russian-style barracks. Dressed in costumes designed by Victor Vasnetsov resembling early Russian prototypes they reenacted an imagined seventeenth century, before a backdrop of early Russia, to set the military-religious entourage of the imperial family apart from the court, state, and Orthodox church.[67]

The revival of seventeenth-century architectural forms by the monarchy both expressed and sustained a myth that distinguished Russian autocracy from the monarchies of the West and gave the Russian emperor a religious mandate for the preservation of his absolute power. The building of revival churches after 1881 sought to demonstrate the vitality of the historical spirit of Muscovite Rus' and affirm the autocrat's title to the national past. After the revolution of 1905, the recreation of the past withdrew behind monastery walls to sustain illusions of omnipotence and mass support that allowed Nicholas II to believe that he still represented and spoke for a Russian nation.

9 Civilization in the City

Architecture, Urbanism, and the Colonization of Tashkent

Robert D. Crews

> Nothing is more striking in representing the civilizing
> work of the Russians in Central Asia than a view of
> Tashkent. A lifetime has passed since summer 1865
> when this important and then thoroughly Asiatic and
> Muhammadan city was conquered by the Russians,
> and today it stands as a partly European city with
> many modern cultural institutions and palaces, so that
> it is well time to bring it before the eyes of the Euro-
> pean.
>
> P. von Stenin, "The New Tashkent, the Russian
> Metropolis in Central Asia," *Globus* (1902)

To European and Russian visitors, the visual pleasure produced by a view of the new
Tashkent lay in its association with the "civilization" of Europe.[1] The panoramic perspective most sought by admirers of this monument to the "civilizing work" of Russian
colonialism framed the juxtaposition of the
"European town" with its "Asiatic and
Muhammadan" neighbor (fig. 9.1).

Deployed in photographs, drawings, maps,
and literary descriptions, these contrasting
views of the comforting regularity and geometric order of the Russian-built town laid
out alongside the "disorder," "chaos," and
"filth" of the narrow and winding streets of
conquered Tashkent appeared to Russian and
European contemporaries to present a narrative of Russian imperial rule. With the introduction of an urbanism concerned with the
production and distribution of space in grids,
radial axes, monumental squares, and parks,
the tsarist regime announced the dawning of
a new era in Central Asia. Its architects and
engineers sought to demonstrate in the
utopian vocabulary inherited from Enlightenment architecture and urbanism the arrival of
"civilization" (*tsivilizatsiia* or *grazhdanstven-*
nost')—of the advent and ascendance of reason, progress, and enlightenment.[2]

The successful performance of a *mission
civilisatrice* hinged upon the creation of representational categories to position the actors
involved. In the area that nineteenth-century
European and Russian geographers called
Central Asia, the tsarist regime drew upon
the most "progressive" models derived from
a common European colonial archive. From
the mid-1860s, Russians arrived there as Europeans, sharing many of the goals and self-
perceptions of other contemporary colonial
elites who undertook to manage the affairs
of non-Europeans through the modern instruments of science and the law.[3] At the turn
of the century, the governor-general of the
territory of Turkestan, Sergei Dukhovskoi,

Richard Wortman, Laura Engelstein, Stephen
Kotkin, Leopold Haimson, Thomas Metcalf, Randolph
Starn, Cynthia Hooper, Erik Zitser, Daniel Rowland,
and James Cracraft offered insightful comments on earlier drafts of this essay between 1994 and 1996. I am
most grateful to them and to the Department of History and Council on Regional Studies of Princeton University and the Fulbright-Hays Commission who supported the research for this article.

117

Fig. 9.1 A View of "Old Tashkent" (from M. V. Lavrov, *Turkestan: geografiia i istoriia kraia* [Moscow, 1914]).

summed up the achievements of tsarist rule, boasting that the Russians had overthrown "with one hand the coarse, arbitrary rule of petty despotic rulers, [and] with the other smashed the fetters of slavery and sowed the healthy seed of humane Christian culture." They had laid "the path to universal progress for the numerous peoples of Central Asia and had covered our dear Fatherland with new glory."[4]

As arts of visual communication and spatial definition, architecture and urbanism lay at the heart of Russian imperial authorities' efforts to cast the conquest of the peoples of the steppe and oases of Transoxania as the advancement of enlightened rule. Since the time of Saint Augustine, Europeans had associated civility with urban life. In the nineteenth century, they refined this legacy, discerning a strict hierarchy of urban forms. Tsarist elites invested the idea of the planned European town with extraordinary qualities as they pursued the conquest and integration of this territory, the regulation and reform of its peoples, and the transformation of its natural environment. The ruling classes of the empire calculated that the visual effects produced by the construction of European-style towns and the arrangement and design of buildings within them could lend definition to social groups and shape their relationship to political authority.

From the era of Peter the Great, Russian rulers' adaptation of European architectural and urban forms represented a strategy for the cultural transformation of Russian society, providing the monarchy with a symbolic vocabulary to identify sovereignty with empire and the West.[5] With the regimented geometry of the state-planned town and the uniformity of its official facades, provincial governors implanted the emblems and instruments of reason, order, and discipline throughout the empire.[6] To the Central Asian built environment tsarist architects also brought an aesthetic inherited from Enlightenment and romantic theorists; they attributed to buildings the power to evoke sensations of awe and fear and the capacity to inspire feelings of devotion, loyalty, and obedience.[7]

The state-directed urbanism of the nineteenth-century European capital city, with its wide tree-lined avenues converging upon the ceremonial and memorial spaces of squares, monuments, and cathedrals, appealed to the values of the military leaders entrusted with the task of subjugating and governing Turkestan. To project imperial might in a contested geopolitical space where local dynasties and the Russian, British, and Ch'ing empires confronted one another, these generals adopted what Spiro Kostof has called "an urbanism of dominion," a neo-baroque theatrical setting for "the staging of power."[8] They required an architecture whose appearance would underscore the permanence and legitimacy of Russian rule to rivals in the capitals of Europe, to skeptical critics at home, and, perhaps most significantly, to themselves and the new imperial subjects whom they labeled "natives" (*tuzemtsy*). These self-styled Europeans sought a built environment that might secure their rule by replicating and naturalizing in Central Asia the hierarchy that seemed to subordinate "Asiatics" to Europeans in colonial societies everywhere. The structures housing the tools of colonial administration—garrisons, barracks, bungalows, palaces, prisons, chancelleries, archives, banks, libraries, and railway stations—were to be constructed beyond, though adjacent to the walls of the "native" town.

What might architecture and the design of a city contribute to the making of a colonial society? This essay argues that the rulers of Russian Turkestan envisioned architecture and urbanism as tools to shape a social order marked by the neat separation and opposition of two communities and to make manifest the contours of a hierarchical society in which the local agents of a national community of Orthodox Russians would exercise domination over Muslim Asians. Russian architects created spatial distance between the rulers and the ruled. In the name of preserving the health of the Russian population, they utilized this separation as a safeguard against contagion and pollution of the social, political, and confessional boundaries dividing the colonizer from the colonized, a hierarchy that required continual definition and articulation.[9]

Imperial officials valued these elements of visual culture as means to differentiate "civilized Europeans" from "natives" precisely because, in day-to-day administration, they relied less upon European law than on native police, courts, and customs, resembling the British authorities in Africa who excelled, as Mahmood Mamdani has shown, "in tapping authoritarian possibilities in culture."[10] The tsarist administration publicly celebrated its civilizing mission in the new city but depended upon Muslim intermediaries to govern Turkestan. Despite official avowals of non-interference in Islamic affairs, reliance on Muslim religious figures made Russian officials critical actors in the mediation of local disputes and transformed contests for religious authority among Muslims.[11]

Architectural representations elided the interdependence of Islam and imperial administration; instead they projected images of a European-style civilizing mission. But these efforts ultimately failed to resolve a number of dilemmas. How would the design and production of urban space make colonial masters of a heterogeneous immigrant society that included Muslim Tatars, Jews, Catholic Poles and, by the turn of the century, social groups who did not embrace the values associated with this image of a colonial Russian nation?

The designers of new Tashkent faced another challenge in deploying these arts of self-identification to attribute identities to others, namely, the tsar's newest subjects. The residents of the city, the consumers of these architectural representations of social identity, reshaped these images in the everyday lived environment.[12] From petitions and literary accounts left by the intended audience of this work, we learn that most indigenous inhabitants of the city rejected the association of new Tashkent with a superior civilization. By the early twentieth century, however, a small elite of Turkestani intellectuals had appropriated elements of this urbanism as a model for the reordering of Muslim life, but together with other Muslim notables, they simultaneously protested its exclusionary effects.[13] Both responses disputed the civilizing claims of the rulers in the new city.

At the same time, daily life entailed the mixing of laborers, artisans, merchants, and domestic servants—of Muslims, Jews, and Christians—from both sides of the city. These interactions, along with workers' demonstrations, riots, Shi'i processions, and indifference to official rites commemorating imperial conquest, challenged the officially prescribed uses of urban space. In the urban fabric of Tashkent, rival strategies of visual communication and spatial production framed a contest among several actors over the meaning and enactment of a colonial hierarchy and the definition of social identities within it. The struggle revolved around architecture, space, and time and their contribution to the molding of communities and the drawing of boundaries between them.

THE UNCANNY WORLD OF EUROPE IN ASIA

With few exceptions, the architects of Russian Tashkent did not appropriate native architectural styles and motifs; nor did they attempt to legitimate their authority by claiming mastery of local tradition, as in the creation of a British Indo-Saracenic architecture in India or in the *villes nouvelles* in French colonies in Africa and southeast Asia in the late nineteenth and early twentieth centuries.[14] Rather, they underscored in their work the intent of the military administration to rule this society from outside, and "above," its aesthetic norms. Sensitive to domestic and foreign criticism of the civilizing capacity of a regime whose own Europeanization dated only to the last century, its architects labored to distinguish the new European city from the architectural vernacular of the neighboring town.[15] To illustrate that Russians were indeed Europeans, they built in the classical style of universal empire. And in an age when progressive opinion expected the ruling classes of European powers to exhibit the cultural characteristics of a particular nationality, these architects elaborated various representations of Russianness as they conceived and inhabited, always in relation to "old Tashkent," what Russian contemporaries commonly referred to as a "European" or "Russian world."[16]

In designing this world for possession, habitation, and self-representation, the makers of new Tashkent also produced a world of anxieties. European and Russian observers read the juxtaposition of new and old Tashkent as an allegory of enlightenment, as the confrontation of light and dark. But the dark spaces that remained haunted authorities in the new city. They generated insecurity and, by the turn of the century, competing views of an ideal spatial order for this colonial society.

Disagreements arose among military officials and civilian physicians, architects, and engineers who differed in their conceptualization of the problem posed by the "labyrinth" of old Tashkent. Professionals raised the question of reordering the built environment to make possible a more rigorous and continuous regulation of its population. They advocated the use of "transparent space"—the spatial production of visibility as a condition of surveillance, occupation, and reform.[17] Concealed from the view of the Russian police officer, census-taker, physician, ethnographer, and statistician, the domestic spaces of the Muslim family lay behind the walls forming what Russians perceived as a "labyrinth of tight, crooked streets and narrow lanes."[18] In the spaces that these imperial authorities could not make visible, they imagined fanaticism, disease, and rebellion.[19]

Anxiety about dark spaces and the inaccessibility of native life also contributed to uneasiness about the temporal dimensions of the urban experience in the new era proclaimed by the advent of Russian rule. The juxtaposition of old and new Tashkent appeared to many Russians, like the early twentieth-century historian of the city, A. I. Dobrosmyslov, to offer visual affirmation of the existence of "two civilizations living side by side—one ancient, if not of Biblical times than at any rate medieval, the other, European."[20] Russians insisted that life in the new city showed the "natives" the way from an ancient or medieval to a modern and European way of life; and from a static and fatalistic conception of time to one marked by belief in the advance of scientific progress and universal civilization. Nonetheless, doubts and uncertainty about achieving this transformation plagued officials and other authoritative observers of native life. In particular, they feared that the four quarters of the old city preserved memories of an earlier age that still held the minds and allegiances of their residents.

As Russian ethnographers and Orientalists discovered, Muslim saints dwelled in their cemeteries. Devotional life focused on the mosques, shrines, and saints' tombs of the neighborhood (*mahalla*) or quarter.[21] Under tsarist rule, the shrines attracted growing numbers of devotees from beyond Tashkent who visited the tombs to offer prayers and hear the teachings of the Sufis responsible for maintaining the holy places. Pilgrims included nomads from the steppe whom tsarist officials struggled to shield from the teachings of the Muslim men of religious learning and piety (*ulama*). Like the monumental architecture of the mosque and the madrasa, the shrines—and their charismatic guardians—sustained the memory of an age when Muslim dynasties ruled Tashkent. At the same time, pilgrimage from the steppe suggested that Islam, rather than the civilization of the new city, prevailed as the dynamic agent of cultural change in Russian Turkestan.

Against the memories embedded in the sacred topography of the old city, the urbanism of new Tashkent proposed a narrative that identified new social identities for its inhabitants. This urbanism may be understood, as Anthony Vidler points out, within a broader history of urban design from the late Renaissance to the Second World War, as "the instrumental theory and practice of constructing the city as memorial of itself."[22] The "memory theater" of the new city aspired to suspend time. Its architects fashioned memorial spaces to transport "the past into the present," to keep alive memories of June 1865, the mythic time when Russian soldiers arrived as conquerors, and the natives bowed down before their new masters.[23]

Yet the past that these memory agents were to revive, reshape, and make continuously manifest had multiple authors and audiences. Just as Russian professionals' plans for the scientific reorganization of Tashkent differed from the symbolic uses proposed by military officials, the Orthodox Church invested these memorial spaces with its own meanings. Some military elites avoided representing the Russian conquest as the epic confrontation of Christendom and Islam. But local Orthodox clergymen utilized the juxtaposition of old and new Tashkent to advance this very reading. When they led the community of the new city in an annual procession of the cross through the old city, Tashkent became the setting for liturgical rites that cast imperial expansion as the sacred victory of Orthodoxy and the Russian people over Islam and the Muslims of the old city. Russian architects and engineers fashioned their city around the memory devices of monuments and cemeteries, but the danger remained that residents would devise their own readings. Worse, they might lack the necessary "will to remember" and ignore the monuments and rites through which Orthodox and military elites struggled to keep the memory of 1865 alive.[24]

THE URBANISM OF THE THEATER, THE HOSPITAL, AND THE MUSEUM

Russian anxieties about the possible failure of their *mission civilisatrice* and their ability to persuade the natives of the "superiority of the intellectual and moral development of [their] conquerors" animated their search for the means to demonstrate the supremacy of Russian rule.[25] For theorists like M. I. Veniukov, "the most important of the historical contributions" of this administration entailed the "maintenance and even elevation of that halo of omnipotence that Russia has long enjoyed in Central Asia, so that the will of the sovereign now appears irresistible to the Central Asian, like the will of fate."[26] Like their British rivals in India, Russian military officials sought a ritual idiom for the representation of imperial authority to peoples whom they presumed to be especially susceptible to "parade and show."[27] To a greater extent than their counterparts to the south, however, these Russian military men also had another audience in mind, that of public opinion in Europe and of educated society in European Russia.

To bring political unity, order, and the rule of law to what the science of ethnography cast as the great "variety of tribes inhabiting Central Asia," the new rulers required a center, a permanent setting for the display of imperial authority. As Captain L. F. Kostenko of the General Staff explained, early Russian administrative practice privileged the distinction between "settled" and "nomadic natives" over that of "tribal" divisions. While these nomads represented "raw material, of which it is easy to do all that one pleases," Kostenko pointed out, "the settled population," by contrast, formed a "hearty body, firmly united by the Muslim religion, which is why it is hard to make it accessible to European civilization." Faced with this challenge, the military chose the "inhabited locales" of the region as the arena for the performance of the confrontation of "civilization" and its supposed antithesis, the "Asiatic city."[28]

A major trading and artisanal center, Tashkent had formed an administrative center of the khanate of Kokand, from which a *beglerbegi* (governor) appointed by the khan ruled the northern *vilayets* (provinces) of this Özbeg kingdom. From 1835, the Kokanese had used it as an outpost in campaigns to subordinate its sedentary and nomadic neighbors. In the quarter-century preceding the tsarist conquest, control of the city changed hands seven times between the Kokanese khan and the Bukharan emir.[29] Following its siege and capture by tsarist troops in 1865, the visual impression created by the war-torn city hardly served the representational needs of the new power in the region. Though Russian forces had inflicted great damage on the town during the siege, "the monotonous picture of Tashkent" nonetheless functioned as an emblem of the disorder, backwardness, and irrationality of a timeless "Orient" in the cultural repertoire shared by educated Russians and Europeans.[30]

Scientific as well as aesthetic criteria determined the military staff's plans for a new Russian settlement. For those entrusted with securing housing for Russian troops, the "Asiatic" city signified disease. Medical experts associated the geography, climate, and government of "the East" with the proliferation of deadly diseases. They interpreted these elements through the lens of contemporary theories of hospital architecture, which proposed that "space could be arranged in such a way as to encourage the spread of disease or to oppose it."[31] Equipped with aerial theories of disease and the spatial norms of late En-

lightenment hospital design, officials identified the built environment of Tashkent as a threat to the health of the Russian military population. The construction of houses, canals, and the arrangement of streets and courtyards seemed to prevent the circulation of air, water, and sunlight.

Alongside environmental factors, the categories of "religion" and "mode of life" entered their analysis of natives' health. Experts like Kostenko paired the danger of contagion with a menacing and authoritarian image of Islam.[32] Writing five years after the conquest, Captain Kostenko suggested a direct relationship between Islamic rites and the spread of disease. "With the prescribed washing five times a day," he argued, "the law-giver had in mind the maintenance of cleanliness and neatness as the main guarantees of human health. Muslims zealously wash themselves, but the result turns out bad: . . . filthier Central Asians are not to be found!" He also linked the built environment and non-European diseases, claiming that the canals of the old city "are infected and give rise to a great number of cutaneous diseases almost unknown in Europe."[33]

By this account, Islam and its ostensibly despotic law (the *shari'a*) bound urban and social space together with the biological, the cultural, and the political. "Further development of Muslim peoples is not possible," Kostenko insisted, "because all activities and actions of people are conditioned by the *shari'a*: food, clothing, housing, state structure, administration, the levying of taxes, politics—all of this is determined once and for all, and improvements in them are not permitted."[34] To ameliorate and correct the natives' mode of life, so that they may "come to life and revive," Kostenko prescribed "the help of outside force."[35]

Initially, however, the military hesitated to intervene to reshape the urban fabric of Tashkent. Privileging the maintenance of order over the reform of native life, these officials tried to avoid what they viewed as unnecessary conflict with Tashkentis. In particular, they feared confrontation resulting from encroachments upon what they presumed to be the all-encompassing domain of Islam. Russian architects largely avoided colonizing Turkestani cities, even though contemporary European architects offered precedents for massive urban reconstruction in the "Hauss-manization" of Paris and similar projects for Istanbul, Vienna, Rome, and other cities.[36] Instead, topographers and engineers began the construction of a settlement just south and east of Tashkent, where they could create a "healthy" environment with barracks built with a sanitary design providing for ventilation and sunlight.[37]

The conquest of Tashkent established the pattern for tsarist urban development in the region.[38] In 1866, the beginnings of a "European quarter" designed by M. N. Kolesnikov began to take shape in a grid following the removal of several homes and other buildings owned by Tashkentis.[39] The first governor-general of the territory, General Konstantin von Kaufman, issued orders prohibiting "residents of the Asiatic part of Tashkent" from claiming land in or near the new quarter without the permission of the district military governor. Calling such claims "illegal," Kaufman explained that "with the growth of the Russian population of Tashkent," "Asiatic buildings" would hinder the expansion of the "border of land set aside for the building of the European section of Tashkent."[40] A network of perpendicular streets divided this land into blocks, creating the conditions for a market in real estate and the delineation of state and private property. As the plan developed, the focus of the grid became Cathedral Square, where the residence of the governor-general, known as "the White House," was built. It became the site of military parades and in 1868 the first Orthodox church in the region, the Church of Saints Joseph and George, whose feast days corresponded with Alexander II's "miraculous salvation" from attempted assassination on April 4, 1866.[41] To the south of this area, engineers constructed the first hospital between 1868 and 1870. In 1888, the Cathedral of the Transfiguration of the Savior came to dominate the square. Designed in the "Russo-Byzantine" style, the cathedral overshadowed the one-story White House.

In 1869, Captain Kostenko boasted that the new Russian Tashkent affirmed "the vitality and civilizing capacity of the Russian tribe [plemia]."[42] Its rectilinear pattern supplied Russian authorities with the means to demarcate and distribute land for the settlement of new Tashkent (now divided by a canal from the old city), but it failed to create the monumental visual impression sought by the new rulers. Recalling his first impressions upon his arrival there in November 1867, Kaufman complained:

> It would be impossible to imagine anything corresponding less to the name "capital city"; it was an enormous wasteland without a single tree, with streets outlined, but still not built. . . . and only a fortress, whose appearance was far from impressive, and a small, narrow church [tserkovka] testified that Russians lived there. And next to this Russian capital . . . lived a native population of one hundred thousand.[43]

The governor-general dwelled on the relationship between the appearance of the new city and the choice made by these subjects between resistance and submission:

> Russian housing, the troops' quarters and institutions—all of this had a temporary character and a disorderly, almost beggarly appearance. Nothing about the view inspired the indigenous population to think about the durability of the conquest; on the contrary, everything gave one reason to maintain hope for a forthcoming liberation from the hands of the Russians, . . . the influence of order and the beginnings that the Russian victory had only just proclaimed were still not sensed, not felt.[44]

To address these perceived failings, Kaufman and his administration set out to transform Tashkent into a site that would produce the visual effect commensurate with the mission of the city as Russia's imperial capital in the Muslim East.

In 1870, the administration approved a new design by another military engineer, A. V. Markov, which departed dramatically

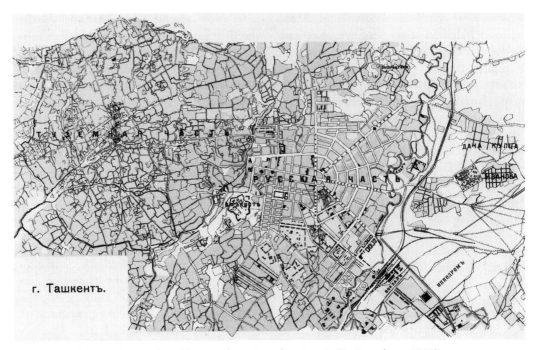

г. Ташкентъ.

Fig. 9.2 Tashkent on the eve of World War I (from *Aziatskaia Rossiia* [St. Petersburg, 1914]).

from the grid that had served as the model for much of the urban development throughout the empire.[45] The designers chose a radial-concentric scheme, with straight, wide, tree-lined avenues reminiscent of the design of St. Petersburg. Extending eastward from the initial rectangular sections of the new city, a series of broad avenues spread out like a fan away from the indigenous city (fig. 9.2). A new Konstantin (also later known as Kaufman) Square, where three axial avenues converged, formed the focal point of this scheme. Along these avenues and the square, architects employed an eclectic range of architectural styles, ranging from the classical to seventeenth-century Muscovite motifs, in the construction of Orthodox churches, palaces, administrative buildings, shops, restaurants, theaters, schools, a museum of regional ethnography and archeology, an astronomical observatory, and public library. Drawing attention to the garden, church, palace, and state architecture that predominated there, the first guidebook to the region informed readers in 1879 that Tashkent could now be called "the capital of the territory of Turkestan."[46]

While the broad avenues arranged in a radial *trivium* improved the defense capabilities of the new city by facilitating the rapid movement of troops, they also provided a more demonstrative setting for the ritual expression of imperial authority. In a departure from the secular and classical idiom that had characterized earlier commemorations of imperial conquest, Orthodox clergymen appropriated the public spaces and memorials of the city to celebrate the capture of the city as the victory of Orthodoxy over Islam. The anniversary of the conquest on June 15 presented a unique opportunity for the Orthodox Church to have officially sanctioned contact with the Muslims of the old city.[47] Church authorities made clear that the procession of the cross through both parts of the city should revive the memories of Orthodox and Muslim alike and that all residents were to play critical roles in this drama of definition and exclusion. As one observer pointed out in the journal of the diocese in 1907, the procession commemorated "an important day in the history of Russian and Asiatic Tashkent. It is gratifying to think," the correspondent continued, "that the Russian population of the town is not forgetting this day and that each year, despite the heat, large numbers of people of different ages and sexes accompany the Church procession."[48] At the same time, the procession represented a "rare display" for residents in the Asiatic part of the city, "especially for the female part of the native population"; and while "the feelings of the Russian and native population are not identical at seeing the procession of the cross," the writer repeated, "the Church procession reminds the one and the other population of an important day in the centuries-old and politically turbulent history of our city."[49]

Each year Orthodox men and women assembled at the Russo-Byzantine Cathedral of the Transfiguration of the Savior. Following church services, the procession of soldiers, officials, and other residents moved through the decorated streets of the new city and crossed into old Tashkent led by clergymen bearing icons, crosses, and liturgical banners. As the procession crossed the spatial divide into the old city, crowds gathered to watch the passing of the Russians. In the reactions of these bystanders, commentators hoped to discern reflections of the elevation of the Russian people in the eyes of the "natives."[50] As the procession passed out of the old city and turned to an outlying military cemetery draped in greenery and flowers, notables of old Tashkent gathered to participate in the requiem liturgy in remembrance, as the *Turkestan Gazette* observed in 1897, of "those who fell in the battle from which the dawn of new life in Central Asia began."[51]

The ceremony at the cemetery set the stage for an annual reconfirmation of the relationship between imperial authorities and their local intermediaries by way of an exchange of ritual declarations of tsarist beneficence and native submission and loyalty. In 1886, governor-general N. O. Rosenbach instructed Muslim officials at the funeral ceremony: "Twenty-one years ago, this region lay in a state of perpetual unrest: the Russian heroes living and dead are the reason for peace and tranquility in all of Turkestan; for this reason you must honor the memory of those buried

here."[52] At the fiftieth anniversary of the conquest of Tashkent in the summer of 1915, the Archpriest A. Markov reflected upon the conquest and its service to Christianity, tsar, and fatherland. Surveying Russia's great achievements during this period, he marveled at how far "our heroes had come in order to bring Christian culture and Russian civilization to this place—to implant peace and legality where despotism and violent law had reigned."[53] As the official account of the day's events at the garden cemetery also reported, a representative announced in the name of the Muslim population that they remembered and valued the happiness and benefits that had been brought them over the course of the last fifty years. Natives were praying for the health of the White Tsar and wanted to express their loyal feelings of gratitude and devotion.[54]

The *Turkestan Gazette* called on Russians, too, to feel a special bond with one another, as "according to the honorable custom of the citizens of Tashkent," they honored "with gratitude the memory of the warriors whose blood secured our city for Russia."[55] Through the deaths of common Orthodox Russian soldiers, the region had been reinvigorated and indeed redeemed. This fusion of military and Orthodox imagery advanced a narrative of a shared past and future for the residents of Russian Tashkent, a city that "appeared almost suddenly," as one contemporary reminded his readers, "its society, so to say, an influx, gathered from almost all ends of our mother [*matushka*] Russia."[56] While Orthodox prelates like Dmitrii, Bishop of Turkestan, celebrated soldiers who had sacrificed themselves "for the Faith, Tsar, and Fatherland," the procession provided those who came after them, including women, an opportunity to demonstrate their patriotism and piety as "pilgrims" to the sacred graves of fallen Orthodox.[57] State officials feared the urban crowd's lack of discipline and may have been wary of collective expressions of a potentially disruptive popular national sentiment in such an imperial context. But in Tashkent state and church elites supported a rite that mobilized a crowd and utilized urban space in a way that aimed more at national than dynastic integration.[58] Though participants joined in the rite for a variety of reasons, the local Orthodox hierarchy scripted this performance, like other public religious displays in Turkestan, as an element of all Russians' divine obligation to exert "cultural influence" on Muslims and to earn their "respect for the Orthodox faith that we profess."[59]

Invoked in the rites that memorialized the subordination of Muslims and played upon the juxtaposition of the old and new cities, the image of the common Orthodox Russian soldier became a permanent and central marker of the urban fabric of new Tashkent as well. In 1883, General Mikhail Cherniaev commissioned M. O. Mikeshin to plan "a monument in honor of those who fell at the taking of Tashkent" to be placed on Konstantin Square, at the convergence of the city's three radial avenues.[60] After studying the history of the storming of Tashkent for his composition, Mikeshin concluded that "without this Russian soldier, under the most unbearable conditions of war, no commanders with troops of other nations could have conquered the region."[61] He chose to represent the event with a single Russian soldier raising an imperial banner to a height of twelve meters. His sketch of the composition called for an inscription dedicating the monument to "the Russian soldiers who valiantly fell during the taking of Tashkent." Though his proposal for the inscription highlighted the role of Alexander III as "sovereign of Turkestan" and featured the imperial double-headed eagle and Orthodox cross, the focus of the work was the common Russian soldier—with an imagined audience of turbaned onlookers (fig. 9.3). An unsuccessful fundraising campaign postponed the execution of the monument, however, and officials soon devised an alternative strategy for representing the conquest. In place of the monument to the fallen soldiers, a plan appeared for a memorial to "the conquerors and organizers of the territory of Turkestan." Military engineers modified Mikeshin's drawing, substituting the figure of a soldier atop the "native defensive wall" for

Fig. 9.3 M. O. Mikeshin's plan for a monument to the Russian soldiers who fell in the taking of Tashkent (from *Niva* no. 31 [1883]).

one raising a banner atop artillery barrels and adding two medallions with the busts of Generals Cherniaev and Kaufman.[62] Executed in a less grandiose fashion than Mikeshin's original project, the monument was consigned to the city garden neighboring the central square (fig. 9.4). In 1913 a larger monument to Kaufman, "the organizer of the territory of Turkestan," and to the "conquerors of Turkestan" took its place on Konstantin Square depicting the general and two soldiers atop a captured fortress tower.

In memorializing the official values of a national community that they hoped to constitute in the new city, Russian officials had not solved the "problem" posed by the old city. The monuments and rituals of the new city celebrated both the locality and a militaristic and Orthodox idea of Russian nationhood

Fig. 9.4 The monument to Russian soldiers erected in the Tashkent city park (from M. V. Lavrov, *Turkestan: geografiia i istoriia kraia* [Moscow, 1914]).

the division of the two parts of the city and its impact upon relations between Russians and "natives." He argued that this arrangement had created an obstacle to economic development and that "the division of administrations and interests of the two parts of one and the same city to a certain degree artificially supports the divide between Russians and natives and hinders the drawing together [*slianie*] of these two peoples [*narodnosti*] that is so desired."[64] Kaufman opposed the total consolidation of the two parts of the town because, given the "tribal heterogeneity of the urban population," elections for local government could prove "dangerous" in Tashkent. Instead, he proposed to utilize the dynastic image of the tsar to integrate this population. Renamed "Aleksandrograd," the two parts of Tashkent could come together in "one whole society."[65] His superiors in St. Petersburg rejected this proposal, however, and with the growth of municipal self-government in the new city, different actors appeared to articulate a new vision of how the two parts of Tashkent should relate to one another.

The increasing authority of scientific knowledge, as elaborated by physicians, architects, and the late nineteenth-century hybrid of these two professions in the "sanitary engineer," lent political weight to these experts after cholera riots broke out in Tashkent in 1892. The successful exhibition of imperial power had relied upon the juxtaposition of a well-ordered European city and what Russian observers repeatedly called a disorderly, diseased, and Asiatic city lacking a rational design. In 1892, however, the cholera epidemic and the protests that followed illustrated the dangers of inattention to old Tashkent and its population. Tsarist police closed Muslim cemeteries, set up disinfection chambers, and tried to inspect homes and examine the men and women of the old city. These and other measures taken in the name of hygiene lent weight to rumors that officials sought the forcible conversion of Muslims to Christianity and even that these doctors had intentionally poisoned the water supply. On June 24, a crowd of some 400 men crossed from the old to the new city to

but excluded residents of old Tashkent, except as the conquered and subordinated. Despite the racially inflected language of imperial administration, it remained possible for many Russians to entertain the ideals of older dynastic models of empire in which the many subject peoples represented the children of the emperor or empress. As attention turned increasingly to administrative issues following the establishment of the city Duma in 1877, officials raised the question of integrating the two parts of Tashkent with greater frequency.[63]

Kaufman was particularly concerned with

protest at the offices of the commandant of the city. Fighting broke out, and the crowd attacked the commandant. The spread of disorder to the new city, what one official called "the unlawful movement of the native crowd into the Russian city," threatened its identity as the metonym of order, reason, and a superior European civilization.[66]

These developments strengthened the hand of medical and engineering professionals who sought to extend their regulatory authority to the residents of the old city. The chief physician of the military hospital insisted that, given the natural environment and the "backwardness" of the Muslim population, "the sanitary work of doctors must go hand in hand with concerns about the organization of the conquered territory."[67] However, the old city frustrated reformers' desires to regulate the health of its population. Much to the consternation of Russian explorers of the old city who sought information about the customs, mores, and health of its inhabitants, the dwellings of the city "lacked" the representational architecture of the facade that these observers hoped might reveal something about these residents' lives.[68] They identified Islamic law and its purported prohibitions against contact with Muslim women as obstacles to the systematic collection of census data, especially concerning birth and mortality rates.[69]

At the turn of the century, the old city and its population still represented a dangerous unknown in the minds of doctors concerned with the health of the new city. To remedy this situation, the Society of Doctors of Turkestan proposed in December 1899 that a hospital be built there. Like other projects initiated by Russian physicians, architects, and civic activists, including the widening and straightening of streets of the bazaar in the old city in 1886–87, this proposal sought to improve the infrastructure of the old city only to the degree that such an effort would also affect the health and security of Russian Tashkent (fig. 9.5).[70] A representative of the Society emphasized this point in arguing that a hospital was necessary in the old city because "the native city represents the constant source of all kinds of infectious diseases and, in case of the appearance of some kind of epidemic, it could remain unknown to the sanitary inspectorate for a long time and, in this way, threaten the Russian part of the city." Moreover, the proposal added, Russian authorities had to take responsibility for providing a hospital for the natives because they had not made it a priority to do so for themselves in the past thirty-five years.[71] These physicians and engineers reframed an argument based on the science of sanitary hygiene for the maintenance of spatial distance between residents of the two parts of the city.

Though the military administration stopped short of wholly endorsing "the sanitary work" and the accompanying reform of domestic (and hospital) space proposed by these professionals, it continued to view the layout of old Tashkent as a threat to the Russian presence. General Dukhovskoi requested support from the War Ministry in 1899 for a plan to cut "a wide and straight prospect in the Asiatic part of Tashkent that would enable convenient communications around the city and assist the proper police supervision of the native population." Adding that Kaufman had first recognized the need for the construction of such a street in 1876 "on economic and, principally, political grounds," Dukhovskoi argued that such a reworking of the urban fabric of old Tashkent had become even more critical after 1898: "It was noticeably felt in particular during the Andizhan events [a rebellion in the nearby Ferghana valley], when echoes of Muslim ferment were also noted among the natives of Tashkent."[72] The General Staff endorsed this proposal, recognizing "as more than desirable that the labyrinth of old Tashkent with its 100,000 residents be cut through with a wide band dividing [it] into two parts and isolating the Muslim population of the city in instances of various sorts that cannot be foreseen."[73] The War Ministry supported Dukhovskoi's security measures enabling the rapid deployment of troops into the old city and even cited precedents of the reordering of cities in the Caucasus, but Sergei Witte, the Minister of Finance, refused to allocate funds

Fig. 9.5 The redesigned bazaar in the "Old City" (1883–1884) (from M. V. Lavrov, *Turkestan: geografiia i istoriia kraia* [Moscow, 1914]).

to purchase the land for the proposed band through the old city.

THE ARCHITECTURAL UNCERTAINTIES OF THE LIVED ENVIRONMENT

The failure to find funds, whether from Witte or the local government, revealed contradictory attitudes about restructuring the relationship between the two cities that persisted well into the twentieth century. Though the "dark spaces" of old Tashkent might still haunt the architects of the new city, the allegory of Enlightenment—the confrontation of dark and light—that educated Russians and Europeans saw in this design depended upon the persistence of "native backwardness." Although the city government rejected Muslim requests for a hospital in their part of the city, the myth of backwardness and Muslims' supposed indifference to matters of health and science reassured officials and professionals in the new city of the continued vitality of their civilizing mission.[74] Moreover, with the exception of the renovation (ordered by Alexander III) of the fifteenth-century mosque of Hoja Ahrar, tsarist authorities rarely restored deteriorating buildings in the old city. They avoided large-scale repairs that might disrupt a tourist's picturesque view of a timeless Orient or dispute the image of a static native world set apart in time and space from the modernity of new Tashkent, what urban professionals celebrated in 1915 as a "typical garden-city"—the equal of the most progressive European and North American thinking about the organization of nature, health, hygiene, and social welfare in urban design.[75]

By the early twentieth century, however, residents of the old city had begun challenging the temporal and spatial identities attributed to the two parts of Tashkent by appropriating key elements of Russian reformers' vision of urban social welfare. In petitions to Senator K.K. Pahlen in 1908–9, leaders claiming to speak in the name of the population of old Tashkent criticized the "indifference of the majority of Christian members of the Duma to the needs of the native city," pointing out that "the latter wallows in dirt up to this day."[76] As a result of this neglect, moreover, the population was forced to drink dirty and diseased water from street and courtyard canals. Petitions railed against the government in the new city who concentrated its resources on the material well-being of the Russian city while denying Muslim residents the means to improve sanitation, health, and the general welfare of the tsar's subjects in the old city. Another addressed the unequal distribution of funds, which left residents with poor and impassable roads because the Russian mayor had refused to answer requests to address the needs of the old city. "Meanwhile," this petition pointed out, "in the Russian part of the city, the network of urban services [blagoustroistvo] is completely different—the streets are beautifully paved and the residents suffer no inconveniences."[77] The most radical of these petitions added that, because old Tashkent had been ignored so long by the Russian city and the municipal government, Muslims should be granted a separate Duma to administer their own affairs.[78]

While identifying the discriminatory effects of the juxtaposition of the two parts of the city, some Muslim petitioners sought to preserve and even strengthen the spatial separation of these two communities. In protesting the regime's disregard for the "most urgent needs" of the old city, they felt compelled to turn to Pahlen because their "spiritual needs" also required addressing. "With profound sadness," Muslim leaders had observed "among the ignorant native population ever-increasing drunkenness, various games of chance, prostitution and other vices, which are strictly forbidden by the laws of our religion and often severely punished."[79] Whereas Russian officialdom had identified Islam and Turkestanis' supposedly undisciplined character as the chief causes of this behavior, this complaint cited exposure to Russian life in the new city. According to these Muslims (as some Russians also admitted), contact with the immigrants had brought not civilization but vice. They added that because these sins were "committed in the Russian part of the town, where trade in alcoholic drinks, public houses and places are concentrated, [and] where gambling carries on, [our] administration and the courts of the native part of the city are completely powerless against the most horrible spread of various mortal sins."[80] By this account, the Russian presence had not only displaced Muslim commercial and industrial enterprises and left the old city in diseased squalor; it had also undermined Muslim society's internal controls and, most important for these petitioners, the authority of its moral guardians.

Among elites on both sides of the spatial divide, anxiety about bolstering strategies of avoidance and separation between the two communities increased in the early twentieth century. Strikes, protests, civil unrest, and the mutiny of the local garrison during the revolutionary tumult of 1905 revealed grave fissures in the society of new Tashkent.[81] Orthodox priests increasingly complained of a decline in "faith and religiosity in the Orthodox working people," the spread of "complete atheism," and indifference to church holidays, so that "the Muslims surrounding us do not feel respect for the Orthodox faith."[82] The missionary and ethnographer Nikolai Ostroumov offered similar criticism of educated society in Tashkent for its "indifference to the conquered city" and to the annual commemoration of its heroic conquest. In 1908, he warned that such complacency made Russian authority appear weak, advising that the natives might grow bolder and seek to expel Russians in a rebellion that could turn the region into a "second Caucasus." He singled out "the wealthy and influential classes and *intelligenty* (including students) [who] do not take part in this procession."[83]

The memory devices of the new city, their images of a cohesive Orthodox nation, and the conquest narrative advanced by the church no longer harmonized with the self-perceptions of many residents of the new city. Indeed some residents clashed with the rulers of the city when they ventured uses of architecture and urban space that challenged the official association of new Tashkent with Russianness, progress, and modernity. An immigrant Tatar community that established itself in the new city ran into conflict with the authorities' efforts to mute the visibility of the Muslim community there by restricting the height of the minaret built for a mosque constructed near the Sunday Bazaar.[84] In 1901, Persian railroad workers held a Shi'i procession mourning the martyrdom of the Imam Husayn. Reports of a procession of bloody Shi'i Muslims flagellating themselves as they proceeded through the streets of new Tashkent particularly disturbed tsarist authorities, frustrating their efforts to maintain a monopoly on the ritual uses of the city.[85] Moreover, the everyday lived environment of the city generated a steady flow of laborers, traders, and prostitutes between the two parts of the city, producing a migration that jeopardized the separation of these two communities. Though Russian sources tended to downplay this dimension, a German visitor emphasized this point in 1902, pointing out that "One encounters the native in the Russian city at every step—as house servant, coachman, peddler, cook, day-laborer, gardener, building contractor, workman, even as wholesale merchant and supplier to the crown."[86]

While such exchanges frustrated readings of this city as a symbol of the opposition of two civilizations, they also posed an ongoing challenge to the social, political, and confessional boundaries dividing Europeans from Asiatics. With great anxiety tsarist officials faced the possibility that the lower strata of old and new Tashkent might in some way join forces, especially in the wake of 1905, against the tsarist order. For the church, the policing of confessional boundaries became an enormous concern in the early twentieth century, when Orthodox immigrants abandoned their inherited faith, adopted Islam, native dress and local languages, and disappeared (from the view of the church) into the "old cities" of Turkestan.[87] Recurrent cases of apostasy, together with the religious indifference that Ostroumov criticized, highlighted the faltering of a civilizing mission. They also presented embarrassing evidence of the fragility of the bonds of Orthodoxy and even of the language and way of life associated with Russian nationality. From the perspective of Tashkent, such cases suggested that cultural change in the region had taken a turn neither anticipated nor directed by tsarist authorities. Other developments confirmed these suspicions when, for example, officials concluded that the influence of Sufi holy men in Tashkent had increased throughout the region, gaining followers in the steppe among nomads ostensibly oriented toward Christianity and Russian "civilization." Meanwhile, in Tashkent itself, these holy men seemed to block the reorientation of time and memory: "[they] resurrect in the minds of the people that old time when Russians did not dare to appear in Central Asia, curse the orders of authorities of a different faith and set the natives against everything Russian."[88]

Anxieties about the civilizing mission and the maintenance of tsarist rule in Central Asia reflected the limitations of architectural representation and spatial definition as means to impose and maintain imperial authority and the hierarchy of social groups and communities that operated as its foundation. Muslims refused census-takers, doctors, and ethnographers access to domestic space and brought "disorder" to the new city to protest officials' handling of the cholera outbreak of 1892. Many Orthodox ignored the annual commemoration of the conquest in the procession of the cross, while others rejected Orthodoxy altogether. Along with an undercurrent of artisans, merchants, and prostitutes from the old city, immigrant Jews and Muslims became visible in the new city. Strikes, mutiny, and irreligion tainted images of national solidarity embedded in the architecture of "Russian Tashkent." In both parts of the city, audiences selectively—and perhaps skeptically—read conflicting meanings into the rites and monuments of the memory theater in the new city.

To counter these moments of doubt, responses from the old city occupied a prominent position in official accounts crafted to affirm the superiority of the civilization represented by new Tashkent and its population. "Twenty-one years have passed," read one speech at the dedication of a monument at the Russian military cemetery, "since we Muslims of the city of Tashkent came under the protection of the White Tsar and the most powerful state in the world—Russia. And for us, too, Muslims [and] natives of Tashkent, this day must be remembered."[89] Perhaps because so many representatives of (and purported spokesmen for) the indigenous population owed their power over fellow Muslims to state patronage, such public proclamations failed to disperse the shadows of doubt that drove tsarist officials further in their resort to ritual and display.[90] Officials often regarded such statements as "cunning flattery," while Count Pahlen, for example, recalled the uncanny feeling produced in him by his "first glimpse of that peculiar subtlety with which the Asian regards the European." An "appearance of outward submission," he remembered, seemed to veil "genuine contempt."[91]

Such exchanges amplified the apprehension and misgivings felt by tsarist officials about the impact of the architecture and design of Tashkent. Their responses suggest a reading of this city as a monument to the constraints of colonial rule. The dissonance that lingered around representations of a cohesive Russian nation, of the "backwardness" of Muslim Tashkentis, and of new Tashkent as the locus of universal civilization unsettled its rulers.

Representational schemes designed to sustain tsarist authority by setting apart and elevating the new masters of Turkestan created the desired associations with contemporary European empires but simultaneously bred anxieties about disease, fanaticism, and rebellion. Photographic and literary representations of the city as metonym of an imperial civilizing mission distorted as much as shaped the experiences and perceptions of its residents.

The juxtaposition of the two parts of the city left a legacy that outlived the tsarist regime. As a symbol of the confrontation of backwardness and progress, the layout of the city shaped revolutionary politics in 1917 and beyond, constricting the possibility of the integration of these two populations and facilitating the exclusion of local Muslims from the exercise of political power.[92] Notions of backwardness and progress had special meaning for the new Soviet regime, and assumptions about the modernity of urban environments like new Tashkent figured prominently in them. To a greater extent than the tsarist regime, however, the Bolsheviks sought alliances with Muslims who shared elements of their modernizing ideology. They included those who, like the Tatar historian and political activist Abdullah Taymas, saw in Tashkent "two cities: one of medieval life and civilization, the other a solid model of modern civilization."[93] The Soviet state managed to "overcome" this lag in culture and time only after World War II. It finally integrated the two parts of the city by extending streets from the old through the new city in the 1950s and 1960s.[94] Despite the perennial scarcity of resources, the decision to redesign the city at last signaled that the exhibition of "backwardness" no longer suited the ideological needs of the regime.

Part 3

Soviet Russia

10 Stalinist Modern

Constructivism and the Soviet Company Town

Greg Castillo

The attempt to devise a physical environment for Soviet socialism and its *novyi chelovek*—literally the "new person," more typically translated as the "new man"—was marked by a procession of clashing architectural styles. Of these, constructivism is given top billing in architectural histories. The movement's favorable reception is based as much upon the interpretations woven around its modernist compositions as on the structures themselves. Constructivism is depicted as an emblem of "The Great Utopia," a vision of the Soviet project predating its totalitarian metamorphosis. Socialist realism, the neoclassical idiom anointed by the party as Soviet modernism's successor, is conventionally deemed the aesthetic and political antithesis of constructivism. String the movements together and you get the orthodox plotting of Soviet architectural history: the tragedy of an avant-garde springtime frozen on Stalin's command.[1]

For its reputation as the antithesis of Stalinist architecture, constructivism's timing is problematic. The movement's apogee of popularity, among both architects and the state enterprises that constituted their client base, crested during the First Five-Year Plan (1928–32). That historic juncture witnessed the rise of the cult of personality and campaigns to collectivize agriculture and industrialize at breakneck speed—phenomena heralding the emergence of a Stalinist state. It was also the period during which most of constructivism's canonic monuments were built or commissioned.

Constructivist architects, like their Soviet patrons, were engaged in two promethean efforts. Their duty was to build an infrastructure that would support industrial modernization and the emergence of a modern proletariat. Visionary designers applied rational planning and machine-age aesthetics to workers' housing and industrial settlements in order to effect an alchemical transformation of society. Modernist design, backed by centralized planning, was to foment a social and economic revolution, simultaneously yielding ideal manufacturing communities and a working-class population that was contented, efficient and unalienated from the means of production. Accordingly, constructivist schemes for "the socialist city" are largely an avant-garde elaboration of what in capitalist contexts is known as "the company town." Far from constituting the antithesis of Stalin-era architecture, these modernist labor utopias instead document constructivism's ultimate complicity in the Stalinization of Soviet society (fig. 10.1).

This interpretation deviates from the Soviet avant-garde's exegesis of its own efforts, and from histories based on those accounts. There are good reasons not to limit our historical grasp to such authorized narratives. Constructivism was much more than the roster of influential personalities, projects, and proclamations that takes center stage in most architectural histories. It was also a potent set of symbols and attitudes forged in Stalin's campaign to build smokestack socialism. These cultural practices, as adopted and transformed by the avant-garde's client population and bureaucratic patrons, helped shape the ongoing experience of that campaign. How Soviet modernism figured in the

Fig. 10.1 A factory and housing in the constructivist mode are the focus of modernization in this panel from Alexander Deineka's two-part poster of 1931, "Let's Turn Moscow into a Model Socialist City of the Proletariat!" Hoover Archives, Iowa.

broader experience of Stalin's First Five-Year Plan is also an aspect of the constructivist legacy.

Attempts to situate that legacy within the Soviet cultural landscape must confront the issue of constructivism's multiple personalities. Was it a countercultural movement or a popular phenomenon? Were its designs visionary exercises or a form of applied research? The dilemma of establishing the movement's parameters is not new; it plagued its adherents as well. It was, in a sense, the price they paid for preeminence. Constructivism's professional organization, the Union of Contemporary Architects (OSA in its Russian acronym), enjoyed triumphs unequaled by other avant-garde factions. Its periodical, *SA (Sovremenaia Arkhitektura)*, was the sole Soviet journal devoted purely to architecture from 1926 through 1930, the

period during which the industrial future of the USSR was debated and decided.[2] OSA leaders Moisei Ginzburg and Aleksandr, Leonid, and Viktor Vesnin secured the patronage of the state's centralized construction bureaucracy and were awarded an enviable number of commissions in its booming market for manufacturing facilities and ancillary structures.

Success bred a rash of imitators. By the late 1920s outsiders like Boris Iofan and Alexei Shchusev were winning commissions by appropriating the stylistic hallmarks of constructivist design. Worse yet was the 1931 treatise published by Iakov Chernikov, another designer without formal connections to the OSA, expounding the "forms and fundamentals of constructivism."[3] Chernikov's work was panned in *SA* as a vulgarization,[4] and late-night meetings of the magazine's editorial board found "everyone . . . speaking out against the new 'stylizers,' the epigones of the 'constructive style' and so on."[5] Despite the OSA's attempts to defend its franchise, by the late 1920s the term "constructivism" had entered the Russian vocabulary as a generic label for "the new architecture," and with good reason, as demonstrated by the ongoing assimilation of OSA design approaches. This inclusive application of the movement's name is abundantly documented, but remains unexplored—and at times even repudiated—by architectural historians.[6] Doing so denies constructivism one of its most spectacular achievements: the leap from proprietary practice to mass culture. In becoming part of a popular discourse, cultural innovations invariably escape the jurisdiction of their originators, and constructivism's galvanizing expressions of a socialist material culture were no exception.

UNIVERSITIES OF LABOR

Industrial technology was at the very heart of early Soviet politics and culture. From the miracles of mass production Bolshevism spun a story about economic, social, and human revolution, and populated it with a Manichaean cast of characters. Lenin summarized the plot in 1920:

> Anyone who has carefully observed life in the countryside, as compared with life in the cities, knows that we have not torn up the roots of capitalism and have not undermined the foundation, the basis of the internal enemy. The latter depends on small-scale production, and there is only one way of undermining it, namely, to place the economy of the country, including agriculture, on a new technical basis, that of modern, large-scale production.[7]

As the leading edge of revolution, the Communist Party took responsibility for shepherding a largely agrarian population through this metamorphosis. Injecting the West's industrialism with communal forms of labor would transform specimens of what Lenin once called "the Russian savage" into the "cultured, conscious, educated workers" essential to socialism.[8]

A politically engaged avant-garde celebrated this goal and gave it aesthetic expression. "Off to the factory, the creator of the highest springboard for the leap into the all-encompassing human culture," effused the authors of the manifesto "From the Constructivists to the World."[9] El Lissitzky, who helped found Switzerland's constructivist architectural association (but declined to join its Soviet equivalent), declared the factory "the crucible of socialization for the urban population" and suggested its new functional parameters:

> By virtue of the exact division of time and work rhythm, and by making each individual share in a large common responsibility, the factory has become the real place of education—the university for new Socialist man.[10]

Lissitzky's comment that factory architecture "is not merely the wrapping for a complex of machines, but something completely new and different" may recall Western modernism's machine aesthetic, but the resemblance is skin deep.[11] Here industrial design is conceived as

the mass production of both objects and *subjects*, the latter created by synchronizing the peasant body to the disciplining rhythms of machinery. The process parallels the militarization of the peasant body analyzed by Michel Foucault, yielding a model proletarian rather than a model soldier.[12]

The notion that environmental conditions mechanically determine human behavior was widely held across Europe and America in the 1920s. In Soviet Russia this conviction held a special meaning for the avant-garde. Aleksandr Vesnin praised engineering's invention of "objects of genius" and called for artists to create devices equal in the "potential energy of their psycho-physiological influence on the consciousness of the individual."[13] Constructivists venerated machine environments for their ordained capacity to transform human nature. The factory was considered the most potent example of the "social condenser"—a term for building types that, while fulfilling basic needs, also instilled socialist modes of behavior and thought. Another example of the genre was the communal housing complex, sometimes known as the *zhilkombinat* or "dwelling-factory." Of course, ad-hoc communality was made a commonplace reality of Soviet urban life in the aftermath of the October Revolution and the ensuing civil war through massive internal migration and economic collapse, which brought an abrupt end to speculative housing construction. But as a new building type, the purpose-built commune was much more than a solution to the Soviet housing crisis. It was seen as a guarantor of restructured familial relationships that would liberate the housewife from bourgeois domestic chores and allow her participation in proletarian labor. OSA member Nikolai Kuzmin was a radical advocate, calling for the "demolition of the family (which operates) as a means of exploitation and oppression."[14] Public laundries, public baths, the creche, and the "factory-kitchen"—a cafeteria that served meals on the premises or packed to go—also had ideological connotations similar to that of the communal house. These communal facilities inculcated a so-

Fig. 10.2 The new woman is equated with the constructivist "social condensers" seen out the window behind her — including a *"Fabrika-Kukhnia"* (factory-kitchen) and a worker's club — in the 1931 poster "Working Woman in the Struggle for Socialism and the Struggle against Religion," by Klinch and Koslinskii. The working woman's glowing future is depicted as a wedge splitting the darkness of religious ignorance (bottom left) and the brutality of an alcoholic husband and staggering chores of a traditional home life. Hoover Archives.

cialist way of life and conserved state investment by aggregating services traditionally duplicated in individual residences (fig. 10.2).

The workers' club was the social condenser formulated as a replacement for church and tavern. Drunks were ejected bodily, drastically redefining the norms of Russian working-class behavior. A "Red Corner" in the club reading room appropriated for portraits of Lenin and Stalin the Russian Orthodox tradition of hanging icons in corners. Similarly, early attempts to invent a body of socialist life ritual patterned club events after religious ceremonies. Marriage was celebrated at the club with a "Red Wedding," birth through an "Octobering" rite.[15] Workers' clubs could be affiliated with communal residences, trade unions, specific neighborhoods, or factories. The late 1920s saw a disproportionate expansion of the latter category, and factory clubs account for many of the most celebrated exemplars of the building type.

Creating social condensers was "the essential objective of Constructivism in architecture," according to Moisei Ginzburg.[16] "Today the concept of 'architecture' only has meaning," he insisted, in its application to "tasks of life-building, of organizing the forms of the new life."[17] This redefinition of the profession was implied in the title "engineer-architect," a term that gained popularity among constructivists in the late 1920s.[18] As with the engineering of structures, architecture's engineering of psyches was to be founded in empiricism. Credence for "psycho-formal" science, while customarily associated with the rationalist school of architects led by Nikolai Ladovsky, was also to be found among OSA theorists. In the seminal 1924 constructivist manifesto *Style and Epoch*, Moisei Ginzburg informed readers that "Modern psychophysiology has established that various elements of form . . . engender emotions of satisfaction or dissatisfaction within us." "From the moment man takes his first steps," Ginzburg wrote, "form exerts a spontaneous influence, which becomes increasingly more clear, distinct, and concrete." The paradigm of architecture as a behavioral science bolstered the design profession's self-image as the Party's indispensable partner in forging a socialist society.[19]

THE AVANT-GARDE ESTABLISHMENT

With *Style and Epoch* Ginzburg began to elaborate a design methodology that he described as constructivist. He outlined a two-part analogy linking the machine on the factory floor with the architecture of the socialist city. Just as mechanical functions organized factory design, so would the factory exert its influence on residential and public buildings, creating a landscape of modernity modeled on industrial paradigms.[20] Ginzburg's theorizing was motivated in no small part by his desire to create the working method for a "monistic architectural system," a hegemonic environmental order Ginzburg considered impossible to achieve under capitalism.[21] "The firm conviction has arisen among all contemporary architects that their different specializations—housing, community buildings, factories—are merely subsections of a homogenous territory," he asserted in *SA*.[22]

This endorsement of total design reflected the possibilities inherent in the patronage of a powerful state, or more accurately, its various ministries and administrative branches. Constructivists were poised to thrive in that new order. The OSA's founders registered their organization with Moscow authorities under the designation "specialists oriented toward industrial buildings."[23] This self-promotional claim was entirely legitimate, as confirmed in OSA's origins. A critical phase of the constructivist movement's incubation took place between 1924 and 1925 at the Moscow Higher Technical College, or MVTU. Its school of architecture, the Faculty of Industrial Building, had been founded by Aleksandr Kuznetsov, called one of "the founders of the Russian school of industrial construction."[24] Kuznetsov hired Viktor and Leonid Vesnin as faculty members in 1923. The Vesnin brothers' résumé of built work included workers' housing at Shatura (1919) and Podolsk (1922); an electrical power station at Saratov (1919); and chemical refineries at Tambov and Kineshma (1915), Nizhni Novgorod (1918), Petuchovo (1921), and Kostroma (1922). Moisei Ginzburg also joined the faculty of MVTU, where he taught architectural theory and history as he composed the constructivist manifesto *Style and Epoch*.

Viktor Vesnin was on the faculties of MVTU and Vkhutemas simultaneously, and his pedagogical goals at both schools stressed the development of skills needed by the Soviet state for its industrialization program. His resolution on "systematically linking tasks set in the faculty with real problems being addressed by various state economic organs" passed unanimously at a 1926 conference of Vkhutemas faculties.[25] At a "First Exhibition of Modern Architecture" held at Vkhutemas the following year, work by Vesnin's students consisted almost exclusively of industrial projects.[26] Students at MVTU heard lectures on spinning mill design and organized field trips to automobile and tractor factories, timber processing plants, and numerous chemical works.[27] This instructional program performed as intended. The Five-Year Plan found Vesnin's students heavily represented in state industrial concerns such as Chemstroi, Energstroi, and Stromstroi.[28] Moisei Ginzburg's career was also capped with a position in one of the new state bureaucracies. At Stroikom (the Construction Committee of the Russian Republic) Ginzburg headed an office established in 1928 to conduct design research on standardized housing. Here he fulfilled an agenda that he had laid out in the premier issue of *SA*, where he had asserted that the real work of the Soviet architect lay in "establishing . . . standards for the organization of new dwellings and towns, rather than the fulfillment of individual commissions."[29]

THE COMPANY TOWN

Contrary to Ginzburg's assertions, the "absolute monism" that he had identified as the goal of his constructivist method had proven not to be impossible under capitalism, just unprofitable. Ironically, Soviet architects initiated their search for a unified, reformist urban order centered on the factory just as many industrialized nations were abandoning the company town, their free-market version of that paradigm. The simplest definition of the company town is one built and operated by a single enterprise. The "works," whether a mill, mine, or factory, often dominated the site visually, and always did so ideologically. Labor relationships were systematically reinforced across the entire spectrum of community structures and services. Workers' identification with management was nurtured with claims of solidarity based on paternalistic bonds. Churches, playing fields, and alcohol-free watering spots served as platforms for indoctrination. The values inculcated were those of management's ideal laborer: hard-working, clean-living, punctual, and dependable. The counterweight to this "culture from above" was an unmediated community spun from shared social traditions, often rural, and the networks of mutual aid that linked workers to each other directly.[30]

Centralized management of urban space provided opportunities to control workers' lives. It also made the company town a proving ground for utopian city planning. The iron foundry of Jean-Baptiste Godin was the site of a Fourierist phalanstery, and company towns built by the Lever and Cadbury corporations became fodder for the Garden City movement. Industrial paternalism clothed itself in the rhetoric of social reform in these "ideal" communities as well. The myth of factory work as an edifying experience permeated the discourses distinguishing the model company town from its philistine predecessor. "The Moral Influence of Manufacturing Establishments," according to American pamphleteers, included the industrious habits and timekeeping skills that accrued to rural folk under a factory's tutelage.[31] Although social science theory and scientific management revitalized the company town's didactic mission at the turn of the century, the aim of these communities remained little changed. A 1918 survey of industrialist patrons reported their majority opinion: "A Housed Labor Supply is a Controlled Labor Supply."[32]

The model company town represented management's gamble that construction and maintenance expenses would be paid back through worker performance and good public relations. Profit was, as always, the bottom line. Yet risks were associated with town building, and industrialists ignored them at their peril. The deadly riots at Pullman had demonstrated that the company town's social contract could be easily broken. In addition, company housing was a fiscal liability. It re-

quired periodic maintenance, produced low returns on investment, and embroiled management in financial and domestic disputes. On isolated sites, however, manufacturers were compelled to provide housing and related facilities or face the possibility of being surrounded by a worker-built shantytown jeopardizing public health and public relations.[33] Such were the circumstances of America's last boom in company-town construction, which ended with the Great Depression. With the help of architects specializing in planned industrial communities, textile mill owners planted new settlements across the Carolinas and rural Georgia and stocked them with the cheap, unskilled labor made feasible by automated machinery.[34] Production practices in these company towns proved inspirational to visiting Soviet cotton industry representatives in the early 1920s, and resulted in a bid to cultivate Taylorism in Russian mills as a new model of socialist labor.[35] But there was no need for Soviet managers to travel to America to absorb the reformist innovations of the late-model capitalist company town. These were available for study in their own backyard.

LESSONS FROM "RUSSIA'S MANCHESTER"

Ivanovo-Voznesensk played a pioneering role in the development of the Soviet company town. Located about 150 miles northeast of Moscow, the community formed the nucleus of a rural textile district dotted with mill towns of pre-Revolutionary provenance. Industry was dispersed across the landscape in towns made up of a factory and its workers' colony: a settlement pattern that foreshadowed the urbanistic ideals later espoused by the Soviet state and many of its avant-garde architects. Barracks were the usual housing type in early nineteenth-century Ivanovo-Voznesensk. Around the turn of the century reformist practices caught on. They were fully implemented by the manufacturing firm of Ivan Konovalov and Son in the company town of Boniachki, where 120 workers' cottages went up in 1913. The settlement was soon served by a school, crèche, and hospital, all built and operated by company management. Ground was broken in 1914 for a "House of the People" as well. It was to include a theater accommodating 1,600, and a club with various recreational facilities. This building program, identical to that of later socialist workers' clubs, proves false the Soviet claim that these were "developed after the Revolution: absolutely independent objects, without model or tradition."[36] Although construction of Boniachki's House of the People was interrupted by war and revolution, this exemplar was connected directly to constructivist praxis. In 1924, as the textile-producing area became a magnet for state spending, Viktor Vesnin was placed in charge of the structure's completion.[37]

As one of the first targets of large-scale Soviet redevelopment, the Ivanovo-Voznesensk region reaped the bounty of an investment scheme that predated Stalin's industrial "revolution from above." Lenin's New Economic Policy (NEP) of 1921 conceded that, for the time being, the USSR's industrial future remained in the hands of peasants. Private control over agricultural production made the peasantry a de facto entrepreneurial class. Soviet power would dwindle until the state came up with something to barter for provisions. Fabric was always in demand by peasants, and the state controlled its production facilities, which had been expropriated in the Revolution's opening act. Calicoes and cheap cotton prints were suddenly of strategic importance to the USSR's survival, a fact soon reflected in the flows of state capital.

Competitions in 1924 and 1925 heralded the reformatting of Russian textile production as a state socialist venture. OSA members were well-represented in a 1924 competition for a Soviet "House of the People" for Ivanovo-Voznesensk, with entries by Ilia Golosov, the Vesnin brothers, and the team of Georgi Vegman and Vassili Krasilnikov, among others. Golosov and Ginzburg also submitted designs the following year for a "House of Textiles" in Moscow. The brief was for the industry's centralized administrative headquarters, which was to contain office space and a hotel, restaurant, and general store. In heralding the proliferation of purpose-built socialist workers' clubs and the elaboration of state manufacturing bureaucracies as well-provisioned fiefdoms, both competitions foreshadowed the institutions of Stalin's era of heavy industry.

In the 1920s, Ivanovo-Voznesensk became a city of "firsts." The earliest Soviet "factory-kitchen" was built in there in 1925. Its nineteen industrial kettles produced 5,000 prepared lunches daily, helping the preponderantly female population of textile workers juggle the demands of family and factory. Workers' clubs began to go up in 1926. The "First Workers' Settlement" of 1924–26, a garden suburb organized around streets leading directly to the mills, could claim the USSR's first purpose-built school (1927), health clinic (1927), and crèche (1928). Contributions by OSA members included a combination company store and bank by Viktor Vesnin (1927), the "Red Bobbin" textile mill by Boris Gladkov and Ivan Nikolaev (1927–29), and a communal housing block by Ilia Golosov (1929).[38]

THE SOVIET COMPANY TOWN

Ivanovo-Voznesensk was a proving grounds for the factory-managed settlement type characteristic of the First Five-Year Plan's *novostroiki*, or new construction sites. In 1929 Stalin announced the "Great Break" (*velikii perelom*) marking a wholehearted plunge into the construction of socialism. The goal was to overtake capitalist nations, and manufacturing capacity was to be the measure. Technological prowess would be a hard-currency import. The superadditive effect of socialism and Western machinery promised unprecedented levels of productivity. The greed of foreign capitalists eager to cash in on the Soviet state's spending spree would yield a delicious irony: the West's eclipse as the USSR emerged, a global industrial superpower.

The Five-Year Plan called for three hundred new cities: two-thirds of them organized around manufacturing plants, the rest around factory farms designed to bring industrial labor and its proletarian lifestyle to agriculture. Parameters for these settlements were set out by Leonard Sabsovich of the State Planning Agency, Gosplan, with the help of Stanislav Strumlin, the chief economist of the Five-Year Plan. Socialist new towns were to collectivize laundry, bathing, cooking, and recreational facilities for communities of 40,000 to 60,000 communal apartment residents.[39] Translating statistics into assimilable images, a Soviet schoolbook written to explain the Plan came up with a townscape familiar to Russian textile workers of the recent past and present. "A socialistic city will be entirely different from the city that we know," it pledged. "Its center will be, not a fortress, or a market, but a factory or an electric station. . . . Every future city will be a workers' village near a factory."[40]

The urban geography may have been reductive, but the analogy was precise. By 1930 the state had stripped individual city soviets of their autonomy over local development, setting the stage for centralized urban planning by large state trusts such as Stroikom and Gosplan's Institute for the Planning of Cities, Giprogor. For architects and planners it was the debut of history's largest new-towns program. Proposals called for the agglomeration of the various individual social condensers into a sort of urban "supercondenser." Competing OSA schemes included the linear city advocated by Ivan Leonidov; a strategy based on urban superblocks combining communal housing and service structures and favored by Nikolai Kuzmin and the Vesnins; and the "disurbanist" approach prescribing an even scatter of mass-produced cabins across the countryside, as espoused by the sociologist Mikhail Okhitovich and, as a late convert, Moisei Ginzburg. All contenders proclaimed the end of metropolitan hegemony over the countryside through their averaging of rural and urban landscapes. Yet, perhaps with the exception of the hermetic fantasies of the disurbanists, these schemes assaulted the overlapping pattern of agrarian and industrial labor long-established in Russia.

Most avant-garde paradigms for the socialist city prescribed a domain in which individuals were organized into a proletariat stripped of all mutual networks of support and subsistence unmediated by the state. With workers living in congregate settlements and employed in industry or its service sector, the traditional household supported by both wages and small-scale farming would disappear. It was a proposal of proven utility to management. Previous Soviet experience at Ivanovo-Voznesensk had shown that workers with ties to the land were not only more likely to be disengaged from mechanistic constructs of time, but also resisted Taylorist rationalization campaigns more easily than workers completely dependent on wages for their subsistence.[41] In addition, the city of social condensers undermined the *artel*, a traditional Russian community of labor which thwarted managerial controls. The *artel* was an alliance of workers, typically from the same village, who banded behind a designated spokesman and shared income, shelter, a female cook, and vodka. Here communal life acted as wage insurance, insulating the less-productive from the goad of piece-rate pay. In 1928, *arteli* at the giant Dneprostroi construction site were condemned as both counterproductive and unnecessary, since the factory-kitchen eliminated the need for workers to emulate "capitalist exploiters" by hiring a cook.[42]

Constructivism's "socialist cities" empowered management at the expense of workers, and, in the case of Aleksandr and Leonid Vesnin's 1930 plan for the Siberian new town of Novokuznetsk, even celebrated this social contract in the configuration of urban space. Their plan features three residential districts composed of communal superblocks offering residential cells of nine square meters to individuals, fifteen to families. All amenities are located in structures connected to housing by enclosed walkways (fig. 10.3). The town's administrative and public buildings, which include a House of Soviets, a technical institute, and state commercial enterprises, are arrayed around a broad square located at the factory

Fig. 10.3 The Vesnins' design for housing collectives at Novokuznetsk appears in the lower left of this 1931 poster by Nikolai Dolgorukov, "Let's Create a Powerful Base for Industrialization in the East!" Hoover Archives.

dered. Technology purchased at great expense arrived at sites lacking an infrastructure of skills and supplies. Machines, it turned out, were *consumers* of industrial development, not simply its means of reproduction. As imported technology failed to work its magic, Soviet managers, pressed to meet untenable quotas, increasingly traded off mechanization for manpower, a resource in abundant supply as peasants fled the land to escape the state's brutal program to collectivize agriculture. The population at industrial settlements soon outstripped housing and services. At the construction site of the Dneper dam (its powerhouse the work of an OSA team headed by Viktor Vesnin) the number of workers on payroll by the end of the Five-Year Plan was 166 percent more than the foreseen maximum.[46] Worse yet, industrial undercapitalization pushed town-building to the bottom of management's list of priorities, with predictable results. As at certain New England mill towns, construction workers remained partially or fully disenfranchised from the factory welfare system. In the USSR, as in the United States a century earlier, new industrial centers found themselves encrusted with a district of "mud huts" built by immigrant labor.[47]

In the etymological sense of being found at no place, the socialist city visualized by constructivists remained truly "utopian." Its tangible legacy was instead a fragmentary collection of individual social condensers. A review of this built heritage reveals that here too, visionary theory overshot its capacity for execution. Constructivist buildings in most cases either fell short of expectations, or fulfilled them in ways typically associated with "high" Stalinism rather than its avant-garde preamble.

Factories, it should be recalled, were the most vaunted of all socialist condensers. Why so few of them were ultimately attributed to constructivist designers deserves a note of explanation. For Bolsheviks, *Amerikanizatsiia* connoted industrial dynamism, and *fordizatsiia* was a buzzword for efficiency.[48] When Soviet delegates on a 1929 visit to Detroit

gates[43] The Vesnin's constructivist rendition of the company town conveys a diagram of hierarchy as clear as any planned by a capitalist magnate.[44] If Selim Khan-Magomedov is correct in his assertion that Sabsovich's notion of the socialist city was originally inspired by the Vesnins' designs for communal housing, Novokuznetsk can be seen as a genealogical culmination of the constructivist company town ideal.[45]

UTOPIA IN TATTERS

Constructivism's city of social condensers was to be realized through rationalized construction, standardization, and mass production. These strategies harmonized with the First Five-Year Plan's vision of a revolution through technology, and it was here that both the Plan and its signature architecture floun-

learned that the Ford plants at Highland Park and River Rouge were the work of Albert Kahn, Inc., the design office was immediately contracted for work in the USSR. It was a highly productive relationship. During the Detroit firm's three years in Moscow it planned over five hundred industrial facilities, and left behind blueprints that accounted for the replication of many others. The list of factories that emerged from the Kahn branch office reads like a roll call of First Five-Year Plan accomplishments: steelworks at Kharkov, Magnitogorsk, and Kuznetsk; aeronautic facilities at Kramotorsk and Tomsk; a chemical works at Kalinin; the automotive colossus at Cheliabinsk, and many more.[49] And these projects represented just one facet of the firm's endeavors. Office staff ran what amounted to a night school, coaching over 4,000 Soviet apprentices after hours on the fine points of facility planning and construction management.[50] Soviet factory design was largely an American import rather than a domestic product.

Excluded from that market, constructivists turned their efforts to the "everyday-life shop," as journalists dubbed the factory's civic apparatus.[51] One component was the factory-kitchen, a social condenser with a virtuous reputation peculiar to Soviet propaganda and Western architectural history (fig. 10.4). The specimen at Dneprostroi, designed by an OSA team headed by Viktor Vesnin, was a filthy place featuring long lines, high prices, and tainted food in portions well below a worker's subsistence-level caloric intake.[52] Magnitogorsk's cafeteria specialized in serving up gastrointestinal epidemics, and conditions at the factory-kitchen at Ivanovo-Voznesensk were grim enough to fuel a general strike.[53]

The public reception of purpose-built collective housing was largely negative as well. The single kitchen shared by eighty apartments in Magnitogorsk's first communal superblock was a place of constant feuding and episodic theft.[54] Workers living in Dneprostroi's purpose-built commune ignored the assignment of washing, cooking, and

Fig. 10.4 "Public Feeding" is depicted as a sanitary, mechanized process occurring behind the scenes at an airy sun-drenched "factory-kitchen" in this poster from the First Five-Year Plan. Hoover Archives.

leisure activities to shared rooms, and reallocated these spaces to house families living in the hierarchical patterns that social condensers were intended to reform.[55] Sensitive to the resistance that enforced collectivity might provoke, Moisei Ginzburg took a different approach to communality. He provided a compact galley kitchen in each unit of the 1927 apartment block of the People's Commissariat of Finance (Narkomfin). Residents could make their own decisions about whether or not to dine at the communal canteen. Encouraging the new way of life without imposing it made this a *dom perekhodnogo tipa*, or "house of the transitional type." Ginzburg's building, the best known of all constructivist residential designs, may have entailed a transition, but it was not to a communal lifestyle. Ginzburg's company housing consisted of fifty units: this for an organization that counted

37,000 employees three years after the building was completed.[56] While the Narkomfin apartments were small by contemporary Western standards, they were nothing less than luxurious for post-Revolutionary Moscow, where flats were usually shared at one family per room. As the building's architect, Ginzburg received one of the two apartments which boasted south-facing windows. His residence was "significantly larger and more elaborate" than the average unit and included a formal dining room, according to the most recent historian of the Narkomfin block, Victor Buchli. The original design was also amended to provide Nikolai Miliutin, the Soviet Commissar of Finance (and theorist of the Soviet linear city), with an eye-popping two-story penthouse unit.[57] Architectural historian Anatole Kopp unwittingly provided a clue to the residential demographics of the housing complex when he wrote that the block was built "for the officials of Narkomfin."[58] As industrialization pulled resources away from consumers and caused general standards of living to plunge, the in-house amenities of buildings like Ginzburg's Narkomfin block and Boris Iofan's modernist Government House (1927–31) provided interiorized consumer landscapes that allowed a managerial elite to enjoy comforts unknown to the rank and file. In Narkomfin's case, the project was to have included a cafeteria, gymnasium, library, day nursery, and roof garden. Little wonder that a group of workers visiting an urban commune are said to have remarked: "They live just like rich folks or like dwellers from another planet."[59] Rather than access to an egalitarian material culture, Ginzburg's "house of the transitional type" heralded a transition to the unrepentant elitism of later Stalinist housing.[60]

Mass conversion to an idealized communal lifestyle, the ultimate objective of the social condenser, also eluded the workers' club. Campaigns to induce workers to retire to clubs at the end of their shift hardly dented rates of proletarian alcoholism. The clubs' concocted rites and festivities, deemed "boring, dreary, and tiresome" even by Soviet observers, soon withered in popularity.[61] But while failing to replace their sacred counterparts ritually, workers' clubs scored major victories in doing so physically. One example could be seen at Leningrad's Putilov works, where the factory's former chapel was remodeled beyond recognition by the local OSA leader Aleksandr Nikolsky to create the Red Putilov Club.

Constructivism's embrace of demolition as an architectural *damnatio memoriae* was implicit in its theory of the social condenser. If a constructivist building was "a workshop for the transformation of man," as El Lissitzky put it, then structures conceived otherwise had the potential to be the new man's unmaking. An article in *SA* bears this out, stating that capitalist workers' housing was designed "to replace authentic, international, working-class thinking by another way of thinking—the petit-bourgeois way of thinking."[62] Since the peasant was the raw material of a nascent proletariat, environments capable of contaminating him with his former nescience had to be demolished. Iakov Chernikov's unauthorized treatise on OSA theory supports this notion, observing that in the constructivist world view "everything superfluous is swept away, everything without direct relationship to the object's aim and purpose has to go."[63] In constructivist designs for the Proletarskii District Palace of Culture, what had to go was the historic Simonov monastery. Its famed pilgrimage churches, the oldest dating to 1405, and its 93–meter-high bell tower had survived blazes set by Napoleon's retreating troops. Dynamite reduced these landmarks to rubble in a single day. The site was cleared for what the Vesnin brothers considered to be one of their most significant works, a club attached to the Likhachev Auto Works near Moscow. The monastery also vanishes in Ivan Leonidov's unbuilt project for the site. This taste for demolition as a strategy for social reform traces another critical continuity between Stalinist architecture's modernist and classicist guises.[64]

The First Five-Year Plan concluded in a nation transfigured. New towns rose at over sixty major industrial sites. Magnitogorsk, a flagship project, was exemplary. Here urban construction and administration was the concern of the factory's KBU, or "Department of Everyday Life." Having appropriated responsibilities formerly entrusted to a local city soviet, the factory now managed the entire urban environment, from housing, health, and social facilities to public transport and sanitation. And it was precisely in this regard that Soviet new towns of the First Five-Year Plan differed from the company town precedent set by Ivanovo-Voznesensk. The absence of an inherited urban infrastructure in cities like Magnitogorsk, rather than liberating the town planner from the impediments of capitalism, frustrated industrial management's attempts to provide residents with even the most basic public services and levels of sanitary hygiene.

Older cities were also transformed by Soviet manufacturing concerns. As the command center of smokestack socialism, Moscow was refashioned into the capital of a company town archipelago. By the early 1930s the city hosted a wide array of institutions related to this national enterprise, including eleven "industrial academies," various production and raw materials research facilities, and headquarters for the Soviet state's sprawling planning and management bureaucracies. Company townscapes also sprouted along the capital's suburban peripheries. One of Magnitogorsk's citizens, a recent transplant, observed that his new home resembled Moscow "a bit farther out [from the city center], say, on the Boulevard of the Enthusiasts, where gigantic construction is going on."[65] As Magnitogorsk's chronicler Steven Kotkin notes, "In the USSR, virtually all towns had become company towns."[66]

Trends toward centralized management were not limited to manufacturing. In 1932 all independent architectural associations were disbanded by Party directive and folded into an All-Soviet Architects' Union, with the neo-classicism of socialist realism as its official idiom. Constructivism now fell out of favor, portrayed by its socialist realist detractors as a heresy incompatible with the Stalin Era. Yet even within this new order, former OSA members continued to participate in Stalin's industrialization campaign. After the death of Leonid Vesnin in 1933, brothers Aleksandr and Viktor became the directors of architectural studios at the Moscow City Soviet. Their facilities were soon taken over by a new patron: the People's Commissariat of Heavy Industry (Narkomtiazhprom).[67] Ginzburg found a position within the Commissariat as well, as the leader of Studio 3 in its architectural department. Leonidov joined Ginzburg's studio in 1934, the same year he drew up what architectural historians now hail as constructivism's lyrical swan song: his competition entry for Narkomtiazhprom's new headquarters.

Established in 1932 as the successor to the Supreme Council of the National Economy (Vesenkha), Narkomtiazhprom was the hub of policy and decisionmaking for the immense empire built around Soviet heavy industry. Its headquarters' proposed location, planted in the heart of the capital, demonstrated the organization's clout. The functional brief included enormous amounts of office space, an assembly hall, several smaller auditoria, a hotel, library, policlinic, and clubs, cafeterias, and restaurants. Competition guidelines called on architects to base their design on a site that entailed the demolition of GUM's elegant turn-of-the-century shopping arcade, along with as much of the rest of the Kitaigorod, Moscow's compact nineteenth-century business district, as they saw fit. The bureaucracy's new headquarters was to front Red Square directly opposite the Lenin Mausoleum. Dom Narkomtiazhprom would screen this ritual landscape from retrograde monuments to Moscow's capitalist past, and celebrate the state's program for heavy industry as the pith of Soviet socialism.

The competition's first-round entries were a roll call of the former avant-garde. The Vesnins took the building's unwieldy program and distributed it into identical slabs rising from a solid multistory base. In the project's ponderous scale, symmetrical disposition, and garnish of heroic sculpture, the Vesnins were clearly attempting to satisfy the vague new injunctions of socialist realism. With the addition of Ginzburg as a new partner, the design team made it into the second (1935) and third (1936) rounds of the competition. But Leonidov's entry, jettisoned by judges after the first round, rendered all other contenders prosaic. Here the building's complex program engendered a menagerie of sculptural form. Three idiosyncratic highrises rose from a stepped slope that served as a viewing stand for mass processions in Red Square, broadened in Leonidov's design from its existing 130-meter width to a 200-meter expanse. A courtyard hollowed into the massive complex would engage an adjoining street and frame a worm's-eye view of the highrises. The most striking of these, a shaft with disc-like appendages, suggests to Catherine Cooke, a historian of the Soviet avant-garde, Leningrad's Rostral Column—a monument to military victory. "Until now the Kremlin and St. Basil's Cathedral have been the architectural center of Moscow," Leonidov explained. "I feel that (they) . . . should be subordinated to the Dom Narkomtiazhprom, and that this building itself must occupy the central position of the city."[68] With a total built volume of over one million cubic meters, the complex would have challenged the planned Palace of the Soviets as the capital's dominant structure. In both word and deed Leonidov demonstrated a clear grasp of the corporate body he was outfitting.

In the end, nothing came of Dom Narkomtiazhprom. After the third round of competition, the site was shifted south to the river's edge, where the hulking Hotel Rossia stands today, built on the abandoned foundations of a final, stillborn Narkomtiazhprom headquarters. The colossal bureaucracy was disbanded in 1938 and split into more than a dozen separate commissariats. The last project built under the auspices of Narkomtiazhprom, the Commissariat's mountainside resort in Kislovodsk, was completed the same year.[69] The architect-in-chief was Ginzburg; landscape design was by Leonidov.

Designs for the Commissariat of Heavy Industry's vacation retreat and unbuilt corporate headquarters constitute critical research documents. Narkomtiazhprom was a prototypical institution of the Stalinist system, co-ordinating an industrialization campaign that by the end of 1934 counted among its employees well over one-half million peasants in forced-labor settlements.[70] Commissariat designs by Leonidov, Ginzburg, and the Vesnins refute the simplistic formulas so often applied to Soviet architecture, which describe its modernist phase as utopian and its neoclassical turn as totalitarian. The recognition that Soviet modernism, like Stalinism, was a complex phenomenon with multiple phases, clarifies the research question facing historians: not *whether* constructivism was a tool of the Stalinist system, but precisely *when* it became one.

The Stalinization of the USSR's industry and avant-garde were parallel events, and logically so (fig. 10.5). Constructivism shared some of its basic premises with Stalin's First Five-Year Plan. These included enthusiasm for mechanical technology that bordered on fetishism, an aversion for the hodgepodge of cultures, economies, and townscapes inherited from the past, the ambition of installing a monolithic industrial society in its place, and the association of all of these with socialism. A body of architectural theory and praxis consistent with this approach emerged in the mid-1920s, at the time of the Party's strategic debate on industrialization. Constructivists were directly employed in the retooling of textile manufacture as a socialist enterprise at Ivanovo-Voznesensk, a project that preceded Stalin's control of the Party. Here the state and its avant-garde architects deployed a reformist company town as the urbanistic paradigm for Soviet industrialism and its paternalistic welfare system. By 1929, with Stalin's call to arms for the assault on an industrial future, architects were ready to offer a vision of the socialist man's new environment and a collection of innovative building types designed to bring that human prototype to life. It is true that these avant-garde visions were realized only in fragments and were ulti-

Fig. 10.5 This photomontage of the early 1930s depicts Stalin as a revolutionary, surrounded by the signifiers of industrial modernity, including shipyards, tractors, and immediately to his right, the constructivist Zuev Worker's Club of 1927–29. By Ilia Golosov. From Barbara Kreis, *Moscau 1917–35* (Munich, 1985).

mately repudiated by their former patron in favor of socialist realist neoclassicism, hailed in 1934 as the only artistic method capable of expressing the emergent Soviet reality. Still, the Soviet avant-garde's complicity in trans-forming the "base" and "superstructure" of Soviet society in accordance with Stalinism is incontrovertible, the orthodoxies of socialist realists and constructivism's contemporary apologists notwithstanding.

11 The Greening of Utopia

Nature, Social Vision, and Landscape Art in Stalinist Russia

Mark Bassin

> That Marxism is so strongly oriented toward technology and science obscures the fact that the sentiments it seeks to exploit are essentially those of anti-industrialism and of hostility to urban civilization. It condemns "the idiocy of rural life," yet it appeals shamelessly to the longing for a purer and uncomplicated agrarian society.
>
> ADAM ULAM

For most of the history of the USSR, Soviet studies in the West devoted very little serious analytical attention to the phenomenon of socialist realism.[1] Specialists and nonspecialists alike were inclined to concur with Nicholas Riasanovsky's severe conclusions about the "dreary poverty" and "unrelieved worthlessness" of its artistic content,[2] and the fact that as an artistic movement it was openly and for the most part eagerly subservient to the dictates of the Communist Party suggested that relatively little was to be gained by studying it. A few brave scholars ventured against the tide to produce substantial studies of socialist realist *belles lettres*,[3] but in the fields of painting and sculpture all interest was focused on the experience of the avant-garde of the post-Revolutionary era, and practically nothing was said about anything postdating 1930.[4] No sooner had Mikhail Gorbachev begun to loosen the tight ideological and censorial corset constraining artists, critics, and historians, however, than this marked reluctance to take Stalinist culture seriously evaporated. A stream of studies about socialist realist art— by Russian as well as Western scholars— began to appear, and a variety of major exhibitions have been organized as well.[5] The most immediate concern of this new attention

is not to challenge the reigning skepticism about the quality of this art (although such a challenge is inevitable and is already intimated in some of these works) but rather to investigate what the content of socialist realist art can tell us overall about the mentality that shaped the Soviet period. To judge only from the work produced so far, there is a great deal to be learned here.

At the same time, but in an entirely different connection, the study of what might be called the cultural representation of landscape has been undergoing a sort of renaissance in its own right. Moving beyond the foundations established by pioneers of the study of landscape art such as Kenneth Clark and Ernst Gombrich,[6] recent researchers from a variety of disciplines have been trying to contextualize historically and in a sense to politicize the analysis of landscape representation. The principal goal, broadly speaking, would be to challenge the commonplace notion that the content of putatively "natural" or pastoral scenes is in some way disengaged

I would like to thank Hugh Prince, Denis Cosgrove, Linda Nochlin, Geoffrey Hosking, Matthew Gandy, and Chris Ely for their careful reading and insightful comments, all of which have greatly enriched this essay.

from the complex web of political, economic, social, and other entanglements that make up what we call civilization. The fact that stylized depictions of the natural world commonly appear to offer precisely such a disengagement may go far in explaining the perennial appeal of landscape art, but the matrices of iconographic representation and meaning are much more complex.

The new literature strives to show how depictions of nature are the products of ideological determination, fully and faithfully reflecting the values, myths, and power relations in those societies or subsets of society that produced them.[7] Far from being conceived in any sort of opposition to the social world, that is to say, landscape or pastoral art in fact reproduces this world, and participates actively in the various contestations among discordant perspectives and interests with which society at large is fraught. As part of this, its attribute as a medium for articulating its message lies not in its actual removal from society but rather in the *appearance* just noted of being removed, for this circumstance lends it a sort of subliminal or masked quality that can render it particularly effective in ideological discourse.[8]

In this essay I have attempted to combine these perspectives, in a study of the function of landscape and nature representation in the art of the Stalin period. My argument is not only that depictions of the natural world formed a consistent part of the "painterly conception" of socialist realist art across a diverse range of themes and subjects, but that the image of nature was manipulated ideologically as a fundamental building block of that particular vision of Soviet society which the art was intended to convey. Socialist realism drew inspiration from the traditions of Russian landscape art of the nineteenth century, which had used nature in order to articulate graphic images of the Russian nation.[9] Although Soviet communism was not a nationalist ideology per se, it responded at various moments to the strong influence of Russian nationalism, and at these moments the elements of nature and landscape in socialist realism provided an important means by which it could articulate these nationalist preoccupations.

"NATURE'S TIRELESS RECONSTRUCTOR"

If there is one aspect of the Soviet Communist project about which we can all agree, it must certainly be the fact that its adherents were driven by the vision that they were destined to change the world. We most commonly understand the "world" in question here in anthropological terms as the social world, in other words a given structure of human organization and pattern of social relations, all of which were to be improved and perfected through a process of radical reorganization. At the same time, however, it is generally appreciated that the transformist intentions that permeated the Communist ethos were directed beyond the human-social realm and onto the natural world as well. The belief in the possibility and desirability of reshaping nature through human agency had figured already among Marx's earliest utterances of the 1840s, and it was an important part of the body of doctrines he left behind.[10] The Russians absorbed it along with the rest of this legacy; indeed, they absorbed it with a special eagerness, driven not only by their anxious fidelity to the letter of the dogma but by the stimulus of their own indigenous views on the relationship of society to the natural world.

Tormented by the perceived hardships of their physical environment—a litany of woes including poor soils, a notoriously difficult climate, inadequate drainage, and vast unmanageable expanses of open land—the Russians over the centuries developed a sense of their natural milieu as harsh and ungiving. In the imagination of many, nature had played the role for Russia not so much of a *mat'*, or nurturing mother, as of a *machekha*, or cruel stepmother. With the emergence of a nationalist movement in the nineteenth century, this inchoate perspective was formalized and provided with an ideological framework, for as Russians became increasingly preoccupied with their perceived *otstalost'* or backwardness *vis-à-vis* the developed West, the belief took hold that it was the natural world itself which was the culprit responsible for their low level of social development.[11] Since that time, the most appealing visions of progress and development for the Russians were those that included the promise of overcoming these natural handicaps by redesigning the natural world, a point illustrated most clearly in the character of Soviet Communism itself. From the rudimentary hydroelectric stations of the early 1920s through the unadorned grandiosity of the "Great Stalin Plan for the Transformation of Nature" of the 1940s, Krushchev's Virgin Land program of the late 1950s, and the massive interbasin water-transfer schemes of the 1980s, Soviet development at all times involved major projects of environmental transformation. Indeed, it could be argued that Soviet modernization actually measured itself in terms of such transformation, and that the ever-elusive notion of "development" was for the Soviets in fact simply another term for the large-scale reshaping of the natural world. The more radically one transformed, that is to say, the higher one demonstrated one's level of development to be.

There is no denying that the Soviet mentality was thoroughly suffused with this transforming impulse. What I would like to suggest in laying out the themes of this essay is that our sensitivity to these elements of the communist *Weltanschauung* has perhaps worked to overdetermine our understanding of other aspects of Soviet culture, in particular in regard to views of the natural world. I propose to explore this question in what may appear to be a rather improbable connection: namely, a consideration of the representation and function of nature in socialist realist art. Socialist realism, famously, was a vehicle for articulating and pressing those ideological principles that the Communist Party decided ought to be guiding Soviet society at any given moment. Without any question, the notion of the human conquest and transformation of the natural world described above was among the most constant and most important of these principles. "Liberated man," declared a history of Soviet art in 1947, "has

ceased to be the ecstatic, but often silent and inactive observer of conditions of nature that are filled with poetic lyricism." Instead, "he has become nature's tireless reconstructor and transformer."[12] A work devoted specifically to landscape art made the same point in more emphatic terms, by illustrating the range of transformist accomplishment from which the artist should derive immediate inspiration:

> Soviet landscape art, like all Soviet art, owes its achievements and new characteristics to the animated and constant connection with life and with the experience of struggle and socialist construction. . . . Socialist construction—which brings the entire country into motion, calls new natural forces and wealth into life, and visibly changes the face of our homeland—has enriched landscape art with a new theme and awoken in it an interest in depicting new subjects and motifs, in reflecting the process of the transformation of nature. Since the establishment of the Soviet Union, vast new expanses of Central Asia and Siberia have been called to life, the Arctic has been conquered, the deserts and wild steppes have been converted into flowering fields and gardens, and gigantic dams and hydroelectric stations have been erected on rivers. The colorful array of small [backward] peasant holdings depicted by old-fashioned landscape art has given way to massive agglomerations of collective-farm fields and seas of ripening grain, . . . dissected by the asphalt ribbons of roads. The masts of high-energy electricity transmitters have marched over ravines and thickets. Alongside of the horse and cart, typical for old-fashioned landscapes, automobiles and tractors, long-distance and commuter trains are becoming features [of landscape art] that are just as typical. In the skies, airplanes have appeared. All of this calls upon the artist to depict it, to uncover new beauties in the landscape.[13]

Insofar as such exhortations were commonplace, there was perfectly good reason to assume that the depiction of nature or the natural landscape in socialist realist art was conceived on the basis of the principle of conquest. Such an assumption would involve two major implications. First of all, the emphasis on the anthropogenic transformation of the natural world assumes a view of the latter as deeply flawed in some way, which in turn suggests that nature would be depicted negatively in this art, and would certainly not represent a favored subject. This indeed is the conclusion of one recent study of the subject, which maintained that in socialist realist art the natural landscape was a "neglected genre."[14] The second implication is the belief that to the extent that nature was depicted at all, its use was exclusively instrumental. The exclusive purpose of including it, in other words, was in order to bring out more effectively the process by which Russia's geographic milieu was yielding to the irresistible forces of human agency, specifically industrialization, mechanization of agriculture, electrification, canal-digging, the extension of transport networks, and so on.

My basic argument in this essay is that such a perspective underestimates the complexity, tension, and ambivalence at the core of what might be called the Stalinist aesthetic of nature and the natural landscape. Socialist realism did indeed portray the conquest and transformation of nature. At the same time, however—and regardless of various and sundry *ex cathedra* annunciations of the cultural authorities to the contrary—this nature could not at all be said to have become a demeaned, unimportant, or even particularly subsidiary category. Far from merely chronicling the relentless extirpation or at least neutralization of the power of the natural elements through human activity, nature as an autonomous entity was actually affirmed and in a peculiar but unmistakable manner even celebrated in Stalinist art, albeit highly idiosyncratically and always toward a precisely articulated ideological end.

The reasons for this derived from Soviet and Russian views of nature, but beyond this they related directly to the practical exigencies of socialist realism as political and ideological propaganda. The suggestion that the natural landscape was a "neglected genre" of socialist realism, therefore, is correct only to the extent that one has in mind a formalized sense of what this genre of landscape art actually represents: namely, the depiction of the natural world essentially devoid of anthropogenic presence, in which the focus is on nature's own autonomous being. Indeed, even this sort of "pure" natural landscape was eventually to find a significant place in socialist realism, as we will see. I would suggest also that despite the common theme of industrial construction which is at the center of much Stalinist art, the latter was very much about landscape as well. Indeed, to the extent that all landscape art—whatever its particular subject or sensibility—is devoted to making a point of some sort about the meaning of the natural world to human society, most of the art of the Stalin period would fit under this rubric.

UTOPIA AND NATURE IN POST-REVOLUTIONARY RUSSIA

Perhaps the best way to begin to illustrate these points is to consider for a moment the treatment of nature in the hyper-modernist Russian avant-garde art of the 1920s, against which socialist realism was ostensibly a reaction. It is here, in fact, that we actually find that intention to negate and extirpate the natural world which is commonly attributed to Stalinism itself. Much of Russian modernism was in fact founded on this particular sentiment, as was modernism elsewhere in the Western world. The natural world was seen in a profoundly negative light, as a sort of prison offering no positive inspiration to the human spirit, which, for its part, strived with justice to conquer and control it.[15] One of the most illustrious talents of the movement, Kazimir Malevich, put the point bluntly in a manifesto from 1915: "To produce favorite objects and little nooks of nature is just like a thief being enraptured by his shackled legs." The real purpose of art, by contrast, was to engender a forceful creativity that could emancipate humankind from these bonds and permit it to organize its own existence freely and rationally. Such a state of human freedom could be attained only to the extent that artists produced forms that themselves were radically free from all "naive ... copies of nature." This in Malevich's view was the simple but supreme perfection of the square as an artistic form. It could be found nowhere in nature; it was exclusively the "creation of intuitive reason." He thus proclaimed it to be "a living regal infant / The first step of pure creation in art."[16] Two years after the October Revolution the suprematist Ivan Kliun wrote in the same spirit about how "the corpse of painterly art, the art of daubed nature, has been laid in its coffin, sealed with the Black Square of Suprematism." Kliun continued triumphantly:

But if the art of painting, the art of expressing nature, has died, then color, paint, as the basic elements of this art, have not died. Liberated from the centuries-old bond of nature, they have begun to live their own life, to develop freely, and to display themselves in the New Art of Color— and our color compositions are subject only to the laws of color, and not to the laws of nature.[17]

Such a nihilistic attitude toward this rather fundamental legacy of world art, however, did not mean that the artists of the avant-garde stood in any sort of political opposition to the post-Revolutionary authorities. Quite to the contrary, they tended to be enthusiastic supporters of the new order, and a large number of them lent their talents for the promotion of specific programs and policies of the Communist authorities. "The best poetic work," affirmed Vladimir Maiakovskii in a 1926 essay on the role of poetry in the new society, "will be written on the social order of the Comintern, and will have the express goal of the victory of the proletariat."[18]

In this spirit, the practitioners of nonrepresentational art contributed their abstract images to the cause of Bolshevism, while those numerous artists who did not follow Malevich's and Kliun's radical principles produced works inspired by such recognizable themes as industrialization and the celebration of the worker. To the extent that these themes were to become emblematic of the 1930s, the latter works anticipated to some extent the emergence of socialist realism itself. Yet they could never really be mistaken for the Stalinist art to come. Those artists who most clearly foreshadowed socialist realism—the so-called "heroic realists" of the Association of Revolutionary Russian Artists, founded in 1922[19]—produced paintings lacking the particular utopian spirit that was the first condition of Stalinist art. The art of the 1920s differed from that of subsequent decades because, throughout most of it, some residual influence of the spirit of the avant-garde was still clearly apparent.

Workers could be featured, as in Iurii Pimenov's *Give to Heavy Industry* (1928) or Aleksandr Deineka's *On the Building of the New Factory* (1926), but their natural human forms were distorted and not depicted realistically. All of the space of the picture not devoted to these human figures is dominated by nonnatural, strictly geometrical forms: sharp and clean angles, straight lines, or perfect circles. Very little if any area in these pictures is given over to the natural landscape itself. The exclusive preoccupation with deliberate and constructive human activity, or the products of that activity, meant that for them, as for the artists of the avant-garde itself, the natural world possessed no significant autonomous value.

In order to appreciate the chasm that separated this dismissive attitude toward nature from the aesthetic sensibilities of socialist realism of the 1930s and beyond, we must consider the foundations of the latter as an ideological system. The first point to be noted is that the self-designation of Stalinist art as "realist" is fundamentally misleading. The term was adopted in order to emphasize the rejection of the abstract or, to speak in the language of the times, the "formalist" art of the avant-garde, as well as to establish a more or less clear link with selected earlier periods in the Russian and Western traditions. Yet rather than striving to depict the world "as it really is," the mission of socialist realism from the outset was to provide graphic and literary representations of the utopian ontology of Stalinism. The writer or artist was charged with translating and depicting this utopian vision in accessible, comprehensible, and convincing ways to the broad masses of the Soviet population. This clearly was a very different project from the preoccupation of a simple-minded "realism" with rendering the precise detail of the perceived world, a point which Andrei Zhdanov himself stressed in a speech to the First All-Union Congress of Soviet Writers in the summer of 1934, where the term "socialist realism" was first officially promulgated. "What obligations," he asked, "does this title impose upon us?"

> First of all, it means that we must know life in order to be able to depict it truthfully in our works of art, and not depict it scholastically, lifelessly, or merely as "objective reality." We must depict reality in its revolutionary development.
>
> In this respect, truthfulness and historical concreteness of the artistic depiction must be combined with the task of the ideological transformation and education of the working people in the spirit of socialism.[20]

As if to underscore this rejection of art as "objective reality," Zhdanov went on to call for a "revolutionary romanticism," which should become "a component part" of the literary and artistic creative process.[21]

Reality, as Stalin taught, was dialectically constituted and in constant flux, and consequently it had no permanence of form. The only true way of portraying it, therefore, was to portray the dynamic social forces that underlay it and determined its path of "revolutionary development." On the one hand, this meant that because the specific character and juxtaposition of these social forces at any given moment could only be authoritatively mapped out by the Party in accordance with the principles of Marxism-Leninism-Stalinism, the "reality" that socialist realism depicted would have to be indicated at all times by the Soviet authorities. As Georgii Malenkov explained in a keynote address at the Nineteenth Party Congress in 1952 on the question of the *tipichnoe* or "typical" in the

real world, "the typical is not that which is encountered the most often, but that which most persuasively expresses the essence of a given social force. From the Marxist-Leninist standpoint, the typical does not signify some sort of statistical mean. . . . The typical is the vital sphere in which is manifested the party spirit of realistic art. The question of the typical is always a political question."

At the same time, the pervasive concern with underlying social forces insured the deeply symbolic and iconographic quality of all socialist realist representation. Despite the apparent naturalness and genuineness of its often extremely carefully crafted and true-to-life images, the muscular construction worker, beaming collective-farm girl, weathered tractor driver, or sleek and leering baron of the evil capitalist past nevertheless serve as nothing more than palpable icons for political, social, and "human" qualities that were understood to be transcendental. This circumstance, as Boris Groys has pointed out, renders Stalinist art rather more reminiscent of medieval realism than of that of the nineteenth century.[22]

To be sure, the indication of the utopian underpinnings of Stalinist art does not necessarily help us distinguish it from the period that preceded it, which—as an extensive literature now makes very clear—was itself inspired by a wide variety of sustained utopian impulses.[23] What is striking, however, is the difference in the nature of the respective utopian perspectives. In his insightful examination of the culture of utopia in Russia during the 1920s, Richard Stites has suggested that in contrast to the plurality of utopian projects up until to the First Five-Year Plan, Stalin's was a "single utopia," a despotic and authoritarian vision that forced itself upon the imagination of the population at large, and could tolerate no alternative.[24] Along with this, we might point to a more substantive distinguishing aspect. The Soviet utopias of the 1920s were all forward-looking. They were, in other words, "plans" and "blueprints," in Stites's expression, which were anticipatory of things to come.[25] In setting them forth, their framers understood themselves to be engaged in the important task of constructing the future, but the consummation of their projects loomed far in the distance and was necessarily out of their immediate reach. Indeed, some utopian thinkers saw the entire value of their efforts to be precisely in the act of envisioning and striving toward a final goal, rather than actually realizing it. The very possibility of this realization could even be called into question without undermining the utopian project itself, as suggested by one of the greatest utopian writers, Aleksandr Bogdanov, in his story *Engineer Menni*: "Utopias are an expression of aspirations that cannot be realized, of efforts that are not equal to the resistance they encounter."[26]

Although less imaginative and elaborate than the science-fiction fantasies and other utopian schemes of the post-Revolutionary period, Stalin's "single utopia" after 1930 nonetheless was an altogether more complicated proposition. At the outset, it also was understood to lie somewhere off in the future, as signaled by Zhdanov's call in the speech just cited for Soviet literature to produce works enabling Soviet citizens "to glimpse [*zaglianut'*] into our future." At the same time, however, it began to be intimated that in all important respects, the Socialist-Communist paradise was already being realized. Indeed, Zhdanov had begun his speech with this very point, asserting that "all essential obstacles which confront us on the road to socialism have been overcome," that the Soviet Union has "accomplished the construction of the basis of a socialist economy," and that "under the brilliant leadership of our great leader and teacher Comrade *Stalin* . . . a socialist order has irrevocably and decisively triumphed."[27] This message—that all of the important preconditions for a classless Communist society in the USSR had already been assembled—was then subsequently hammered home incessantly on all ideological fronts. Soviet society, it was claimed, had moved definitively beyond the ills of inequality and exploitation, of deprivation, hunger, and misery that plagued the rest of capitalist and precapitalist civilization, and had already begun to enjoy those blessings of social harmony, material abundance, and a saturated *Lebensfreude* that Marx had promised nearly a century earlier. Effectively, the vision of utopia had become a tautology, such that the Soviet Union began to regard itself as "its *own utopia*": an ideal order in which, as Blomqvist puts it, "the existing society *is* the future society."[28] In the earliest years of Stalin's regime, this still-evolving picture of Soviet society as a real existing utopia maintained something of an awkward coexistence with the older and more familiar utopian anticipation of things to come: its triumph by the mid-1930s was a major landmark in the triumph of the Stalinist mentality overall.

Although the notorious characterization of the artist as an "engineer of the human soul" commonly associated with Stalin in fact had its roots in the avant-garde mentality of the post-Revolutionary period, the duties of this engineer underwent a significant change after 1930 that corresponded to the shift in utopian vision just indicated.[29] For the avant-garde, the artist-engineer would literally help design and construct the new world. Socialist realism, however, expected something entirely different. In the Stalinist system, the artist-engineer would assist the state by providing the popular imagination with graphic images of a putative Soviet "reality" which was nothing other than a "picture of life . . . invented by the Party" itself.[30] It is precisely this shift that Gassner and Gillen have in mind when they speak of the transition from "utopische Ordnungsentwurf" to "Versöhnungsideologie." Effectively, this involved situating a socialist utopia in the midst of contemporary Soviet existence, a challenge which, however daunting, was met and readily assimilated by the artistic community. "For the first time in many centuries," wrote an art textbook piously in 1950, "reality and the artistic ideal no longer contradict each other, . . . for never before has there been an epoch in which the very basis of historical reality has been beautiful."[31]

The suggestion that the ideal society was supposed to be immanent in some way as a part of present-day Soviet reality had one implication which proved to be vital for the thematic character of socialist realism. Because utopian visions involve social orders which are by definition perfect and cannot be improved, there is a logical bias in them toward preserving the status quo and against change.[32] Yet insofar as these envisioned societies remain situated unambiguously in the future, the immediate effect of utopian inclinations is to seek radical transcendence of the present, and they are therefore revolutionary. This revolutionary quality was lost in Stalinism, which was obsessed instead with the classically conservative interest in preserving the overall framework of the social order—if not necessarily the specific personnel—as it already existed. To this extent, the Stalinist order, like the "Thousand-Year Reich" of German Fascism, represented an " 'eternal order' utopia," in which "everything is already achieved, [and] there is nothing left to strive for."[33] The ideal condition for such a society self-evidently was stasis or absolute lack of movement, and by the same token the gravest threat was the progress of time itself, which might flow out of control at any moment into unforeseen channels. For this reason the attempt to halt this march received the highest ideological priority.

The principal means toward this goal was to collapse time by effacing the distinctions between past, future, and present, a process which, if successful, would produce an entirely new chronological dimension encompassing at once the past history and the future of humankind, and which consequently would have neither anywhere else to go nor anything else to become. Hence the automatic and incessant emphasis in Soviet propaganda on evoking the "world-historic" and "eternal" quality of the principal features of the Soviet system at any given moment, however ephemeral they might actually prove to be: its leaders, its organizations, its edicts, its *podvigi* or heroic accomplishments, and so on. Even socialist realism itself was eternalized and blended into the stream of universal history as "the sole heir to all of the very best in the treasury of world literature"—this at the very moment when Zhdanov was making the first public announcement of its existence.[34]

It was in pursuit of these tasks of bringing out the already-existent "beauty" of Soviet life and the conquest of time[35] that socialist realism conceived its aesthetic of landscape and the natural world. Simply put, nature was understood to be a powerful and evocative subject which, if properly manipulated, could support, embellish, and even legitimize the entire Stalinist utopian vision. There were various impulses behind this new preoccupation with nature, not the least of which related to the critical issue of how most effectively to instrumentalize the graphic arts for the purposes of propaganda on the domestic front.

Far better than the artists of the avant-garde, the Party understood that at the very least, art could have the desired didactic effect only to the extent that it could communicate with its audience, and it could do this only if it spoke a language they understood and appreciated. Whatever other virtues the cerebrally abstract or quasi-abstract styles of the 1920s may have possessed, easy accessibility and inherent appeal to mass popular taste were not among them. The genial insight of socialist realism lay in its realization that very new ideological messages could be most successfully conveyed by adapting styles and genres that were already familiar and accepted. In stark contrast to the avant-garde's categorical rejection of all past art forms, therefore, socialist realism was founded stylistically upon an explicit call for a return to the classics, by which was meant primarily the nineteenth-century Russian traditions of the *peredvizhniki* and the Academic school but also included Greek and Roman antiquity and the Renaissance as well. "Socialist realism," as Ivan Gronskii affirmed (with the bluntness one would expect from the editor of *Izvestiia)*, "is Rubens, Rembrandt, and Repin put to serve the working class,"[36] whereby the "service" to be rendered was nothing else than the depiction of Stalin's utopia of the present. Among other things, this had the result of quickly absorbing back in the artistic mainstream a large number of older Russian artists who had been trained in traditions of the late nineteenth century and had never really strayed from them. These included artists such as Isaak Brodskii and Aleksandr Gerasimov, who would become high priests of the socialist realist art.

This return to tradition was not, as is sometimes thought, an indication of a conservative or genuinely traditionalist bias in socialist realism, as opposed to the radicalism of the avant-garde. Quite to the contrary, it was the clearest indication of how much more absolutely radical socialist realism was prepared to be than anything put forward in the 1920s, although it was indeed a paradox of Stalinism that this radicalism was directed toward an end that was itself profoundly conservative: stasis and self-preservation at all costs. "The radicalism of Stalinism is most apparent in the fact that it was prepared to exploit the previous forms of life and culture [toward its own ends], whereas even the avant-garde detractors of the past knew and respected the heritage to such a degree that they would rather destroy than utilize or profane it."[37] As it turned out, none of the traditional genres that socialist realism sought to adopt and co-opt was more broadly familiar and appealing than the rich legacy of landscape painting in Russian art. The latter half of the nineteenth century had witnessed a remarkable flowering of landscape art, developed in the work of Isaac Levitan, Ivan Shishkin, A.I. Kuindzhi, and numerous others.[38] This art had always proved compelling for Russian sensibilities, for in it was conveyed not only the apprehension and dread that Russians have traditionally associated with the natural environment but fond attachment as well. Moreover, this genre provided an extremely important means for the articulation of a nationalist vision, insofar as it described a society and culture that was deeply sculpted into the natural environment, and by the same token helped define a natural non-anthropogenic landscape which was unmistakably and quintessentially Russian.[39] Beginning in the 1930s, practitioners of socialist realism returned to this tradition and resurrected important elements of it for the purposes of the day.

Together with this full appreciation of the instrumental value of landscape for disseminating a political-artistic vision, the engagement with the natural world in Stalinist art reflected a genuine aesthetic of nature in its own right. This aesthetic rested on a new or renewed vision of the natural world and its relationship to the human realm. At its heart was a sort of dialectical process, which Katerina Clark has described in her insightful work on socialist realist literature.[40] According to the Russian reading of Marx, under socialism and eventually communism humankind is elevated to become the conqueror of the natural world. Stalinism, however, brought out a subtle dimension in this proposition that had been lost in the single-mindedness of the 1920s, namely that this conquest can be heroic and truly grand only if that which is being conquered was formidable and grand to begin with. In this way, the natural world was transformed into a kind of yardstick by which communist society measured and evaluated itself, and the magnificence of the former directly reflected and confirmed the magnificence of the latter. This new attitude was reflected in a shift in sensibilities throughout Soviet culture, as what Clark terms the "cult of the machine" of the 1920s was replaced by the "cult of the garden" in the 1930s. "In Soviet literature the natural world began to supplant the machine.... Metaphors from nature began to supplant machine metaphors in the press and in official speeches as well."[41] In Soviet art, the result was an incipient pastoralism, advanced tentatively at first but growing ever more self-confident and emphatic. This did not mean that the theme of the conquest of nature was discarded, but it did involve a far-reaching redefinition of terms, such that this conquest could now be carried out without in any way violating or even affecting the purity, beauty, or harmony of the natural world.

That a dynamic interconnection between nature and socialist society was perceived to be vital in socialist realist art is indicated among other things by the fact that practically no settings were entirely removed from the natural elements. Despite the explosive growth of cities during this period,[42] explicitly urban themes were never very popular, and there are similarly extremely few paintings of industry set *inside* a factory. Only pictures depicting great leaders directing indoor political assemblies were consistent exceptions. In socialist realism nature acquired a central importance, to which was attached a degree of positive glory. From this standpoint, the turn back to the landscape traditions of the nineteenth century was not as purely instrumental and opportunistic as it might appear, for the earlier period had similarly endeavored to depict the glorious qualities of Russia's natural world. It had not been preoccupied, to be sure, with the Marxist-modernist notion of the conquest and control of natural elements, but insofar as Stalinist culture itself was capable of considerable ambivalence on this point, it did not present a major obstacle.[43]

Socialist realism never represented and was never restricted to a single artistic style or mode of representation. Its purpose was didactic, and it could tolerate a broad range of different subjects and styles, providing they were ideologically effective and conformed to its minimal requirements for "realism" and social-political engagement. As a text on the Soviet theory of art proclaimed in 1950, "the ideal of socialist realism lies not in any artistic norm, but in the real, practical reconstruction of life. . . . Soviet art has no aims other than the aims of the people, no ideals other than those of the Bolshevik Party."[44] Landscape and the natural world, accordingly, were represented across a range of genres. Out of these, four in particular may be identified as exemplifying the way in which nature was utilized and ideologized.

INDUSTRIAL CONSTRUCTION

In spite of the absolute precedence that the drive to industrialize took over every other endeavor throughout Stalin's peacetime reign, the theme of industrialization presented a problem for realization in socialist realist art. The problem was threefold. To begin with, the construction of factories and hydroelectric dams, the laying of railway tracks, installation of electrical cables, and so on were the most obvious demonstrations possible of the straightforward conquest of nature, and while entirely legitimate in their own right, these themes allowed less room than others for bringing out the complex nuances of the relationship between Soviet society and the natural world that socialist realism required. Moreover, the fact that industry in some form was in the process of being constructed at all logically meant that it was not yet fully in place and functioning, which in turn meant that Soviet society was not yet fully developed and had not achieved the communist ideal. This latter point was a subtle one, to be sure, and not really problematic as long as the prospect of developed communism still officially lay at least partially in the future, but by the middle of the 1930s this moment had passed. Finally, industrial construction and development was inherently a dynamic and transformative process, qualities that did not easily fit with the growing insistence in socialist realism on stasis in Soviet society. All of this did not mean that industrialization as such was neglected, but it does help to explain the fact that it formed neither as large nor as significant a category in socialist realist art overall as might have been expected in view of the clear political and economic priority accorded the process.

A peculiar result of these tensions can be seen in Arkadii Rylov's *Tractor at the Logging Site* (1934) (fig. 11.1). Rylov, who had trained under Kuindzhi in the 1890s, was one of those landscape painters of the pre-Revolutionary school who were eclipsed during the 1920s and to whom socialist realism offered new, if highly circumscribed and carefully dictated opportunities. The deadpan tone of the picture's title is misleading, for what is depicted is in fact a stunning view of a pristine and snowy coniferous forest of the Russian *taiga*, with the brilliant sunlight playing in the boughs of a tree in the foreground. The two tractors winding their way through the center of the scene are partially obscured, and we have no view of that part of the forest that has been obliterated in order to obtain the mass of felled tree trunks that they drag in train behind them. The

Fig. 11.1 Tractor at the Logging Site, A. Rylov, 1934. Reproduced from a small poster, published by Sovetskii Khudozhnik (Moscow) in 1984.

painting conveys no sense whatsoever of struggle or conflict between the natural environment and the human activity which is in fact transforming it. Quite to the contrary, the message is one of almost undisturbed harmony, as if industrial development and the construction of socialism—represented in this case by the simple presence of tractors in a forest—could itself be a thoroughly pastoral and natural affair. This impression is enhanced by the fact that the sunlight dances serenely on the dead and stripped logs as well as the living forest. Indeed, the beauty and peace of the forest scene serves to beautify and perhaps even legitimize the industrial activity; again, the fact that the process of logging actually destroys the forest is not a part of the painter's conception.

The manner in which the natural world could be depicted so as to lend powerful enhancement to the process of industrialization is exemplified in a celebrated picture by Serafima Riangina entitled *Higher and Higher*

(1934) (fig. 11.2). The picture depicts a man and woman laying electrical cables up the side of a high mountain. They are pictured on a ladder, their expectant and satisfied faces turned upward, striving with their cables toward the very summit of the range. The great yawning height of the mountains and the drama of the summit that the pair is approaching are all symbolic of the resplendent heights of the communist order being built in the country at the time. The neat row of pylons visible in an alpine valley in the background of the picture testifies to the fact that the mountains are being "conquered" by industrial activity, but at the same time the natural grandeur of the latter is quite undiminished. It serves to reinforce positively the splendid quality of the industrial and social achievement. The same dynamic interaction between industrialization and the natural world is apparent in K.D. Trokhimenko's "Workers of the Dneper Hydroelectric Station"(1937) (fig. 11.3). A brigade of four

Fig. 11.2 *Ever Higher*, S. Riangina, 1934. A. G. Fedotova, *Zhivopis' pervoi piatiletki*. Khudozhnik i vremia (Moscow, 1981), Plate 90.

a shovel, a primitive saw, and an axe. With this rudimentary equipment—ludicrously inappropriate for the massive engineering project in question—and their unmistakably peasant origins, the artist sought to reduce the workers to the same undeveloped and pristine level as the yet-to-be-tamed river itself, and in so doing to appropriate for them some of its own unadulterated elemental power.[45] Invoking what Katerina Clark has termed "the neo-primitivism of Stalinist political culture," Trokhimenko's picture suggests that the coming assault upon the river would be a true *stikhiinyi*, or elemental meeting of equals.[46] To be sure, the eventual outcome was not in question, but the source of the workers' victory would come not so much from modern technology as from their own primal-natural strengths.

The art of late Stalinism was even more obsessed than the pre-war period with the challenge of reducing dynamism and slowing the movement of time. The picture *On the Great Stalinist Construction Site* (1951) gives some indication of how even the depiction of industrial activity could be manipulated toward this end. The picture was painted by the "brigade" method popular after the war, in which a team of artists worked together on different parts of a single painting.[47] In this case six individuals joined their efforts under the direction of Pavel Sokolov-Skalia. The picture shows a massive construction site on the banks of a river, presumably the preliminary phase in the construction of a hydroelectric dam. A large group working on the site is depicted, but quite unlike the pictures just noted, this group is arranged in terms of a very carefully indicated social-political hierarchy. The hierarchy centers on three principal characters: the leader of the work team (young, strong, and vital, clad in a simple T-shirt), the engineer-technician (with eyeglasses, a necktie, and white coat), and the party representative (in the classic cap and buttoned-up tunic of an agitator). The motion and activity logically inherent in the scene cannot be entirely eliminated, but the presence of the three main characters works effectively to channel and control it, as the

workers fills the foreground, with a wintry Dneper river and broad Ukrainian sky occupying the rest of the canvas. A small building of some sort can be seen in the distance, apparently a base of operations for the project, but the actual construction of the dam has not yet begun, and the still-pristine state of the river is underscored by the presence of a herd of horses milling on its banks. The landscape conveys a sense of boundless expanse and the power of the elements, once again enhancing the quality of the human undertaking to bring them under its control. Significantly, the brigade of workers is pictured in traditional native attire, and the only tools they carry are those to be found in a peasant hut—

Fig. 11.3 *Workers at the Dniepr Hydroelectric Station*, K. Trokhimenko, 1937. *Gosudarstvennyi muzei ukrainskogo izobrazitel'nogo iskusstva USSR. Al'bom* (Kiev, 1971), Plate 75.

rest of the individuals all orient themselves toward and center their attention upon this trinity. Hardly a move is made without a glance at the leader, or at least a glance at someone glancing in that direction. The landscaping of the scene, which places the site on a vast natural bend in the river's banks against a backdrop of graceful bluffs overlooking the water, skillfully manages to insert the construction site into the inherent natural majesty of the waterway, and in so doing goes some way to appropriate the latter's timelessness for the social activity.

AGRICULTURE AND THE COLLECTIVE FARM

In contrast to industrial motifs, rural settings and agricultural pursuits were ideal for illustrating the sort of qualities that socialist realism sought to emphasize. The agricultural countryside was an arena in which modernization and industrialization—indicated vari-

ously by mechanized farm equipment, evenly and neatly plowed fields, indications of electrification, or modern Soviet clothing—could both be depicted without rupturing the impression of an organic and healthy connection between rural Soviet society and the land. Nor, it must be said, did the circumstance that in the 1930s the countryside was actually the locus of the worst ravaging, famine, and mass decimation of human life in the USSR present any particular problem for the ideological manipulation of the image. The positive potentialities were clearly brought out in Sergei Gerasimov's famous *A Collective Farm Festival* (1936–37). In this picture, a large group from the farm is enjoying a picnic. Political authority in the picture is represented by the presence of a local political agitator, to whom the group pays calm but rapt attention. The recent mechanization of the countryside is signaled not (as was customary) through the image of a tractor or combine harvester but rather by the presence of a bicycle in the foreground. The group is large and diverse, the table is lavishly decked, the faces are uniform mirrors of joy and happiness, and the entire scene breathes an atmosphere of easy leisure, satisfaction, and harmony. This mood is brilliantly amplified by the location of the group in the midst of the rolling and lushly fertile meadows of the Russian countryside, bathed in the bright summer sunshine. The social and ideological harmony between the individual *kolkhozniki* is palpably intensified by the ease with which they blend as a whole into the natural landscape.

This image of a rural cornucopia—what Vladimir Papernyi aptly termed an "agricultural pathos of fertility and productivity"[48]—was a popular one in Russia, and it spread rapidly to the non-Russian republics as well. This can be seen in the picture *A Collective Farm* Toi *[Festival]*" (1937) by the artist A. K. Kasteev. Here as well, the themes of beneficent Communist authority, material abundance, and profound social harmony are portrayed, now with a distinctive national emphasis as some people drink kumis out of bowls while others watch a performance of native folk dances. The mechanization of agriculture is more deliberately depicted here than in Gerasimov's painting, in the form of two large harvesters, several trucks, and an automobile, but again the entire human scene is situated harmoniously within a larger panorama of the expansive green fields hazily bordered by mountains looming gently in the background. Together, festival and landscape form one unitary and profoundly pastoral entity. If the "conquest" of nature is being depicted in these two pictures, then it certainly represents something quite different from the conventional image.

An interesting variation on the collective farm motif can be seen in Taras Gaponenko's famous *To Dine with the Mothers* (1935). A brigade of women working in the fields takes a break as a wagon arrives carrying their young babies. The women crowd around the wagon, as it is time to feed them. A woman and a man occupy one side of the foreground, the man tossing the child happily in the air as the woman fingers the top button of her heavy blouse, obviously about to get on with the business of nursing. The picture plays on a number of different themes. On the one hand, the group of young mothers and babies, and in particular the anticipation of one mother's breast about to be bared, is a subtle but powerful enhancement of the image of fertility and abundant nourishment with which socialist realism endeavored to associate the countryside and by extension all of Soviet society. This same image was evoked more prosaically in pictures such as Gerasimov's by the prospect of tables groaning under mountains of food. Moreover, by associating work in the fields so deliberately with breast-feeding—some of the mothers have not yet put down their field implements—*To Dine with the Mothers* sought to imbue the former activity with some of the organic wholesomeness and naturalness of the latter. In this connection, it is significant to note that the babies were delivered to the field not in a motorized vehicle but in a horse-drawn wagon, although a tractor is visible in the background. Finally, of course, the picture helped articulate the then still-emerging Stalinist view of the place and function of women, with its heavy stress on child-bearing and-rearing (abortions having been banned in 1936), in addition to whatever other activities women might pursue.

The highly uncomplicated ethos of joy, abundance, and harmony in a freshly mechanized and collectivized countryside evoked by these pictures from the 1930s was carried over after 1945 as well. The Ukrainian artist Tatiana Yablonskaia, for example, won a Stalin prize in 1950 for her painting *Grain* (1949) (see fig 11.4), which pictured a group of sturdy, beaming women at harvest time, shoveling a vast shimmering ocean of grain into sacks for shipment on the waiting trucks. *They Are Writing about Us in* Pravda (1951) by Aleksei Vasil'ev depicted a group of young collective farm workers contentedly sharing a fat watermelon on the lush green meadows of the Russian heartland, their motorcycle resting casually in the background. In the work of numerous other artists, however, the image of the countryside underwent a notable trans-

Fig. 11.4 Grain, T. Iablonskaia, 1949. *Iskusstvo Sovetskogo Soiuza* (Leningrad, 1982), p. 544.

formation after 1945. As part of this, the most tangible indications of the profound Soviet transformation of the countryside—the mechanization and modernization of agricultural life—began to recede and fall away. In painting after painting, trucks, combine harvesters, bicycles, T-shirts, and silverware evaporated from the collective farm landscape, replaced by hoes, horse-drawn carts, *rubashki* or traditional peasant shirts, and wooden spoons, all of which served as an unmistakable indication that even the precious fruits of industrialization were ultimately expendable for the politico-aesthetic project of socialist realism. Stasis had become an absolute priority, and the authors of the pictures realized that the best way to stop time was to eliminate all signs of change and effectively embed the present and the future firmly in the past, and the best way to accomplish the latter was to embed the entire scene as deeply and inextricably as possible in the natural world. Images of a smoking tractor or a sleek party representative could never foster a sense of transcendence and eternity, but a scythe, a crude earthen jug, or a flowing beard certainly could.

The new model image, exemplified by pictures such as Arkadii Plastov's *Haymaking* (1945), Fyodor Shurpin's *Resurrection* (1945), or Aleksandr Bubnov's *Corn* (1948), was that of traditionally clad laborers working with hand tools in an unkempt agricultural environment, with none of the neatly divided fields and even, well-ploughed furrows that so clearly betokened mechanization. The mood of glib and simpleminded joy that was characteristic in the 1930s vanished as well, replaced by a more genuine feeling of tranquility, harmony with the natural elements, and modest contentment. This is particularly true in those pictures such as Plastov's *Harvest* (1945) (fig. 11.5), which depict families eating together in the fields. This scene is hardly that of the extravagant collective farm picnic of an earlier decade—Plastov's family eats with crude wooden spoons in the traditional fashion out of a single common pot, and in the absence of proper glasses a young boy drinks directly from an earthen jug—but there is a serenity in the picture nonetheless. This serenity, indeed, is powerful, but there are at least two aspects in all of these scenes which rupture their idyllic atmosphere and insure that they have not been removed entirely from the flow of time. The most striking

Fig. 11.5 Harvest, A. Plastov, 1945. *Iskusstvo Sovetskogo Soiuza* (Leningrad, 1982), p. 440.

is the fact that only children, women, and elderly people are featured, a silent but powerful statement about the demographic legacy of the war for Soviet society which would not have been missed by any viewer. The second aspect is the fact that although the most obvious signs of the "Sovietization" of the countryside are by and large gone, subtle indications remain, most commonly the gratuitous use of the color red for some central object, often a girl's dress, kerchief, or hair ribbon.[49] In spite of these elements, however, these rural scenes from post-war art moved socialist realism significantly closer to the creation of a full pastoral utopia, a goal that was pursued deliberately in another genre to be considered below.

THE BODY IN STALINIST ART

A very effective motif through which socialist realism could establish the positive connection of Soviet society with the natural world had nothing to do with landscape per se, and instead involved carefully stylized depictions of the human form. The "naturalness" of the body was brought out in a familiar fashion by stressing qualities of health, energy, fitness, and spontaneous beauty, all of which were mobilized so as to reflect upon and enhance various aspects of the Soviet project itself. Healthful and fit bodies could help eternalize the Stalinist present, for like the Russian countryside itself they possessed a quality that was transcendental. Indeed, the human form offered a sort of double opportunity for capturing timelessness. On the one hand, its biological and anatomical characteristics constituted an organic natural entity and thus could not be exclusively situated either historically or socially. At the same time, however, depictions of the body could suggest parallels with and even establish connections back to classical periods of antiquity. The "creation of an eternal link to the past" was a device pursued to great effect by the artists of the Third Reich, who sought to create out of the Olympian bodies of Greek and Roman art the prototype of the "New German,"[50] and the Russians used such a link for their own purposes as well. A particularly effective example is Aleksandr Samokhvalov's *Woman Metro-Builder with a Pneumatic Drill* (1937). The form of a fair-haired young woman fills the picture, taking a rest with her drill held casually in her hand. Her torso is clothed in a light T-shirt, and thus her gracefully powerful shoulders and trim muscular body are clearly visible, accented in particular by a line of taut muscle across her abdomen. Not content with this rather labored infusion of blonde health and fitness into the daily routine of Moscow's working class, however, the artist has gone further. Some sort of heavy protective cloth is draped around her broad hips, and it falls around the lower part of her body in graceful folds that are easily reminiscent of the flowing robes of Greek and Roman sculptures. This classical allusion is enhanced by the fact that although her body faces the viewer directly, her face is turned in a striking profile. Bown has referred to this figure as a prototype for the "New Soviet Woman": we may go further and see in Samokhvalov's picture the attempt to create a veritable proletarian Athena.[51]

The most common thematic context for presenting the body was that of *fizkul'tura* or physical education. In a telling parallel to Nazi Germany, physical fitness and mass athletics became something of an obsession for Soviet society during the 1930s.[52] As in Germany, bodily fitness was celebrated for the qualities of self-discipline, teamwork, and control that it purportedly fostered in its practitioners.[53] At the same time, by developing the natural strengths and physiological potentials of the human organism, *fizkul'tura* offered another way of demonstrating how the new Soviet society nurtured a salubrious bond between the individual and the natural world. In contrast to the stern and generally masculine physical perfection of German representations, however, the prototype of preference for this role in Stalinist art was what might best be called the amateur athlete:

someone in obviously highly trained physical condition but a proletarian "from the ranks" nonetheless. In many paintings, socialist realist artists created archetypes of such amateurs, commonly female and almost uniformly fair-complexioned and blonde. Numerous examples can be seen in other pictures by Samokhvalov, such as *Girl in a Football Jersey* (1932) and *Girl Athlete* (1933), or in Sergei Luchishkin's *Keep Fit, Girls* (a panel from his pentaptych *Constitution Days* [1932]). The identification of the wholesomeness of the fit Soviet body with the wholesomeness of the natural world is brought out quite explicitly in Aleksandr Deineka's *Freedom* (1944). The picture depicts a group of athletic young women in sports dress running in a competition through the countryside. Some are ascending the bank of a broad river that, along with the open sky, fills the background, while others have cleared the bank and emerged onto a grassy meadow in the foreground. Sunshine drenches the entire scene, and there is a palpable feeling of harmony between the breathless and healthy activity of the girls and the tranquillity of the landscape across which they are racing.

Although socialist realism did not follow fascist Germany in the frequent depiction of the naked body, nudity figured nonetheless in Stalinist art, and indeed it played a significant role as part of the ideological symbology we are considering.[54] The painting *Tractor Drivers* (1943) by Arkadii Plastov is a telling example. Like the rest of Plastov's work that we have noted, this picture depicts a collective farm scene, but the subject is rather different. In the foreground runs a small stream, and standing on its sandy bank two young women have taken off their clothes, preparing for a dip. An unattended tractor idling in the background to the right indicates that they are taking a break from their morning work. Their healthy, glowing, and apparently spur-of-the-moment nudity, together with the bucolic prospect of the lazy stream, generate a contrast of sorts with the tractor, a contrast amplified by the presence of a traditional horse-drawn cart balancing off the tractor in the background to the left. There is a suggestion here of a challenge or at least a contrast to the cult of mechanization in favor the purer qualities of organic nature, represented among other things by the naked body. As a rule, nudity in socialist realism was associated with leisure; even when naked soldiers were the subject, as in Deineka's *After Battle* (1944), they were depicted not in stern and commanding poses but rather relaxing in the shower. Nudity as a temporary release from the rhythm of work forms the theme another picture by Deineka, *Lunch-Break in the Donbas* (1935). A group of male workers have taken off their clothes and are frolicking with a large ball in the river. In the background, along the distant bank, a smoking train rushes along drawing cars of coal or iron ore. The natural vigor, dynamism, and virtue of their blonde trim bodies at joyful play is obviously intended to enhance and even anthropomorphize the more serious motion of the train, and by extension the process of industrialization itself. Dmitrii Zhilinskii's *The Bridge Builders* (1959) is nearly identical in conception, depicting a group of naked and tanned workers splashing in the water with a large inner tube, framed against their construction site that rises off a bridge in the background.

A STALINIST PASTORAL

Although socialist realism sought from its inception to establish clear connections with pre-Revolutionary traditions in Russian art, its borrowings from the earlier period were extremely eclectic. In regard to depictions of the natural world, Stalinist art of the 1930s co-opted many elements of the late-nineteenth-century genre of landscape painting but at the same time remained critical of the genre itself and was unwilling to embrace it fully. The reasons for this reluctance are easy enough to appreciate. It is obvious that traditional scenes of the Russian countryside with its birch forests, lethargic rivers, vast expanses, and stalwart but unmodernized peasantry could hardly convey the essential elements of the Stalinist utopia as it was being articulated in the era of the first Five-Year

Plans. The successful birth of a "new reality" had to be confirmed, and regardless of the fact that in the final analysis this Soviet reality was supposed to fit quite as harmoniously with the natural world as had the Russia of landscapists such as Levitan and Shishkin, its precise contents could not but differ. Depictions of magnificent alpine heights, in other words, were acceptable only if dotted with electrical pylons, and snowy scenes of the wild *taiga* had to be dissected by a string of tractors. Representation of landscapes that did not contain some clear and positive evidence of the new order were roundly criticized by the watchdogs of socialist realism for a lack of social engagement. It was more than likely that the stubborn authors of these sorts of traditional non-Stalinist landscapes in the 1930s—artists such as Aleksandr Morozov and Nikolai Krymov—were in fact seeking to avoid their political-aesthetic "responsibilities" to the Soviet state.[55]

This rejection of landscape art melted away virtually overnight as part of the sea change in Stalinist ideology and propaganda precipitated by the outbreak of war. In view of the need to mobilize the population physically and psychologically to meet the extraordinary demands of a desperate war effort, the government was prepared to discard the Soviet "filter" and appeal directly to nationalist-patriotic sentiments of devotion to the Russian homeland. This went even to the extent of tolerating a revival of the Orthodox church. In view of these exigencies, the artistic legacy of pre-Revolutionary Russia became even more useful and relevant for the purposes of socialist realism than it had been up to this point. The landscape genre of Russian art in the nineteenth century had developed as part of a broad nationalist movement. One of its fundamental objectives was to deliver characteristic representations that could serve as pictorial archetypes, a process of envisioning Russia through painted images which gave expression to the patriotic feelings of the artist and were intended to inspire viewers in their attachment to the homeland. This sort of articulated nationalist-nativist dimension was at odds with the spirit of the 1930s, but it was precisely what became necessary after 1940. Formerly a politically suspect refuge for artists unwilling to engage the noble task of glorifying the construction of socialism, the "unfiltered" depiction of the Russian landscape now became something of a thematic priority.

In January 1942 a major exhibition of landscape paintings entitled "Landscape of our Motherland" opened in Moscow and proved to be enormously popular. Two months later, in March, a Stalin Prize was awarded to Vasilii Baksheev, a celebrated painter of *berezka* forests whose work in the 1920s and 1930s showed the undiluted influence of the *peredvizhniki* Vasilii Polenov and Aleksei Savrasov, under whom he studied in the 1880s. Baksheev went on to receive the Order of the Red Banner of Labor in the following year.[56]

A picture by Arkadii Plastov, *A Fascist Plane Flew Over* (1942) (fig. 11.6) provides an example of how the themes of Russian landscape and war could be combined. A unkempt open field fills most of the picture, while a small birch grove occupies part of the background. This is a traditional country scene: a number of wild animals wander across the field, and although a lone haystack in the distance indicates some sort of farming activity there is no sign of the technological or social reorganization of agriculture under the Soviets. A prostrate and apparently lifeless figure is sprawled in the front corner of the picture, with a small splash of red on his head indicating what must be a fatal wound. Faintly in the receding sky, an airplane is flying away, obviously having just killed the Russian peasant. A dog at the dead man's side howls mournfully. The picture's primary purpose is to illustrate the rapacious nature of the German aggressors, but it does so not by having them destroy a major railway hub, a water reservoir, hydroelectric station, or munitions factory—any of which would have been a far more likely and devastating target—but rather by rupturing the peaceful and deep serenity of the Russian land with a single carefully aimed bullet.

In Nikolai Romadin's *The Herd* (1944), by contrast, there is no suggestion at all that war is ravaging the country. It is a simple landscape, which shows a scattered herd of cows grazing across a wild meadow. A stream and its sandy bank can be seen in the background. Not only is there no sign of the Soviet transformation, there is no human presence whatsoever. Entirely in the spirit and tradition of the nineteenth century, the elemental virtues of the Russian nation are signaled here by subtle association with the innate qualities of the natural environment, and the fact that such a scene could be depicted several decades after the revolution confirms that these national qualities were as resilient as ever. In 1946, Romadin was honored with a Stalin prize for a series of wartime landscapes entitled *The Volga: A Russian River*.

Quite unlike the official toleration of the Orthodox church, which proved to be ephemeral and did not survive the end of the war, landscape painting was endorsed in the late Stalin period and entered into the socialist realist pantheon of accepted and respected genres. Freed from the overriding imperative of mobilization for the war effort, the pictures often became more stylized, formal, and majestic (or at any rate grandiose). The stylistic continuities with the work of nineteenth-century artists became more pronounced, to the point that in some cases it was extremely difficult to identify anything in the Stalinist landscape to distinguish it from one produced before the Revolution. This circumstance could conceivably be taken as an abandonment of socialist realism altogether, in practice if not in name, but such a conclusion does not take into account the changes in the ideological climate in the late 1940s and early 1950s. From the moment that Stalin raised a toast at the war's end to the Russian people as "the greatest of the Soviet nations," it was clear that the glorification of the Great Russian ethos would continue in some form as a leading ideological theme. There was no lack of celebration of the *vsesoiuznyi* Soviet accomplishment, to be sure, but at the same time the particular qualities of Russia as a nation—its language, history, military traditions, and so on—became a subject of con-

Fig. 11.6 A Fascist Plane Flew Over, A. Plastov, 1942. *Iskusstvo Sovetskogo Soiuza* (Leningrad, 1982), p. 432.

stant praise and even adulation. The glories of Russia's natural environment represented an important expression of these qualities. Thus, the persistence and even intensification of landscape art did not in fact signal a departure of any sort from the strictures of socialist realism. It indicated rather the continued faithful compliance with a set of official ideological priorities which had themselves changed notably since the 1930s.

In one regard in particular, Russian pastoral art after 1945 not only continued to pursue an important function of socialist realism in the 1930s but was able to achieve a certain consummation not possible before. The point has been made above that as part of its striving for the immortalization of the Soviet order, Stalinist art had sought from the outset to "conquer" time. *Fizkul'tura* festivals and collective-farm arcadias, to say nothing of industrialization itself, could at best be only partial means to this end. In depictions of the Russian landscape, however, socialist realism finally located a near-perfect means for accomplishing this task. Aleksandr Gritsai's *A Stormy Day in Zhiguli* (1948–1950), for example, is composed entirely in the grand style of traditional depictions of the Volga by Repin and others. Its emphasis is on the immensity of the river, the rocky bluffs rising out of its banks, and the vastness of the Russian sky which frames the entire scene. The link backward to pre-Revolutionary antecedents is subtly but effectively enhanced by the artist's decision to depict a rainy day, for while in the nineteenth century the use of turbulent elements was a common romantic device with which to bring out the innate *Sturm und Drang* of the natural world, socialist realist art unswervingly preferred bright and undisturbed sunshine. Indeed, with the exception of so-called "leader art," or paintings depicting the persona of various Soviet heroes, there are practically no pictures in which the weather is noticeably inclement, a circumstance understandable in view of the uses of the natural world described in this essay.[57]

In Gritsai's painting, however, heavy dark clouds billow ominously, and the water of the river foams white with agitation. The only sign of human presence is a lone grey boat on the waves, dwarfed by the immensity of the river. Upon inspection, we can see that it is apparently a barge from the Soviet period, but in marked contrast to the combine harvesters, turbines, bicycles, high-tension electrical cables, radios, and other technological paraphernalia enthusiastically featured in the art of the 1930s, there is nothing very "new" about this vessel. The artist has given us almost nothing in this picture to tell us exactly *when* it is supposed to be situated—or rather, he is telling us that the scene is located simultaneously in different periods, in the Soviet present as well as the eternal Russian past. As a result, the deliberate effect of timelessness comes across very powerfully. Gritsai, it should be stressed, was in no way exceeding official guidelines in producing this picture. His work was blessed with official commendation at the highest levels, and for this picture in particular he was awarded a Stalin prize in 1951. Nor was he tied exclusively to landscape art. Like all loyal socialist realist painters, he was prepared to accommodate the full range of thematic needs determined by the party, as indicated by the fact that he received the prize again in 1952 for supervising a brigade painting entitled *A Meeting of the Presidium of the Academy of Sciences*. Landscape art, to repeat, had become normalized within the framework of Stalinist art.

An even more remarkable attempt to articulate a timeless Soviet pastoral can be seen in Vasilii Yakovlev's *Svistukha* (1948). The picture presents a bucolic country scene, with rolling meadows and fields stretching far off into the background, where they meet the broad Russian sky at the horizon. The foreground is occupied by a peasant farm, where the human presence is not incidental as in Gritsai's Volga but rather the central focus of the picture. In all respects, Yakovlev's farm is a positive archetype of the typical Russian homestead. The spacious wooden house can obviously accommodate the family comfortably, and while the house has a well-worn look about it—the roof has been extensively (but carefully) patched—altogether the scene makes a sturdy and even cozy impression. The fences are uneven and appear to be a bit rickety, but in fact their unevenness allows them to follow the rolling contours of the landscape naturally and faithfully, and thus they enhance the impression of the farm's close fit into the natural world. A smiling woman has just finished milking a cow, her daughter is playing with a goat in the yard, in front of the house a man carries buckets in the traditional manner on a pole slung across his shoulder, and other members of the family are visible on the porch and in the windows. The picture depicts a total rural idyll, which breathes an atmosphere of wholesomeness, tranquillity, and quiet prosperity.

There is only one vaguely discordant feature in Yakovlev's painting. Even more than *A Stormy Day in Zhiguli*, *Svistukha* is resolutely ambivalent as to when it is supposed to be situated. The entirely unmechanized and apparently noncollective character of the homestead suggests at first that the scene predates the Revolution. We have seen, however, that since the early days of World War II, socialist realism had been busy removing tractors and T-shirts from the Soviet countryside and reintroducing horse-drawn carts, hand implements, traditional clothing, and traditional agricultural relations. From this standpoint, there is really nothing in the picture to prevent it from being intended as a contemporary Soviet scene as well. Indeed, in the same way that socialist realist paintings of the 1930s evoked a positive image of Soviet agricultural life through the harmony of the agricultural collective and the material abundance of the farm, so *Svistukha* evokes the same image in a more subdued way through the suggestion of enduring family ties and a harmony with the eternal rhythms of the natural landscape. The point is that we are not able to date this scene. The artist's attempt to eternalize the scene is successful. Finally, in this painting we are confronted with one of the major paradoxes of Stalinist art. The same socialist realism which during the 1930s sought above all else to demonstrate the presence and effect of the Soviet transformation in every aspect of national life had by the end of the next decade begun to produce works that strove to obliterate all indication of this very transformation. In either case, however, we should note that socialist realism's instrumental function—to bring out the "beauty" of putative Soviet reality—remained unchanged.

In conclusion, let us note the considerable disparity in the Soviet experience between the aesthetic ideology of socialist realism and actual practice in regard to the natural world. The point was made at the outset that the prospect of the modernization and industrial development that Soviet communism was determined to bring to the country was founded on the belief in the virtually unlimited ability of a socialist society to transform its environment. This remained a unquestioned article of faith down to the 1980s at least, and in all events was absolutely axiomatic during the Stalinist period considered here, when it not only underlay the industrialization goals and norms of the Five-Year Plans but engendered a variety of grandiose and fantastic schemes of environmental transformation as well.

All of this activity, however, coexisted apparently quite harmoniously with the efforts of socialist realism to evoke a picture of Soviet society as "nature-friendly," non-destructive, and even loving of the natural environment. This paradox can be seen most clearly in the late Stalin period, at which time a thoroughly pastoral and bucolic view of the Russian nation such as Yakovlev's *Svistukha* was successfully appealing to the same public imagination that was supposed to be stirred by the contemporaneous unveiling of the "Great Stalin Plan for the Transformation of Nature." This disparity—which may be noted in fascist Germany as well—forms a problem requiring further investigation; for the moment it may be taken as an indication of the profound complexity of social views of the natural environment, as well as the tight interconnectedness of these views with most fundamental preoccupations of the society.

12 The Rise and Fall of Stalinist Architecture

Andrew Day

ARCHITECTS AND THE STALIN REGIME

Historians of Soviet architecture tell us that during the reign of Communist Party General Secretary Joseph Stalin, architects occupied a privileged place among the country's artists and professionals.[1] These scholars agree that throughout this era, architects had an exceptionally close relationship to the Party-state's leaders, who took a direct hand in shaping their designs, spent extravagantly to carry out their grandest projects, and rewarded them handsomely for their compliant contributions to the "construction of socialism."[2] According to scholarly consensus, this relationship was unique, and an examination of its features reveals a great deal about the way the Stalin system worked.

But curiously, those who have studied it make little effort to explain its origins—they seem simply to assume that lavishing power, money, and prestige on architects is a natural tendency of regimes of the Stalin sort.[3] They also pay little attention to explaining how it worked in practice, or to specifying its effects on particular projects, beyond repeating well-worn, unsubstantiated anecdotes about Stalin's supposed contribution to the Moscow Hotel project, and Moscow Party chief Lazar Kaganovich's alleged reworking of the design for the Red Army Theater.[4] Nor do they offer any account of the reasons for architecture's sudden decline in status—by the early 1950s, architects played little role in designing most buildings, and had been removed from positions of authority over planning and urban-development matters—treating this as the natural consequence of Stalin's death in 1953.

Why do these scholars show so little interest in looking at these questions in any detail? There seem to be two reasons. First, they follow established architectural history convention, focusing on the formal analysis of individual masterworks while devoting much less attention to these works' production and the context in which it took place. Second, they hold to the curious view that under Stalin, architects and politician-patrons played less of a role in shaping the built environment than did the abstract force (which they call either "totalitarianism," "Stalinism," or "Culture 2")[5] that, in their opinion, determined the political and cultural character of the era. When making pronouncements about what should be built and where, they suggest, politicians were merely giving voice to this force's needs,[6] while architects did little more than translate these utterances into built form. Neither process, they imply, involved or even

For their thoughtful comments and suggestions on this piece, I would like to thank Arthur McKee, David Engerman, Mark Johnson, Peter Holquist, and Mark von Hagen, as well as the other participants in the "Architecture and the Expression of Group Identity in Russia" conference, particularly Emma Widdis, Robert Crews, and Greg Castillo. For helping me in the course of my research on Stalin-era architecture and urbanism, I am indebted to the staff members of the Russian State Economic Archive (particularly Boris Borisovich Lebedev), the Russian Republic branch of the State Archive of the Russian Federation, the Russian State Archive of Literature and Art, the Russian National Library, and Columbia University's Avery Library. Finally, for providing the financial support that enabled me to carry out this project, I am grateful to the Columbia University Graduate School of Arts and Sciences and the Harriman Institute.

permitted any sort of interpretation. For them, it is almost as though individuals played no role in creating the era's buildings, ensembles, and cityscapes, the plans for which descended, fully formed, from on high, and then were quickly and completely executed without significant human intervention.

Closer examination reveals that the Stalin-era Soviet-built environment was shaped by design and patronage decisions that were the product of complex, dynamic, and often contentious interactions, both among architects competing for support for their projects, and between architects and their politician patrons. The evidence also shows that the architecture profession was neither raised high by Stalin's accession to power, nor brought low by his death. Rather, these shifts in fortune were largely the result of architects' initial success, and later failure, at carrying out a series of projects that politicians considered particularly important; another key factor was the regime's decision, in the late 1940s, radically to reshape its urban planning and development policy.

It appears, then, that there was nothing broadly extraordinary about either the relationship between architects and the Stalin regime, or Stalin-era architectural practice. Both did, however, have certain features that were most unusual, and, in fact, uniquely Stalinist—that is, they were unique products of the Stalin-era Soviet socialist project. And an account of their origin and workings can indeed tell us a good deal about that project. To date, however, scholars have neither properly identified them nor correctly explained their broader significance. In endeavoring to do so, it is instructive to examine the history, and prehistory, of one of the period's most celebrated projects: the early postwar effort to build a magnificent new center in the battle-ravaged city of Stalingrad.

THE ROMANCE OF THE BLANK SLATE

On January 31, 1943, Soviet forces captured German Field Marshal Friedrich von Paulus at Stalingrad, effectively bringing to an end months of bitter fighting for control of the city. Hundreds of thousands had been killed, wounded, or taken prisoner in the course of the battle, and the city itself had been almost totally destroyed, having borne the brunt of several onslaughts by German forces trying desperately to break through to the Volga. A little more than a month after von Paulus's surrender, a census taken by local officials showed that of Stalingrad's 450,000 prewar residents, only 1,515 remained in the city.[7]

Politicians and urban development officials moved quickly to begin rebuilding Stalingrad, the symbolic significance of which was enormous: it was, after all, not only the site of a key victory in the war against the Nazi invader, but also the city of Stalin. Within a few months, almost all the country's leading architects and planners had been put to work drafting rebuilding plans for the city. In May, the People's Commissariat of the Communal Economy (NKKKh), the state body then in charge of urban development policy in the Russian Republic (RSFSR), commissioned preliminary projects from the architects Boris Iofan (the designer of the celebrated but never built Palace of Soviets), Alexei Shchusev (who built Lenin's Mausoleum), and Karo Alabian (the head of the USSR Academy of Architecture), as well as lesser-known specialists working in its own planning department. Regime leaders selected Alabian's project to serve as the basis for further work, and commissioned him to turn it into a new general plan for the city. By midsummer, he had secured the assistance of several other prominent architects, including Viktor Gel'freikh (who had worked with Iofan on the Palace of Soviets project) and Lev Rudnev (the designer of Moscow's Frunze Military Academy).[8] By year's end, he and his team had finished their work, and in February 1944, the RSFSR government approved their plan for use as a blueprint for Stalingrad's reconstruction.[9]

The rapidity with which this plan was drawn up and ratified seemed to augur well for the future of the project, and those involved in it spoke of it with optimism, even excitement. Yes, they agreed, it would be an enormous endeavor, but one that offered a unique opportunity: they would take advantage of the emptiness of the site to create not only a new Stalingrad, but a new kind of city. By this, they meant that they intended to create a city that would be truly "socialist," in the then-standard sense of the term—that is, one whose rational layout, modern infrastructure, and well-designed buildings would make it an efficient productive and administrative center; whose well-appointed apartment houses, parks, and cultural facilities would make it a pleasant place to live; and whose appearance would be so magnificent as to convince visitors and residents of the power and historically progressive nature of the Soviet project.[10]

PREWAR SOVIET ARCHITECTURE AND URBANISM

Not since the era of the First Five-Year Plan (1929–32) had architects, planners, and their politician patrons shown such enthusiasm for the idea that the way to make cities socialist was to build them from the ground up. During these years, the fledgling Soviet regime sponsored the construction of dozens of such cities on virgin sites throughout the Soviet Union, putting most of them next to one of the factories and mines whose output was critical to fulfilling Plan targets. The powerful industrial ministries built the majority of them, often working from comprehensive blueprints drawn up by leading experts in the nascent field of urban planning. With the enthusiastic support of the modernization-obsessed Party-state, these specialists drew up reams of plans that made extensive use of such cutting-edge rationalistic strategies as zoning and comprehensive population density, green space, and transportation planning.[11]

Interest in the new-cities project began to wane somewhat in the early 1930s, when the regime turned its attention to reshaping Moscow in such a way as to make it a symbol of the modernity and power of the Soviet order.[12] At the behest of top politicians, leading planners and architects now devoted much of their energy to developing and ap-

plying a series of techniques for achieving the "socialist reconstruction" of existing urban areas. Early on, many specialists (including such foreigners as Le Corbusier) argued that the only way to make such cities truly rational was to raze and then rebuild them.[13] But this strategy met with official rejection. By this point, politician-patrons had become markedly less enthusiastic about demiurgic, scientistic urban planning, in part because of the practical difficulties involved in carrying out many of the projects drawn up by its adherents, and in part because they had begun to heed the arguments of some architects and planners (particularly the members of the recently formed All-Union Society of Proletarian Architects, or VOPRA) that buildings and cityscapes crafted in accord with abstract-rational criteria, rather than historical aesthetic standards, were "alien" or even "anti-Soviet," because such designs ignored local traditions, the celebration of which regime leaders had recently begun to sponsor.[14] They had also begun to come around to the view that much of cities' existing built environments should be preserved, not only because leveling and rebuilding them seemed unfeasible, but also because doing so would help to protect the Soviet "cultural heritage," which, in keeping with the regime's new enthusiasm for local tradition, was now considered to include much that was created in the pre-1917 period. Socialist reconstruction, they maintained, should not entail razing existing cities but should aim to improve them, by making them more beautiful, expanding and integrating their transportation networks, and adding new, modern housing and administrative and cultural facilities.[15]

Politicians, and architects, and planners in turn nonetheless denied that socialist reconstruction's aims were anything less than radical. While much would be preserved, they claimed, cities would still be transformed. Every decision about what to build and what to keep would be taken in accord with the strictures of comprehensive plans, drawn up by specialists whom the regime had empowered to ignore such "subjective" factors as unexamined tradition and the caprice of landholders,[16] and to heed only "objective" technical criteria in their work. Once these plans had been completed, the Soviet state would implement them rapidly, completely, and in coordinated fashion. As a result, planning would effectively enable blank-slate development even in existing cities. Working together, planners, architects, and political leaders would turn every city into a completely integrated ensemble, rational in its every aspect, and thus a monument to the power and progressive character of total, centralized, and historically conscious political-administrative authority, and, in this, a sine qua non symbol of Soviet socialism. Such was this system's power that socialist reconstruction—like its inspiration, the ongoing effort to use planning to transform the country's economy—could fail only if subverted from within, by "wreckers," the Bolshevik project's hidden enemies, whom the regime would neutralize by ferreting out and punishing them as traitors.[17]

Given these assumptions, it is not surprising that those whom the regime put in charge of socialist reconstruction sought to impress their superiors by making concerted use of strategies that had the most immediate and visible effects. Three techniques were particularly popular, and were widely used even in cities whose general plans had not yet been completed. Local officials sponsored the carving of broad, straight avenues through older, down-at-the-heels districts, and also the wholesale razing of churches, private homes, and other buildings deemed symbolic of outmoded ideals. They commissioned architects to fill in the gaps with magnificent new political-administrative and residential complexes, which were universally historicist in appearance (modernism was now considered emblematic of an alien technocratic ideal) and often so large as to be completely out of scale with their surroundings. As to historic preservation, they set aside a select number of older structures to be protected and restored, generally working from recommendations drawn up by architects.[18]

By the late 1930s, such measures had visibly changed Moscow and dozens of other So-

viet cities. All involved in socialist reconstruction hastened to celebrate these changes as a sign of its success—and thus of their own diligence and skill in putting the planning ideal into practice.[19] Their claims, however, were exaggerated. From the outset, socialist reconstruction was hindered by a number of major problems, chief among them the sheer enormity of the task at hand and constant delays caused by politicians who imposed unrealistic and often conflicting imperatives on planners and then changed their demands at the last minute. As a result, by decade's end, planners had finished but a few city general plans,[20] and of the handful that had made their way through the complicated ratification process, most were already outdated, having been outrun by the extraordinarily rapid pace of urbanization.[21] Moreover, officials charged with implementing plans (and, wherever one was lacking, with enforcing various lesser-order controls on development) saw their authority regularly and repeatedly violated, in the main by the Moscow-based ministries and agencies that carried out most construction, and which were politically so powerful as to be able to circumvent or ignore most such strictures.

Planners, architects, and urban-development administrators alike recognized the existence of these problems, and spoke and wrote about them freely, in speeches to various forums and articles in both the professional and general press. Indeed, they tended to supplement their declarations that socialist reconstruction was a resounding success with grumbling about the myriad difficulties they had experienced in trying to carry out particular projects.[22]

This seeming disjuncture can only be understood as a product of the era's schizophrenic political culture. No one dared suggest that socialist reconstruction was less than a resounding success, because to do so would have meant suggesting that the administrative-command ideal, which it supposedly embodied, might be flawed. So whenever a person complained about its problems, he or she presented them as exceptional, and said either that they were the result of mistakes in execution, or, more frequently, that they could be traced to the devious actions of socialism's hidden enemies. By so doing, the complainant was shielded from blame, showed fealty to the administrative-command ideal, and made a show of responding to the regime's demand that all Soviet citizens help ferret out supposedly omnipresent wreckers.[23]

Also by way of responding to this demand, the leaders of NKKKh, the Party's Control Commission, and the Union of Soviet Architects sent special investigative brigades to a number of cities in an effort to determine who was responsible for hindering work on various major socialist reconstruction projects; in this way, they too showed themselves to be vigilant while transferring blame for socialist reconstruction's problems to others. (As a result of these inquisitions, countless officials were fired and countless plans were reworked, which in most instances seems to have delayed rather than sped planning, and to have hindered rather than helped attempts to put tighter controls on development.)[24] For their part, local officials rushed to complete whatever projects they could, with the aim of showing themselves to be moving the socialist reconstruction of their cities aggressively forward. Even more than before, the emphasis was on representation—that is, on showing that cities were being transformed into symbols of Sovietness—and on achieving immediate effect. As a result, politician-patrons became dependent on architects to help them carry out what was still ostensibly a city-planning endeavor, calling on them to design monumental administrative buildings and apartment houses that could be put up in rapid succession on central streets and main squares,[25] and, often, to add new historicist facades to prominent modernist buildings erected only a few years earlier.[26]

ARCHITECTS TO THE FORE

In March of 1939, Stalin put an end to the hunt for wreckers, declaring, in a speech to the Eighteenth Party Congress, that "grave mistakes" had been made in the course of the drive to root out socialism's foes, and that the

regime would "have no further need of resorting to the method of mass purges."[27] No longer compelled to blame socialist reconstruction's problems on careless mistakes and hidden enemies, its stewards began to seek ways to solve them in systematic fashion.

They were particularly concerned to strengthen and centralize administrative control over planning and development. NKKKh, for example, stripped local officials of the authority to develop plans for Stalingrad and Sverdlovsk, placing it in the hands of the Moscow-based State Planning Institute (Giprogor).[28] In various cities, party and state officials vested a single institution or office with the power to regulate planning, building design, and construction; Moscow's city council led the way by creating a new Architecture-Planning Directorate, then putting it in charge of all activity in all these areas.[29] The leaders of NKKKh and the RSFSR State Planning Commission (RSFSR Gosplan), meanwhile, proposed replacing existing republic-level planning organs with a new all-Union ministry-level agency, to be called the Committee on Planning and Urban Construction Affairs, and giving it the power to supervise the drawing up and implementation of all city general plans.[30]

The regime took no action on this proposal in advance of the war's outbreak. But in 1943, with victory seemingly in sight, it was resurrected by several leading planners and architects, who called on the Party-state to launch the rebuilding effort by establishing such an agency. Alabian took the lead on this issue, putting a novel spin on prewar pro-centralization arguments: he suggested that to guarantee rebuilding's practical and aesthetic success, the Party-state should give architects full authority over all aspects of shaping and reshaping the built environment.[31]

In September of 1943, the USSR Council of People's Commissars (SNK), the Soviet government's supreme executive body, created a new agency, the State Committee on Architecture Affairs, that was meant to do just this.[32] In the prewar period, socialist reconstruction's problems had made politicians inordinately dependent on architects in their efforts to transform Soviet cities; now, by setting up the State Committee, the regime moved in effect to formalize this relationship. As Soviet president Mikhail Kalinin explained in an open letter to State Committee president Arkadii Mordvinov, the country's leaders believe that the politico-symbolic imperatives involved in rebuilding were so great that they considered it "essential that this endeavor rest in the cultured hands of architects."[33]

SNK and the State Committee took a series of steps to ensure that this would be the case. Rather than putting a bureaucrat in charge of the new agency, SNK gave the post to an architect, Mordvinov. It also set up the post of chief architect in dozens of cities where there had been no such office in the prewar period, gave those appointed to these jobs full responsibility for supervising the implementation of their cities' rebuilding plans, and made them answerable in this not to local political authorities, but to the State Committee and its republic-level subsidiaries.[34] The State Committee, meanwhile, engaged prominent Moscow and Leningrad architects to draw up plans for the largest of the cities that had been destroyed or damaged during the war, even though most of these men had no planning experience.[35]

From the outset, the State Committee placed special emphasis on the speedy development and implementation of plans for rebuilding the centers of war-damaged cities, treating these projects as the key part of its effort to fulfill the regime's demand that urban reconstruction proceed as quickly as possible, and place specific symbolic goals first. It organized a series of high-profile center-ensemble design competitions, intending that entries provide city chief architects with ample creative input that would help them draw up final plans for these areas. To ensure that center ensembles would be rebuilt right away, it ran these competitions according to an accelerated schedule; in many cities, they were completed well before the drawing up of general reconstruction plans. And in its competition briefs, it prescribed that entrants give their projects a very specific symbolic thrust, by organizing their proposed ensembles

around two visually dominant structures: a state administrative building or complex (qua symbol of the Soviet political order) and a prominent war monument.[36]

DEVELOPING A PLAN FOR STALINGRAD'S CENTER

Of all these projects, the effort to rebuild Stalingrad's center would seem to have had the greatest chance of success. The State Committee treated it as a top priority. The "blank slate" site excited project architects, and gave them a good deal of freedom in their work. The city's general rebuilding plan was already complete by the time the State Committee launched a center-ensemble competition. The State Committee had given one man, Alabian, full control over the process of fleshing out this plan. And in his work, Alabian had the luxury of drawing on the talents of most of the country's leading architects.

In the end, though, this project was something of a failure, and one that showed the State Committee's inability to run socialist reconstruction in such a way as to overcome the problems that had plagued it in the prewar period. Moreover, this failure helped convince regime leaders they had erred by placing so much faith in architects, and led them not only to remove architects from positions of authority over planning and urban development, but also to take most aspects of building design out of the hands of the architectural profession, as if to punish its members for the mistakes of their most illustrious peers.

Problems surfaced early on, touched off by a seemingly unrelated development: the regime's move, in the late wartime period, drastically to limit public discussion of the war, and to propagate a new official story of its nature and purpose. The new narrative treated the battle against Nazi Germany not as a world-historical ethno-cultural death struggle defined by suffering and loss (this theme had been a common feature of wartime propaganda and cultural products), but as a conflict between political systems, victory in which was due to the brilliant leadership of Stalin and the Party. As such, the regime held, more energy should be devoted to celebrating the Soviet political order than to examining and commemorating the war, which should be treated as, in effect, merely the latest stage in socialism's development. In seeking to ensure that this would happen, it paid particular attention to establishing control over the production of works of culture and scholarship. Most of its efforts were negative; they ranged from sponsoring attacks on artworks that failed to toe the new line to forcing the Institute of History to cancel plans to produce a comprehensive study of the war.[37]

During this campaign's earliest stages, several participants in the Stalingrad general plan competition produced projects that would have given the new center a symbolic thrust that was out of keeping with the new narrative. These projects reflect what had been, until recently, a certain professional consensus on how the architects of new city-center ensembles should translate the old narrative into built form.[38] Treating the Stalingrad site as a blank slate, they proposed radically reworking its prewar layout in such a way as to make a new war monument or monuments its clear visual focus. Shchusev, for example, suggested that the city center be transformed into a memorial complex commemorating those who had died fighting to stop the German Army's advance to the Volga (fig. 12.1).[39] Boris Iofan, meanwhile, proposed rearranging the city's street network (which, before the war, had described a rough grid) into a star pattern, such that all roads, and thus all sightlines, would lead to a towering monumental column many times larger than the surrounding buildings. Even Giprogor's planners, whose work was normally staid and technocratic, were caught up in the spirit of the moment. One Giprogor wartime project would have recentered the city's built environment on a new elliptical memorial plaza, immense in size (its axes roughly two hundred and four hundred meters long), and decorated with rows of fountains and a commemorative obelisk. In another project, Giprogor proposed slicing a

new, four-and-a-half-kilometer–long main avenue at an angle through Stalingrad's existing street grid; the avenue would have linked the center with, and reoriented all sightlines toward, nearby Mamaev Hill, which had been the site of a key skirmish a few months before.[40]

Following his colleagues' lead, Alabian presented the center-ensemble portion of his 1943 general plan as radical in intent; its purpose, he claimed, was to create "an entirely new sort of city." He proposed creating a series of grand squares and "magisterial" avenues, and clearing river embankments of existing structures so that they could be used as parks. He suggested basing a new center ensemble on three public spaces, connected in a line running eastward from the Volga. His plan was to clear away riverbank rubble to create a new Square of Glory, then connect it to the existing Square of Fallen Fighters, several hundred meters away, by means of a new tree-lined pedestrian boulevard, the Alley of Heroes. He proposed surrounding each of the center's major public spaces with new, monumental political-administrative buildings. Chief among them would be a new House of Soviets, whose tower he intended to be the city's tallest structure; he set aside a plot for it on the southern perimeter of the center's main plaza, the Square of Fallen Fighters. As to commemorating the war, he wanted to place a relatively modest victory arch at the spot where the Alley of Heroes opened onto the Square of Fallen Fighters (fig. 12.2).[41]

His claims to the contrary, Alabian's plan was hardly transformationist in thrust. Most obviously, he broke with his peers in proposing that the city's pre-war street grid not be reworked. (He had good practical reason to eschew this radical measure: while few streets had escaped without heavy damage, it had become obvious by this time that many of them could be quickly cleared of rubble, repaired, and put back into service.) More significantly, he decided that the House of Soviets, rather than a war monument, should be the new center's focal point. He may have done this because he was ordered to do so by some leading politician whose directions on

Fig. 12.1 Aleksei Shchusev, Stalingrad center project (detail), 1944 (N. B. Sokolov, A. V. Shchusev, *Gosu-darstvennoe izdatel'stvo literatury po stroitel'stvu i arkhitekture*, 1952, p. 288)

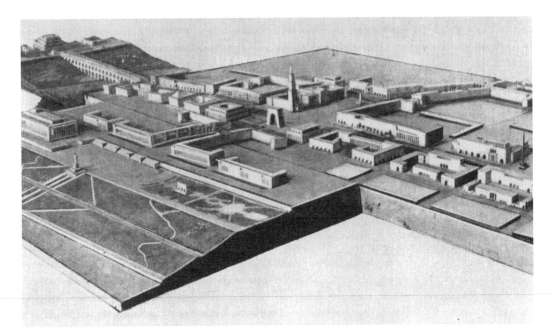

Fig. 12.2 Karo Alabian, Stalingrad center project, 1944. (L. B. Karlik, *Karo Alabian*, Aiastan, 1966, n.p.)

this matter have gone unrecorded. This is unlikely, however, since whenever any regime leader said anything about architecture, planning, or urban development, his words were quickly taken up and endlessly repeated, both in speeches and in print, by architects and planners concerned to show that their projects did the best possible job of translating this utterance into built form, and so deserved official patronage. It is more likely that Alabian was simply more sensitive to the changing political winds than were his fellow competition entrants, and so was quicker to realize that in order to ensure his project's victory, he needed to craft a center ensemble whose main symbolic function was to celebrate the Soviet state, not commemorate the war. Indeed, he was so concerned to do so that he even proposed removing from the Square of Fallen Fighters a mass grave containing both Civil War and World War II victims, along with a memorial obelisk that honored their sacrifice.[42]

Alabian's project marked the beginning of a shift in standard practices for commemorating the war in built form. In managing the Stalingrad center competition, the architecture establishment worked to ensure that participants would submit projects that reflected this shift. In early 1944, the Academy of Ar-

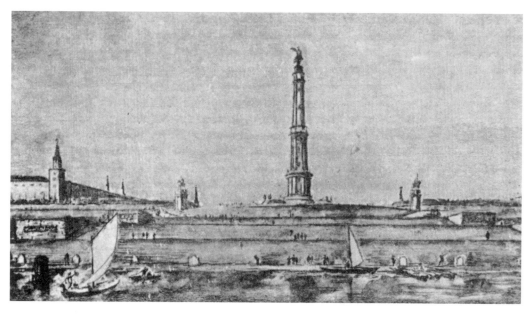

Fig. 12.3 Lev Rudnev, Stalingrad center project, 1946 (V. G. Gel'freikh, "O proektakh tsentra Stalingrada," *Arkhitektura i stroitel'stvo* 15–16 [1946], p. 8)

chitecture's Presidium declared, in a set of guidelines for competition entrants:

> The architectural center of Stalingrad cannot be defined by a monument alone. It is imperative that a political-administrative center be developed, into which both ensembles of political-administrative buildings and monuments have been organically integrated.[43]

The leaders of the State Committee and its Russian Republic subsidiary, meeting in joint session later that year to draw up a formal brief for the competition's first round, went still further on this score, ordering that new monuments be placed only on the riverside Square of Glory, and that the Square of Fallen Fighters be surrounded only with political-administrative buildings, and used only for official rallies.[44] And in its October 1945 brief for the competition's next-to-last, invitation-only stage, the State Committee added another restriction, ordering entrants to include no more than two monuments in their projects—one celebrating victory and the other a statue of Stalin.[45]

By the spring of 1946, the members of the State Committee's Stalingrad center competi-

tion jury were falling over one another to show their fidelity to the new orthodoxy. Meeting in April to review final-round entries, jury members spent much of their time criticizing entrants for doing too much to commemorate the war, and too little to celebrate the Soviet political order. Iofan and Rudnev were among those whose entries came in for criticism on this score; each had proposed that the riverside war monument be the center's dominant structure, and that the Square of Glory be the center's largest public space (fig. 12.3).[46]

The jury found particular fault with one entry, that of Stalingrad chief architect Vasilii Simbirtsev. Simbirtsev not only proposed leaving the existing memorial in place (fig. 12.4), but also suggested that the new House of Soviets be set far back from the Square, so that its tower would not draw too much attention from the obelisk. He also argued that the Square must be treated as a specifically *memorial* space, with the obelisk and grave as its focus; by so doing, he said, his proposed design would "create a sort of cult of the dead of Stalingrad" (fig. 12.5).[47]

The memorial obelisk had been the defining element of the Square of Fallen Fighters

Fig. 12.4 Memorial obelisk, Square of Fallen Fighters, Stalingrad (*Stalingrad*, Moscow, 1956, n.p.)

Fig. 12.5 Vasilii Simbirtsev, Stalingrad center project, 1946 (V.G. Gel'freikh, "O proektakh tsentra Stalingrada," *Arkhitektura i stroitel'stvo* 15–16 [1946], 7)

since the Civil War era, when, in a ceremony organized by local political leaders, it was placed atop a common grave of Red Army men who had died fighting the Whites. In 1943, soon after the Soviet Army had driven the Germans out of the city, the bodies of several soldiers who had died in the fighting were buried under a small marker a few meters away. And in February 1946, local officials organized the interment of three more war heroes on the site; they were laid to rest directly under the old obelisk.[48] Simbirtsev noted that "every meter of [the Square's] land is drenched with the blood of fallen heroes"; his project gave concrete expression to local sentiment in favor of preserving it largely as it was.[49]

The jury sternly reminded him that because the Square of Fallen Fighters was meant to be a political-administrative center, it could not be turned into a "necropolis."[50] Gel'freikh neatly summarized the criticisms of his fellow jurors when he stated that Simbirtsev was guilty of falling into "naturalism"—meaning by this that the architect had essentialized the war experience as one whose significance lay not in the final victory of communism, but in the sufferings of ordinary Soviet people.[51]

After reviewing the competition entries, Alabian drew up his own detailed center plan, which he presented to a December 1946 meeting of the State Committee leadership. Perhaps hoping to blunt potential criticism of his proposal to remove the obelisk and the graves beneath it, he argued that, like Simbirtsev, he wanted to make the Square of Fallen Fighters a historical space. In drawing up his project, he claimed, his primary goal had been to "give expression to the history of Stalingrad, its historical and political meaning in the history of our country."[52] But he maintained that doing so was not merely a matter of preserving what had been there before. He asserted,

> It is understandable that some local comrades, for entirely natural reasons, love their old city and its monuments, which were put up in the past, and this pleases them. But it seems to me that Stalingrad

should, in this district, have more monumental structures than existed there before the war, and so I cannot agree with their point of view.

In any case, he averred, the graves had to be moved for "technical reasons"—by which he meant that space needed to be cleared for a new building that was a critical element of his center plan—and doing so would in no way detract from the character of the memorial, since the site on which it now stood was "of no historical importance."[53]

But in the months since the competition jury's last meeting, the leaders of the State Committee had changed their minds about this part of Alabian's plan; in the interim, it seems, Simbirtsev and local officials had convinced them that the obelisks and graves could be left in place without changing the planned ensemble's basic symbolic thrust. Even Gel'freikh had come around to this point of view, and had joined the Stalingrad city council in formally recommending that the State Committee compel Alabian to provide for their preservation.[54] After hearing Alabian out, the State Committee ordered him to modify his plan to do just this. And it gave final approval[55] to the project only after he had agreed, in writing, to save as much of the existing memorial complex "as possible."[56]

Simbirtsev and his allies had taken a certain professional and personal risk by objecting to an officially approved design for a politically important project. But doing so was not unheard of. Leading architects mounted similar challenges to many of the Stalin era's most prominent projects, including those for the Lenin Library and the Palace of Soviets.[57] While they rarely managed to secure major changes in the designs to which they objected, their right to raise such objections seems to have been generally accepted, so long as they presented their challenges as intended to ensure that the building or ensemble in question properly represented the principles for which it was supposed to stand.

Several months later, in February of 1947, Alabian's plan would come under a more concerted, more effective attack, one that would lead to significant delays in the rebuilding effort. In an *Arkhitektura i stroitel'stvo* piece on the entries to a Stalingrad House of Soviets design competition,[58] Lev Rudnev took the dispute over the center to a new level, criticizing Alabian's project on explicitly politico-symbolic grounds. He chastised Alabian for proposing to make the new House of Soviets relatively modest in height, and for proposing that it be placed on the side of the square rather than at its rear, where this symbol of the "indestructibility of the Soviet system" would face the Volga, and thus be the ensemble's obvious centerpiece (see fig. 12.3). He argued that Alabian's plan was fundamentally flawed because it was marked by an improper "contradiction between the meaning of the House of Soviets building, as the leading architectural structure in the city, and the site which has been allocated to it." Worse still, he claimed, anyone looking at the ensemble would find his gaze passing quickly over the House of Soviets, then fixing on another structure—the planned riverside war monument. If built as currently planned, he contended, the center ensemble would be invested with improper "symbolic content," and would fail to convey a properly Soviet sense of "boldness, happiness, and optimism."[59]

In recent years, Rudnev had become a tireless advocate of the idea that every rebuilt city center should be organized in strictly hierarchical, symmetrical fashion around a single visually dominant structure that symbolized the Soviet political order. In 1944, to cite one example, he had argued that Voronezh's decimated center should be reorganized around a new state-administrative building that would tower over its surroundings.[60] In an early 1946 project, to cite another example, he had proposed reshaping Riga's war-damaged center in such a way as to refocus sightlines on an enormous new war museum, which, in recently annexed Latvia, would have stood as a stark symbol of Soviet power.[61]

That he was afforded a forum for his attack on the Alabian plan may indicate that he had some sort of support from a high-level politician or politicians. Given the absence of

evidence to this effect, however, another explanation is more likely. With the onset of the cold war, the regime had intensified its efforts to root out and punish its supposedly ubiquitous internal enemies. As in the 1930s, this led, among other things, to the production of a flood of artworks that celebrated the Soviet order in the most fulsome possible fashion, and to a flood of articles and books lauding these works, produced by artists, journalists, and critics who were concerned either to show their political devotion to a regime they legitimately believed to be under threat, or to protect themselves in advance against allegations that they were among communism's hidden enemies. Most probably, Rudnev and the editors of *Arkhitektura SSSR* were motivated by just these concerns.

Whatever the case, his salvo had rapid effect. In March of 1947, about a month after the article appeared, the Stalingrad city council launched a new, closed House of Soviets competition.[62] No doubt aware that Rudnev's star was on the rise,[63] and perhaps also that Alabian's was on the wane,[64] it awarded first prize to Rudnev's plan to build—at the rear of the Square of Fallen Fighters—a House of Soviets modeled on Moscow's new *vysotnye zdaniia* (fig. 12.6).[65] Once it had done this, it then asked the RSFSR Council of Ministers (the RSFSR's highest-level executive body) to reverse the State Committee's approval of the Alabian plan, on the pretext that Rudnev's proposal needed to be taken into account. M. I. Rodionov, the Council's chair, came to the city to examine the site and hear local complaints. Soon thereafter, the Council ordered that the plan be revised, and put Simbirtsev in charge of doing so.[66]

In March of 1949 the State Committee and its Russian Republic subsidiary signed off on a revised center plan, which Simbirtsev had developed together with a team of architects led by Rudnev. The plan provided for moving the House of Soviets as per the latter's suggestion, and for preserving the obelisk and graves. As to the center's prescribed political-administrative function, it proposed setting the House of Soviets back from the edge of the Square of Fallen Fighters, which would

Fig. 12.6 Lev Rudnev, Stalingrad House of Soviets project, 1947 (V. Shkvarikov, "Neustanno povyshat' kachestvo zastroiki gorodov," *Arkhitektura SSSR* 3 [1952], pp. 4–5)

not only make the new building appear more impressive, but also create an open area, adjacent to the Square, that could be used for official parades and rallies.[67]

BUILDING STALINGRAD'S NEW CENTER

By creating the State Committee and giving it unprecedented authority over planning and development, the regime sought to ensure that postwar rebuilding would be rapid and coordinated, and would prioritize politico-symbolic goals. But by 1949, it was clear that the new system had had the exact opposite effect on rebuilding's showcase project. Even though both the USSR and RSFSR governments had made completing Stalingrad's center a "first-order" priority,[68] the State Committee had needed nearly six years just to complete and ratify a plan for the area, which was still filled with ruins. Much of the city's periphery, meanwhile, had already been rebuilt by the industrial ministries.

Members of the State Committee had expressed concern about these delays in several closed meetings;[69] others now began to complain about them in public. An emboldened Simbirtsev was at their forefront. In two widely publicized speeches, one delivered in 1947, the other in 1948, he argued that to solve the problems afflicting both the Stalingrad project and urban reconstruction as a whole, authority over planning and development had to be further centralized, and placed in more capable hands. But he turned this argument against those who, a few years earlier, had used it to take control of the rebuilding effort. He lashed out at the Moscow architects who ran the State Committee, accusing them of causing a myriad of local-level problems by failing to coordinate their planning efforts with the central ministries, which controlled construction. He also accused both the State Committee and the central ministries of showing no interest in cities' practical needs. His solution: putting city chief architects in charge of all aspects of urban development.[70]

Politicians ignored this suggestion, but moved to act on his and others' complaints about the slow progress of the Stalingrad center project. Beginning in early 1948, the USSR and RSFSR Councils of Ministers issued a series of decrees intended to force construction patrons to complete a number of short-order projects within the confines of the center.[71] For their part, local authorities helped out by organizing "volunteer" building brigades and sponsoring work speedups on various center-ensemble sites.[72]

With Simbirtsev's plan in place, these measures did have some effect. Various buildings began to go up along the perimeter of the Square of Fallen Fighters.[73] The city government used both paid and "volunteer" labor to replant the Square and the adjacent Alley of Heroes, and to rebuild the central Volga embankment.[74] But a number of key city-center projects languished. The central stretch of Stalin Prospect, intended to serve as Stalingrad's main north-south avenue, continued to be blighted by uncleared ruins, as did the perimeter of the Alley of Heroes. And no one seems to have been doing anything concrete to move the House of Soviets project forward.

Stalingrad was not the only city where work had stalled on building a new center ensemble. In some cities, planning was delayed by battles over politico-symbolic questions. In Riga, for example, the planning process dragged on for years, held up by endless debates about how a new center ensemble should commemorate the war, and about which existing buildings were sufficiently historic to merit preservation. In various other cities, planners completed center-ensemble blueprints in relatively short order, but these ended up being ignored, either because they were too general to be of use, or because local officials lacked the tools to implement them.[75]

Despite these and other similar problems, it would seem to have been premature, so soon after war's end, to decide that they showed that the State Committee had failed to do a competent job of managing postwar rebuilding. Yet this is exactly what the country's political leaders did. In July of 1949, the regime abolished the State Committee, transferring its responsibilities to the new Ministry for Urban Construction (Mingorstroi). The Supreme Soviet decree establishing Mingorstroi declared this step necessary to "securing state control over . . . urban planning and development."

Throughout the Stalin era, of course, regime leaders were obsessed with putting all areas of Soviet life under the direct control of the central party-State. But this would not seem to have been their aim in this case—rather, they wanted to strip architects of authority over planning and development, and to make certain that in the future, those managing these areas would pay far less attention to the aesthetic-symbolic features of buildings and ensembles, and far more to getting them built as quickly as possible. Unlike the 1943 decree setting up the State Committee, the edict outlining Mingorstroi's duties contained no reference to either planning or development having any aesthetic-symbolic purpose whatsoever. It also ordered Mingorstroi to reduce expenditures on building design, and to do so by promoting the increased use of standardized projects, which meant more look-alike buildings and less work for architects. And significantly, the regime put a construction professional (K. M. Sokolov, who had previously served as Minister of Construction and Road Construction), rather than an architect, in charge of the new ministry.[76]

It is unclear whether the country's political leaders truly believed they had erred by placing so much power in the hands of architects, then telling them to focus on aesthetic-symbolic concerns in rebuilding war-damaged cities. But it is obvious that they wanted to make architects the scapegoats for ongoing problems with this, socialist reconstruction's signal postwar endeavor.

In 1950, Mingorstroi took a series of aggressive steps to overcome these problems. It launched a campaign to force local authorities in cities throughout the Union to finish those general plans that had not as yet been completed, so that patrons would know where and what they could build. It ordered that plans already in place be revised to eliminate provisions to build new parks and magisterial-style main streets; its goal was to free up resources that could then be devoted to other, more "essential" projects, and particularly housing construction, which had recently become a regime obsession.[77] It also mandated that cities loosen restrictions on building height, in the hope that this would enable patrons to achieve economies of scale in construction by making new buildings taller.[78] And in reviewing both new and revised plans, its officials paid little attention to anything but quantitative building targets, which they insisted be high, and project deadlines, which they insisted be soon.[79]

Not long after Mingorstroi was established, the new ministry's leaders sent a group of investigators to Stalingrad to assess the situation there. In its report, the team complained that "in spite of the fact that construction is being carried out in great volume . . . there is a complete lack of attention to ensuring that new streets and squares are created as ensembles." It described the state of work on the center in bleak terms:

> None of the main streets or squares has been built on or has itself been completed and landscaped. In the main, they are wastelands covered with the uncleared ruins of destroyed buildings, and neither they nor their various parts have anything resembling the appearance of having been completed. [Most notably,] only one-quarter of the perimeter of Fallen Fighters Square has been built up.[80]

City officials fell back on familiar tactics in trying to show that they were indeed transforming the center. Not long after the completion of the Mingorstroi report, they moved to speed the completion of work on several new apartment houses along Peace Street (not far from the Square of Fallen Fighters), ordering that two stories be added to each during construction so that this "ensemble" would be more impressive (fig. 12.7).[81] The city also hurried along the construction of an ensemble

of seven- and eight-story apartment houses along the Alley of Heroes.[82]

But other showcase projects remained stalled. Little was being done to put up the monumental political-administrative edifices that were supposed to transform Stalin Prospect, for example, due to a lack of both approved designs and funding.[83] Not until the mid-1950s was the street's central stretch cleared of the detritus of buildings that had been destroyed in battle.[84]

As to the House of Soviets project, leading architects and urban-development bureaucrats continued to refer to it as proof that in time, Stalingrad would get the monumental center ensemble that everyone agreed was the city's due.[85] But while drawings of the planned building showed up occasionally in the professional press,[86] work on the project seems to have proceeded at a relaxed pace. Only in May 1950 did the city council bother to draw up a set of specifications to guide Rudnev's team of designers,[87] and four years later, V. Masliaev, the head of the city government's main architecture studio, said that work was still at the "draft project" stage.[88] Rudnev seems in fact never to have generated anything resembling a final plan for the building—by 1953, six years after his initial salvo against Alabian, he had yet to submit even preliminary technical specifications to central authorities for their review. While city officials occasionally complained about Rudnev's lack of activity,[89] no one seems to have been particularly concerned with hurrying him along. In any case, in various professional fora, the idea of putting up such a building had begun to come under attack as wasteful and frivolous.[90] Soon after Stalin's death, it was quietly dropped,[91] effectively bringing to a close the effort to give Stalingrad a grand central ensemble.

BUILDING SOCIALISM

The evidence shows that standard histories of Stalin-era architecture present a highly inaccurate picture of architects' relationship to the regime. While correct in arguing that for much of the period in question, this relation-

Fig. 12.7 Apartment houses, Peace Street, Stalingrad, completed 1950 (V. Shkvarikov, "Neustanno povyshat' kachestvo zastroiki gorodov," *Arkhitektura SSSR* 3 [1952], p. 8)

ship was unusually close, they fail to identify its origins, its character, its duration, the reasons for its collapse, or its effects on the way architects worked. In so doing, they also fail adequately to explain what its history tells us about the nature and workings of Stalinism.

Contrary to historiographical commonplace, this relationship was primarily rooted not in some natural affinity of Stalin-style regimes for architecture, but in two chance occurrences. In the mid-1930s, when local officials ran into problems carrying out the grand urban-development projects that were intended to make cities socialist, they turned to architects for assistance. Architects responded by crafting a series of small but impressive monumental ensembles, and pasting historicist facades on modernist buildings; in so doing, they helped their patrons show that whatever its problems, socialist reconstruction was moving forward. Soon thereafter, the regime rewarded the architecture profession by putting it in charge not only of rebuilding war-damaged cities, but also of urban planning and development as a whole.

In order to earn this support, architects did not have to surrender control over their designs. Indeed, the case of the Stalingrad center project shows that architects had a significant degree of creative autonomy, and that leading politicians almost never involved themselves in even the highest-priority projects.

This absence of meddling "from above" did not mean that the design process was as simple and smooth as some scholars have suggested, or that designs were quickly and fully realized. As we have seen, the design stage of important projects could be tortuously protracted and complex because architects, bureaucrats, and local politicians often fought bitterly and at length over how to fine-tune plans to make them politically acceptable. And even when they were finalized, a number were never carried through to completion, as a result of lack of funding.

By the late 1940s, such problems convinced the regime that the urban-development effort had been mismanaged, and it reacted by lashing out at the architecture profession, in whose "cultured hands" it had placed this effort a few short years before. It removed architects from positions of authority over urban development, and greatly reduced their role in building design. At about the same time, it also began to divert resources away from many of architects' showcase projects and into residential construction. Both these changes took place several years before Stalin's death, which, historians' assumptions to the contrary, seems to have nothing to do with architecture's fall from grace.

Clearly, then, the evidence paints a very different picture of the relationship between architects and the regime, and of architectural practice, than the one we find in the historiography. What does it tell us about them specifically Stalinist?

In order to answer this question, we must look first at how the era's political culture shaped the environment in which architects and other creative and technical professionals worked. The character of this political culture was determined first and foremost by the Stalin regime's three driving obsessions: transforming every aspect of Soviet life to make it socialist, defending socialism against foes both overt and hidden, and mobilizing the entire population to assist in both endeavors. It also insisted that socialism be built and defended in certain ways, and in accord with certain assumptions. It demanded the total involvement of all actors at all times, and in all situations, no matter how seemingly far-removed from the realm of the political. It maintained that whatever was not demonstrably *of* socialism was necessarily opposed to it, and insisted on the omnipresence of hidden enemies whose goal was the total destruction of the Soviet project. It lavished power, status, and in some cases material wealth on those who made significant contributions to its projects; it called those who didn't "wreckers," "enemies," and "traitors," and punished them with loss of status, imprisonment, and even execution.

The regime also insisted that in carrying out these endeavors, its subjects must always follow both the spirit and the letter of official directives. But it did not and indeed could not explain exactly how, in every single situation,

they should do so. Some imperatives were clear—everyone "knew," for example, that socialism could not exist in a country without a powerful heavy-industrial sector, meaning they had to help build one. Others, however, were more vague—what did it mean, for example, to create a more just society? Marxism-Leninism's canonical works set certain goals (placing political power in the hands of workers, establishing some sort of societal control over production and distribution, and so forth) but rarely said much about how to achieve them. Some guidance on the latter score could be gleaned from various official pronouncements and policy decisions. Over the course of the late 1920s and 1930s, for example, a series of regime statements and edicts laid out a fairly detailed (if not always coherent) vision of how state power should be used to manage and modernize the economy. In most situations, however, official directives and sacred texts provided little help, and regime leaders were too busy to be able to give detailed instructions; architects, planners, and local officials, for example, had almost no such guidance when they set out to make Soviet cities socialist.

In such instances, one tried to fall back on precedent. One wanted always to be able to say that one had only said or done those things that had, on some prior occasion, won approval "from above," meaning they qualified as properly socialist. Thus Iofan and Shchusev, for example, took care to ensure that their Stalingrad center projects commemorated the war in a way consistent with accepted precedent. Given the regime's insistence that whatever was not entirely socialist was by definition antisocialist, failing to take such care could mean leaving oneself open to being denounced by neighbors, peers, or subordinates as insufficiently loyal to the Soviet project, which could have a wide range of consequences, all of them negative.

Desperate to increase its control over the general population, and to secure proof for its claim that omnipresent wreckers were to blame for socialism's significant problems, the regime encouraged denunciations, treating denouncers as valued defenders of socialism, and punishing the denounced as enemies. It turned its subjects into agents of surveillance and control, and put at their disposal the full power of the state's investigative and repressive apparatuses. The effects were enormous. Millions of the denounced were jailed or executed, while lesser professional and personal harm came to countless others, including Alabian, who lost the Stalingrad center commission after he was effectively and subtly denounced by Rudnev. Throughout Soviet society, nearly everyone became exceptionally fearful and cautious.

Inaction, however, was not an option—in every situation, one was compelled to do something, because the regime equated passivity with wrecking. As a result, all areas of public life, and even much of private life, came to be dominated by the rote repetition of statements and actions that had previously been ratified as acceptable ways to aid the construction and defense of socialism. And many people devoted enormous energy to doing things that enabled them to make a show of helping to build socialism, even though their actions made little or no real contribution to this effort. Officials in postwar Stalingrad, for example, rushed to complete small-scale projects such as the Peace Street apartment houses, and sponsored a plan to build a *vysotka*-style skyscraper that they knew no one would pay for.

In situations where one could not follow these paths of least resistance, one proceeded by finding some relevant official pronouncement or ideological principle, deriving from it an utterance or action that seemed to be useful to solving the problem at hand, and then hoping for official ratification of one's attempt to translate doctrine into practice. This is why Alabian, in crafting his design for Stalingrad's center, made celebrating the Soviet political order, rather than commemorating the war, its symbolic focal point, hoping that by so doing, he would win over the jury by showing his project to be more in keeping with the new official war narrative than those of his fellow competition entrants.

If one failed, the consequences could be grave. But if, like Alabian, one was successful, one had effectively defined or redefined some aspect of socialism, and the rewards for doing so could be enormous. For the ambitious and fearless, this was the path to advancement. Under Stalin, those who rose to prominence and power were those who sought and received official sanction for their innovative approaches to making some aspect of Soviet life socialist.

Many of these people were technical and creative professionals. From the first, the regime realized that without their assistance, it could never hope to achieve its goal of rapidly turning backward Russia into the world's most advanced country. To win their support, it accorded them leading role in the effort to define and build socialism, and also granted them certain privileges, the most important of which was a real degree of professional autonomy. This autonomy was limited, of course, but included, among other things, the right to argue among themselves (and, occasionally, with their politician patrons) about how their profession should build socialism within its area of expertise. As a result, Simbirtsev was able to escape punishment for challenging the Alabian Stalingrad center project, even though his challenge was, in effect, also a challenge to the way the regime had chosen to commemorate the war.

This arrangement was perpetuated neither by the constant use of coercion nor by frequent high-level interventions into professional affairs. Rather, it was largely self-enforced, by specialists whose motivations were ambition and the fear of being denounced by colleagues or subordinates. Concerned to win support for their ideas and projects and to demonstrate their political reliability, they devoted themselves to translating the regime's directives and ideological principles into canons of standard practices—such as those intended to make cities socialist—and then applying them in their work. In this way, every aspect of technical and creative activity became, and remained, professionalized on explicitly ideological grounds, which helped the regime achieve its goal of tapping specialists' talents while maintaining close control over their work.

The example of architecture shows that not all professions were equal in the regime's eyes, and that it was willing to give additional autonomy and authority to those it believed capable of making important contributions to its pet projects. This case also shows that when favored professions failed to deliver, the regime not only did not hesitate to withdraw this support, but also had no compunction about treating them as enemies of socialism.

These tendencies did not die with Stalin. In the wake of his passing, his successors moved quickly to build a base of popular support by distancing themselves from Stalin, which they did by blaming socialism's problems on him, many of his close associates, and many of his regime's signal policies, and rushing to give support to those professions whose work seemed capable of helping to solve socialism's problems. In 1954, as part of this effort, Nikita Khrushchev, Stalin's successor as general secretary, moved to give construction professionals still more authority over architecture, planning, and urban development. He also launched a campaign denouncing many of the practices and projects that had long been central to socialist reconstruction. In so doing, he emphasized that under Stalin, not a single major project had been carried out in full, and that much of what was supposed to have been done had never even been started.

Picking up on what was by then an established line of argument, he placed much of the blame on architects. The architecture profession's basic practices, he insinuated, were fundamentally antisocialist, because they had led to the waste of huge amounts of time, money, and energy, which could and should have been devoted to socialist reconstruction's more worthwhile projects, particularly those in the area of residential construction.[92]

In a certain sense, Khrushchev was right: judged by the high standards set by its patrons, socialist reconstruction was indeed a failure, and architecture practice was partly to blame. But this does not mean that either was not socialist. Stalin-era Soviet socialism—Stalinism—was never merely an abstract doctrine, a compendium of tenets drawn from sacred texts and regime edicts and pronouncements. It was, rather, a complex, dynamic civilization whose defining characteristics were effects of the regime's attempt to create, in short order, a society utterly distinct from and superior to those of the past and the contemporary capitalist West. Both objects of Khrushchev's scorn were quintessential products of this effort's ambitions and contradictions; their built legacy was a symbol of its achievements and failures. And in this, they were nothing if not Stalinist.

Part 4

Post-Soviet Russia

13 Conflict over Designing a Monument to Stalin's Victims

Public Art and Political Ideology in Russia, 1987–1996

Kathleen E. Smith

In 1987 the renowned Russian poet Yevgeny Yevtushenko took up the theme of commemorating victims of Stalinism. His poem "Monuments Still Not Built" challenged Soviet politicians to consider that "there can be no rebuilding without rebuilding memory." With a burst of optimism about the potential of perestroika, he declared that "the time of honest marble" had come.[1] Indeed, political liberalization led by Mikhail Gorbachev opened the way for frank reevaluations of Soviet history. The possibility of winning public acknowledgment of the innocence of those who suffered during the purges inspired a powerful national civic movement. Formed with the assistance of liberal intellectuals, including Yevtushenko, the Memorial Society set itself the concrete and apparently feasible task of raising a monument to Stalin's victims based on donations and design ideas from the public. It also adopted the more abstract and seemingly unrealistic goal of fostering democratization in the Soviet Union. Ironically, the totalitarian political system crumbled in 1991—due in part to civic activism—but as of 2000 a national monument commemorating victims of political persecution had not been built.

Political reform facilitated the design competition for a monument commemorating those who suffered in the Gulag, but also unleashed increasingly significant and distinct group identities that undermined the consensus behind honoring Stalin's victims. Moreover, although political liberalization made the dream of a civic monument possible, market-oriented economic reform simultaneously hampered the effort. The divergent views on how to remember the past that were revealed by design competitions for a monument, however, offer insight into competing understandings of national identity. Those monuments built since perestroika similarly demonstrate the bases of new nationalisms in Russia.

It should come as no surprise that the attempt to commemorate Stalin's victims through the construction of a memorial generated controversy. The genre of monumental art tends to be political. Monuments serve as sources of national pride for aesthetic reasons and for their content, their contribution to defining the national heritage. Both the public and politicians treat each monument as "a statement about the nature of the nation."[2] By immortalizing certain historical individuals or events, those who make monuments attempt to perpetuate an interpretation of the past, to consolidate an unambiguous vision of national history and identity.[3]

Political changes, however, can alter the making and meaning of public art. After all, notes W. J. T. Mitchell, "The very conditions that allow art to come into being—the sites of its display, circulation, and social functionality, its address to spectators, its position in systems of exchange and power—are themselves subject to profound historical shifts."[4] The breakdown of Communist Party rule in the former Soviet Union was one such in-

The research for this paper was funded by Hamilton College and the National Council for Soviet and East European Research. The author is grateful to Natal'ia Malykhina, Elena Zhemkova, and Boris Belenkin of the Interregional Memorial Society for their assistance.

stance where political reform transformed the conditions for making and appreciating art. In particular, by allowing civic associations to emerge and to promote their own interests and self-conceptions, the authorities opened up monumental art to new and competing visions of national and group identity.

Under the old Soviet system the prerogative to commission monumental art belonged to Communist Party officials. Soviet leaders, beginning with Lenin, recognized the role that public art could play in defining new national heroes and values.[5] Lenin himself helped draw up the first list of figures to be honored with statues. The final version of Lenin's list consisted of sixty-seven names and included obvious choices, such as Karl Marx and Friedrich Engels, and unexpected figures, such as Frederic Chopin and Nikolai Gogol. The Bolsheviks' eclectic program left artists great stylistic freedom and some leeway in choice of theme and site. Moreover, the sculptors' representative to the artists union pressed the political leadership "to destroy the conventional jury and to settle for public review of the model projects." Ordinary viewers sharply criticized many of the early monuments and as a result some statues—including a distorted, futuristic figure of Bakunin—were torn down.[6] Stalin, however, changed the conditions for making art. Subject matter and style were strictly monitored by party ideologists; party officials, not the general public, acquired the deciding vote in vetting public art.

From the 1930s onward, the Soviet state sponsored monuments to revolutionary leaders, military victories, outstanding national historical and cultural figures, and scientific achievements such as space flight. With their utopian ideology, Communist Party leaders preferred positive monuments. The leadership's taste ran to realistic, gigantic, and symbolically unambiguous sculpture. Designers were limited to a small number of politically correct motifs—Lenin, the hammer and sickle, five-pointed stars, workers or soldiers—from which to create their compositions; thus their works took on a certain homogeneity. An example of the resulting

"totalitarian kitsch" is the monument to victory in World War II at Stalingrad (Volgograd)—described by an astute American observer as a "gargantuan snarling motherland figure, wielding an immense sword."[7]

The underground art scene that evolved beginning in the 1960s offered little innovation in the field of monumental art. Perhaps it is no accident that dissident or non-conformist artists of the 1960s through the 1980s were more often drawn to painting, drawing, and conceptual installations than to sculpture—though some experimented with kinetic and non-figurative works.[8] Sculpting or casting large pieces required studio space and art supplies available only to members of the official creative unions. Moreover, small works could be displayed in private apartments, but monuments' realization hinged on party permission to use public space. Thus, when he fell out of political favor in the 1970s, the sculptor and monumentalist Ernst Neizvestny reluctantly chose to go abroad so that he could continue to work.[9]

Given the paucity of daring experimental work by Soviet sculptors, it is not surprising that the first real challenge to party-dictated monumental art in the 1980s came not from artists in regard to style, but from politically conscious citizens in regard to content. When Gorbachev loosened the Communist Party's restrictions on speech and association in 1987, a group of youthful would-be civic activists united around the idea of commemorating the victims of communism. Although the Memorial Society coalesced around a broad agenda—to promote democratization of Soviet society, to aid survivors of the purges, to educate people about the "blank spots" in official history—the element of Memorial's program that truly captured the public imagination was the proposal to build a monument to Stalin's victims.[10]

Constructing a public memorial to victims of repression would serve many purposes at once. Monuments are popular everywhere for their capacity to counter "anxiety about memory left to its own devices" by "anchor[ing] collective remembering, a process dispersed, ever-changing, and ultimately intangible, in highly concentrated, fixed, and tangible sites."[11] If the victims of Stalin were immortalized in metal or stone, perhaps it would be harder to officially "forget" them, as had happened after Nikita Khrushchev fell from power in 1964. Moreover, the authorities' permission for a memorial would equal an acknowledgment that those arrested under Stalin were innocent. Insofar as monument building legitimizes "by extension the notion of the people who possessed and rallied around such a memory," successful construction of a memorial would also testify to the solidarity of survivors and their allies who had come together to rescue the past.[12] Furthermore, monuments often become physical centers for new rituals, which in turn can foster organizations and new common interpretations of the past. At a monument to victims of political persecution, survivors, victims' families, and others could mourn, remember, and even draw lessons from the past together.

The advent of glasnost permitted a lively debate about the content of public art, and also revealed the superficial nature of the artistic consensus behind the officially approved genre of socialist realism. Some art critics called for a moratorium on gigantic, trite sculptures and when Memorial announced its plans, one prominent architect openly questioned whether Soviet artists were up to the challenge of creating a monument that "embod[ied] popular memory—which is sincere, quiet, stern, humble—versus propaganda history which is wordy, didactic, grandiose and aggressive."[13] Memorial Society organizers hoped that by orchestrating a fundamental shift in the power to commemorate they would be rewarded with innovative designs. To empower survivors and to gather a multitude of perspectives on the past, they chose a diverse jury and an open design competition. They solicited entries both from professional artists and from ordinary citizens. Those who lacked artistic abilities were even invited to describe in words their concept of a monument.

Over a thousand entries, ranging in shape from scale models to pencil drawings and in scope from brief suggestions for a statue to detailed descriptions of whole memorial ensembles, poured in to Memorial from across the country. The results of the call for proposals reflected the difficulty of adapting an art form that is generally positive and self-congratulatory to mark a tragedy—a problem evident in controversies over the design of memorials to the Holocaust, as well as in the acrimonious debate over the American Vietnam Veterans memorial.[14] The entries in the Memorial Society's contest exposed major differences in how Soviet citizens understood their history and in their choice of values to be enshrined. Besides the conflict between loyal communists, who saw Stalin as an aberration in the otherwise admirable history of Soviet rule, and fervent anticommunists, who argued that Lenin had initiated the Soviet concentration camp system, one also finds competition between pluralist and nationalist principles. The monument designs also reveal that neither amateurs nor professionals had come to terms with the legacies of socialist realism. Wittingly or unwittingly, most were still working in the old Soviet monumental language.

Despite some politicians' fears that memories of purges would provoke criticism of the whole communist experience, a monument to the victims of repression did not have to be intrinsically anti-Soviet. In his treatment of the purges, Nikita Khrushchev consistently encouraged people to draw anti-Stalinist but pro-Leninist conclusions, that is, to condemn Stalin's excesses but to praise the party's candor and resilience in acknowledging its past errors. Khrushchev himself raised the idea of building a monument to victims at the 22nd Communist Party Congress in 1961. Though he never followed through on this idea, Khrushchev had set a pattern in his speeches of not identifying any culprits besides Stalin and Beria, paying homage to loyal party, state, military, and non-party victims of Stalin's repressions (in that order). He also carefully ignored the passivity of the party and of most victims in the face of the purges. By elevating a subset of victims based on their loyalty to socialism (and even to Stalinism) and by celebrating those who had previously displayed some special merit, Khrushchev emphasized heroic and patriotic values.

Selectivity regarding victims would allow artists to work within the Soviet tradition of positive monuments. One might immortalize the good, brave Communist prisoner, while avoiding any depiction of culprits, any disturbing suggestions of the party's accountability for the purges. Hence, one entry in the Memorial competition bears the inscription "To you who fought for socialism and became innocent victims of lawlessness" (see fig. 13.1).[15] Or one might focus on the party's triumphal repudiation of the cult of personality, like the design that showed the 20th Party Congress—where Khrushchev made his "secret speech" denouncing Stalin and the terror—as a bolt of lightning splitting open a Stalinist prison (fig. 13.2). Several other contemporary proposals had Stalin cowering as Gorbachev, an old Bolshevik, or other untarnished revolutionary figures stood in judgment.[16] These designs presented the possibility of casting the Communist Party in the role of victim and moral authority rather than that of persecutor.

Those people who believed that the Soviet system could overcome its mistakes also clung to the notion that victims could be divided into pure and impure. For example, a sailor sent in a model that he saw as representing each person's choice between the truth and the lie. A path with a crystal clear slab with "Lenin" lettered in gold would be followed by red marble slabs bearing "the names of the most outstanding people from our homeland and the international communist movement who were killed during the years of the cult of personality." A second path would begin with Stalin's name carved in black stone, followed by names of "executioners and those guilty of slander."[17] But the impossibility of sorting ordinary victims into "true" and "untrue" meant that the author of this project still ended up using crude political markers and singling out elite victims of the purges for special recognition. Unlike the American Vietnam Veterans memorial, which

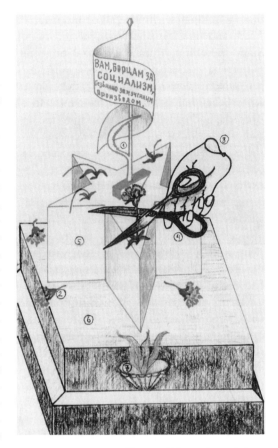

Fig. 13.1 Monument "To you, fighters for socialism, innocent victims of lawlessness." Design by Aleksandr Sheremetev. Courtesy of Interregional Memorial Society Archives.

sought to heal divisions over the past by naming all those U.S. soldiers who died in Vietnam in equal fashion, this design would be exclusive and partisan. Visitors who rejected the path of Stalinism could only choose the path of Leninism; alternative political allegiances would have no avenue for expression.

For decades, Communist officials attempted to foster in Soviet citizens the belief that the nation and the party were one. But the majority of civic proposals for a monument in the 1980s did not seek to glorify the Communist Party. Instead, one finds clear efforts to replace purely communist symbols with apolitical, populist, or national motifs, as well as attempts to denigrate Soviet rule (the latter will be addressed in the next section). Many survivors and relatives who were

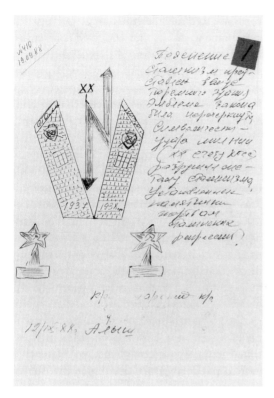

Fig. 13.2 Monument design by A. Alyshev. Courtesy of Interregional Memorial Society Archives.

critical of the Communist Party's failure to prevent the terror or to halt the purges before Stalin's death still shared the party's belief that the monument should honor something lest it promote nothing but despair about the Soviet experience. The search for points of pride in the past led many back to memories of World War II, when Soviet citizens had fought selflessly against the evident evil of Nazi aggression. Still other people, however, turned to prerevolutionary history. Across the USSR renewed interest in historical "blank spots" went hand-in-hand with exploration of national identity.[18] For Russians this meant a revival of pride in religious and cultural traditions.

Numerous monument proposals drew on religious culture, almost always Russian Orthodoxy. Some designers found inspiration in Christian images of martyrdom. Georgii Trubetskoi, for instance, pictured a monument in the shape of a huge cross (20 meters long) borne by life-size human figures dressed to

represent different professions and nationalities, but all with the face of Christ.[19] Another entry combined Soviet and Christian symbols by depicting a five-pointed star nailed up on a cross, blood dripping from its wounds. Many proposals incorporated aspects of church architecture, especially bells and candles, and religious funeral rites (see fig. 13.3).[20]

On a basic psychological level, a symbolic funeral or grave would compensate all relatives who had no real remains to bury. Frequently designs for grave sites revolved around Christian imagery—one plan, for example, featured a model of Christ on the cross surrounded by holders where visitors could place lit candles, thus creating the semblance of the interior of an Orthodox church. One person even suggested that the resurrection of the Cathedral of Christ the Savior dynamited by Stalin would be the best monument.[21] It would be a mistake to attribute all use of Orthodox imagery to strong Russian nationalist sentiments, but monument designs that expected Soviet citizens to unite around such symbols sought to revive an older Russian visual language. Religion, after all, had been an anathema to communist ideologists and was associated with prerevolutionary Russia and its values.

A second attempt to find a popular symbolic language can be seen in contest entries that tried to separate out patriotic from communist imagery and rituals. Deliberately nonpolitical statements of grief were often cast within the realist traditions of Soviet art, and in particular in the stereotyped forms repeated endlessly in monuments to victims of World War II. One Muscovite, who argued that the nation needed to remember both famous and unknown victims, suggested that the memorial take the form of "many, many little eternal flames" stretching out through an arch and seen through the grate of a prison window. The memorial, she opined, should also feature a *"bratskaia mogila"* (common grave). A museum to the purges could be built elsewhere, but she proposed that this memorial be placed at the Kremlin walls next to the Aleksandrovskii garden. Thus, she incorporated traditional Soviet patriotic images in

Fig. 13.3 Monument design by Aleksandr N. Vasilevskii. Courtesy of Interregional Memorial Society Archives.

her design and physically placed it next to the existing Tomb of the Unknown Soldier of World War II. Other projects mimicked the Moscow monument to the unknown soldier: one included "camp dust," instead of earth from Leningrad mass war graves; another inscribed the names of notorious camp sites, instead of "hero cities," on stone cubes.[22]

A monument to victims that fit in easily with existing tributes to the triumphs of Soviet rule, however, did not suit democratically oriented organizers of the design competition. The first Memorial Society organizers envisioned a memorial complex composed of a monument, museum, archive, and library for research on the causes of human rights abuses. They saw a monument as merely a complement to civic action—the real guarantee against a return to totalitarianism—and to research—the embodiment of a continuing search for truth. The Memorial movement with all its activities thus could be seen as the

best way to remember the purges. As regards a monument, just as they endorsed confrontational politics, the radical democrats within Memorial wanted a form of commemoration that would challenge people's complacency.

Liberal activists recognized that Stalin alone could not bear full responsibility for the purges. In carrying out mass repressions, he had relied on the cooperation of party loyalists and policemen and on the conformity of the masses. The complicity that characterized life in a totalitarian state could not be "shouted," and hence did not fit with triumphal, positive art.[23] As the activist Nina Braginskaia noted in her review of the monument competition, "Usually, commemoration in sculpture or architectural form suggests greatness, heroism, and glory, but being crushed by a machine does not in and of itself make a person a hero."[24] Similarly, a frustrated letter writer complained to Memorial that to put forth a positive lesson the theme of the competition would have to be changed. The monument, he argued, should not commemorate victims but rather be "a symbol of civic resistance to the violence of totalitarianism." In other words, freedom fighters rather than passive victims should be the role models for future generations.[25]

Artists struggled with the problem of turning monumental art into a vehicle for expressing a critical evaluation of complex and tragic events. Several tried to sidestep the problem by rejecting sculptural forms. One proposal was that Lubianka square be renamed "Democracy Square" and made into a sort of Hyde Park Corner—thus turning a place that caused people to fall silent in fear into a site for exercising the right to free speech.[26] Another idea called for every town or family that suffered in the purges to plant a tree or post a plaque on a tree in memory of their losses—like several other designs, it attempted to bring home the activity of coming to terms with the past by advocating the creation of many local monuments instead of a single national memorial. Changing the symbolic face of Moscow alone might imply that only the capital's elite needed to reform their thinking.[27]

A second clear trend among those who saw a memorial as a means of encouraging critical thinking was to subvert monumental forms to match their subversive ideas. To commemorate the Holocaust, young German sculptors have created "anti-monuments" or "counter-monuments," including an obelisk that gradually sank into the ground, to express "deep distrust of monumental forms in light of their systematic exploitation by the Nazis."[28] Soviet citizens similarly suggested monuments that took the shape of downward spirals, maelstroms, and pits in the ground, as opposed to typical sculptural markers that thrust up toward the sky, breaking up the cityscape.[29] One innovative design would have turned the tables on visitors who identified themselves exclusively with victims of Stalinism. It suggested an interactive memorial in which visitors would find themselves marching among life-size figures from the May Day parade of 1937 and then would encounter a forced march of prisoners. Mirrors along the route would reflect back the image of the visitors so that they would see themselves both as members of the conformist mob creating the illusion of monolithic support for the dictator and then as equally anonymous cogs in the Gulag.[30] This design would have graphically reminded visitors that they could have just as easily been among those cheering Stalin as among those cursing the regime from their prison cells.

Liberal intellectuals expected that would-be designers, having been freed from the ideological and artistic strictures of the Brezhnev era, would find an image that provoked catharsis by producing both terror and pity in its viewers. But for the most part, proponents of a memorial that promoted democratic principles found it easier to explain what they did not want than to describe their ideal monument. Experts fell back on abstract terms to express their hopes: a good monument would convert terror and even anger into spiritual renewal, would form a bulwark against the return of repression, would have an "all-human" element, a point of view that crossed the bounds of time and space.[31] They were profoundly disappointed with the extremely common but unsophisticated designs proposed by amateurs that adopted the perspective of the prisoner and reproduced the prison cell or labor camp, complete with barbed wire, watch towers, and guard dogs. Democratically oriented activists and critics also insisted that the monument be inclusive as regarded victims, and not privilege one religious tradition. Professionals also rejected entries that tried to shake up viewers by using communist symbols in crudely negative ways—such as a design that joined a swastika with a hammer and sickle.[32]

The national monument to victims of repression long campaigned for by Memorial is still unbuilt. The jury, disappointed with the predominance of crude and Brezhnevite proposals, could not pick a winner. Having rejected the old monumental style, the democrats who dominated Memorial's leadership awaited the creation of a new idiom capable of expressing the complexity of the purges. They also awaited an influx of funds, since the depreciation of the ruble greatly reduced the worth of their treasury. But they did manage in 1990 to mark a site in Moscow for a future monument with a boulder from the first political concentration camp in the USSR. The stone from the Solovetskii prison camp is humble, uncontroversial, and almost invisible through the shrubbery on a tiny traffic island in the middle of a busy intersection (fig. 13.4).

Yet the choice of a location for a monument represented a significant decision. The proposals for placing the monument to victims had highlighted the fundamental divisions in interpretations of the purges and hence in functions of the monument itself. Contestants interpreted sacred ground variously as Red Square, for its proximity to Lenin's mausoleum; the square in front of the government house (*dom na naberezhnoi*), where many prominent party victims had lived before their arrests; the site of the Moscow Swimming Pool, where the Cathedral of Christ the Savior stood until it was destroyed in 1931; the Kremlin walls near the Tomb of the Unknown Soldier; Poklonnaia

Fig. 13.4 Memorial Society's monument—consisting of a boulder from the Solovetskii prison camp—in Moscow's Lubianka Square. Photo by the author.

Hill, the home of a new gigantic monumental ensemble commemorating victory in World War II; or within or in front of the Lubianka, where it would have provided a contrast to the statue of Feliks Dzerzhinskii, the founder of the Soviet secret police.[33] Memorial went with the democrats, choosing Lubianka Square, where the monument would be visible to contemporary state security officers from their office windows.

Even before the Soviet regime collapsed once and for all in August 1991, the concurrent processes of political and economic reform had once again begun to alter the conditions for making public art. First of all, the enthusiasm and consensus behind anti-Stalinist activism faltered in the 1990s. Gorbachev's gradual concessions regarding rehabilitation and free speech sapped some of the urgency from the anti-Stalinist cause. Confident that they had shattered the taboos about criticizing the Soviet past, democratic activists moved on to other issues. Some of them channeled their energy into direct confrontations with the Communist regime. Oth-

ers sought challenges in the new entrepreneurial realm.[34]

Meanwhile religious and secular nationalism grew in popularity and intensity. Nationalists began to chafe at democrats' fondness for Western ideas, their modern artistic tastes, and their seemingly constant disparagement of Russian and Soviet history. In response, they looked for points of pride in national history and culture. The very weakening of the old regime forced people to move beyond criticizing the existing government to defining what they wanted from a future state—in the process, the broad anti-Stalinist civic movement gave way to smaller, more politically polarized groups. The growing estrangement between Russian nationalists, both religious and secular, and those pursuing a pluralist modern vision of the nation is quite evident in the development of monumental art since the end of Soviet rule.

Nationalists, or "patriots" as they prefer to be called, have supported the construction of numerous monuments. The range of nationalists' interests can be seen in the work of their favorite sculptor, Viacheslav Klykov. Between 1989 and 1996, Klykov erected monuments to two members of the Romanov family, the Russian writer Ivan Bunin, the Russian saints Cyril and Methodius, and the legendary World War II hero Marshal Zhukov—each one a larger-than-life, realistic portrait.[35] Klykov, an unabashed supporter of autocracy, fought to place his works—and in essence his philosophy—in the symbolic heart of the Russian state. He sought to place Zhukov on Red Square but settled for the adjacent Manezh square; he tried to get permission to erect Nicholas II in the Kremlin or on the central Borovitskaia square, but was firmly rebuffed.[36] Nevertheless, Klykov's centrally located monument to Cyril and Methodius has become the accepted location for Orthodox church officials and nationalists to celebrate Slavic Literacy Day.

Nationalist groups and families of veterans have also financed the creation of small memorials to Russian soldiers whose sacrifices in World War I, on the side of the White Army in the Civil War, and in Afghanistan were ignored by the Soviet regime.[37] Patriots nowadays rarely mention the history of the purges, presumably because Russian behavior during this tragic period gives them little cause for celebration. They prefer heroic subjects and traditional monumental style to foster public pride in Russia's military, cultural, and religious heritage.

With the exception of Moscow's mayor Iurii Luzhkov, democratic leaders and groups, by contrast, do not seem to have put much stock in monumental art or in patriotic propaganda in general. In the wake of the democrats' defeat of the August 1991 coup attempt by hard-line Communists, many Soviet statues were torn down, including the monument to Dzerzhinskii that towered over Memorial's stone marker in Lubianka square. But the government took no positive steps to use public art to commemorate its triumph. As the curator Irina Bazileva observed in 1995, Moscow was "more a site of restoration than innovation." By restoration Bazileva meant not only the trend for literally returning prerevolutionary street names and

statues and rebuilding old shrines, but also the continued proliferation of monuments in the old triumphal, realistic style. Yeltsin's government gave virtually no material support to the kind of conceptual art championed by dissident artists.[38] Innovative ideas for a new monumental propaganda solicited by the infamous inventors of Sotsart (a sort of pop art that takes off on Soviet rather than capitalist icons) Vitaly Komar and Alexander Melamid, for instance, remain only paper fantasies.[39]

Aside from a monument to 1960s idol Vladimir Vysotskii on Moscow's boulevard ring, no prominent liberals are commemorated in the capital's central public spaces. The most visible new monument in Moscow is to Peter the Great. Smaller works honor cultural figures who were not highly prized by the Soviet state—namely the nineteenth-century writers Feodor Dostoevsky and Anton Chekhov and lyric poet Sergei Esenin. Only plaques commemorate modern liberal heroes. Inconspicuous markers adorn the last residences of Andrei Sakharov in Moscow and Joseph Brodsky in St. Petersburg. The heirs and admirers of nonconformist literary and political figures seem to prefer museums as a means to foster remembrance. The Anna Akhmatova house museum in St. Petersburg has hosted controversial exhibitions, and the newly opened, privately funded Sakharov museum and human rights center includes a research library and meeting space for use by current civic activists.

Democratization in Russia freed artists from censorship and permitted citizens to organize into interest groups. But the demonstrated ability to please the public or to impress art critics does not presently determine which pieces of monumental art will be built. Public hearings and open design commissions have once again vanished. The simplest way to get a piece of public art installed is to donate it to a city or to get a unilateral decision in its favor from a city mayor.[40] Although the process of gaining approval to erect a monument has been decentralized, with more power residing at the city level, democratic principles seldom govern current decisionmaking regarding public art. The power to make public art, like the power to do many other things in Russia today, lies in access to private money and to the executive branch of government at any level. As a consequence of the increased importance of financial and political patronage, a few sculptors—most notably Zurab Tsereteli, Viacheslav Klykov, and Mikhail Chemiakin—have begun to dominate the field of monumental art all out of proportion to the artistic merits of their recent works.

Nevertheless, the new patronage system has produced two monuments to Stalin's victims, neither of which was subject to public vetting. The first, by the Russian émigré artist Mikhail Chemiakin, was installed in St. Petersburg in April 1995. Like most of his works, Chemiakin's monument to the victims of political persecution draws on historical Petersburg themes and images. The monument consists of two sphinxes, reminiscent of those decorating the imperial Petersburg Academy of Arts, with half-human and half-skeletal faces [fig. 13.5]. Between the two sphinxes, four blocks of marble are stacked to form a prison wall with a small window barred by a cross-shaped iron grate. The whole ensemble stands on the bank of the Neva river across from the Kresty prison, through which many of Leningrad's political prisoners passed.[41]

Despite the sphinxes' artistic link to old St. Petersburg, they have not been very warmly received. Chemiakin did not seek material or moral support from the public to build his monument. He raised the necessary funds from a local private bank and relied on the mayor's intercession to get planning approval. Now it seems that residents feel estranged from the artist who has admitted that he rarely visits his native city and considers himself too well-established to participate in competitions.[42] The sharpest rebuke came from Memorial spokesmen, who were upset that Chemiakin did not invite purge survivors to attend the dedication of the sphinxes and that he used the inscription that the St. Petersburg Memorial had engraved on the cornerstone marking the site intended to someday

Fig. 13.5 Detail from Mikhail Chemiakin's monument to victims of political persecution. Photo by the author.

hold its own tribute to Stalin's victims. Angered by Chemiakin's disrespect for their years of efforts to represent the wishes of purge survivors, Memorial organizers fired off letters of protest to local governmental institutions and newspapers demanding that the city create a mechanism for consulting with the public about new monuments.[43]

A second monument to victims of repression was dedicated in Magadan on the eve of the final round of the 1996 presidential elections. The internationally renowned sculptor Ernst Neizvestny created a towering, seventeen-meter-high *Mask of Sorrow* for this city, which had once served as the gateway to the far eastern section of the Gulag. The huge cement mask weeps tears, each drop a tiny human face. Visitors can climb up into the interior of the mask, where there is a solitary prison cell and, in a chapel-like space, a bronze figure of a girl prostrate in front of a large cross.[44] Pointing to stone markers featuring symbols from a variety of confessions and a hammer and sickle for communists at the monument's base, Neizvestny insisted that his design does not privilege the Orthodox faith, but simply reflects his Russian heritage.[45]

Neizvestny from the start refused to participate in Memorial's competition. He preferred to work directly with the local activists and officials in Magadan, Ekaterinburg, and Vorkuta who had invited him to design a monument for them. He thought that he could realize his personal vision on the basis of donations and support from local governments, but all three of his projects stalled in the 1990s for lack of funds. The sculptor prevailed on Yeltsin to donate some of his book royalties to the project in 1994, but only an infusion of funds from the federal government allowed Neizvestny to finish one of his three monuments. In exchange, pro-Yeltsin officials—to the dismay of many in the crowd—turned the monument's dedication ceremony into a final campaign rally.[46]

In the late 1980s, thousands of Soviet citizens affirmed Yevtushenko's avowal that "the time of honest marble" had arrived by sending in money and design advice to Memorial's contest to select a monument to Stalin's victims. As the old regime collapsed, Soviet loyal-ists, Russian patriots, and liberal democrats abandoned the joint project of commemorating victims of repression in favor of pursuing their own separate interests. It seemed to all but the most committed nationalists that the time for monumental propaganda had passed. And yet today Russia can boast of two substantial monuments to Stalin's victims.[47] Chemiakin and Neizvestny built their monuments without public review and thereby escaped having to cope with conflicting ideas of what a monument to victims should be like. It is obviously easier for an artist to serve his or her personal creative vision than to cater to the wishes of others. But the essence of the civic monument as imagined by Memorial—to turn the survivors of totalitarianism from the objects of history into subjects—was lost.[48] If, as their financial support of Neizvestny's *Mask of Sorrow* suggests, democratic politicians have finally realized the merit of public art as a means of propagating some kind of patriotic culture, then they need to consider reinstating a system that empowers citizens. Without mechanisms for public review of monumental art, they may exacerbate social resentment of the wealthy and powerful who seem to have government's ear. They may also fail to find images that truly resonate with their constituency.

14 Architecture, Urban Space, and Post-Soviet Russian Identity

Blair A. Ruble

Late-nineteenth-century and late-twentieth-century Russian cities share two characteristics that distinguish the citybuilding of these periods from other eras. First, the role of the state to shape the city diminished, expanding the capacity of individuals to choose and to shape their immediate environment. Second, confusion over the content of Russian identity led to a frantic search for appropriate architectural antecedents that could impose order on the bewildering turmoil surrounding the meaning of "Russianness." This essay will seek to explore both dimensions of post-Soviet urban reality through the lens of a single provincial city, Yaroslavl.

PROPERTY AND URBAN SPACE

The politics of property stand at the center of the conflict over the role of the state in Russia's post-Soviet future, just as it once did in the divisive battles over Imperial Russia's industrial possibilities. Only the state can shape the city in a world without individual and corporate private property rights. At present, the who, what, when, where, and how of property relations in a new Russia have yet to be established. Examining issues of space reveals a great deal about how post-Soviet politics are being played out. Those politics, in turn, can offer valuable insights into how space reflects the values and power structures of a given society.

New post-Soviet Russian realities are becoming visible in the very stones of Yaroslavl. It is apparent from what has been taking place in this Volga River city that housing will be privatized as the municipality and the various enterprises that once controlled and managed apartment buildings now seek to divest their responsibilities to residents. Quarrels have erupted across Russia over the most just distribution of responsibility and cost among state agencies, individual citizens, and their families. Participants in these discussions appear only vaguely concerned with the psychological, economic, and political consequences of private custody over the primal resource of shelter. Even those who are familiar with North American debates over property taxes, mortgage deductions on income tax, and the myriad of other issues that rouse homeowners can only begin to imagine the transformation of Russian political and economic life that will follow in the wake of the privatization of state housing.

Land-use decisions and urban planning that have ignored financial constraints are giving way to a new preoccupation with land cost. Planners must learn how to incorporate private actors into their vision of the future. Enterprise managers must recalculate how much land they must occupy to accomplish their economic mission. New private banks—highly concentrated in Moscow—are setting their own policies. Where people live and work will be quite different in the years to come as hundreds and thousands of individual and institutional decisions find expression in the city's physical form. Those living patterns, in turn, influence how people think

Portions of this article are drawn from materials found in Blair A. Ruble, *Money Sings! The Politics of Urban Space in Post-Soviet Yaroslavl* (New York, 1995).

about themselves, thereby shaping post-Soviet identities.

The face of Russia is changing. The devolution of political and economic decisionmaking that has marked the past half-decade or so of Russian political and economic life elevates the importance of individual choice in shaping the future Russian city. Any movement, no matter how irregular, toward the creation of market mechanisms in the Russian economy carries with it a new set of problems all too familiar to Western city dwellers. Market mechanisms also create a renewed opportunity for the private realm to gain pride of place in urban development. Personal preferences as well as profits and property will grow in importance as Russian cities respond to a more market-oriented system of economic organization.

An examination of urban form and the processes by which it has come into being reveal a great deal about its creators. The building of a city involves every aspect of human existence. It blends the economic with the political, and the social with the cultural, into the material expression of otherwise abstract and remote "tendencies" and "forces."

The shaping of a city places societal changes in particularly sharp relief. The physical order of the city undergoes continuous modification, even in as small a detail as the shape of a lamppost. Indeed, one sign of hope for many Yaroslavtsy during the present-day "time of troubles" is that "historically accurate" lampposts have been installed throughout the center of town.

People's understanding of the city in general—and of a specific city in particular—evolves even as the physical environment remains more or less constant. Kevin Lynch observed in 1959 that the city is not only "an object which is perceived (and perhaps enjoyed) by millions of people of widely diverse class and character, but it is the product of many builders who are constantly modifying the structure for reasons of their own."[1] The result for Jonathan Raban is an "emporium of style" in which "there is no single point of view from which one can grasp the city as a whole."[2] The public nature of the urban environment permits the observer to penetrate the various influences shaping that world.

Lynch and Raban both assumed that cities are the public manifestation of an infinite number of private visions and decisions. The city is imagined by thousands—resident and visitor, official and citizen. An examination of the principles and motivations underlying their decisions exposes the public and private forces that shape society. Russia's Soviet experience, however, devalued the standing of private decisions in shaping the urban form. State agencies and government planners appropriated city building as their own. The dreariness, tedium, and banality of the modern Russian city is a natural consequence of this appropriation.

The devolution of political and economic decision-making that has marked the past half-decade or so elevates the importance of individual choice in shaping the future Russian city. The private realm is gaining ground in urban development, much as it did a century ago. These trends are evident in the typical post-Soviet Russian provincial city of Yaroslavl.

YAROSLAVL AS A RUSSIAN "MIDDLETOWN"

Yaroslavl was founded in 1010 at the confluence of the Volga and Kotorosl' rivers some 150 miles northeast of Moscow. Its current population is approximately 640,000 residents, spread out along the banks of the Volga for several miles.

The city is the capital of the Yaroslavl Oblast (Region), which is home to some one and one-half million residents—including those of the city of Yaroslavl itself. The region generally lies between the Volga River, running from the northwest to the southeast, and the Moscow Region to the south and west. The region's employment patterns remain fairly typical for Russian provinces as a whole.

Yaroslavl's economy evolved over the centuries, moving the city from a reliance on trade and handicrafts to its emergence as a significant manufacturing center after the completion of a major rail line to Moscow in 1870. The first Russian automobile—the Lebed (Swan)—was scheduled to have rolled off a Yaroslavl assembly line in 1917. That effort collapsed in the chaos of the Bolshevik Revolution and the Civil War. The local economy nonetheless came to rely heavily on major factories connected with the automotive industry, including the Soviet Union's most important diesel motor, tire, and auto-paint factories, as well as a major oil refinery.

Yaroslavl remains fairly atypical for a Russian city of its size in one way that is rather helpful for this discussion.[3] Unlike towns located farther west and south, Yaroslavl was essentially untouched by World War II. The town suffered greatly during the Russian Civil War (1918–21), and a few German bombing raids were directed at local factories and rail yards. Stalinist industrialization policies and later inattention to historical monuments also took their toll on the Yaroslavl townscape. Yet it is far more possible to read the city's history in its physical structure than is the case in many other provincial Russian cities of similar size and significance. The elemental character of a pre-Soviet trading town still defines the city core. A Stalinist "rust belt" factory town belches pollution nearby, while Brezhnev-era blighted moonscapes delimit newer districts farther away from downtown. A distinctive physical text endures, providing inestimable clues to nearly a millennium of habitation.

THE INDIVIDUAL MAY CHOOSE

A number of physical changes have already occurred in Yaroslavl's spatial organization over the course of the past half-decade as a consequence of an expansion of property rights on the one hand, and a diminution in the influence of central planning authorities on the other. Individual choice is making its impact felt on the city's physical development.

Housing patterns in post-Soviet Yaroslavl are now being determined by the market: money matters. The percentage of formerly state housing that has been privatized inched up to over 30 percent for the entire Federation by the end of 1995. The Russian Federation Presidential Administration reported that 32 percent of all apartments eligible for privatization throughout the Federation had been privatized by the end of 1994. In Yaroslavl, 29 percent of all eligible housing units had passed into private hands.

What sort of housing do people actually want? The results of a 1993 survey of housing preferences suggest some of the ways in which the city's future development may be rather different from its Soviet past.[4]

The 1993 survey respondents appear to have strongly positive attachments to the city's historic downtown districts. One-half (50.1 percent) of the respondents identified older districts as their first preference as a place to live, as opposed to 42.1 percent who would chose the newer high-rise districts of the Brezhnev and later eras if they had an opportunity to live anywhere in town. A remarkably low 7.8 percent expressed primary preference for the city's semi-rural suburban districts, while over one-half (52.4 percent) declared that the suburbs were the least desirable areas in which to live.

Yaroslavtsy similarly attached a remarkably high importance to the issue of historical preservation, with an astonishing 71.2 percent of those queried responding that the issue was "one of the most important problems" for the city, and another 26.4 percent calling historic preservation one of the city's "secondary problems." While strikingly high, these figures are nonetheless lower than those for environmental concerns, as 95.1 percent of those responding identified that issue as one of the city's most important, and an additional 3.5 percent viewed it as being of secondary importance.

The salience of preservation issues complements a view of the city that values central historic neighborhoods over newer, high-rise districts surrounding the city core. Interestingly, however, the strong preference for the pre-war central city as a place of residence is cast in a different light when social class and especially generational perspectives are brought to bear on the issue.

The survey suggests that the highest-income respondents had the greatest interest in living in suburban districts, as did self-identified "entrepreneurs." Such groups are likely to exert increasing influence over the city's physical and economic development, as Yaroslavl implements post-Soviet investment and ownership practices. More telling is the strong correlation between age and the preference for residing in central historic districts. Younger Yaroslavtsy, especially those of the post-Soviet cohort under 21 years of age, express the strongest interest in newer urban neighborhoods and even in semi-rural suburban districts.

While support for historic preservation remains strong in every social group, it too reflects complex income and generational patterns that might not bode well for the future of central Yaroslavl. Once again, those who are most likely to control post-Soviet development are among the least identified with the need to preserve the city's historic form. The difference between the pattern of responses on preservation issues and preferences for residing in central historic neighborhoods is that the youngest cohort of respondents, those who came of age since Mikhail Gorbachev rose to power more than a decade ago, have emerged as the strongest advocates of preservation programs. While this pattern suggests a possible base of support for future activities intended to protect central historic districts, it should not lessen alarm over the future viability of central Yaroslavl as a place to live and, perhaps, even to work. These same respondents are among those least likely to want to reside in central neighborhoods. Not surprisingly, identification with preservation issues is strongest in those areas with the largest number of historic monuments (primarily sixteenth- and seventeenth-century churches).

Taken together, there appears to be considerable support for new patterns of urban development among those Yaroslavl residents most likely to be directly involved in reshaping their city during the post-Soviet transition. Suburban areas are likely to grow despite the extraordinarily small number of respondents who currently favor the Russian version of suburbia. Both preference for residing in central districts and supportive attitudes for historic preservation, while strong throughout the survey's respondents, are the weakest among those generational and income groups most likely to determine Yaroslavl's future in a market-oriented economy.

The physical form of Yaroslavl is already being transformed by the privatization of municipal and enterprise apartments and the construction of single-family cottage settlements. A new, decentralized, boundless urban form familiar to urban and suburban residents of capitalist societies is coming into being. The precise contours of this future post-Soviet city may not yet be well-defined, but its vague outline may already be discerned. The individual is already emerging as the most potent actor in the city-building process. Urban Russians are living—and will continue to live—differently. Individual choice is shaping the city.

WHO OWNS GOD?

The end of the Soviet regime created new opportunities for religious organizations of all denominations to seek return of former houses of worship that had fallen under state control. Many preservation specialists, for their part, expressed concern over the ability of religious institutions to properly maintain these numerous historic structures.[5] Vicious battles consequently erupted in Yaroslavl and elsewhere between the Orthodox Church and cultural institutions housed in former religious institutions. There have been some positive outcomes to these struggles. For example, a felicitous merger of museum and religious facility was negotiated at Moscow's historic Andronikov Monastery, which had served as the Andrei Rublev Central Museum of Ancient Russian Culture and Arts since the late 1950s.

Tensions and suspicions linger on as such successful accommodation between cultural and religious leaders has proven all too rare. In Yaroslavl, the issue of the return of religious property led to particularly bitter con-

Fig. 14.1 Church of Elijah the Prophet, 2001. Photograph by Aleksandr Khodnev.

frontations between preservation officials and representatives of the Russian Orthodox Church. Painful disagreements over the conveyance of the city's largest religious building—the Church of Elijah the Prophet—to Orthodox authorities illustrate many of the harsh controversies that have come to divide the local preservation movement.

The Church of Elijah the Prophet (fig. 14.1) had been a museum for much of the Soviet era. Orthodox officials demanded that this structure, the most prominent and prestigious in the city, must be returned to its original purpose and serve as a place of worship. People's Deputy Father Mikhail Mikhailovich Peregudov drew on his standing within the Orthodox Church and his position on the Yaroslavl Regional Soviet to guide the process of partial transfer of title through to completion in late 1990 and early 1991. Some local cultural notables—such as Yaroslavl Art Museum curator Irina Bolotseva—led a charge against this transfer. Discussions raged in the press, on local television, and at various government and religious commissions and com-

mittees all the way up to the most senior governing bodies of the Russian government and the Orthodox Church in Moscow.

A 1990 article by Bolotseva appearing in the major local paper of the period, *Severnyi rabochii* (*The Northern Worker*), established the parameters of debate.[6] Acknowledging that there were reasonable grounds for supporting the transfer of title—the structure was built as a house of worship, the Soviet government had abused and irreparably damaged scores of historic buildings, justice demands that stolen property be returned to its rightful owner—Bolotseva contrasted the 1,000-year history of the Russian Church with the 200-year history of her own institution.

Local gentry and intellectuals established the Yaroslavl Art Museum in the eighteenth century in order to protect icons and religious artifacts from abuse by daily worshipers. One of the oldest art museums in Russia, the Yaroslavl collection had demonstrated, according to Bolotseva, a record of considerable accomplishment that should allay any doubts about its dedication to protecting Russia's patrimony for all Russians. The Bolshevik desecration of churches enhanced the cultural significance of those buildings, icons, frescos, and artifacts—such as the Church of Elijah the Prophet—that had survived under the Museum's protection. Finally, she noted, there was as yet no legal basis for returning the property to its previous owner, the Church.

A firestorm of controversy ensued.[7] The passionately supercharged issue of the meaning of "Russianness" conditioned much of this debate. As an undergraduate history student at Yaroslavl State University explained, "the Church of Elijah the Prophet has emotional meaning for all Yaroslavtsy, even if they do not believe in God. The [Orthodox] Church should not be permitted to assert a new ideological monopoly over the meaning of Russia for Russians."[8]

In the end, the conveyance documents for the church stipulated that its maintenance and management were the combined responsibility of the city council, the region's preservation administration, and local prelates. Religious services may not be conducted during the winter so as to limit the damage to the building's inestimable frescos by snow, mud, and bulky outer garments. It was only in 1993—after most property demands by local religious institutions had been resolved—that relations between some more moderate religious officials and their more restrained colleagues among preservation groups began to improve.

A bitter legacy of recrimination remains as local authorities across Russia decide the fates of scores of religious buildings. The task is enormous. There were 1,200 operating churches in Yaroslavl province (Iaroslavskaia guberniia) in 1912, as opposed to only 130 remaining open to parishioners in 1993.[9] Meanwhile, the powerful and once united Yaroslavl historical preservation movement has become sharply divided and contentious.

Russian Federation legislation eventually established more precise guidelines for title transfer to religious organizations. Museums and religious officials have nonetheless tangled over the fate of religious artifacts as many disputes over the disposition of real property were being resolved. Writing in *Vash vvbor*, a national journal devoted to regional affairs, Bolotsova once again sounded the alarm.[10] She protested plans to empty out icons from the Yaroslavl Art Museum for use in churches around the region. She acknowledged that many icons from the thirteenth through nineteenth centuries came to the Museum through state confiscation programs during the 1920s and 1930s—most actively in 1928. The Museum had saved hundreds of precious paintings and frescos from destruction. While they are not always stored in ideal conditions, she continued, they nonetheless receive professional care. The Orthodox Church could not similarly protect the hundreds of icons that were scheduled for transfer, at least in the short term.

In a Russia searching for new lenses, differing views of the present and hopes for the future naturally sustain differing views of the past. Similar quarrels occur, of course, in many historic towns and cities around the world. The problem of the moment in Yaroslavl is to establish mechanisms that will facilitate their constructive resolution. The degree of openness permitted by whatever procedures that eventually emerge will partially determine precisely how urban space will be reinvented in Yaroslavl's post-Soviet future.

THE POLITICS OF MONUMENTS

Post-Soviet Yaroslavl has endured four protracted battles over civic symbols since 1989. First, there was a vicious fight over redrawing the city's seal. Then, the city leaders dedicated a monument to their town's founder—Yaroslav the Wise—in the face of public protest. Next, the mayor unveiled a statue of the Old Testament Holy Trinity on the site of the historic Cathedral of the Assumption. Finally, the city sponsored the construction of a chapel commemorating the 1611 passage through the city of Kuz'ma Minin's and Dmitrii Pozharskii's citizens' liberation army.

The last City Soviet—which served from

the city's first Soviet-era competitive elections in 1989 until November 1993—had been paralyzed by discussions of the historic authenticity of the city's seal. The coat-of-arms featured a bear with an ax jauntily tossed over his shoulder, in reference to a legendary wrestling match at the confluence of the Volga and Kotrosol' Rivers in 1010.[11] The Soviet deputies argued endlessly over the precise position of this paw or that, of the size and shape of the ax, of the appropriate balance between warning and welcome in the bear's grin. The exhausted delegates eventually settled on a new "historically correct, non-Soviet" symbol for their town that is not nearly as embraceable as its "unauthentic, Soviet" predecessor.

An analogous battle ensued over a monument honoring the winner of the legendary wrestling match, Kievan Prince Yaroslav the Wise. On October 23, 1993, Russian Federation President Boris Yeltsin, making his first major political appearance since the tragic battle at the Russian Parliament three weeks before, joined political and religious leaders from the Russian Federation, Belarus, and Ukraine in the shabby square at the front of Yaroslavl's main post office. There, in the frost of an early-autumn afternoon, they dedicated a new monument to Yaroslav the Wise, creator of the first written Slavic legal code and city founder.[12]

The statue itself had provoked something of a controversy in the city. Its cost of $40,000 struck some as an extravagance, given the city's severe fiscal constraints. Others argued bitterly about the statue's design. The largest group of critics merely urged that Yaroslav be moved to the site overlooking the Volga where legend places the wrestling match of lore.

City officials chastened by the dispute over the city seal had formed a blue-ribbon commission, inviting leading cultural, civic, and religious figures from Yaroslavl, Belarus, and Ukraine to participate in their deliberations. These figures included representatives of the Orthodox Church in Russia and in Ukraine as well as of the Ukrainian Uniate Church. Convinced that they had finally figured out how to run such competitions, the city leaders were lulled into a false sense of security by the scanty press coverage and mild public interest in their deliberations.

The city's architects and planners had decided to draw on European design principles to bring some modicum of order to the sprawling, ill-defined open space in front of the city post office. The "square," left over from an awkward juncture of various construction projects over the centuries, had presented something of a design problem. A relatively recent bridge across the Kotorosl' dumped traffic from Moscow into a rather large, typical Russian trading *dvor*. This disorder simply would not do in a city striving for increased tourism from abroad. Hence, the city decided to place the monument in a traffic circle that would provide a focal point for the rather awkward public space greeting tourists arriving in their cars. The only problem was that many Yaroslavtsy—unschooled in the architectural principles of the Italian Renaissance—rather enjoyed their ungainly square. Distinct Russian and western notions of urban space had once again come into conflict.

City authorities had their way in the end, and Yaroslav the Lawgiver now provides a modicum of Western-style rationality to a main public space in central Yaroslavl (fig. 14.2). The aesthetic principles of the professionals won out over populist impulses. The statue, which shows Yaroslav cradling a model of the city in his arms, is reminiscent of the famous Byzantine mosaic portrait in Hagia Sophia of Constantine presenting his city to the Savior. New form was given to a prominent neighborhood in this historic town. But the war over monuments did not come to an end. Rather, the entire saga repeated itself within two years.

The city's seventeenth-century Cathedral of the Assumption (Uspenskii Sobor) overlooking the confluence of the Volga and Kotorosl' rivers had been Yaroslavl's primary cathedral and most holy site. Severely damaged during the Bolshevik shelling of the city at the time of a White Guard rebellion in 1918, the cathedral was demolished in 1934 to make

Fig. 14.2 Monument to Yaroslav the Wise, 2001. Photograph by Aleksandr Khodnev.

way for a gargantuan, five-hundred-unit apartment complex that was never built.[13] Competing political groups throughout the Gorbachev era and into the post-Soviet period argued vociferously over how best to honor the destruction of the city's most important cultural monument. Proposals to rebuild the cathedral eventually gave way to economic reality. Mayor Victor Volonchunas allocated the funds for a statue to be placed within a cement outline of the building's original foundations.

The winning design was a statue of the Old Testament Holy Trinity, reminiscent of Orthodox iconography. All the participants in the local cultural wars immediately went into battle once again. Russian Orthodoxy does not traditionally exhibit physical representations of the Trinity. Better, some proposed, to place the statue off by the city's unused Roman Catholic church because, after all, such representations are by their very nature of the West. Better still to leave the site vacant, a tragic reminder of the destruction of the Soviet era. Mayor Volonchunas prevailed, and the statue was unveiled in May 1995 (fig. 14.3).

A fourth controversy followed in 1997, as the city joined forces with the Orthodox hierarchy to build a memorial chapel on the shores of the Kotorosl' River at the ford through which Dmitrii Pozharskii and

Fig. 14.3 Monument to the Holy Trinity, 2001. Photograph by Aleksandr Khodnev.

Kuz'ma Minin led their army of angry citizens to drive Polish and Swedish occupiers from Moscow (fig. 14.4). The chapel's design had been the subject of yet another heated debate over symbols. An initial sketch showed the chapel crowned by a double-headed eagle, representing the power of the old Russian state.[14] This ornament was eventually replaced in the final version by an Orthodox cross, reportedly intended to emphasize the religious nature of Pozharskii and Minin's victory over Roman Catholic infidels from the West. The chapel was dedicated at precisely the same moment in September 1997 when Mayor Luzhkov was presiding over Moscow's triumphant 850th Anniversary celebrations, as if to suggest that the Russian provinces might again have to rescue their capital from Western occupiers.

Given all of Yaroslavl's and Russia's perplexing problems, pitched battles such as these over monuments and symbols may appear to be rather curious. They point to the very heart of Russia's post-Soviet conundrum.

Russian politicians such as Mayor Volonchunas intuitively understand that the present Russian regime lacks an ideological center, something that gives meaning to the new Russian state. Deep divisions run through Russian society over the very meaning of Russia and Russianness; in short, over identity. The rejection by some Russians of so much that is Western and the embrace of nationalism so evident in public opinion polls point in a similar direction.

MYTH AND CEREMONY IN POST-SOVIET RUSSIA

What will fill this void? Are statues of Yaroslav the Wise and the Trinity sufficient? Who precisely are the Russians? What does the adjective "Russian" mean? How can the Russian Federation secure an emotional bond with the people and culture after whom it has been named? And what about the other nationalities making up the Federation's consti-

Fig. 14.4 Chasovnik honoring Minin and Pozharskii, 2001. Photograph by Aleksandr Khodnev.

tuent republics? Where does *"nash"* ("our") begin and end? What is to be included and who shall be excluded? How these questions are answered should give more than enough material to those interested in the expression of group identity to keep busy in the years ahead. Just as all seemed to be contended in the industrializing Russia of the late nineteenth century, everything seems the object of battles once more in the post-Soviet Russia of the late twentieth century.

For all but a limited period at the end of the last century and this, the Russian state sought to lift "the sovereign" into another realm where he or she displayed the superior qualities of a being entitled to rule.[15] The messy order of capitalist development undermined the symbolic distance between ruler and ruled a century ago. The capitalist Russian townscape had only begun to assert a more coherent symbolic expression by the time the Imperial state had begun to collapse. The Romanov dynasty never quite succeeded in establishing new forms of expression that

could complement the realities of the industrial city. Moscow's neo-Russian architecture and romantic realism in other arts began to bridge the chasm between public nationalist expression and the individual taste of those with the resources to shape the city. This story is beginning to be repeated with capitalism's return.

Russian space is being reorganized, with private capital and individual choice overtaking state decree and collective preference as the driving forces shaping the Russian city. A new symbolic language will emerge as architectural, institutional, and ceremonial organization delineate new boundaries and codify new functions for the post-Soviet Russian state and society.

Single-family dwellings designed from glossy photographs in North American and European magazines betray the fantasies of individual builders. The search for appropriate monuments to give meaning to the fledgling post-Soviet Russian regime exposes that state's shallow philosophical and ideological roots. Politicians intuitively understand that bears, lawgivers, and angels hold out the hope of giving fresh national meaning to cities molded by the desire of socialist planners to stamp out all forms of localism. Monuments may not provide a meaningful substitute for hard thought about the form and content of the Russian state. They nonetheless reveal just how important such deliberation can be in a period of national reformation.

Notes

Introduction

1. *Journal of Interdisciplinary History* 17, no. 1 (Summer, 1986): 1; F. Haskell, *History and Its Images: Art and the Interpretation of the Past* (New Haven, 1993), 10.

2. Benedict Anderson, *Imagined Communities: Reflections on the Origin and Spread of Nationalism*, rev. ed. (London, 1991). For a stimulating set of essays on the theme of nationalism, see *Becoming National: A Reader*, Geoff Ely and Ronald Grigor Suny, eds. (New York, 1996), especially the excellent introduction.

3. " 'The Souls of the Righteous in a Bright Place': Landscape and Orthodoxy in Seventeenth-Century Russian Maps," *The Russian Review* 58, no. 1 (January, 1999): 1–25.

Chapter 1 Peter the Great and the Problem of Periodization

1. Nicholas V. Riasanovsky, *The Image of Peter the Great in Russian History and Thought* (New York, 1985), 152–65 (154 for the phrase quoted); and further, Edward C. Thaden, *The Rise of Historicism in Russia* (New York, 1999), especially 174–97.

2. S.M. Solov'ëv, *Istoriia Rossii s drevneishikh vremën*, 15 vols. (Moscow, 1962–66), vol. 9, 541–53; originally published St. Petersburg, 1851–79.

3. I quote from the edition of Kliuchevskii's *Kurs russkoi istorii* published as the first five volumes of V.O. Kliuchevskii, *Sochineniia v vos'mi tomakh* (Moscow, 1956–59), vol. 4, 201, 220–21. On Kliuchevskii see further Riasanovsky, 166–76. Kliuchevskii's influence extends to the current leader of Petrine historians in Russia, E.V. Anisimov, as is manifest in the latter's *Vremia petrovskikh reform* (first ed. Leningrad, 1989); see also the English edition of same, Evgenii V. Anisimov, *The Reforms of Peter the Great: Progress through Coercion in Russia*, trans. J.T. Alexander (Armonk, N.Y., 1993).

4. I. Grabar' et al., *Istoriia russkago iskusstva*, 4 vols. (Moscow, n.d. [1910–12]), profusely illustrated.

5. W.C. Brumfield, *Gold in Azure: One Thousand Years of Russian Architecture* (Boston, 1983), is a prominent example. Nor is the cause of a coherent periodization of Russian architectural history advanced in the revised and expanded edition of this work published a decade later: Brumfield, *A History of Russian Architecture* (Cambridge, 1993), valuable though it also is in other respects, particularly illustration.

6. For this very useful term—"rusticalization" (*Rustikalisierung*), meaning the "barbarization of forms" or the "disintegration of style under the impact of new factors, whether aesthetic or sociological in nature"—see V.V. Stech, "Rustikalisierung als Faktor Stilentwickelung," in *XIIIe Congrès international d'histoire de l'art: Résumés présentées au congrès* (Stockholm, 1933), 210–13.

7. A task attempted in J. Cracraft, *The Petrine Revolution in Russian Architecture* (Chicago, 1988).

8. Kaufmann, *Court, Cloister and City: The Art and Culture of Central Europe 1450–1800* (Chicago, 1995), 417, 424.

9. Cracraft, *Petrine Revolution*, 155, 70.

10. E.H. Ter Kuile, "Architecture," in J. Rosenberg et al. *Dutch Art and Architecture 1600 to 1800* (Baltimore, 1966), especially pp. 221–29 (p. 225 for the words quoted).

11. Bernard le Bovier de Fontenelle, as quoted in Cracraft, *Petrine Revolution*, p. 1.

12. The progression of styles is amply demonstrated in the later chapters of Brumfield, *History of Russian Architecture*.

13. Cf. R.J. Tuttle, "Vignola," in J. Turner, ed., *The [Grove] Dictionary of Art*, vol. 32 (London, 1996), pp. 502–8.

14. T.A. Bykova and M.M. Gurevich, *Opisanie izdanii grazhdanskoi pechati (1708–1725)* (Moscow/Leningrad, 1955), nos. 29, 61, 720; N.A. Evsina, *Arkhitekturnaia teoriia v Rossii XVIII v.* (Moscow, 1975), 37.

15. See Manuela Khan-Rossi et al., *Domenico Trezzini e la costruzione di San Pietroburgo* (Lugano, 1994), lavishly illustrated, with essays by various scholars, original documents, and bibliography.

16. *Pis'ma i bumagi imperatora Petra Velikogo*, 13 vols. (St. Petersburg, 1887–1992), vol. 7, pt. 1, no. 2994 (p. 32); ibid., pt. 2, p. 600; ibid., pt. 1, no. 3412 (pp. 375–77); ibid., pt. 2, p. 1236.

17. Discussion based on a copy of the Moscow 1712 edition at the Russian State Library, Moscow.

18. See my related volumes, *The Petrine Revolution in Russian Imagery* (Chicago, 1997), and *The Petrine Revolution in Russian Culture* (Cambridge, MA, forthcoming [2004], devoted to verbal culture).

19. See the bibliographies in Cracraft, *Revolution in Architecture* and in Brumfield, *History of Russian Architecture*, for comprehensive listings.

Chapter 2 The Throne of Monomakh

1. In all references to the Tsar's Pew in official ceremonials from the Cathedral of the Dormition (the earliest from 1622 with commentary on practices from more than a century earlier), the verbs consistently used with respect to the Throne are *stoiati / stavitisia / stati* "stand" and not *sidieti / saditisia / siesti* "sit;" cf. A.P. Golubtsov, *Chinovniki Moskovskogo Uspenskogo Sobora*, ChOIDR, 1907, 28–32 and passim.

2. Sigmund Freiherr von Herberstein, *Rerum Moscoviticarum Commentarii* (Vienna, 1557), reprinted 1969, 96.

3. *PSRL*, v. 25 (Moscow and Leningrad, 1949), 302.

4. Cf. S. M. Zemtsov and V. L. Glazychev, *Aristotel' F'oravanti* (Moscow, 1985), 91–93.

5. I have in mind Russian travelers, foreign dignitaries, individual members of the higher clergy, and possibly his second wife, Sophia Paleologue, niece of the last Byzantine emperor. See, for example, the testimony of Ignatii of Smolensk (late fourteenth century) in George P. Majeska, *Russian Travelers to Constantinople in the Fourteenth and Fifteenth Centuries* (Dumbarton Oaks, 1984), 109 (cf. commentary, pp. 422–23, 430–33). The sixth- and tenth-century descriptions of Paulus Silentarius (*Descriptio ecclesiae sanctae Sophiae et ambonis*, PG, v. 86, lines 580–85) and Constantine VII Porphyrogenitus (*De cerimoniis aulae byzantinae* in *Le Livre des Cérémonies*, ed. Albert Vogt [Paris, 1935–39], 70–73), respectively, have been interpreted by most scholars as indicating that the *metatorion*, the site of the emperor's throne, was located in the southeastern bay of Hagia Sophia adjacent to the southern wall. Cf. Rowland J. Mainstone, *Hagia Sophia: Architecture, Structure, and Liturgy of Justinian's Great Church* (London, 1988), 223–25, 231–33.

6. Herberstein's description of Vasilii III standing without throne in the Cathedral of the Dormition appears to indicate that the grand prince simply had no special pew before the installation of the Monomakh Throne by Tsar Ivan IV. Therefore there is no expectation of its mention prior to 1551, contra I.M. Sokolova, "Tsarskoe mesto pervogo russkogo tsaria: Zamysel i forma," *Rossiia i khristianskii vostok* 1 (1997), 136.

7. For example, T.V. Tolstaia, *Uspenskii sobor Moskovskogo kremlia* (Moscow, 1979), 30, and

G.N. Bocharov, "Tsarskoe mesto Ivana Groznogo v moskovskom Uspenskom sobore," *Pamiatniki russkoi arkhitektury i monumental'nogo iskusstva: Goroda, ansambli, zodchie*, ed. V.P. Vygolov (Moscow, 1985), 46.

8. I.M. Snegirev, *Pamiatniki moskovskoi drevnosti* (Moscow, 1841–45), 26.

9. The descriptive, extended version of the coronation ceremony mentions a special, temporary royal pew erected to the right-hand (south) side in front of the iconostasis (*i potom ugotovaiut' tsrskoe miesto na desnei stranie*), which is torn apart by the people after the ceremony and taken as souvenirs of the coronation (*i togda to tsrskoe postavlenoe miesto vs' narod obdiraet, koizhdo, khto vozmet", na chest' tsrskago postavlenia*), E.V. Barsov, *Drevne-russkie pamiatniki sviashchennogo venchaniia tsarei na tsarstvo* (Moscow, 1883), 43, 66. The text cited here is based on the Church Typikon copy (16th c.). Supralinear letters are underscored.

10. *PSRL* v. 34 (Moscow, 1978), 189.

11. St. Petersburg Public Library, M.P. Pogodin Collection, No. 1567. I have not yet had the opportunity to examine this manuscript personally and therefore I am obliged to rely on the transcription by Snegirev and the apparently minor corrections of same by Zabelin (see n. 16).

12. I. Zabelin, "Reshenie voprosa o Tsarskom meste, ili tak nazyvaemom Monomakhovom trone v Uspenskom Sobore," *Moskvitianin*, 1850, no. 11, 54–55 (reprinted in "Tron, ili Tsarskoe mesto Groznogo v Moskovskom Uspenskom Sobore," *Otchet imperatorskogo Rossiiskogo Istoricheskogo muzeia imeni Imperatora Aleksandra III v Moskve za 1907 god*, 1908, 68–69).

13. *Sie zhe Tsar'skoe miesto, ezhe est' prestol", ustroen" byst' v lieto 7060 (1551) miesiatsa Sentevriia v 1 den' v piatoe lieto derzhavy tsarstva i gosudarstva ego*. Indirect evidence in support of a completion date earlier than 1570 comes from events connected with Ivan IV's defeat of Novgorod in the winter of 1570. He not only ordered a Tsar's Pew to be built near the Prelate's Pew in Novgorod's Cathedral of the Holy Wisdom, but, in an action that would perk up the mood of any Freudian historian, he had the baldachin of the former transferred to his own Pew, replacing the cross with a golden dove. The prelate himself, Archbishop Pimen, was stripped of his rank and banished to Riazan' (*PSRL*, v. 3 [St. Petersburg, 1841], 163, 169; cf. Iu. I. Nikitina, "Monumental'no-dekorativnaia rez'ba molennykh mest iz Novgorodskoi Sofii," *Pamiatniki kul'tury. Novye otkrytiia: Pis'mennost', Iskusstvo, Arkheologiia, Ezhegodnik 1986* [Leningrad, 1987], 350). It is highly unlikely that the tsar would have a Tsar's Pew built in Novgorod's Cathedral of the Holy Wisdom without a previously existing analogue in Moscow's cathedral church.

14. The occasional equivalence of the phrase *liutyi*

zver,' "fierce beast," and *lev,* "lion" is taken up in O.P. Likhacheva, "Lev—liutyi zver'," *TODRL* 48 (1993), 129–37. The author is apparently unaware of "Fragment."

15. Zabelin is confident that a deeper symbolism is present but leaves its determination to archeology, "Reshenie voprosa," 69. The juxtaposition of a crouching lion or lion cub and a hyena is apt, these two animals being natural enemies in a common habitat, but the unclear reference of *oskrogan* makes any resolution unlikely.

16. V. Schepkin "Khudozhestvennoe znachenie Trona," in "Tron, ili Tsarskoe mesto Groznogo v Moskovskom Uspenskom Sobore," *Otchet imperatorskogo Rossiiskogo Istoricheskogo muzeia imeni Imperatora Aleksandra III v Moskve za 1907 god,* 1908, 77–78.

17. The panel inscriptions are reproduced from Snegirev, *Pamiatniki,* 29. I have emended the text as recommended by Zabelin in "Reshenie voprosa," 54. Zabelin was primarily concerned about the order in which Snegirev presented the material, that is, first the inscription from the double doors, then that from the cornice, rather than the other way around, which he considered the correct one. He notes that the errors in Snegirev's transcription are minor, save one (*gobi > tobie,* which he corrects). The manuscript copy itself was done somewhat carelessly in his opinion.

18. *Blagoviernyi Velikii Kniaz' Vladimer" Kievskii Manamakh" soviet" tvoriashe so Kniazmi svoimi i Boliary, poviedaia im" khrabrost' praroditel' svoikh", kako imali dan' s" Tsariagrada.*

19. *Blagoviernyi Kniaz' Velikii Vladimer" zbiraet" voevody iskusny i blagorasudny i postavliaet" chinonachal'niky, tysushchniki, sotniki, piatdesiatniki, elika voiskomu iskusu po . . . [potrebno?].*

20. *Velikago Kniazia Vladimera voiska edut" vo oblasti Frakiistii.*

21. *Velikago kniazia Vladimera voevody pristupisha k" Frakiiskou gradu.*

22. *Velikago kniazia Vladimera voevody plenivshe vesi Frakiiskiia.*

23. *. . . i vzvratishasia so mnogim" bogatestvom".*

24. *Togda bie v" Tsarigradie blagochestivyi Tsar' Konstiantin" Manamakh" i v to vremia bran' imeia s Persy i s Latynoiu.*

25. *Blagoviernyi Tsar' Konstiantin" Manamakh" sostavliaet" soviet" mudryi i Tsar'skii i otriazhaet" posly svoia k Velikomu Kniaziu Vladimeru Vsevolodichu v Kiev", Neofita, Mitropolita ot Asia Efes'kago i s" nim" dva Episkopa Meletin'ska i Mitulinska i stratiga Antiokhiiskago Igumena Ierusalim"skago Ieustafiia i inykh" svoikh".*

26. *Blagoviernyi Tsar' Konstiantin" daet" chestnyia dary Mitropolitu Neofitu i Episkopom" i poslannikom", i otpusti ikh iz Tsariagrada v Kiev" k" Velikomu Kniaziu Vladimeru Vsevolodichu.*

27. *Otpushchennym zhe im", byvshim" Neofitu*

Mitropolitu so Episkopy i s" predrechennymi poslanniki iz Kon'stiantina grada, vnidosha v korab' plovushche k Kievu.

28. *Priidosha poslanniki ot" Tsariagrada vo grad" Kiev" ko Kniaziu Vladimeru Vsevolodovichu i prinesosha k nemu Tsar'skie chestnyi i iny mnogi dary i proshakhu u nego mira.*

29. *Vienchal" bie blagoviernago Velikago Kniazia Vladimera Vsevolodovicha Manamakha Sviatyi Mitropolit" Neofit".*

30. *Kniga o izbranii . . . tsaria . . . Mikhaila Fedorovicha* (Moscow, 1672).

31. *Skazanie o kniaz'iakh vladimirskikh,* ed. R.P. Dmitrieva (Moscow, 1955).

32. *. . . da naritsaeshis' otsele Bogovenchannyi Tsar'! Venchan" sim" Tsar'skym" ventsem" rukoiu Sviateishago Mitropolita Kir" Neofita i so Episkopy, i ot" togo vremeni Kniaz' Vladimir" Vsevolodich" narechetsia Manamakh" i Tsar' Velikiia Rosia, i prebyst' s" Tsarem" Konstiantinom" prochee vremia v miru i liubvi i ottole i donynie tiem" ventsem" Tsar'skim" venchaiutsia velitsyi Kniazi Vladimerstii.*

33. Cf. Averil Cameron, "The Construction of Court Ritual: The Byzantine *Book of Ceremonies,*" in *Rituals of Royalty: Power and Ceremonial in Traditional Societies,* ed. David Cannadine and Simon Price (Cambridge, 1987), 130–31; Daniel Rowland, "Biblical Military Imagery in the Political Culture of Early Modern Russia: The Blessed Host of the Heavenly Tsar," *Medieval Russian Culture, Vol. 2,* ed. Michael S. Flier and Daniel Rowland (Berkeley, 1995), 183–84.

34. Zabelin, "Reshenie voprosa," 67. See, for example, M. D'iakonov, *Vlast' moskovskikh gosudarei: Ocherki iz istorii politicheskikkh idei drevnei Rusi* (St. Petersburg, 1889), 77–78.

35. *RIB,* vol. 3 (Moscow, 1876), col. 311: *Da u tsarskogo zh" miesta obraz" Blagoslovenno voinstvo Nebesnago Tsaria na zolotie v kiotie. . . .* [And right by the Tsar's Pew is the icon "Blessed is the Host of the Emperor of Heaven" on a gold background in a case.] This particular inventory is now dated to 1609–11; see T.S. Borisova, "O datirovke drevneishei iz sokhranivshikhsia opisei Uspenskogo sobora," in *Uspenskii sobor Moskovskogo kremlia: Materialy i issledovaniia* (Moscow, 1985), 258.

36. The most detailed studies remain the articles by Zabelin ("Reshenie voprosa") and Schepkin "Khudozhestvennoe znachenie," published together in "Tron, ili Tsarskoe mesto Groznogo v Moskovskom Uspenskom Sobore," in *Otchet imperatorskogo Rossiiskogo Istoricheskogo muzei imeni Imperatora Aleksandra III v Moskve za 1907 god,* 1908, 67–79 plus 20 tables and one engraving.

37. Bocharov, "Tsarskoe mesto," 46; cf. André Grabar, "Trônes épiscopaux du XIe et XIIe siècle en Italie méridionale," *L'art de la fin de l'antiquité et du moyen age,* vol. 1 (Paris, 1968 [reprint of 1954 article]), 383–90.

38. Bocharov, "Tsarskoe mesto," 44.

39. Shchepkin, "Khudozhestvennoe znachenie," 73.

40. Ibid., 73–75.

41. The connection between the Tsar's Pew and the Zion is apparently not unusual; some of the decorative motifs on the Tsar's Pew and Prelate's Pew in Novgorod are found on the twelfth to fourteenth century zions in Novgorod's Cathedral of the Holy Wisdom (Nikitina, "Monumental'no-dekorativnaia rez'ba," 355).

42. I. A. Sterligova, "Ierusalimy kak liturgicheskie sosudy v drevnei Rusi," in *Ierusalim v russkoi kulture,* ed. Andrei Batalov and Aleksei Lidov (Moscow, 1994), 50.

43. See Nikitina, "Monumental'no-dekorativnaia rez'ba," 359–61.

44. *Re(che) G(ospod)', az" izbrakh' tia Tsaria, vziakh tia za desnitsu tvoiu i ustroi tebe obladati liudmi moimi vo vsia dni zhivota tvoe(go). Ashche khodishi po zapoviedem" moim" i tvorishi voliu moiu, dam" tebie serdtse smyslenno i mudrost' i budeshi iako nie by tako ni edi(n") v tsariekh" prezh tebe i po tebie ne budet", i ashche tvorishi sud" i pravdu posredie zemlia i slyshishi vozdykhanie i slezy sushchikh" v skorbie imat" i upravlenie stvorishi im", vskorie umnozhiu liet" zhivota tvoego i dam" tobie odolienie na vragi i dam" tobie na zemli na umnozhenie plodov" zemnykh" i vozstavliu semia tvoe i ustroiu tsarstvo vashe i prestol" vash" do vieka i budu vam" vo ottsa i vy budete mi v syny. K sim" zhe ezh . . . i ne prosishi u mene, dam" ti slavu i bogatstvo i pokoriatsi iazytsi. Ashche priidet" nepravda vashe, nakazhu vas", milosti moeia neot"imu ot vas".*

45. For the transmission of Agapetus in Muscovite Rus' through Iosif Volotskii and Metropolitan Makarii, see Ihor Ševčenko "A Neglected Byzantine Source of Muscovite Political Ideology, *Harvard Slavic Studies* 2 (1954), 141–79, reprinted in Ihor Ševčenko, *Byzantium and the Slavs in Letters and Culture* (Cambridge, Mass., and Naples, 1991), 49–87, esp. 64–73; and David B. Miller, "The Coronation of Ivan IV of Moscow," *Jahrbücher für Geschichte Osteuropas* 15, n.s., 1967, 567–68.

46. . . . *glt' bo gs' bg" prorokom", az" vozdvigokh tia s pravdoiu tsria i priiakh tia za ruku, i ukriepikh tia.* Barsov, *Drevne-russkie pamiatniki,* 57.

47. *gsdi bzhe nsh', tsriu tsrstvuiushchim i gsd' gospodstviushchim, izhe Somoilom" prorokom" izbrav" raba svoego dvda i pomaza togo v" tsria nad" liudmi svoimi israilia,* Barsov, *Drevne-russkie pamiatniki,* 51.

48. I. Ia. Kachalova et al., *Blagoveshchenskii sobor* (Moscow, 1990), 60.

49. The development of the dome and domelike structures from the earliest representations of heaven as a cosmic house is discussed in great detail in E. Baldwin Smith, *The Dome: A Study in the History of Ideas,* Princeton Monographs in Art and Archaeology, no. 25 (Princeton, 1950). The symbols of heavenly paradise were transferred along with the dome to whatever space was later sacralized, e.g., martyrium, the church as a whole, reliquaries, presentational sites for prelates and rulers (see especially 16–29, 54–57, 79–94).

50. Ibid., 79–83.

51. Bocharov, "Tsarskoe mesto," 55.

52. The carving of a pyramid of pomegranates in a container as a symbolic life spring is found in early Coptic art. Similar images make their way into Byzantine art from the Near East. See Friedrich Muthmann, *Der Granatapfel: Symbol des Lebens in der Alten Welt* (Bern, 1982), 124–28.

53. Michael S. Flier, "Filling in the Blanks: The Church of the Intercession and the Architectonics of Medieval Muscovite Ritual," *Kamen' kraeOg"l'n Rhetoric of the Medieval Slavic World,* ed. Nancy S. Kollmann et al., [*Harvard Ukrainian Studies* 19, nos. 1–4, 1995], 120–37.

54. Sokolova, "Tsarskoe mesto," 143. This position is now repeated in I. M. Sokolova, *Monomakhov tron* (Moscow, 2001), 32–35.

55. E. V. Barsov, *Drevne-russkie pamiatniki sviashchennogo venchaniia tsarei na tsarstvo . . .* (Moscow, 1883, reprinted The Hague and Paris, 1969), 62.

56. *Kniga o izbranii . . .* See a reproduction of this page in Irina Polynina and Nicolai Rakhmanov, *The Regalia of the Russian Empire* (Moscow, 1994), pl. 52.

Chapter 3 Architecture and Dynasty

1. The most recent investigator of politics from 1584 to 1605 stresses Boris's political skill and strength both before and after his election as tsar in 1598. In particular, he claims that Boris was in control of the Military Chancellery (Razriadnyi prikaz), the main organ entrusted with fortress construction, as discussed below. See A. P. Pavlov, *Gosudarev dvor i politecheskaia bor'ba pri Borise Godunove* (Moscow, 1992), especially 55–56.

2. For a recent survey of these projects, see William C. Brumfield, *A History of Russian Architecture* (Cambridge, 1993), 89–106, 114–19, 122–29, with further references. For the dynastic connections of the Church of the Intercession (St. Basil's), see Michael Flier, "Filling in the Blanks: The Church of the Intercession and the Architectonics of Medieval Muscovite Ritual," *Harvard Ukrainian Studies* 19 (1995), 120–37.

3. Pavlov convincingly argues that Boris had clearly established his dominance even in the Duma by the 1590s, after his victory over the Shuiskies. For his arguments and references to his predecessors (especially S. F. Platonov and R. G. Skrynnikov) who stressed Boris's weak position in the Duma, see Pavlov, *Gosudarev dvor,* 50–85.

4. For a description of these efforts, see R. G. Skryn-

nikov, *Boris Godunov* (Moscow, 1978), 112–16. Valerie Kivelson makes this point in her *Autocracy in the Provinces: The Muscovite Gentry and Political Culture in the Seventeenth Century* (Stanford, 1996), 213–14.

5. E.G. Shcheboleva, "K voprosu o 'godunovskoi shkole' v drevnerusskoi arkhitekture kontsa XVI-nachala XVII v.," *Pamiatniki russkoi arkhitektury i monumental'nogo isskustva*, V.P. Vygolov et al., eds., (Moscow, 1991), 28. V.V. Kirillov estimates that, while lack of evidence permits only an estimated range of new towns founded "in the sixteenth century" of 45–70, by 1620 there were 180 new towns. Given the disruptions of the Time of Troubles and the following years, it seems likely that the large majority of these 110–35 towns were built under Boris Godunov: "Organizovannoe stroitel'stvo gorordov v Moskovskom gosudarstve," in N.F. Gulianitskii, ed., *Gradostroitel'stvo Moskovskogo gosudarstva* (Moscow, 1994), 7. The list of fortified towns founded between 1584 and 1605 found in the text below is also based in part on V.V. Kostochkin, *Gosudarev master Fedor Kon'* (Moscow, 1964), 9–33, and on what is still the most reliable source on this subject: A.A. Zimin, "Sostav russkikh gorodov," *Istoricheskie zapiski* 52 (1955), 336–47. As Zimin's notes make clear, the sources sometimes offer conflicting dates for the founding of towns; my dates should be taken as approximate.

6. G.V. Alferova, *Russkie Goroda XVI–XVII vekov* (Moscow, 1989); Kirillov ("Organizovannoe," 43) also discusses the dominant role of the central chancelleries in producing sketches (*chertezhi*) and precise instructions for the construction of new towns. An excellent example of a published documentary record of the process is found in D.I. Bagalei, *Materialy dlia istorii kolonizatsii i byta stepnoi okrainy Moskovskogo gosudarstva*, 2 pts. (Khar'kov, 1886, 1890), pt. 1, 5–13. I gladly thank Edward Keenan for this last reference.

7. M.B. Mikhailova and A.P. Osiatinskii, "Goroda Srednego i Nizhnego Povolzh'e," in Gulianitskii, *Gradostroitel'stvo*, 87–102.

8. T.S. Proskuriakova, "Goroda Sibiri i Priural'ia," ibid., 103–40.

9. Gulianitskii, *Gradostroitel'stvo*, 59–60, 160–63, 168–69, 243–44; N. F. Gulianitskii, ed., *Drevnerusskoe gradostroitel'stvo X–XV vekov* (Moscow, 1993), 329–30.

10. The information on Astrakhan' below is based chiefly on Mikhailova and Osiatinskii, "Goroda srednego," 87–92. These authors refer (p. 88) to a five-domed cathedral built "on the border of the sixteenth and seventeenth centuries," but then state that the builder was Dorofei Mineevich Miakishev. Since Miakishev was the builder of the late *seventeenth-century* church, there seems to be some confusion here. On the Miakishev's church, see A.V. Vorob'ev, *Astrakhanskii kreml'* (Astrakhan', 1958), 20–23. I have

been unable to find any other independent information on Godunov's church in Astrakhan'.

11. Brumfield, *History*, 109–13; N.I. Brunov, A.I. Vlasiuk, and A.G. Chiniakov, *Istoriia russkoi arkhitektury* (Moscow, 1956), 145.

12. Daniel Rowland, "Biblical Military Imagery in the Political Culture of Early Modern Russia: The Blessed Host of the Heavenly Tsar," *Medieval Russian Culture, Vol. 2*, Michael S. Flier and Daniel Rowland, eds. (Berkeley, 1994), 182–212.

13. On Boris's generosity to, and patronage of, Moscow's German Settlement, see Francine-Dominique Leichtenhan, "Les Étrangers à Moscou aux XVI et XXVII siècles," *Revue de la Biblioteque Nationale* 40 (1991), 13–14. (I am glad to thank John LeDonne for this reference.) Isaac Massa tells us how avid Boris was to make connections (presumably including trade connections) with the natives of the Russian north: *Detectio Freti Hudsoni, or Hessel Gerritsz's Collection of Tracts by Himself, Massa, and de Quir*, Fred. John Millard, ed. (Amsterdam, 1878), 9–15.

14. On this theme, see Stanislaus von Moos, *Turm und Bollwerk: Beitrage zu einer politischen Ikonographie der italienschen Renaissancearchitektur* (Zurich: Atlantis, 1974); James Cracraft, *The Petrine Revolution in Russian Architecture* (Chicago: University of Chicago Press), 56–66; Aleksei Ivanovich Nekrasov, *Ocherki po istorii drevnerusskogo zodchestva XI-XVII veka* (Moscow, 1936), 325–31; Christopher Duffy, *Siege Warfare: The Fortress in the Early Modern World*, 2 vols. (London, 1979–85), 1:173.

15. L.A. Iuzefovich, *Kak v posol'skikh obychaiakh vedetsia* (Moscow, 1988), 73. I am grateful to Maria Salomon Arel for reminding me of the location of this reference.

16. I. Zabelin, *Istoriia goroda Moskvy* (Moscow, 1902), pt. 1, 160–61. A.P. Pavlov (*Gosudarev dvor*, 54) describes Boris's successful efforts to persuade the commercial-artisanal population of Moscow to switch their support from the Shuiskies to the Godunovs.

17. *Skazanie Avraamiia Palitsyna*, O.A. Derzhavina and E.V. Kolosova, eds. (Moscow-Leningrad, 1955), 252. Palitsyn reports that Boris announced loudly during the liturgy, "O Father and Great Patriarch Iov, let God be a witness to this: no-one in my kingdom will be poor or destitute (*nishch ili beden*)." Boris then removed his shirt, and promised that he would divide his last shirt with everyone. Palitsyn called these words "loathsome to God (*Bogomerzosten*)."

18. Maureen Perrie, *Pretenders and Popular Monarchism in Early Modern Russia: The False Tsars of the Time of Troubles* (Cambridge, 1995), 63. The Pretender also claimed the support of the Volga towns, with some (but not full) justification (ibid., 73). This resistance to Boris may have been resistance to the Moscow center rather than to Boris personally, since these towns continued to oppose the government

in Moscow well after Boris had left the scene. See ibid., 117, 135–36.

19. Boris Polevoi has provided a useful survey of the history of both the Gerritsz maps and the Bol'shoi chertezh with citations to other literature: "Concerning the Origin of the Maps of Russia of 1613–1614 of Hessel Gerritsz," in Lindsey Hughes, ed., *New Perspectives on Muscovite History* (London and New York, 1993), 14–21.

20. On maps and map-making as a state-building enterprise, see Benedict Anderson, "Census, Map, Museum," Chap. 10 in the second edition of his *Imagined Communities* (London and New York, 1991), 163–85. James C. Scott described the power of maps to transform the countryside they describe in "State Simplifications: Nature, Space, and People," a talk delivered at Harvard University on March 14, 1996. Perrie (*Pretenders*, 63) points out that by the time of Boris's death, many southern border towns still consisted almost entirely of military servitors. Agriculture and trade had not yet followed.

21. On the religious (and other) obligations of the tsar, see Daniel Rowland, "Did Muscovite Literary Ideology Place Limits on the Power of the Tsar (1540s–1660s)?" *The Russian Review* 49 (1990), 125–55, here especially pp. 131ff. This article provides references to the rich literature on the subject.

22. On pilgrimages, see Nancy S. Kollmann, "Pilgrimage, Procession, and Symbolic Space in Sixteenth-Century Russian Politics," in Flier and Rowland, *Medieval Russian Culture*, 163–81.

23. Boris also had his name inscribed on the top of the Holy Trinity Cathedral in Pskov, the domes of which he had had gilded. See the *Piskarev Chronicle*, *PSRL* 34 (Moscow, 1978), 202.

24. *Vremennik Ivan Timofeeva*, O. A. Derzhavina, ed. (Moscow, 1951), 64–65.

25. On a "Godunov School" of architecture, see Shcheboleva, "K voprosu," and the seminal P. A. Rappoport, "Zodchii Borisa Godunova," in *Kul'tura drevnei Rusi: posviashchaetsia 40–letiiu nauchnoi deiatel'nosti Nikolaia Nikolaievicha Voronina* (Moscow, 1966), 215–21.

26. See especially A. L. Batalov, "Osobennosti 'Italianizmov' v Moskovskom kamennom zodchestve rubezha XVI–XVII vv.," *Arkhitekturnoe nasledstvo* 34 (1986): 238–45. Batalov distinguishes between two groups of late-sixteenth-century churches, one directly and consciously influenced by the Archangel Michael Cathedral, a group he associates particularly with the Godunovs, and the other based on the intermediate influence of Ivan IV's constructions at Aleksandrovskaia Sloboda and additions to the Kremlin Annunciation Cathedral.

27. A. M. Lidov, "Ierusalimskii kuvuklii: O proiskhozhdenii lukovichnykh glav," *Ikonografiia arkhitektury*, A. L. Batalov, ed. (Moscow, 1992), 57–68.

28. A. L. Batalov, "Grob Gospoden' v zamysle 'Sviataia Sviatykh' Borisa Godunova," *Ierusalim v russkoi kul'ture*, A. Batalov and A. Lidov, eds. (Moscow, 1994), 154–73. This article is a model of painstaking scholarship. Its conclusions seems particularly consonant with Timofeev's thought and word usage, both of which emphasized liturgical matters. I gladly thank Marina Swoboda, who has just completed an excellent dissertation on Timofeev, for her cogent opinions on this subject expressed in private communications with the author.

29. The argument that the Petrovskii chertezh map resembles the New Jerusalem of the Apocalypse is also made by M. P. Kudriavtsev: *Moskva—Tretii Rim: istoriko gradostroitel'noe issledovanie* (Moscow, 1994), 135–40; 205–7. Kudriavtsev also points out the remarkable similarity between the Ivan III Bell Tower as rebuilt by Boris and contemporary representations of the Church of the Holy Sepulcher in Jerusalem (ibid., 200–201). There is a problem with the first argument, however, at least as it relates to Godunov's reign. The Petrovskii chertezh itself, which does clearly show a square, twelve-gate pattern reminiscent of the New Jerusalem, is a later version of the map of Moscow published by Gerritsz in 1613. This earlier map, and still earlier versions published as early as 1610, bear a slighter resemblance to the Heavenly Jerusalem. For reproductions of these maps, with illuminating discussion, see M. V. Posokhin et al., *Pamiatniki arkhitektury Moskvy: Kreml', Kitai Gorod, Tsentral'nye ploshchadi* (Moscow, 1982), 51–59.

30. Ushakov and Klement'ev's careful description is printed in I. E. Zabelin, *Materialy istorii, arkheologii, i statistiki goroda Moskvy*, pt. 1 (Moscow, 1884), cols. 1255–71. The quoted passage is in col. 1262. On the Palace of Facets in general, with full reproductions of the currently visible murals that were painted in the 1880s following the 1672 description, see Aida Nasibova, *The Faceted Chamber in the Moscow Kremlin* (Leningrad, 1978).

31. Note the connection between temple-building and a God-chosen dynasty: when David was informed by Nathan the prophet that he would not be able to build the temple, Nathan also announced God's choice of David's dynasty as the vessel of Godly rule (2 Samuel 7). The term "Holy of Holies" technically refers to the innermost room or sanctuary of the temple, where the Ark of the Covenant was kept (1 Kings 6:23–28; 8:6–7).

32. A. L. Batalov and T. N. Viatchanina, "Ob ideinom znachenii i interpretatsii Ierusaminskogo obraztsa v Russkoi arkhitekture XVI–XVII vv." *Arkhitekturnoe nasledstvo* 36 (1988), 25, make the point that liturgical texts connect Solomon's Temple with the Church of the Holy Sepulcher in contemporary Jerusalem as prefiguration and fulfillment.

33. Daniel Rowland, "Moscow—The Third Rome or the New Israel?" *The Russian Review* 55, no. 4 (October, 1996), 591–614.

34. The last sections of the *Piskarev Chronicle* were first published by O.A. Iakovleva ("Piskarevskii letopisets," *Materialy po istorii SSSR, II, Dokumenty po istorii XV–XVII vv.*, [Moscow, 1955], 5–210); the text was published in full in *PSRL* 34 (Moscow 1978), 31–220. The section on the reigns of Fedor and Boris is found in ibid., 194–205. On the nature and authorship of various parts of the chronicle, see M.N. Tikhomirov, "Piskarevskii letopisets kak istoricheskii istochnik o sobytiiakh XVI–nachala XVII v.," in his *Russkoe letopisanie* (Moscow, 1979), 232–47.

Chapter 4 Catherine the Great's Field of Dreams

Abbreviations:

APDM	Arkhiv Pavlovskogo dvortsa-muzeya
Hermitage	Gosudarstvennyi Ermitazh, otdel rukopisi
NIMAKH	Nauchno-issledovatel'skii muzei Akademii Khudozhestv
PSZRI	Polnoe sobranie zakonov Rossiiskoi imperii
RGADA	Rossiiskii gosudarstvennyi arkhiv drevnikh aktov
RGIA	Rossiiskii gosudarstvennyi istoricheskii arkhiv
SIRIO	Imperatorskoe russkoe istoricheskoe obshchestvo. Sbornik

1. John Claudius Loudon, *Encyclopaedia of Gardening* (London, 1827), 56.

2. Sir William Chambers, *Designs of Chinese Buildings, Furniture, Dresses, Machines, and Utensils* (London, 1757). William and John Halfpenny, *Rural Architecture in the Chinese Taste* (London, 1751). Charles Over, *Ornamental Architecture in the Gothic, Chinese, and Modern Taste* (London: Printed for Robert Sayer, 1758). William Wright, *Grotesque Architecture, or, Rural Amusement Consisting of Plans, Elevations, and Sections, for Huts, Retreats, Summer and Winter Hermitages, Terminaries, Chinese, Gothic, and Natural Grottos* (London, 1767).

3. Georges Louis Le Rouge, *Details des nouveaux jardins a la mode* (Paris, 1776–88).

4. Especially, Jean Francois de Neufforge, *Recueil elementaire d'architecture, contenant plusieurs etudes des ordres d'architecture d'apres l'opinion des anciens et le sentiment des modernes, differents entrecolonnements propres a l'ordonnances des facades, divers exemples de decorations exterieures et interieures, a l'usage des monuments sacres, publics, et particuliers.* 10 vols. (Paris, 1757–80).

5. *Pis'ma Ekateriny II k Grimmu.* SIRIO, vol. 23 (St. Petersburg, 1878), 157.

6. Thomas Weiss and Harri Günther, *Das Gartenreich an Elbe und Mulde: Staatliche Schlösser und Gärten Sachsen-Anhalt, Wörlitz, Oranienbaum, Luisium* (Murnau, 1994), 180–207.

7. SIRIO, vol. 25, p. 157.

8. Ibid., p. 207.

9. Hermitage. Collection of Ch.-L.Clerisseau drawings. Design of a Roman house. Explanations, p. 1.

10. Vladimir Ivanovich Piliavskii, *Giacomo Quarenghi: a cura di Sandro Angelini.* (Milan, 1984).

11. SIRIO, vol. 23, p. 157.

12. Dimitri Olegovich Shvidkovsky, *The Empress and the Architect: British Architecture and Gardens at the Court of Catherine the Great.* (New Haven and London, 1996), 11–39.

13. G.L. Le Rouge, *Details*, cahier 1, p. 1.

14. Erikh Fedorovich Gollerbakh, *Detskosel'skie dvortsy—muzei i parki* (St. Petersburg, 1922), 85.

15. I. Glushkov, *Ruchnoi dorozhnik* (Moscow, 1802), 20.

16. E.F. Gollerbakh, *Detskosel'skie dvortsy*, 82.

17. A. Khrapovitskii, *Dnevnik* (St. Petersburg, 1874), 244–45.

18. RGIA, fond 487, opis 3, 1787, ed.khr. 14.

19. Ibid., fond 486, opis 37, ed.khr. 344, p. 5.

20. V.N. Taleporovskii, *Charl'z Kameron* (Moscow, 1939), 23.

21. Mikhail Ivanovich Pyliaev, *Zabytoe proshloe okrestnostei Peterburga* (St. Petersburg, 1889), 473.

22. *Tsarskoe selo v poezii* (St. Petersburg, 1922), 4.

23. Quoted from E.F. Gollerbakh "Kameron v Tsarskom sele," in E.F. Gollerbakh and N.E. Lansere, eds., *Charl'z Kameron: Sbornik Statei* (Moscow, 1924), 13.

24. Charles Cameron, *The Baths of the Romans Explained and Illustrated* (London, 1772).

25. Gavriil Romanovich Derzhavin, *Sochineniia* (Moscow, 1986), 132.

26. RGADA, fond 14, opis 1, ed.khr. 250, part 1, pp. 80–81.

27. RGIA, fond 1399, opis 1, ed. khr. 704, pp. 1–3.

28. S.S. Bronshtein, *Arkhitektura Goroda Pushkina* (Leningrad, 1938), 38–46.

29. *Ukaz ob obrazovanii pri Tsarskom sele goroda Sofiia*, single sheet, dated St. Petersburg, 1780. See also PSZRI, vol. 20, article 14358.

30. RGADA, fond 14, opis 1, ed.khr. 250, part 1, pp. 34–75.

31. Charles Joseph de Ligne, *Pis'ma, mysli i izbrannye tvoreniia* (Moscow, 1809), 108.

32. I. Glushkov, *Ruchnoi dorozhnik*, 13, 65.

33. RGADA, fond 14, opis 1, ed.khr. 250, part 7, p. 6.

34. RGADA, fond 14, opis 1, ed.khr. 250, part 3 (2), p. 158.

35. Quoted from E.F. Gollerbakh, N.E. Lansere, eds., *Charl'z Kameron*, 41.

36. Hermitage, department of drawings, ed.khr. 11072.

37. RGIA, fond 485, opis 3, ed.khr. 5, p. 1.

38. J.C. Loudon, *Encyclopaedia of Gardening*, 57–58.

39. D.O. Shvidkovsky, *The Empress and the Architect*, 228.

40. D. O. Shvidkovsky, "Grandmother's Garden for the Heir to the Imperial Throne," *Garden History* (Spring, 1996), 107–13.

41. Jean-Marie Perouse de Montclos, *Ecole nationale superieure des beaux-arts (France) "Les Prix de Rome": concours de l'Academie royale d'architecture au XVIIIe siecle* (Paris, 1984).

42. Jean-Marie Perouse de Montclos, *Etienne-Louis Boullée* (Paris, 1994), 103.

43. Claude Nicolas Ledoux, *L'Architecture considerée sous le raport de l'art des moeurs et de la legislation* (Paris, 1804), Preface.

Chapter 5 Russian Estate Architecture and Noble Identity

1. Catherine the Great, letter to Baron Friedrich Melchior Grimm, 1779; cited in Antoine Chenevière, *Russian Furniture: The Golden Age, 1770–1840* (New York, 1988), 22.

2. Dimitri Shvidkovsky (D. O. Shvidkovskii) explicates the tutelary aspect of Tsarskoe Selo in his article "K voprosu o prosvetitelskoi kontseptsii sredy v russkikh dvortsevo-parkovykh ansamblakh vtoroi poloviny vosemnadtsatogo veka," in *Vek Prosveshcheniya* (Moscow, 1983).

3. Makhaev emphasized that the new style was "without much ornamentation." See B-va, "Iz istorii odnogo ugolka na Volge," *Rodnoi krai* (June 8, 1922), 3.

4. See Anthony Cross's review of my *Life on the Russian Country Estate* in the *Times Literary Supplement* for August 9, 1996.

5. See Iu. Anisimov, "Olgovo," in *Podmoskovnye muzei* 4 (Moscow-Leningrad, 1925), 7–65.

6. Alexander B. Kurakin to Alexei B. Kurakin; cited in A. Golombevskii, "Pokinutaya usad'ba: Selo Nadezhdino, byvshee imenie knyazei Kurakinykh," *Starye gody* 1 (1911), 14.

7. *Arkhiv Knyazya Vorontsova* (40 vols., Moscow, 1870–95), vol. 6, p. 304.

8. *Sbornik imperatorskogo russkogo istoricheskogo obshchestva* (148 vols., St. Petersburg, 1867–1916), vol. 13, p. 256.

9. See D. D. Lotareva, "Marino: usad'ba russkogo aristokrata," *Mir russkoi usad'by* (Moscow, 1995), 166.

10. One noble memoirist, speaking of her rural childhood on a very small estate, recalled being mortified when a traveling noble chose a local merchant's house over their own for an overnight halt. The reason, she explained, was that they had lost their entertaining space—the all-important gostinnaya—when her sister was born and it was turned into the girls' bedroom.

11. Cited in A. Golumbevskii, "Pokinutaya usad'ba," 15.

12. Cited by B. I. Gavrilov, "Neskazanno veselee vsekh moikh dereven'," *Mir russkoi usad'by* (Moscow, 1995), 114.

13. Cited by D. D. Lotareva, "Marino," 159–60.

14. See A. G. Vvedenskaya, "Usad'ba kniazei Kurakinykh," *Mir russkoi usad'by* (Moscow, 1995), 205–6.

15. Count M. D. Buturlin, "Zapiski," *Russkii arkhiv* 3 (1898), 403–4.

16. See Martha and Catherine Wilmot, *The Russian Journals of Martha and Catherine Wilmot* (London, 1934), 202.

17. See figure 19 of my *Life on the Russian Country Estate* (New Haven, 1995) for the Podmoklovo church, under reconstruction in 1992; and p. 404 of A. N. Roussoff's *Memoirs of Alexander Wolkoff-Mouromtzoff* (London, 1928), for a description and photograph of the Balovnevo church.

18. See Natalya Skornyakova, "Russian Country Estate Through the Eyes of the Artist," *Russian Heritage* 2 (1993), 38–43.

19. Prince A. A. Bezborodko to Count Semen Vorontsov, 1798; in *Arkhiv Knyazya Vorontsova*, vol. 13, p. 379.

20. Cited in N. Makarenko, "Lyalichi," *Starye gody* (July–Sept. 1910), 132.

21. Le Marquis de Custine, *La Russie en 1839* (4 vols., Brussels, 1843), vol. 3, p. 150.

22. See G. K. Vagner and S. V. Chugunov, *Riazanskie dostopamiatnosti* (Moscow, 1989), 130–36.

Chapter 6 The Picturesque and the Holy

1. Only a brief list of recent studies of tourism and travel is possible here. The following texts focus on the history of tourism more than on contemporary travel practices: Malcolm Andrews, *The Search for the Picturesque: Landscape Aesthetics and Tourism in Britain, 1760–1800* (Stanford, 1989), James Buzzard, *The Beaten Track: Literature and Tourism in Europe, 1800–1918* (New York, 1993), Anne Farar Hyde, *An American Vision: Far Western Landscape and National Culture, 1820–1920* (New York, 1990), Eric J. Leed, *The Mind of the Traveler: From Gilgamesh to Global Tourism* (New York, 1991), Sara Mills, *Discourses of Difference: An Analysis of Women's Travel Writing and Colonialism* (New York, 1993), Ian Ousby, *The Englishmen's England: Taste, Travel and the Rise of Tourism* (New York, 1990), Mary Louise Pratt, *Imperial Eyes: Travel Writing and Transculturation* (New York, 1992), John F. Sears, *Sacred Places: American Tourist Attractions in the Nineteenth Century* (Amherst, 1989).

2. For useful texts on Russian travel literature see Sara Dickinson, "Imagining Space and the Self: Russian Travel Writing and Its Narrators, 1762–1825" (Ph.D. diss., Harvard University, 1995), V. I. Korovin, ed., *Landshaft moikh voobrazenii* (Moscow, 1990), T. Roboli, "*Literatura 'Puteshestvii'*" in *Russkaia*

proza: sbornik stat'ei (Leningrad, 1926), 42–73, Andreas Schonle, "Authenticity and Fiction in the Russian Literary Journey, 1790–1840" (Ph.D. diss., Harvard University, 1995), Reuel K. Wilson, *The Literary Travelogue: A Comparative Study with Special Relevance to Russian Literature from Fonvizin to Pushkin* (The Hague, 1973).

3. When did tourism first appear as a viable phenomenon in Russia? In one unambiguous answer, 1995 was claimed as the 100th anniversary of Russian tourism. A conference, advertised in glossy posters on Petersburg Metro trains, commemorated the event. According to conference organizers, Russian tourism began precisely in 1895. The date is based on the founding of a bicycle touring society, which later became the "Russian Society of Tourists." Since some variety of tourism had been practiced for more than a century before 1895 in Western Europe, and since the founding of modern tourism is usually attributed to Thomas Cook in the 1840s, designation of the year 1895 for the definitive commencement of tourism in Russia must be viewed with skepticism. It is difficult to determine when domestic tourism came into widespread practice in Russia, but to locate the origins of Russian tourism in 1895 is to ignore a century's worth of slow growth of the idea and industry. See *Peterburzhets Puteshestvuet: sbornik materialov konferentsii 2–3 marta 1995 goda* (Saint Petersburg, 1995). In fairness to the participants, few of the contributions were tied to 1895 as the definitive origin of Russian tourism.

4. V. A. Sollogub, *Tarantas* (Moscow, 1955), 13. It should be remembered that other parts of the Empire, particularly Finland, the Caucasus, and the Crimea, presented a more attractive destination for Russian travelers at this time.

5. Fyodor Dostoevsky, *Winter Notes on Summer Impressions*, trans. Richard Lee Renfield (New York, 1955), 35.

6. D. I. Matskevich, *Putevyia zametki. Gruzino. Novgorod. Barovichi. Ustiuzhno* (Saint Petersburg, 1851), 44–45.

7. Recent studies of the European Grand Tour include, for example, Jeremy Black, *The British Abroad: The Grand Tour in the Eighteenth and Nineteenth Centuries* (New York, 1992) and Lynne Withey, *Grand Tours and Cook's Tours: A History of Leisure Travel, 1750–1915* (New York, 1997). Also see Chloe Chard, *Pleasure and Guilt on the Grand Tour: Travel Writing and Imaginative Geography, 1600–1830* (Manchester, 1999).

8. Sollogub, *Tarantas*, 13. This passage was a favorite of the powerful literary critic Vissarion Belinskii. He alluded to it with approval more than once in his review of the novel, as it suited his tendency to condemn the general impoverishment of the Empire.

9. On the picturesque and picturesque tours in Britain see Andrews, *The Search for the Picturesque*,

Ann Bermingham, *Landscape and Ideology: the English Rustic Tradition, 1740–1860* (Berkeley, 1986), Steven Copley and Peter Garside, *The Politics of the Picturesque: Literature, Landscape and Aesthetics since 1770* (New York, 1994), Gina Crandell, *Nature Pictorialized: "The View" in Landscape History* (Baltimore, 1993); on France see Nicholas Green, *The Spectacle of Nature: Landscape and Bourgeois Culture in Nineteenth-century France* (New York, 1990). For a recent examination of a Russian example of the picturesque see Andreas Schonle, "Gogol, the Picturesque, and the Desire for the People: A Reading of Rome," *The Russian Review* 59 (October, 2000), 597–613.

10. Nestor Kukolnik, *Khudozhestvennaia gazeta* 2 (1837), 32. Kukolnik goes on to list Russia's potential picturesque sites and to urge the publication of an album of picturesque Russian views, but it would be half a century before such a work finally appeared.

11. Complaints about accommodations in Russian provincial hotels and roadside inns were so common as to be familiar to even the casual reader of nineteenth-century Russian literature. As Mikhail Pogodin said about Russia on his way to Europe: "There's nothing new to say about the road: it's the same highway, the same distances, the same ugly buildings. . . . The same filth and unpleasantness at the inn." Pogodin, *God v chuzhikh kraiakh (1839)* (Moscow, 1844). Foreign travelers often reacted with alarm to roadside accommodations.

12. S. Mashinskii, ed., *S. T. Aksakov: Sobranie sochinenii v piati tomakh*, vol. 4 (Moscow, 1966), 288–89. See also Andrew Durkin, *Sergei Aksakov and Russian Pastoral* (New Brunswick, N.J., 1983), 83–85.

13. I have in mind the passage that begins "Russia! I see you from my wondrous beautiful afar." For this translation see Nikolai Gogol, *Dead Souls*, trans. David Magarshack (London, 1961), 231–32.

14. It should be noted that the travel writers of the first half of the nineteenth century had been preceded by a generation of travel writers who are often lumped together under the heading of sentimental travelers. These epigones of Nikolai Karamzin tended to emphasize their own inner states and emotional responses over external, pictorial depictions of the places they visited. Thus they are of less interest to the current discussion.

15. In addition to epigrams, Pushkin had Svin'in in mind when he wrote the story "The Little Liar," and he is also said to have given Gogol the idea for *The Inspector General*, based on a story Svin'in had told him about his travels in Bessarabia. Svin'in was criticized in part because he was prone to exaggeration, perhaps also because of his penchant for placing output above accuracy in his work. For a short essay on Svin'in see Abbott Gleason, "Pavel Svin'in," in Marc Pachter, ed., *Abroad in America: Visitors to the New Nation, 1776–1917* (Washington, D.C. 1976), 12–21.

16. A recent edition of the Russian *Picturesque United States* has been published in English, with a useful introduction, under the title *Traveling Across North America 1812–1813: Watercolors by the Russian Diplomat Pavel Svin'in*, trans. Kathleen Carroll (New York, 1992). See also Pavel Svin'in, *Sketches of Moscow and St. Petersburg* (Philadelphia, 1813).

17. A good example of Svin'in's garden description is found in the travel article "Ropsha" in *Otechestvennyia zapiski* 10 (1821), 125–40.

18. *Liubit' otechestvo—velit Priroda i Bog / A znat' ego—vot chest', dostoinstvo i dolg.*

19. Pavel Svin'in, "Ob'iavlenie," in *Otechestvennyia zapiski* 29 (1826).

20. N. M. Karamzin, "Istoricheskie vospominaniia i zamechaniia na puti k troitse i v sem monastyre," in *Zapiski starogo Moskovskogo zhitelia* (Moscow, 1986), 285.

21. Karamzin's *History of the Russian State* was widely read after its first volume was published in 1816. Other evidence of the interest in history during the 1810s and 1820s is the great popularity of the gothic-historical novels of Aleksandr Bestushev (later Marlinskii) as well as the historical novels of Mikhail Zagoskin. A new interest in historical architecture is discussed in T. A. Slavina, *Issledovateli russkogo zodchestvo: Russkaia istoriko-arkhitekturnaia nauka XVIII-nachala XX veka* (Leningrad, 1983). Slavina remarks on the significance of *Fatherland Notes* in furthering the study of historical architecture and archaeology.

22. Svin'in, "Novgorod," in *Otechestvenniyia zapiski* 17 (1821), 328–62.

23. Svin'in, "Stranstvyia v okrestnostiakh Moskvy," in *Otechestvennyia zapiski* 22 (1822), 5.

24. A. N. Murav'ev, *Puteshestvie po sviatym mestam russkim: v dvukh chastakh* (St. Petersburg, 1846; reprint, Moscow, 1990).

25. See G. N. Gennadi, *Spisok knig o russkikh monastyr'iakh i tserkvakh* (St. Petersburg, 1854).

26. Cited in *Peterburzhets puteshestvuyet: sbornik materialov konferentsii 2–3 marta 1995 goda* (St. Petersburg, 1995), 53.

27. See Viacheslav Korb, "*Blagochestivyi stranik*" in Murav'ev, *Puteshestvie*, 389.

28. Murav'ev's travel writing was praised by his famous contemporary Pushkin, and later it was even admired by Chernyshevsky.

29. This preoccupation with the everyday lives of the unprivileged majority in the 1840s was characteristic not only of the Slavophiles but equally so of their opponents, Belinskii's championing of the "natural school" being an obvious example.

30. Gogol', "Nuzhno proezdit'sia po Rossii," in M. A. Maslin, ed., *Russkaia idea* (Moscow, 1992), 107.

31. See, for example, D. I. Matskevich, *Putevyia zametki*, O. P. Shishkina, *Zametki i vospominaniia russkoi puteshestvenitsi* (St. Petersburg, 1848), V. V. Passek, *Ocherki Rossii* (Saint Petersburg, 1838).

32. S. P. Shevyrev, "Pokhozhdenie Chichikova, ili Mertvyia Dushi. Poema N. Gogolia," in V. K. Kantora and A. L. Ospovata, *Russkaia estetika i kritika 40–50–x godov XIX veka* (Moscow, 1982), 58–61.

33. Stepan Shevyrev, *Poezdka v Kirillo-Belozersk monastyr': vakatsionnye dni professora S. Shevyreva v 1847 godu* (Moscow, 1850), vol. 2, p. 2.

34. Ibid., vol. 2, p. 56.

35. Ibid., vol. 1, p. 80.

36. Ibid., vol. 2, pp. 133–34.

37. Nikolai Dobroliubov, "Vpechatleniia Ukraina i Sevastopolia," in *Polnoe sobranie sochinenia*, 278–84.

38. On the development of tourism in Russia see G. P. Dolzhenko, *Istoriia Turizma v dorevoliutsionnyi Rossii i SSSR* (Rostov-na-Donu, 1988), 20, and "Istoricheskii ocherk," in *Entsiklopediia Turista* (Moscow, 1993), 8.

39. N. M. Karamzin, *Letters of a Russian Traveler, 1789–1790*, trans. Florence Jonas (New York, 1957), 99.

40. Ibid., 61.

41. There is a large body of literature on the historical development of American landscape imagery. Some studies useful to the present text are Stephen Daniels, *Fields of Vision: Landscape Imagery and National Identity in England and the United States* (Princeton, 1993), Angela Miller, *Empire of the Eye: Landscape, Representation and American Cultural Politics* (Ithaca, N.Y., 1993), and Barbara Novak, *Nature and Culture: American Landscape and Painting, 1825–1875*.

42. See, for example, Irving Babbitt, *Rousseau and Romanticism*, 4th ed. (New York, 1959); Green, *The Spectacle of Nature;* Simon Schama, *Landscape and Memory* (New York, 1995); Raymond Williams, *The Country and the City* (London, 1972).

43. For a cultural history of the gentry estate, see Priscilla Roosevelt, *Life on the Russian Country Estate* (New Haven, 1995).

44. Although Haxthausen argued in the 1840s that landowners were returning in great numbers to their estates, his contention is not well supported by documentary records. Still, many landowners did spend time on their estates, and in most cases their business interests remained bound to agriculture. See Jerome Blum, *Lord and Peasant in Russia from the Ninth to the Nineteenth Century* (New York, 1968), 386–414.

45. Dmitri S. Likhachev, *Reflections on Russia*, trans. Christina Sever (Boulder, Colo., 1991), 16.

46. Gogol, *Dead Souls*, 113.

Chapter 7 Constructing the Russian Other

1. Theophile Gautier, *Tresors d'art en Russie ancienne et moderne* (Paris, 1859). For analysis of this abortive venture, and for Gautier's Russian travel impressions, written for the French journal *Moniteur*, see the critical edition of his *Voyage en Russie*, published in various editions between 1867 and 1901

(*Voyage en Russie*, Paris, 1901). See also Lauren O'-Connell, "Viollet-le-Duc in Context: French Readings of Russian Architecture in the Nineteenth Century," *Center* 19 (1999), 120–23.

2. Eugène Emmanuel Viollet-le-Duc, *L'Art russe: ses origines, ses éléments constitutifs, son apogée, son avenir* (Paris, 1877).

3. Analyzed in Lauren M. O'Connell, "A Rational, National Architecture: Viollet-le-Duc's Modest Proposal for Russia," *Journal of the Society of Architectural Historians* 52 (1993), 436–52. See p. 436, n. 1 for a review of the *L'Art russe* literature.

4. Eric Hobsbawm, "Inventing Traditions," in *The Invention of Tradition*, ed. Eric Hobsbawm and Terence Ranger (Cambridge, 1983), 1–14.

5. See Edward Said, *Orientalism* (New York, 1978), and the vast literatures of Orientalist and postcolonial theory it generated with regard to the power imbalance implicit in the imperium/colony relationship between the European Orientalizer and his or her subject. On "Orientalism" in nineteenth-century European art and architecture, see Rana Kabbani, *Europe's Myths of Orient* (Bloomington, Ind., 1986); John Mackenzie, *Orientalism: History, Theory and the Arts* (Manchester, 1995); Mark Crinson, *Empire Building: Orientalism and Victorian Architecture* (London, 1996); *Orientalism: Delacroix to Klée*, ed. Roger Benjamin (New South Wales, 1997); and Frederick Bohrer's review article, "Europa und der Orient, 800–1900," and "Exotische Welten, Europaische Phantasien," *Art Bulletin* 73 (1991), 325–30.

6. Natalis Rondot, *Musée d'art et d'industrie. Rapport fait à la Chambre de Commerce de Lyon* (Lyon, 1859), 32. The museum proposed in Rondot's report was founded in 1864, and converted to the Musée Historique des Tissus, devoted exclusively to the silk industry, in 1891 (Léon Galle, *Natalis Rondot: Sa vie et ses travaux* [Lyon, 1902], 344). On the latter, see Henri d'Hennezel, *Le Musée historique des tissus de Lyon* (Paris, 1922).

7. Natalis Rondot, *Excursions en Champagne* [1839] (Reims, 1903), 1–5; *Publications de M. Natalis Rondot* (Lyon, 1893), 16.

8. Galle, 341–44. For debates on industrial arts education in the nineteenth century, see Elizabeth McCauley, *Industrial Madness: Commercial Photography in Paris, 1848–1871* (New Haven, 1994), Chap. 6; and Patricia Mainardi, *The End of the Salon: Art and the State in the Early Third Republic* (Cambridge, 1993). On the catalyzing role of the expositions of 1851 and 1855 in particular, see A. N. F12 2441, Report by the Sécretaire perpetuel de l'Académie des Beaux-Arts, with excerpts from the proceedings of the April 9, 1859, meeting of the Academy.

9. See L. O'Connell, "Architecture and the French Revolution: Change and Continuity under the Conseil des Bâtiments Civils, 1795–99," Ph.D. diss. (Cornell University, 1989), Chap. 5; and Françoise Choay, *The Invention of the Historic Monument* (New York, 2001).

10. *Russkii Biograficheskii Slovar* (St. Petersburg, 1908), 533–34. An obituary published in the April 1881 issue of *Zodchii* (10 [1881]) gives his death as "22 June," presumably of the previous year.

11. See Victor de Boutovsky [sic], *Histoire de l'ornement russe, du Xe au XVIe siècle d'après les manuscrits*, 2 vols. (Paris, 1870); and Wendy Salmond's "Design Education and the Quest for National Identity in Late Imperial Russia: The Case of the Stroganov School," *Studies in the Decorative Arts* 1 (1994), 2–24. See also her *Arts and Crafts in Late Imperial Russia* (Cambridge, 1996).

12. Natalis Rondot, "Musée d'Art et d'Industrie de Moscou," *Gazette des Beaux-Arts* (1868), 82.

13. Ibid., 83.

14. *Stroganovskii ikonopisnyii litsevoi podlinnik. Izdanie litografii pri Khudozhestvenno-promyshlennom Museum* (Moscow, 1869). See also the most recent reprint and translation, *An Iconographer's Pattern Book: The Stroganov Tradition* (Torrance, Calif., 1992).

15. Commission impériale de Russie, *Catalogue de la Section russe à l'Exposition universelle de Paris* (Paris, 1878), 23.

16. Eric Hobsbawm, *Nations and Nationalism since 1780: Programme, Myth, Reality* (Cambridge, 1990). See also Clifford Geertz, The *Interpretation of Cultures* (New York, 1973), 235–55; and *Nationalism: A Report by a Study Group of Members of the Royal Institute of International Affairs* (New York, 1965), xvi–xx, 1–7.

17. On the history and challenge of ethnographic self-description in Russia, see Yuri Slezkine, "Naturalists versus Nations: Eighteenth-Century Russian Scholars Confront Ethnic Diversity," in *Russia's Orient: Imperial Borderlands and Peoples, 1700–1917*, ed. Daniel Brower and Edward Lazzerini (Bloomington, Ind., 1997), 27–57.

18. Rondot, "Musée d'art et d'industrie de Moscou," 85. "En Russie les ornements procèdent de deux sources opposées: les uns du goût occidental, français, ou allemand; les autres du goût national."

19. Ibid. "Se rapprochent du style byzantin, d'autres portent le cachet asiatique, d'autres encore ont le caractère russe proprement dit."

20. As Milan Hauner has noted, in *What Is Asia to Us? Russia's Asian Heartland Yesterday and Tomorrow* (Boston, 1990), 15, n. 3. See also *Russia's Orient*, Introduction, xi–xx. For important critiques of Said's construct in the European context see also James Clifford, "On Orientalism," in his *The Predicament of Culture: Twentieth Century Ethnography, Literature and Art* (Cambridge, 1988), 255–76; Dennis Porter, "Orientalism and Its Problems," *Colonial Discourse and Post-Colonial Theory: A Reader*, ed. Patrick Williams and Lara Chrisman (New York, 1994), 150–61; and Frederick Bohrer, "Inventing Assyria:

Exoticism and Reception in Nineteenth-Century France," *Art Bulletin* 80, no. 2 (1998), 336–56. See also important correctives to Said's original paradigm in his own later work, such as *Culture and Imperialism* (New York, 1993) and *Reflections on Exile and Other Essays* (Cambridge, Mass., 2000).

21. See, for example, Annie E. Coombes, *Reinventing Africa: Museums, Material Culture and Popular Imagination in Late Victorian and Edwardian England* (New Haven, 1994), 217–21.

22. Interestingly, this conflation of subjectivities, which is intrinsic to Russia's geohistorical position, suggests it as an instructive analogue to a more recent strain of postcolonial analysis, that trained on "hybridity" and the commingling of cultural identities in the European colonial setting. See, for example, in terms of architecture, Swati Chattopakhyay, "Blurring Boundaries: The Limits of 'White Town' in Colonial Calcutta," *Journal of the Society of Architectural Historians* 59, no. 2 (June 2000), 154–79, and Zeynep Çelik, "Colonialism, Orientalism, and the Canon," *InterSections: Architectural Histories and Critical Theories*, ed. Iain Borden and Jane Rendell (London, 2000), 124–49.

23. Mark Bassin, "Russia between Europe and Asia: The Ideological Construction of Geographic Space," *Slavic Review* 50 (1991), 1–17.

24. Bassin, "Russia between Europe and Asia," 5; and Nicholas Riasanovsky, "Asia through Russian Eyes," *Russia and Asia*, ed. Wayne S. Vucinich (Stanford, Calif., 1972), 14–18.

25. Bassin, "Russian between Europe and Asia," 11–12.

26. Katya Hokanson, "Literary Imperialism, *Narodnost'* and Pushkin's Invention of the Caucasus," *Russian Review* 53 (1994), 340. See also Susan Layton's reservations about the binary self/other relationships assumed in Hokanson's analysis, in "Nineteenth-Century Russian Mythologies of Caucasian Savagery," in *Russia's Orient*, 80–100.

27. Swati Chattopakhyay describes a similar subjectival ambivalence, an analogous mix of attraction and revulsion in the domestic life of the British Raj in Calcutta in Chattopakhyay, "Blurring Boundaries."

28. As in n. 11.

29. Rondot, "Musée d'art et d'industrie de Moscou," 85. "A une époque ou la Russie nous paraissait ne pas avoir d'histoire."

30. Ibid.

31. Ministère de l'Agriculture et du Commerce, *Exposition Universelle de 1878 à Paris. Rapports du Jury International*. Group II, Classe 9. L'Imprimerie et la librairie, par Emile Martinet (Paris, 1880), 67–68, 75–78.

32. The historiography of Russo-Tatar relations shows that Russian interpretations of the Mongol period have tended to run in step with the political objectives of the Russian state. Demonization of the Mongol Tatars served the interests of Imperial and Soviet leadership alike, and nineteenth and twentieth-century scholarship has tended to reflect their biases in discounting, or deeming strictly deleterious, the Mongol influence on Russian society and culture. Thus while Nicholas Riasanovsky might term the period of Mongol rule "the most traumatic historical experience of the Russian people" (Riasanovsky, "Asia through Russian Eyes," 5), subsequent scholarship has suggested that the Mongol period might more accurately be viewed as "a complex, multifaceted, and long-term relationship between two peoples who were often but by no means always hostile" (Charles Halperin, *Russia and the Golden Horde: The Mongol Impact on Medieval Russian History* [Bloomington, Ind., 1985], 128). See also, by the same author, "Soviet Historiography on Russia and the Mongols," *Russian Review* 41 (1982), 306–22; and "George Vernadsky, Eurasianism, the Mongols, and Russia," *Slavic Review* 41 (1982). See, as well, Donald Ostrowski, "The Mongol Origins of Muscovite Political Institutions," *Slavic Review* 49 (1980), 525–42.

33. Fonds Viollet-le-Duc, Letter of Rondot to Viollet-le-Duc, March 14, 1872.

34. See, for instance, Eugène Emmanuel Viollet-le-Duc, *Histoire de l'Habitation humaine* (Paris, 1875); Lauren O'Connell, "Eugène Emmanuel Viollet-le-Duc," *International Dictionary of Architects and Architecture*, 2 vols. (Detroit 1993), vol. 2, pp. 958–60; and O'Connell, "A Rational, National Architecture."

35. Fonds Viollet-le-Duc, Letter of Rondot to Viollet-le-Duc, April 12 and 23, 1872. Eugène Emmanuel Viollet-le-Duc, "Du Mouvement d'art en Russie," *Encyclopédie d'architecture: revue mensuelle des travaux publics et particuliers*, 2e série (Paris, 1872), vol. 1, pp. 74–76.

36. Viktor Butovsky, *Russkoe iskusstvo i mneniia o nem E. Violle-le-Diuka, frantsuzskago uchenago arkhitektora i F. I. Buslaeva, russkago uchenago arkheologa* (Moscow, Tip. A. Gatsnuka, 1879), 4.

37. Fonds Viollet-le-Duc, Letter of Rondot to Viollet-le-Duc, May 29, 1875. For analysis of the materials sent by Butovsky to Viollet, which included books, drawings, and photographs commissioned by the Museum of Art and Industry, see Lauren O'Connell, "Viollet-le-Duc on Drawing, Photography, and the 'Space Outside the Frame,' " *History of Photography* 22, no. 2 (1998), 139–46.

38. Viollet-le-Duc, *L'Art russe*, 88.

39. Viollet-le-Duc, *Lettres inédites de Viollet-le-Duc recueillies et annotées par son fils* (Paris, 1904), 154. "J'ai sur les arts de l'extrême Orient des données du plus haut intérêt, grâce à la collection de M. Cernuschi qui a bien voulu la mettre à ma disposition, et j'ai trouvé là des solutions qui, je crois, ne peuvent être contestées."

40. See Théodore Duret, *Voyage en Asie* (Paris,

1874), 1–4; Giuseppe Loti, *Henri Cernuschi: Patri-ote—Financier—Philanthrope, Apôtre du bimé-tallisme* (Paris, 1936), 13, 23–55; and Maurice Quentin-Bauchart, *Les Musées Municipaux: Palais des Beaux-Arts, Musée Carnavalet, Maison Victor Hugo, Musée Galliera, Musée Cernuschi* (Paris, 1912), 172–73.

41. In a letter of 7/19 May 1876, Butovsky charges Karamzin with repeating the German view that "les habitants de la Russie étaient des sauvages, vivant dans les forêts comme des bêtes fauves." (Fonds Viol-let-le-Duc, Letter of Butovsky to Viollet-le-Duc). On Karamzin's debt to German historiography, see Irina Grudzinska Gross, "The Tangled Tradition: Custine, Herberstein, Karamzin, and the Critique of Russia," *Slavic Review* 50 (1991), 989–98.

42. Fonds Viollet-le-Duc, Letter of Rondot to Viol-let-le-Duc, April 23, 1876. "Cette théorie, dit-il, est définitivement condamnée. Le finnois, le tartare, ne se rencontrent que dans quelques parties de la Russie, on ne le trouve pas du tout dans la Russe proprement dite."

43. Fonds Viollet-le-Duc, Letter of Butovsky to Viol-let-le-Duc, April 25, 1876. "Quand vous dites 'les bases de l'art russe sont évidemment établis sur les arts les plus anciens de l'extrême orient' ce sont des paroles d'or."

44. Ibid. "C'est pourquoi on peut présumer aussi que la Russie dans son ancien temps à la suite du com-merce que se faisait avec l'extrême orient dû en subir beaucoup d'influence dans son art."

45. Ibid. "On ne peut pas contester l'influence de l'ancien extrême orient: mais on doit se mettre bien en garde de dire qu'il y aurait une influence des tartares, des finnois, et de toutes autres races sauvages, car cela serit soutenir les fausses opinions allemandes, dictées plutôt par la politique, que par une étude de l'art, juste et vrai."

46. See Mark Bassin, "Russia and Asia," in *Cam-bridge Companion to Modern Russian Culture*, Nicholas Rzhevsky, ed. (Cambridge: Cambridge Uni-versity Press, 1998). On the relationship between Rus-sia's economic and political interest in China and at-tention to Chinese culture and society, see Andrew Malozemoff, *Russian Far Eastern Policy, 1881–1904* (Berkeley, 1958), 1–40; and Richard N. Frye, "Orien-tal Studies in Russia," in *Russia and Asia*, 30–51.

47. On the *vostochniki*, see Malozemoff, *Russian Far Eastern Policy*, 41–50; and Hauner, *What Is Asia to Us?*, 48–63. Note that in looking to the East for cultural kin, Viollet also anticipates some elements of the "Eurasianist" philosophy of the 1920s. But unlike Viollet, the Eurasianists insisted on the existence of a distinct geopolitical and cultural unit that was neither European nor Asian. Most important, Viollet's con-struct lacked the imperialist political implications of both *vostochniki* and Eurasianist positions. On the Eurasianists, see Bassin, "Russia and Asia"; and Ri-

asanovsky, "The Emergence of Eurasianism," *Califor-nia Slavic Studies* 4 (1967), 72.

48. Fonds Viollet-le-Duc, Letter of Butovsky to Vio-llet-le-Duc, April 25, 1876. "Si on dit aussi que l'art russe est un art greco-romano-asiatique dans lequel domine l'élément *asiatique* on sera peut-être dans le vrai, mais il faudra alors faire bien comprendre que le mot asiatique s'addresse aux anciens peuples de l'Asie, tels que: Perse, Babylone, ancienne Arménie, [illegible], Inde, etc., peuples civilisés et non aux tatares ou finnois, qui sont arrivés de l'Asie centrale n'ayant aucun art et n'ont apporté que quelques formes asiatiques."

49. David Lowenthal, *The Past Is a Foreign Coun-try* (Cambridge, 1985), 336. Lowenthal writes of the "desire to affirm continuity with a pre-colonial her-itage and to 'restore' non-Western traditions"; for the Russian case one might substitute pre-Petrine for pre-colonial, and non-European for non-Western.

50. Viollet-le-Duc, *L'Art russe*, 102. "Quand on dit aux russes qu'ils sont asiatiques, cette épithète n'a au-cune signification . . . quel est le peuple de l'Europe qui n'est pas un composé de races diverses?"

51. Ibid., 104. "Il serait ridicule de trouver mauvais que le Chinois, dont la structure architectonique re-pose sur l'emploi du pisé et du bambou, n'ait pas bâti le Parthénon, qu'il serait insensé de reprocher à l'Hél-lène, qui construisait en pierre et en marbre, de n'avoir pas élevé une pagode à l'instar des édifices boudhiques de Pékin." See also, in this context, Lau-rent Baridon's discussion of Viollet-le-Duc's debt and contribution to the developing science of anthropol-ogy in *L'imaginaire scientifique de Viollet-le-Duc* (Paris, 1996), 43–58.

52. Fonds Viollet-le-Duc, Letter of Rondot to Viol-let-le-Duc, May 23, 1879. "Personne veut admettre l'influence de l'art de l'Asie, comme si l'Asie représen-tait la barbarie!" The word *asiatchina* (Asianness) re-tains a pejorative tone in contemporary Russian usage, signifying backwardness and lack of cultiva-tion.

53. Ibid. "A la seule parole qu'il existait une influ-ence de l'extrême orient, il a eu la peur que la Russie pouvait être repoussé en Asie."

54. Ibid. "Il crie, il se démène, il est prêt à s'arracher les cheveux. . . . C'est à mourir de rire comme il com-prend cet exemple."

55. As reported in letters of Butovsky to Viollet-le-Duc of January 31/February 12, 1878, and March 6/18, 1879.

56. Fonds Viollet-le-Duc, Letter of Butovsky to Vio-llet-le-Duc, April 17/29, 1879.

57. As in n. 36.

58. Fonds Viollet-le-Duc, letter of Rondot to Viol-let-le-Duc, May 23, 1879. "Vous avez déterminé en Russie un mouvement qui ne fait que commencer, on entreprend des recherches et des études nouvelles, et votre livre est le point de départ de ces travaux."

59. E. Violle-le-Diuk, *Russkoe iskusstvo: ego is-tochniki, ego sostavnye elementy, ego vyschee razvi-tie, ego budushchnost'*, trans. N. Sultanov (Moscow, 1879).

Chapter 8 The "Russian Style" in Church Architecture as Imperial Symbol after 1881

1. E.A. Borisova, *Russkaia arkhitektura vtoroi poloviny XIX veka* (Moscow, 1979), 100, 101; Konstantin Ton, *Tserkvi, sochinennye arkhitektorom Ego Imperatorskogo Velichestva Professorom Arkhtektury Imperatorskoi Akademii Khudozhestv i chlenom raznykh akademii Konstantinym Tonom* (St. Petersburg, 1838), n.p.

2. The most thorough treatment of the history of the building is E. Kirichenko, *Khram Khrista Spasitelia v Moskve* (Moscow, 1997).

3. Ibid., 61–63; Borisova, *Russkaia arkhitektura*, 106–9.

4. *Svod zakonov rossiiskoi imperii* 12 (St. Petersburg, 1857), 49. The provision is article 218 of the *Stroitel'nyi Ustav*.

5. For a discussion of the differences, see my article, "Ofitsial'naia narodnost' i natsional'nyi mif," in N. N. Mazur, ed., *Rossiia / Russia: kul'turnye praktiki v ideologicheskoi perspektive, Rossiia, XVII—nachalo XX veka.* 4, no. 11 (1999), 233–44.

6. In 1881–94, the number of churches rose from 41,500 to 46,000. A. Iu. Polunov, *Pod vlast'iu ober-prokurora: gosudarstvo i tserkov' v epokhu Aleksandra III* (Moscow, 1996), 52; in 1870–90, the number of churches increased from 38,613 to 45,037 and the number of chapels from 13,228 to 18,979. The figure for churches for 1898 is 46,000. Igor Smolitsch, *Geschichte der russischen Kirche, 1700–1917* 1 (Leiden, 1964), 709.

7. On the architectural theorists of the 1870s see E. I. Kirichenko, *Arkhitekturnye teorii XIX veka v Rossii* (Moscow, 1986), 152–278; on Pugin and architectural realism, see Robert Macleod, *Style and Society: Architectural Ideology in Britain, 1835–1914* (London, 1971), 9–12; also Catherine Cooke, "Russian Perspectives," in *Eugène Emmanuel Viollet-le-Duc, 1814–1879,* (London, 1980), 60–63.

8. B. M. Kirikov, "Khram Voskreseniia Khristova (k istorii russkogo stilia v Peterburge)," *Nevskii Arkhiv: istoriko-kraevedcheskii sbornik* 1 (1993), 216–17.

9. On Viollet and the controversy around his books see Lauren M. O'Connell, "A Rational, National Architecture: Viollet-le-Duc's Modest Proposal for Russia," *Journal of the Society of Architectural Historians* 52, no. 4 (December 1993), 436–52; O'Connell, "Viollet-le-Duc and Russian Architecture: The Politics of an Asiatic Past" this volume; and E. Viollet-le-Duc, *L'Art russe* (Paris, 1877), 164–71, 178.

10. Viollet-le-Duc, *L'Art russe*, 8, 148–49.

11. See, for example, Margaret Belcher, "Pugin Writing," in Paul Atterbury and Clive Wainwright, eds., *Pugin: A Gothic Passion* (New Haven, 1994), 115–16; Thomas R. Metcalf, *An Imperial Vision: Indian Architecture and Britain's Raj* (Berkeley, Calif., 1989), 139–40.

12. Three recent studies have provided excellent discussions of the church's architecture and significance: Kirikov's article cited in n. 6 and two articles focusing on the history and the iconography of the church by Michael S. Flier: "The Church of the Savior on the Blood: Projection, Rejection, Resurrection," in Robert P. Hughes and Irina Paperno, eds., *Christianity and the Eastern Slavs* (Berkeley, Calif., 1994), vol. 2, pp. 25–48, and Flier "At Daggers Drawn: The Competition for the Church of the Savior on the Blood," in Michael S. Flier and Robert P. Hughes, eds., *For SK: In Celebration of the Life and Career of Simon Karlinsky* (Berkeley, Calif., 1994), 97–115.

13. In April 1882 the mayor of St. Petersburg informed the City Duma that he had received notification from the St. Petersburg governor that the Minister of the Interior had conveyed the tsar's wish that the cathedral be built "in Russian style." *Moskovskie Vedomosti,* April 9, 1882; A.A. Parland, *Khram Voskresenie Khristova sooruzhennoi na meste smertel'nogo poraneniia v Boze pochivshego Imperatora Aleksandra II na ekaterinskom kanale v Sankt-Peterburge* (St. Petersburg, 1909), 2.

14. Flier, "The Church of the Savior on the Blood," 27; Flier, "At Daggers Drawn," 98.

15. For the projects of the second competition see the volume of Zodchii for 1884. Ignatii's account is cited in *Zhizneopisanie arkhimandrita Ignatiia (Malysheva), byvshego nastoiatelia Troitse-Sergievoi pustyni* (St. Petersburg, 1899), 84.

16. Kirikov, "Khram Voskreseniia Khristova," 230–33; I. Grabar', *Istoriia Russkogo Iskusstva*, vol. 9, Book 2 (Moscow, 1965): 269. "Kokoshniki" are decorative arches that resemble the Russian woman's hat, the kokoshnik. "Shirinki" are oblong panels recessed in exterior walls.

17. Flier, "The Church of the Savior on the Blood," 32–43.

18. This theme was made explicit in sermons and official statements in the months after the assassination. For example, Father Ignatii, in an appeal for contributions for the building of the church, emphasized that the entire people bore the shame, and to a large degree the responsibility for the death. *Zhizneopisanie arkhimandrita Ignatiia, (Malysheva), byvshego nastoiatelia troitse-sergievoi pustyni* (St. Petersburg, 1899), 92. When betrayed by the Jews, Ignatii explained, Christ cried out, asking what the people had done. "Alexander's blood also cried out, My people what have you done? For my whole life, I have cared for you and your well-being, and you condemned me to death. My thoughts and heart were devoted to you. . . . I made the expiatory sacrifice—the body and blood of Christ cleansing every sin, and you murdered me."

Appolon Maikov's poem "March 3, 1881" published in *Moskovskie Vedomosti* 71, no. 3 (March 12, 1881), also expresses a sense of collective shame:

Oh beloved Tsar! Oh remain after death
Our protector!
May Your bloody image show us our emptiness
Our vacillating and weakness for all time!

19. A. A. Parland, "Khram Voskreseniia Khristova," *Zodchii* (1907), 375–76; Parland, *Khram Voskreseniia Khristova*, 3; Flier, "The Church of the Savior on the Blood," 43–45; George P. Fedotov, *The Russian Religious Mind* (Belmont, Mass., 1975) vol. 2, p. 110.

20. A. A. Fet, *Polnoe sobranie stikhotvorenii* (St. Petersburg, 1912), 397:

The snares of the Pharisee are powerless,
What was blood, has become a cathedral,
And the site of the horrible crime,
Has become our eternal shrine!

21. For example, the Cathedral of the Transfiguration, built in 1888 in Tashkent, most Orthodox churches in Poland, and Fedor Shekhtel's 1898 Church of the Savior in Ivanovo-Voznesensk.

22. A. I. Vlasiuk has shown that architectural practice in the second half of the nineteenth century developed its own momentum and was hardly constrained by the 1841 Construction Statute. Vlasiuk, "Evoliutsiia stroitel'nogo zakonodatel'stva Rossii v 1830-e—1910 gody," in *Pamiatniki russkoi arkhitektury i monumental'nogo isskustva* (Moscow, 1985), 226–46; the construction statute, however, remained on the books: *Svod zakonov Rossiiskoi imperii* (St. Petersburg, 1900), Part 2, vol. 12, p. 180.

23. S. Shul'ts, *Khramy Sankt-Peterburga: istoriia i sovremennost'* (St. Petersburg, 1994), 177–78; M. Preobrazhenskii, *Revel'skii Pravoslavnyi Aleksandro-Nevskii Sobor* (St. Petersburg, 1902).

24. Viollet-le-Duc, *L'Art russe*, 115–17.

25. N. Sultanov, "Vozrozhdenie russkogo iskusstva," *Zodchii* 2 (1881), 9; Borisova, *Russkaia arkhitektura*, 308.

26. Iu. V. Trubinov notes this resemblance, *Khram Voskresenie Khristova (Spas na Krovi)* (St. Petersburg, 1997), 40–41.

27. See the suggestive remarks on inflation and copiousness in the art of monarchy in Randolph Starn and Loren Partridge, *Arts of Power: Three Halls of State in Italy, 1300–1600* (Berkeley, Calif., 1992), 166–74.

28. L. N. Benois wrote that during Alexander III's reign, "Petersburg, Peterhof, Warsaw, etc., were graced with new churches, the lack of which was felt acutely, especially in the capital." "Zodchestvo v tsarstvovanie Imperatora Aleksandra III," *Nedelia Stroitelia*, November 27, 1894, No.48: 245. On the increased emphasis on Moscow as the political center of autocracy see my article, "Moscow and Petersburg: The Problem of Political Center in Tsarist Russia," in Sean Wilentz, ed., *Rites of Power; Symbolism, Ritual*

and Politics Since the Middle Ages (Philadelphia, 1985), 244–74.

29. Louis Réau, *Saint Petersburg* (Paris, 1913), 67–68; Flier, "The Church of the Savior on the Blood," 30.

30. *Utrachennye pamiatniki arkhitektury Peterburga-Leningrada; katalog vystavki* (Leningrad, 1988), 31–39; Shul'ts, *Khramy Sankt-Peterburga*, 52, 79–82, 104, 106, 119–21, 173–74, 177–80, 200, 203–4, 212, 218; Polunov, *Pod vlast'iu ober-prokurora*, 76.

31. Shul'ts, *Khramy Sankt-Peterburga*, 81–82, 120–21.

32. See Nadieszda Kizenko, *The Making of a Modern Saint: Father John of Kronstadt and the Russian People* (University Park, Penn., 2000); Simon Dixon, "The Church's Social Role in St. Petersburg," in Geoffrey A. Hosking, ed., *Church, Nation and State in Russia and Ukraine* (London, 1991), 167–92; Jeffrey Brooks, *When Russia Learned to Read: Literacy and Popular Literature, 1861–1917* (Princeton, 1985), 300–1, 306–11.

33. Parland, *Khram Voskreseniia Khristova*, 14; Grigorii Moskvich, *Petrograd i ego okresnosti* (Petrograd, 1915), 62–63.

34. Réau, *Saint Petersburg*, 68; Shul'ts, *Khramy Sankt-Peterburga*, 121.

35. *Stroitel'*, (1896), 559–66, 667–95; Kirichenko, *Arkhitekturnye teorii XIX veka v Rossii*, 254–55.

36. These edifices as well as others in the national style are discussed in V. G. Lisovskii, *Natsional'nyi Stil' v arkhitekture Rossii* (Moscow, 2000), 197–211.

37. *Niva*, 24 (1894): 569.

38. *Zodchii* 8 (1893), Plates 1, 2, 6; (1903), 30–31. Shul'ts, *Khramy Sankt-Peterburga*, 180. William Craft Brumfield, *The Origins of Modernism in Russian Architecture* (Berkeley, Calif., 1991), 129.

39. *Zodchii* (1889). 74–77; On Vorontsov-Dashkov see B. V. Anan'ich and R. Sh. Ganelin, "Aleksandr III i naslednik nakanune 1 marta 1881 g," in *Dom romanovykh v Rossii, Istoricheskii opyt russkogo naroda i sovremennost'* 2 (St. Petersburg, 1995), 205.

40. *Zodchii* (1893), Plates 21–23; Shul'ts, *Khramy Sankt-Peterburga*, 173–74. I thank Priscilla Roosevelt for drawing my attention to the nobility's reproduction of the official Russian style on their estates.

41. The requirements are indicated in articles 205 and 206 of the "Stroitel'nyi Ustav." *Svod Zakonov Rossiiskoi Imperii* (St. Petersburg, 1857), 47. The procedures are suggested in the memoranda: "Po otnosheniiu Ministerstva Vnutrennikh Del o postroike tserkvi vo imia Skorbiashchei Bozhiei Materi v selenie Imperatorskogo steklannogo zavoda na naberezhnoi r. Bol'shoi Nevy," RGIA, 797–63–225; and "O postroike kamennoi tserkvi na naberezhnoi obvodnogo kanala bliz Varshavskogo Voksala v S-Petersburge," RGIA, 799–25–1289 (1903). The first church on the Obvodnyi Canal, completed in 1894, was dedicated to the marriage of Nicholas and

Alexandra; the present church, begun in 1904, marked the birth of Tsarevich Aleksei. Shul'ts, *Khramy Sankt-Peterburga*, 121.

42. The most comprehensive study of the use of church architecture to express Russian imperial domination is Piotr Paszkiewicz, *W sluzbie Imperium Rosyjskiego 1721–1917 : funkcje i tresci ideowe rosyjskiej architektury sakralnej na zachodnich rubiezach Cesarstwa i poza jego granicami* (Warsaw, 1999).

43. *Riga und seine Bauten* (Riga, 1903), 181–84.

44. Edward Thaden, "The Russian Government," in Edward Thaden, (ed.) *Russification in the Baltic Provinces and Finland, 1855–1914* (Princeton, 1981), 67–70; Toivo U. Raun, "The Estonians," in Thaden, ed., *Russification*, 323–25.

45. Preobrazhenskii, *Revel'skii*, 3–4; Raun, "Estonians," 325.

46. "Po voprosu o postroike sobora v g. Revele, Estliandskoi gubernii," RGIA, 797–91–6.

47. "Al'bom vidov tserkvei Estliandskoi gubernii, sooruzhennykh pod vedeniem Revel'skogo nabliudatel'nogo komiteta po postroike tserkvei, prichtovykh i shkol'nykh zdanii" (Revel, n.d.); Adres-kalendar' na 1889 g. (St. Petersburg, 1889), 285. Shirinskii-Shikhmatov later rose to the positions of provincial governor, member of the State Council, official in Nicholas II's court, and Chief-Procurator of the Holy Synod. A. A. Mosolov, *Pri dvore poslednego Rossiiskogo imperatora* (Moscow, 1993), 244, 273.

48. Piotr Paszkiewicz, "The Russian Orthodox Cathedral of Saint Alexander Nevsky in Warsaw," *Polish Art Studies* 14 (1992), 64–65, 67.

49. Ibid., 65–66.

50. V. A. Nil'sen, *U istokov sovremennogo gradostroitel'stva Uzbekistana: xix-nachalo xx vekov*, 49–52, 64–65; Robert Crews, "Civilization in the City: Architecture, Urbanism and the Colonization of Tashkent." Conference Paper, 5.

51. *Zodchii* (1889), Plates 35–38.

52. Austin Jersild, "From Frontier to Empire: The Russification of the Causasus, 1845–1917," unpublished manuscript. Chap. 12, 493 n. 124.

53. On Russian national churches abroad see Piotr Paszkiewicz, *W sluzbie Imperium Rosyjskiego 1721–1917*, passim.

54. *Stroitel'* (1900), 536.

55. *Podvor'e russkoi pravoslavnoi tserkvi v Karlovykh varakh* (Prague, 1987); *Zodchii* 21 (1881), Plates 49–50.

56. Metcalf, *Imperial* Vision, 24, 57, 86–88, 113–15, 128, 140, 245, 249–50. It is interesting to note that the favorite building style of the indigenous merchant elite in Bombay was the English Gothic, which they thought would bring them closer to their colonial rulers. Metcalf, 90–98.

57. *Zodchii* (1905), 497–98.

58. Ibid. (1911), 23–24; William Craft Brumfield, "The 'New Style' and the Revival of Orthodox Church Architecture, 1900–1914," in William C. Brumfield and Milos M. Velimirovic, *Christianity and the Arts in Russia* (Cambridge, 1991), 105–23; Brumfield, *The Origins of Modernism*, particularly chaps. 4 and 6; one of Aplaksin's neo-Russian churches is shown in Shul'ts, *Khramy Sankt-Peterburga*, 106–7, two are mentioned in *Utrachennye pamiatniki*, 36.

59. The monastery had been a center of the Uniate faith. In 1831, after the monks had joined the Polish insurgents, Nicholas I had placed it under the Orthodox church administration. Brumfield, *The Origins of Modernism*, 105–7; *Entsiklopedicheskii Slovar' Brogauz-Efron* (St. Petersburg, 1898), vol. 48, p. 767; John Curtiss, *Church and State in Russia: The Last Years of the Empire* (New York, 1940), 255.

60. *Istoriia Feodorovskogo Gorodetskogo monastyria (Nizhegorodskaia guberniia) i postroenie v S-Peterburge khrama v pamiat' 300 iubileiia tsarstvovaniia imperatorskogo Doma Romanovykh* (St. Petersburg, 1913), 113–24.

61. S. Krichinskii, "Khram v pamiat' 300 letiia doma Romanovykh," *Zodchii* (1914), 122–23; *Niva* 5 (1914), 97; "Snimki vidov tserkvi postroennoi v pamiat' 300–letiia tsarstvovaniia Romanovykh," GARF, 601–1–1841; Georgii Lukomskii, "Khram v pamiat' 300–letiia tsarstvovaniia doma Romanovykh," *Appolon* 5 (1914), 47–49; "Zhurnaly komiteta dlia ustroistva prazdnovaniia trekhsotletiia Doma Romanovykh," RGIA, 1320–1–30, 5–6, 43–45.

62. *Pamiatniki arkhitektury prigorodov Leningrada* (Leningrad, 1983), 126–29. Vladimir Pokrovskii's unrealized project for a Military-Historical Museum in St. Petersburg is an example of this, Ekaterina Abrosova, "Arkhitektor Vysochaishego Dvora Vladimir Aleksandrovich Pokrovskii," *Tsar'ino: Pravoslavnyi istoriko-kraevedcheskii almanakh*, vol. 98, Vyp. 4, pp. 44–46. Also see Vladimir Maksimov's unrealized projects for the building complex of the Railroad Guards' regiment and a hotel complex at Tsarskoe Selo. Arkadii Krasheninnikov, "Russkii zodchii Vladimir Nikolaevich Maksimov, (1882–1942)," *Tsar'ino: Pravoslavnyi istoriko-kraevedcheskii almanakh*, vol. 98, Vyp. 4, p. 74.

63. Kirichenko, *Russkii stil'*, 305–8, 310–11, 366–68.

64. Abrosova, "Arkhitektor," 55–56; One of the principal sponsors of the church was the chief of the Tsarskoe Selo palace administration, Michael Putiatin, a former officer of the Preobrazhenskii Guards and Marshal of the Court. Putiatin was a lover of Russian antiquities, who had helped organize the tsar's visit to Sarov and had designed the shrine for the saint's remains. He closely supervised the decoration of the church and insisted that the iconostasis be in Old Russian style. The church warden was Captain N. Loman, the author of the popular account of the coronation and a popular biography of Alexander II, and an associate of Rasputin. Général Alexandre

Spiridovitch, *Les dernières années de la cour de Tsarskoe-Selo* (Paris, 1928–29), vol. 1, p. 352, vol. 2, pp. 253–62; Mosolov, 28, 118.

65. On Maksimov, his buildings, and his tragic fate under Stalin see Krasheninnikov, "Russkii zodchii Vladimir Nikolaevich Maksimov," 63–83.

66. *Feodorovskii gosudarev sobor v Tsarskom Sele.* Vol. 1: *Peshchernyi Khram vo imia prepodobnogo Serafima sarovskogo* (Moscow, 1915); *Rodina* (Sept. 16, 1912), 538; Spiridovitch, *Les dernières années,* vol. 2, pp. 253–60; Maurice Paléologue, *Alexandra-Féodorowna, impératrice de Russie* (Paris, n.d.), 51–52; A. N. Naumov, *Iz utselevshikh vospominanii, 1868–1917* (New York, 1954–55), vol. 2, p. 226.

67. S. Ia. Ofromisova, "Tsarkaia sem'ia, (iz detskikh vospominanii)," *Russkaia Letopis'* 7 (Paris, 1925), 240–41; I. M. Shadrin, "Pridvornaia Pevcheskaia Kapella i Imperatorskii Dvor do Velikoi Voiny 1914–1917 gg," BAR, Shadrin Collection, 55. On the theatricalization of church architecture in the neo-Russian style and particularly in Pokrovskii's Fedorov Sobor, see A. V. Ikonnikov, *Istorizm v arkhitekture* (Moscow, 1997), 304, 310.

Chapter 9 Civilization in the City

1. Epigraph from "Das neue Taschkent, die russische Metropole in Zentralasien," *Globus* 82, no. 12 (1902): 181.

2. Manfredo Tafuri, *Architecture and Utopia: Design and Capitalist Development,* trans. Barbara Luigia La Penta (Cambridge, Mass., 1976); Jörg Fisch, "Zivilisation, Kultur," in *Geschichtliche Grundbegriffe: Historisches Lexicon zur politisch-sozialen Sprache in Deutschland,* ed. Otto Brunner, Werner Conze, and Reinhart Kosselleck, vol. 7 (Stuttgart, 1992), 679–774; and Raymond Williams, *Keywords: A Vocabulary of Culture and Society* (New York, 1985), 57–60. A broader investigation of Russian Tashkent may now be found in Jeffery Frank Sahadeo's exhaustive study: "Creating a Russian Colonial Community: City, Nation, and Empire in Tashkent, 1865–1923," Ph.D. diss., University of Illinois at Urbana-Champaign, 2000.

3. On the "Europeanization" of Russian attitudes and policies that accompanied tsarist expansion in Asia, see Andreas Kappeler, *Russland als Vielvölkerreich: Entstehung, Geschichte, Zerfall,* 2d ed. (Munich, 1993), especially 139–76.

4. Rossiiskii gosudarstvennyi voenno-istoricheskii arkhiv [RGVIA], fond 1396, opis' 2, delo 448, list 3.

5. James Cracraft, *The Petrine Revolution in Russian Architecture* (Chicago and London, 1988); Richard S. Wortman, *Scenarios of Power: Myth and Ceremony in Russian Monarchy,* vol. 1 (Princeton, 1995); and on the relationship between building forms and the marking of social difference, see Norbert Elias, *Die höfische Gesellschaft* (Neuwied, 1969), 68–101.

6. Robert E. Jones, "Urban Planning and the Development of Provincial Towns in Russia, 1762–1796," in *The Eighteenth Century in Russia,* ed. J. G. Garrard (Oxford, 1973), 321–44; and Daniel R. Brower, *The Russian City between Tradition and Modernity, 1850–1900* (Berkeley and Los Angeles, 1990). On the motif of Catherinian cities as outposts of civilization, see A. M. Panchenko, "'Potemkinskie derevni' kak kul'turnyi mif," *XVIII vek* 14 (1983): 93–104; and Wortman, *Scenarios of Power,* 139–142.

7. See Anthony Vidler, *The Architectural Uncanny: Essays in the Modern Unhomely* (Cambridge, Mass., and London, 1992), 71–77.

8. *The City Shaped: Urban Patterns and Meanings through History* (Boston and Toronto, 1991), 209–77, here, 271.

9. Mary Douglas, *Purity and Danger: An Analysis of Concepts of Pollution and Taboo* (New York and Washington, 1966). Studies stressing the instability of these categories include Ann Laura Stoler, "Rethinking Colonial Categories: European Communities and the Boundaries of Rule," *Comparative Studies in Society and History* 31, no. 1 (1989), 134–61; Mrinalini Sinha, *Colonial Masculinity: The "Manly Englishman" and the "Effeminate Bengali" in the Late Nineteenth Century* (Manchester and New York, 1995); and Gyan Prakash, ed., *After Colonialism: Imperial Histories and Postcolonial Displacements* (Princeton, 1995).

10. *Citizen and Subject: Contemporary Africa and the Legacy of Late Colonialism* (Princeton, 1996), 25.

11. These interactions are examined more closely in Robert D. Crews, "Allies in God's Command: Muslim Communities and the State in Imperial Russia," Ph.D. diss., Princeton University, 1999.

12. On the role of the reader and city-dweller as "cultural consumer" of texts and urban spaces, see Michel de Certeau, *The Practice of Everyday Life,* trans. Steven Rendall (Berkeley and Los Angeles, 1984).

13. See, for example, Z. Radzhabov, *Iz istorii obshchestvenno-politicheskoi mysli tadzhikskogo naroda vo vtoroi polovine XIX i v nachale XX vv.* (Stalinabad, 1957), 309–11; and, more generally, Adeeb Khalid, *The Politics of Muslim Cultural Reform: Jadidism in Central Asia* (Berkeley and Los Angeles, 1998).

14. See Anthony D. King, *Colonial Urban Development: Culture, Social Power and Environment* (London, 1976); Thomas R. Metcalf, *An Imperial Vision: Indian Architecture and Britain's Raj* (Berkeley and Los Angeles, 1989); Gwendolyn Wright, *The Politics of Design in French Colonial Urbanism* (Chicago and London, 1991); Nezar AlSayyad, ed., *Forms of Dominance: On the Architecture and Urbanism of the Colonial Enterprise* (Aldershot and Brookfield, 1992); and Paul Rabinow, *French Modern: Norms and Forms of the Social Environment* (Cambridge, Mass. and London, 1989).

15. As educated society in the tsarist capitals was

well aware, Europeans like the influential Orientalist Hermann Vámbéry derided the Russian capacity to perform the "civilizing mission," pointing to an "*Asiatismus*" lying half-concealed in the Russian character. *Der Islam im neunzehnten Jahrhundert* (Leipzing, 1875), 291–98.

16. V. I. Masal'skii, *Turkestanskii krai*, vol. 19 of *Rossiia: Polnoe geograficheskoe opisanie nashego otechestva* (St. Petersburg, 1913), 610. On the emergence of "Russian style" architecture, see the essays in this volume by Lauren M. O'Connell and Richard Wortman. Of course, Russian elites were not alone in confronting the aesthetic dilemmas posed by the search for an architectural form to represent the "spirit" of a nation. See, for example, Thomas Nipperdey, "Nationalidee und Nationaldenkmal in Deutschland im 19. Jahrhundert," *Historische Zeitschrift* 206, no. 3 (1968), 529–85.

17. See Michel Foucault, *Power/Knowledge: Selected Interviews and Other Writings 1972–1977*, ed. Colin Gordon (New York, 1980), 146–65; and the response by Vidler, *Architectural Uncanny*, 167–75, here, 167–69.

18. See, for example, the description in I. I. Geier, *Ves' russkii Turkestan* (Tashkent, 1908), 219.

19. Gauri Viswanathan's remarks about the vulnerability of the British in India suggest some parallels. She notes that "representation of Indians as morally and intellectually deficient" also imposed constraints upon such a regime, for "depicting the natives as irrational, inscrutable, unstable and volatile, doomed British rulers to inhabiting an imagined, dreaded world of imminent rebellion and resistance." *Masks of Conquest: Literary Study and British Rule in India* (New York, 1989), 10–11.

20. *Tashkent v proshlom i nastoiashchem: istoricheskii ocherk* (Tashkent, 1912), 73–74. See, also, Johannes Fabian, *Time and the Other: How Anthropology Makes Its Object* (New York, 1983).

21. M. Ruzieva, "K istoricheskoi topografii Tashkenta," *Obshchestvennye nauki v Uzbekistane* 6 (1966): 66–69; "Les Ichâns de Tachkent," *Revue du monde musulman* 13, no. 1 (1911): 128–46; and N. G. Mallitskii, *Tashkent mähällä vä mävseläri*, trans. Usman Kochqar (Tashkent, 1996).

22. Vidler, *Architectural Uncanny*, 179.

23. Mona Ozouf, *Festivals and the French Revolution*, trans. Alan Sheridan (Cambridge, Mass. and London, 1988), Chap. 7, and here, 167.

24. Pierre Nora, "Between Memory and History: Les Lieux de Mémoire," trans. March Roudebush, *Representations* 26 (1989), 7–25, here, 19.

25. N. Frideriks, "Turkestan i ego reformy," *Vestnik Evropy* 3, no. 6 (1869), 694.

26. "Postupatel'noe dvizhenie Rossii v Srednei Azii," *Sbornik gosudarstvennykh znanii*, ed. V. P. Bezobrazov, vol. 3 (St. Petersburg, 1877), 86.

27. See Bernard S. Cohn, "Representing Authority in Victorian India," in *The Invention of Tradition*, ed.

Eric Hobsbawm and Terence Ranger (Cambridge, 1983), 165–209.

28. *Sredniaia Aziia i vodvorenie v nei russkoi grazhdanstvennosti* (St. Petersburg, 1870), 54.

29. W. Barthold, "Tashkent," *The Encyclopedia of Islam* vol. 4, (Leiden, 1934) pp. 687–89; F. Azadaev, *Tashkent vo vtoroi polovine XIX veka: ocherki sotsial'no-ekonomicheskoi i politicheskoi istorii* (Tashkent, 1959); and Baymirza Hayit, *Turkestan zwischen Russland und China* (Amsterdam, 1971), 21–38.

30. Dobrosmyslov, *Tashkent v proshlom i nastoiashchem*, 134; and P. I. Pashino, *Turkestanskii krai v 1866 godu: putevye zametki* (St. Petersburg, 1868), 97.

31. See François Delaporte, *Disease and Civilization: The Cholera in Paris, 1832*, trans. Arthur Goldhammer (Cambridge, Mass. and London, 1986), 17.

32. See his *Turkestanskii krai: opyt voenno-statisticheskogo obozreniia turkestanskogo voennogo okruga: materialy dlia geografii i statistiki* (St. Petersburg, 1880), 390–91.

33. Kostenko, *Sredniaia Aziia*, 86.

34. Ibid.

35. Ibid.

36. Carl E. Schorske, *Fin-de-Siècle Vienna: Politics and Culture* (London, 1980); and Zeynep Çelik, *The Remaking of Istanbul: Portrait of an Ottoman City in the Nineteenth Century* (Berkeley and Los Angeles, 1986).

37. See RGVIA, f. 1399, op. 1, d. 1; and f. 1402, op. 2, d. 2.

38. By the late 1870s, the Russians had planned five major new cities alongside the existing towns of Tashkent, Samarkand, Margelan, Andizhan, and Namangan. Kokand, whose interior Russians partially redesigned, formed an exception to this pattern. G. N. Chabrov, "Russkie arkhitektory dorevoliutsionnogo Turkestana (1865–1916 gg.)," in *Arkhitekturnoe nasledie Uzbekistana*, ed. G. A. Pugachenkova (Tashkent, 1960), 221–29; V. L. Voronina, "Deiatel'nost' russkikh gradostroitelei v Turkestane vo vtoroi polovine XIX v.," *Arkhitekturnoe nasledstvo* no. 25 (1976), 79–84; and V. A. Nil'sen, *U istokov sovremennogo gradostroitel'stva Uzbekistana XIX—nachalo XX vekov* (Tashkent, 1988).

39. Tsentral'nyi gosudarstvennyi arkhiv Respubliki Uzbekistana [TsGARU], f. 1, op. 16, d. 3; Nil'sen, *U istokov*, 38–40; and Dobrosmyslov, *Tashkent v proshlom i nastoiashchem* 71–73.

40. TsGARU, f. 36, op. 1, d. 16, d. 224, ll. 5–5 ob.

41. In 1866, the governor-general initiated a "voluntary subscription throughout the whole empire for the construction of Orthodox churches in Turkestan," in order "to lay a firm foundation for the strengthening of the salutary and mores-softening influence of the Orthodox faith in a region whose predominant population is fanatical in [its] religious ideas." *Strannik* (Nov. 1866), 70; and *Turkestanskie eparkhial'nye*

vedomosti no. 9 (1 May 1907), 204. The church apparently commemorated St. Joseph the Hymnographer (c. 810–16) and St. George the martyr.

42. L. Kostenko, "Svedeniia o russkom Tashkente," *Russkii invalid* no. 95 (1869) in *Turkestanskii sbornik* vol. 28 (St. Petersburg, 1870), 53.

43. Cited in E.M. Tolbukhov, "Ustroitel' turkestanskogo kraia," *Istoricheskii vestnik* 8, no. 5 (1913), 893.

44. *Proekt vsepoddanneisheishogo otcheta Gen.-A"iutanta K. P. fon-Kaufmana I po grazhdanskomu upravleniiu i ustroistvu v obliastiakh turkestanskogo general'-gubernatorstva 7 noiabria 1867–25 marta 1881 g.*, ed. P. I. Khomutov (St. Petersburg, 1885), 6.

45. Nil'sen, *U istokov*, 40–41; and Chabrov, "Russkie arkhitektory," 222–23.

46. See the description in V. P'iankov, ed., *Turkestanskii kalendar' na 1880 god: spravochnaia knizhka* (Tashkent, 1879), 130–31; and Nil'sen, *U istokov*, and Chabrov, "Russkie arkhitektory."

47. Kaufman prohibited Orthodox clergymen from pursuing missionary work. Moreover, in 1872, Vernyi (to become Alma-Ata under the Soviets), not Tashkent, was chosen as the seat of the diocese of Turkestan. V. V. Bartol'd asserted that it was Kaufman who prevented its location in Tashkent. He also argued that not only the church but the municipal government of Tashkent viewed the placement of the bishop in Vernyi as "a violation of the city's rights as capital." *Istoriia kul'turnoi zhizni Turkestana* (Leningrad, 1927), 167.

48. "Krestnyi khod v vospominanie 42-i godovshchiny vziatiia goroda Tashkenta," *Turkestanskie eparkhial'nye vedomosti*, nos. 14–15 (15 July 1907), 369.

49. Ibid.

50. See, for example, N. P. Ostroumov, *Sarty: etnograficheskie materialy* (Tashkent, 1908), 95.

51. *Turkestanskie vedomosti*, 19 June 1897.

52. Quoted in Ostroumov, *Sarty*, 95.

53. *Turkestanskie vedomosti*, 17 June 1915.

54. Ibid.

55. *Turkestanskie vedomosti*, 17 June 1905.

56. P'iankov, *Turkestanskii kalendar'*, 130.

57. *Turkestanskie eparkhial'nye vedomosti* 5 (15 October 1906), 46; and *Turkestanskie vedomosti*, 17 June 1905. Compare George L. Mosse, *Fallen Soldiers: Reshaping the Memory of the World Wars* (New York and Oxford, 1990); on the participation of women in patriotic rituals, Linda Colley, *Britons: Forging the Nation 1707–1837* (New Haven and London, 1992), 237–281; and Mary Ryan, "The American Parade: Representations of the Nineteenth-Century Social Order," in *The New Cultural History*, ed. Lynn Hunt (Berkeley and Los Angeles, 1989), 131–53.

58. On tsarist officials' suspicion of popular nationalist sentiment in a dynastic state, see Hans Rogger, "Nationalism and the State: A Russian Dilemma," *Comparative Studies in Society and History* 4

(1961–62), 253–64; and on the "national myth" of Russian monarchy, see Richard Wortman, " 'Offitsial'naia narodnost' i natsional'nyi mif rossiiskoi monarkhii XIX veka," *Rossiia/Russia* 3 (1999), 233–44.

59. *Turkestanskie eparkhial'nye vedomosti* 1 (15 August 1906), 10; and 11 (1 June 1907), 266.

60. RGVIA, f. 1396, op. 2, d. 448, l. 8.

61. RGVIA, f. 400, op. 1, d. 1230, l. 2; and "Pamiatnik v chest' pavshikh pri vziatii Tashkenta," *Niva* 31 (1883), 747.

62. RGVIA, f. 1396, op. 2., del. 448, ll. 9–12.

63. The imperial statute of 1870 establishing a limited measure of municipal autonomy was modified for application in Tashkent in 1877. The city was divided on a territorial basis; two-thirds of the seats in the Duma were allocated to new Tashkent, with the remaining one-third for the old city. See Bartol'd, *Istoriia*, 163–65.

64. RGVIA, f. 400, op. 1, d. 520, l. 3.

65. Ibid., ll. 3–4.

66. See TsGARU, f. 1, op. 31, d. 30, l. 32; and Sahadeo, "Russian Colonial Community," on military and mob violence against Muslims.

67. *Protokol torzhestvennogo zasedaniia Obshchestva turkestanskikh vrachei* 3 (1899), 10–11.

68. On the frustrations experienced by Europeans who read cities like Cairo and Algiers in search of a "visible exterior" as a representation of an "invisible *vie intérieure*" of "Muslim and Oriental life," see Timothy Mitchell, *Colonising Egypt* (Berkeley and Los Angeles, 1988).

69. See N.S. Lykoshin, "Naselenie i smertnost' v tuzemnoi chasti g. Tashkenta," *Sbornik materialov dlia statistiki Syr'-Dar'inskoi oblasti* (Tashkent, 1892), 397–423.

70. On the reconstruction of the bazaar, see Nil'sen, *U istokov*, 24–25; and Bartol'd, *Istoriia*, 172.

71. *Protokol ekstrennogo zasedaniia Obshchestva turkestanskikh vrachei* 13 (1899), 51.

72. RGVIA, f. 400, op. 1, d. 2446, ll. 1–1 ob.

73. Ibid., l. 11 ob.

74. *Musul'manskaia gazeta*, 8 January 1913.

75. On the Hoja Ahrar mosque, see Dobrosmyslov, *Tashkent v proshlom i nastoiashchem* 77; Nil'sen, *U istokov*, 24; and Bartol'd, *Istoriia*, 204. On new Tashkent as a "garden-city," see *Izvestiia Tashkentskoi gorodskoi dumy* 1 (15 June 1915), 91.

76. Rossiiskii gosudarstvennyi istoricheskii arkhiv [RGIA], f. 1396, op. 1, d. 96, ll. 36–37.

77. Ibid., l. 145.

78. Ibid.

79. Ibid., l. 37. In 1889, a Muslim newspaper identified Tashkent as one of the cities in the empire where the sight of Muslim prostitutes had become commonplace. *Perevodchik/Tercüman*, 5 November 1889.

80. Ibid.

81. See Sahadeo, "Russian Colonial Community."

82. *Turkestanskie eparkhial'nye vedomosti* 11 (1

July 1907), 263–66. A lecture, "On Christian Patriotism," sponsored by the local Society for Religious and Moral Education took aim at "cosmopolitanism" and those "rejecting nationality and national feeling" and advocated Christian love for one's own people and fatherland. Ibid., 7 (1 June 1907), 133.

83. *Turkestanskie vedomosti*, 11 June 1908. Another critic wrote that the "Russian citizen must firmly remember, no matter to what political party he may belong, that he lives in Turkestan, that his task is not to change or reform the existing conditions of political life but [lies instead] in cultural influence upon the local native [*inorodcheskii*] element." *Turkestanskie eparkhial'nye vedomosti* 1 (15 August 1906), 10.

84. In 1868, 120 Muslims (mostly Tatar soldiers) petitioned for permission to maintain a *mullah* in the "European quarter" because the *ulama* of the old city refused to say prayers or perform other rites for them. In the 1880s, their mosque became a source of dispute; the original plan called for a minaret of some twenty-nine meters, but the authorities refused to allow one taller than fourteen meters. TsGARU, f. 36, op. 1, d. 456, ll. 3 ob.-10; and TsGARU, f. 1, op. 16, d. 1562, ll. 8–8 ob. The establishment of a Jewish community further complicated "national" representations of the urban landscape. See TsGARU, f. 36, op. 1, d. 874; and "Tashkent" in *Evreiskaia entsiklopediia*, vol. 14 (St. Petersburg, n.d.), col. 773.

85. TsGARU f. 18, op. 1, d. 1158a, l. 1. On this celebration, see Roy Mottahedeh, *The Mantle of the Prophet: Religion and Politics in Iran* (New York, 1985), 173–79.

86. Stenin, "Das neue Taschkent, die russische Metropole in Zentralasien," 183.

87. TsGARU, f. 19, op. 1, d. 5688 and d. 29299; f. 18, op. 1, d. 2394; and G. A. "K perekhodu pravoslavnykh v Islam," *Turkestanskie vedomosti* 94, 1909, reprinted in *Turkestanskii sbornik* 507 (St. Petersburg, n.p., 1909), 1–2. See Fredrik Barth on the "continual expression and validation" of boundaries in the maintenance of ethnic difference. *Ethnic Groups and Boundaries: The Social Organization of Culture Difference* (London, 1969).

88. TsGARU, f. 19, op. 1, d. 3316, l. 1. Tatars also appeared to be usurping the Russian cultural mission by establishing reformist (*usul-i jadid*) schools, newspapers, and printing presses. See Bartol'd, *Istoriia*, 165–66; Adeeb Khalid, "Printing, Publishing, and Reform in Tsarist Central Asia," *International Journal of Middle East Studies* 26 (1994), 187–200; and Abdullah Battal-Taymas, *Kazan Türkleri* (Ankara, 1966), 171–73.

89. RGVIA, f. 400, op. 1, d. 1089, l. 3.

90. Two Tashkentis stand out in accounts of the annual ceremony: Mukhitdin-Khodzha (Muhiddin Kadı), an Islamic law court judge, and Seid Karim Seid Azimbaev (Seyid Azimbey), a merchant, philanthropist, and mosque patron. In 1888, Mukhitdin also spoke at the opening of the Hoja Ahrar mosque,

praising the governor-general's "tolerance" toward Islam. Both apparently supported Russian schools and the study of the Russian language. Another contemporary, A. Zeki Velidi Togan, identified them as members of a "money aristocracy" and an "*ulama* aristocracy" on "the side of the Russians." *Bugünkü Türkili (Türkistan) ve yakın Tarihi* (Istanbul, 1942–47), 272–74. See also Bartol'd, *Istoriia*, 165–66, 184–85, and 204.

91. Frideriks, 702; and *Mission to Turkestan: Being the Memoirs of Count K. K. Pahlen, 1908–1909*, ed. Richard A. Pierce, trans. N. J. Couriss (London, 1964), 2.

92. On 1917 in Tashkent, see Adeeb Khalid, "Tashkent 1917: Muslim Politics in Revolutionary Russia," *Slavic Review* 55, no. 2 (1996), 270–96; and Marco Buttino, "Turkestan 1917: La révolution des russes," *Cahiers du monde russe et soviétique* 32, no. 1 (1991), 61–78.

93. Abdullah Taymas, *Rus Ihtilâlinden Hâtyralar 1917–1919* (Istanbul, 1947), 33–34.

94. See T. F. Kadyrova, *Sovremennaia arkhitektura Uzbekistana* (Tashkent, 1974).

Chapter 10 Stalinist Modern

1. For a discussion of the historiography of constructivism see Greg Castillo, "Classicism for the Masses: Books on Stalinist Architecture," *Design Book Review* 34/35 (Winter/Spring, 1995), 78–88.

2. Catherine Cooke, " 'Form is a Function x': The Development of the Constructivist Architect's Design Method," *Architectural Design* 53, no. 5/6 (May/June 1983), 40.

3. Iakov Chernikov, *The Construction of Architectural and Machine Forms* (Leningrad, 1931); English translation in Catherine Cooke, "Chernikov: Fantasy and Construction," *Architectural Design* U54, no. 9/10 (1984), 24.

4. A. Mikhailov, "Review of *The Construction of Architectural and Machine Forms*" *SA* 5/6 (1931), 27; cited in Cooke, *Chernikov*, 46.

5. Lidiia Komarova, "Arkhitekturny fakul'tet Vkhutemasa: masterskaia A.A. Vesnina," in A. V. Stepanov, *Vkhutemas-Markhi 1920–80* (Moscow, 1986), 33–35; translation in Catherine Cooke, *Russian Avant-Garde Theories of Art, Architecture, and the City* (London, 1995), 175.

6. A fuller accounting of constructivism must grapple with its self-elected practitioners, representations in the mass media (by turns adulatory and hostile), and even its converts outside the USSR (Switzerland's constructivist "ABC" association, founded by El Lissitzky, being the clearest example). Scholars who find this collection of varied and sometimes contradictory phenomena too unwieldy should remember that a monolithic definition of constructivism requires significant and unambiguous identifying criteria. Attempts to rout out what the architectural historian

Catherine Cooke has called "catholic" uses of the constructivist label assume that OSA membership is the authoritative criterion. The dilemmas resulting from this premise are abundantly documented in the literature, where a grab-bag of prescriptions for design methodology are all called "constructivist" without any corroborating evidence of group consensus. In fact, the heterogeneity of OSA praxis, ranging from the functional traffic charts employed by Ginzburg to the intuitive free-space planning of Leonidov, suggests exactly the opposite. Leonidov's career pinpoints another internal contradiction in the use of OSA membership as the exclusive criterion for constructivist practice. His design for Dom Narkomtiazhprom, the Soviet Ministry of Heavy Industry, is often cited as constructivism's culminating masterpiece. But the competition that produced this design was held in 1934, two years after the Party's organizational liquidation of OSA. Once a constructivist, always a constructivist? By that criteria, Leonidov's 1940 project for the headquarters of Izvestiia, a symmetrical courtyard design garnished with applied neoclassical filigree, would also qualify as constructivist.

7. V. I. Lenin, "Report on the Work of the Central Executive Committee and Council of People's Commissars to the III All-Russian Congress of Soviets," 22 December 1920; cited in Anne D. Rassweiler, *The Generation of Power: the History of Dneprostroi* (New York, 1988), 14.

8. V. I. Lenin, "Letter to I. I. Skvortsov-Stepanov, 19 March, 1922, and "Report on the Work of the Central Executive Committee"; cited in Rassweiler, *Generation of Power*, 25, 15.

9. K. Medunesky, V. and G. Stenberg, *From the Constructivists to the World* (Moscow, 1921); cited in H. Gaßner and E. Gillen, *Zwischen Revolutionskunst und Sozialistichem Realismus* (Cologne, 1979), 114, my trans.

10. El Lissitzky, *Russia: An Architecture for World Revolution*, trans. Eric Dluhosch (Cambridge, Mass., 1970), 57–58.

11. Ibid.

12. Michel Foucault, *Discipline and Punish* (New York, 1977), 135–37, 195–228.

13. Alexander Vesnin, "Credo" (unpublished manuscript dated April 1922); cited in Cooke, *Russian Avant-Garde*, 98.

14. V. Kuzmin, "O rabochem zhilishchonom stroitel'stve," *SA* 3 (1927); cited in Vladimir Paperny, "Men, Women, and the Living Space," in William C. Brumfield and Blair A. Ruble, eds., *Russian Housing in the Modern Age* (Cambridge, 1993), 161.

15. Richard Stites, *Revolutionary Dreams: Utopian Vision and Experimental Life in the Russian Revolution* (New York, 1989), 110.

16. Moisei Ginzburg, "Report on the First Conference of the Union of Contemporary Architects, Moscow," *SA* 5 (1928); cited in Anatole Kopp, *Constructivist Architecture* (London, 1985), p. 70.

17. Moisei Ginzburg, "Konstruktivizm kak metod laboratornoi i pedagogicheskoi rabooty," *SA* 6 (1927), 160–66; cited in Cooke, *Russian Avant-Garde*, 102.

18. Katerina Clark, "Engineers of Human Souls in an Age of Industrialization: Changing Cultural Models, 1929–41," in William Rosenberg and Lewis Siegelbaum, eds., *Social Dimensions of Soviet Industrialization* (Bloomington, Ind., 1993), 254.

19. Moisei Ginzburg, *Style and Epoch*, trans. Anatole Senkevich, Jr. (Cambridge, Mass., 1982), 96.

20. Ibid., 109.

21. Moisei Ginzburg, "Konstruktivizm v arkhitekture," *SA* 5 (1928), 143–45; cited in Cooke, *Russian Avant-Garde*, 102–3.

22. Moisei Ginzburg, "New Methods of Architectural Thought," *SA* 1 (1926), 1–4; cited in Cooke, *Russian Avant-Garde*, 130.

23. Cooke, *Russian Avant-Garde*, 164.

24. Igor A. Kazus, "Architektur-Avantgarde im Ural und in Siberien," in Christian Schädlich and Dietrich W. Schmidt, eds., *Avantgarde II: Sowjetische Architektur 1924–1937* (Stuttgart, 1993) 63, my trans.

25. Ia. A. Kornfeld, "Academic Conferences in the Vkhutemas," *SA* 5/6 (1926), 135–37; cited in Cooke, *Russian Avant-Garde*, 183.

26. Cooke, *Russian Avant-Garde*, 169.

27. "Student Society, Industrial Building Department, Faculty of Constructional Engineering, MVTU," *SA* 5/6 (1926), 141; cited in Cooke, *Russian Avant-Garde*, 182.

28. Kazus, "Architektur-Avantgarde im Ural," in Schädlich and Schmidt, *Avantgarde II*, 63.

29. Ginzburg, "Architectural Thought"; cited in Cooke, *Russian Avant-Garde*, 130.

30. John Garner, "Introduction," in John Garner, ed., *The Company Town* (New York, 1992), 4–14.

31. Gwendolyn Wright, *Building the Dream: A Social History of Housing in America* (New York, 1981), 61, 65.

32. Ibid., 184.

33. Garner, "Introduction," in Garner, *The Company Town*, 9.

34. Margaret Crawford, "Earle S. Draper and the Company Town in the American South," in Garner, *The Company Town*, 143.

35. Chris Ward, *Russia's Cotton Workers and the New Economic Policy: Shop-Floor Culture and State Policy 1921–1929* (Cambridge, 1990), 144–45.

36. Michel Ilyine, "L'architecture du club ovrier," *Architecture d'aujourd'hui* 8 (November 1931), 17.

37. Igor N. Chlebnikov, "Architektur der zwanziger und dreißiger Jahre im Industriegebiet von Ivanovo-Voznesensk: Sozialutopische Aspekte und die Avantgarde," in Schädlich and Schmidt, *Avantgarde II*, 44.

38. Chlebnikov, "Ivanovo-Voznesensk," in Schädlich and Schmidt, *Avantgarde II*, 47–52.

39. S. Frederick Starr, "Visionary Town Planning During the Cultural Revolution," in Sheila Fitzpatrick, ed., *Cultural Revolution in Russia, 1928–1931* (Bloomington, Ind., 1984), 210–11, 230.

40. M. Ilin, *New Russia's Primer: The Story of the Five-Year Plan*, trans. George S. Counts and Nucia P. Lodge (Boston, 1931), 153–55.

41. Chris Ward, "Languages of Trade or Languages of Class? Work Culture in Russian Cotton Mills in the 1920s," in Lewis H. Siegelbaum and Ronald Grigor Suny, eds., *Making Workers Soviet: Power, Class, and Identity* (Ithaca, 1994), 208–9, 215.

42. Rassweiler, *Generation of Power*, 100.

43. Kazus, "Architektur-Avantgarde im Ural," in Schädlich and Schmidt, *Avantgarde II*, 59.

44. Compare, for example, this Soviet company-town plan with that of the British company town of Saltaire, described in Spiro Kostof, *The City Shaped* (Boston, 1991), 169–71.

45. Khan-Magomedov, "Schöpferische Konzeptionen," in Schädlich and Schmidt, *Avantgarde II*, 20.

46. Rassweiler, *Generation of Power*, 133.

47. The New England experience is cited in Wright, *Building the Dream*, 61–72. The Soviet legacy of mud huts is recounted in Steven Kotkin, *Magnetic Mountain: Stalinism as a Civilization* (Berkeley and Los Angeles, 1994), 175–78.

48. Stites, *Revolutionary Dreams*, 148–49.

49. Federico Bucci, *Albert Kahn: Architect of Ford* (Princeton, 1993), 92.

50. Grant Hildebrand, *Designing for Industry: The Architecture of Albert Kahn* (Cambridge, Mass., 1974), 129.

51. Kotkin, *Magnetic Mountain*, 123.

52. Rassweiler, *Generation of Power*, 151–53.

53. For Magnitogorsk see Kotkin, *Magnetic Mountain*, 172; on Ivanovo-Voznesensk: Jeffrey Rossman, "Worker Resistance Under Stalin: The Collapse of Shop-Floor Morale and the Strike Movement of April 1932" (Ph.D. diss., University of California at Berkeley, in progress).

54. Kotkin, *Magnetic Mountain*, 174.

55. Rassweiler, *Generation of Power*, 105.

56. Hiroaki Kuromiya, *Stalin's Industrial Revolution* (Cambridge, 1988), 294.

57. Victor Buchli, "Moisei Ginzburg's Narkomfin Communal House in Moscow: Contesting the Social and Material World," *Journal of the Society of Architectural Historians* 57, no. 2 (June 1998), 160–81.

58. Anatole Kopp, *Constructivist Architecture in the USSR* (New York, 1985), 71.

59. A. Grigorovich, *Zhivëm (bytovye kommuny)* (Moscow, 1930), 12; cited in Stites, *Revolutionary Dreams*, 219.

60. For a more detailed discussion see Greg Castillo, "Gorki Street and the Design of the Stalin Revolution," in Zeynep Çelik, Diane Favro, and Richard Ingersoll, eds., *Streets: Critical Perspectives on Public Space* (Berkeley and Los Angeles, 1994), 57–70.

61. Stites, *Revolutionary Dreams*, 110–12.

62. A. L. Pasternak, *SA* 4/5 (1927); cited in Kopp, *Constructivist Architecture*, 62.

63. Chernikov, *Architectural and Machine Forms*, in Cooke, *Chernikov*, 79.

64. It is interesting to note that one of the few competition entries that elected to retain most of the monastery's structures was that by Georgii Golts, famed as a Socialist Realist.

65. B. I. Nikolsky, *Magnitogorskii Rabochii* (December 21, 1936); cited in Kotkin, *Magnetic Mountain*, 390.

66. Kotkin, *Magnetic Mountain*, 103.

67. Selim Khan-Magomedov, *Aleksandr Vesnin and Russian Constructivism* (New York, 1986), 189.

68. Ivan Leonidov, English translation in Andrei Gozak and Andrei Leonidov, *Ivan Leonidov* (New York, 1988), 115–16.

69. Histories of Soviet modern architecture usually refer to such buildings as a "sanatoria," a term that defers to the Stalinist linguistic and propagandistic precedents.

70. Sheila Fitzpatrick, "The Great Departure: Rural-Urban Migration in the Soviet Union, 1929–33," in Rosenberg and Siegelbaum, *Soviet Industrialization*, 24.

Chapter 11 The Greening of Utopia

1. Epigraph from Adam Ulam, "Socialism and Utopia," in Frank E. Manuel, ed., *Utopias and Utopian Thought: A Timely Appraisal* (Boston, 1966), 116–34, here 119.

2. Nicholas V. Riasanovsky, *A History of Russia*, 2d ed. (New York, 1969), 634.

3. Herman Ermolaev, *Soviet Literary Theories 1917–1934: The Genesis of Socialist Realism* (Berkeley, 1963); C. Vaughan James, *Soviet Socialist Realism. Origins and Theory* (London, 1973); Geoffrey Hosking, "The Socialist Realist Tradition," in his *Beyond Socialist Realism: Soviet Fiction since Ivan Denisovich* (London, 1980), 1–28; Edward Mozejko, *Der Sozialistische Realismus Theorie. Entwicklung und Versagen einer Literatur-Methode* (Bonn, 1977); Katerina Clark, *The Soviet Novel: History as Ritual*, 2d ed. (Chicago, 1985); Hans Günther, *Der Verstaatlichung der Literatur: Entstehung und Funktionsweise des sozialistisch-realistischen Kanons in der sowjetischen Literatur der 30er Jahre* (Stuttgart, 1984).

4. A significant exception is H. Gassner and E. Gillen's excellent essay "Vom utopischen Ordnungsentwurf zur Versöhnungsideologie im aesthetischen Schein: Beispiele sowjetischer Kunst zwischen dem 1.Fünfjahrplan und der Verfassungskampagne 1936/37," in Gernot Erler und Walter Süss, eds., *Stalinismus. Probleme der Sowjetgesellschaft zwischen Kollektvierung und Weltkrieg* (Frankfurt/New York, 1982), 272–341.

5. The most monumental of these studies is

Matthew Cullerne Bown's massive *Socialist Realist Painting* (New Haven, 1998), which includes over 500 illustrations. Also see *The Aesthetic Arsenal: Socialist Realism under Stalin* (New York, 1993); Vladamir Papernyi, *Kul'tura dva* (Ann Arbor, 1985); Boris Groys, *Gesamtkunstwerk Stalin* (Vienna, 1988), published as *The Total Art of Stalinism. Avant-Garde, Aesthetic Dictatorship, and Beyond*, trans. Charles Rougle (Princeton, 1992); Thomas Lahusen and Evgeny Dobrenko, eds., *Socialist Realism Without Shores* (Durham, N.C., 1997); Igor Golomstock, *Totalitarian Art in the Soviet Union, the Third Reich, Fascist Italy, and the People's Republic of China*, trans. Robert Chandler (London, 1990); Hans Günther, ed., *The Culture of the Stalin Period* (London, 1990), Part 2; Matthew Cullerne Bown, *Art Under Stalin* (New York, 1991); Brandon Taylor, *Art and Literature Under the Bolsheviks*, 2 vols. (London, 1992); Matthew Cullerne Bown and Brandon Taylor, eds., *Art of the Soviets: Painting, Sculpture, and Architecture in a One-Party State, 1917–1992* (Manchester, 1993); A.I. Morozov, *Konets istorii. Iz istorii iskusstva v SSSR 1930–kh godov* (Moscow, 1995). Also see the exhibition catalogs *Soviet Socialist Realist Painting: 1930s–1960s*, Oxford Museum of Modern Art (Oxford, 1992); *Agitation zum Glück. Sowjetische Kunst der Stalinzeit* (Bremen, 1994); Dawn Ades, ed., *Art and Power: Europe under the Dictators 1930–1945*, Hayward Gallery (London, 1995); Vern Grosvenor Swanson, *Hidden Treasures: Russian and Soviet Impressionism 1930–1970s* (Scottsdale, Ariz., 1994). For an examination of some of the themes in the present article from a rather different perspective, see Mark Bassin, " 'I Object to Rain That Is Cheerless': Landscape Art and the Stalinist Aesthetic Imagination," *Ecumene* 7, no. 3 (2000), 313–36.

6. Kenneth Clark, *Landscape into Art* (London, 1976); Ernst Gombrich, "The Renaissance Theory of Art and the Rise of Landscape," in his *Norm and Form: Studies in the Art of the Renaissance* (Chicago, 1966), 107–21.

7. Chris Fitter, *Poetry, Space, Landscape: Towards a New Theory* (Cambridge, 1995); Denis Cosgrove, *Social Formation and Symbolic Landscape* (Totowa, N.J., 1984); Denis Cosgrove and Stephen Daniels, eds., *The Iconography of Landscape: Essays on the Symbolic Representation, Design, and Use of Past Environments* (Cambridge, 1988); Nicholas Green, *The Spectacle of Nature: Landscape and Bourgeois Culture in Nineteenth-Century France* (Manchester, 1990); W. J. T. Mitchell, ed., *Landscape and Power* (Chicago, 1994); Martin Warnke, *Political Landscape: The Art History of Nature*, trans. David McLintock (Cambridge, 1995); Stuart Wrede and William Howard Adams, eds., *Denatured Visions: Landscape and Culture in the Twentieth Century* (New York, 1991).

8. Ian Jeffrey, *The British Landscape 1920–1950* (London, 1984); Ann Bermingham, *Landscape and Ideology: The English Rustic Tradition, 1740–1860* (Berkeley, 1986); Sarah Burns, *Pastoral Inventions: Rural Life in Nineteenth-Century American Art and Culture* (Philadelphia, 1989); Albert Boime, *The Magisterial Gaze: Manifest Destiny and American Landscape Painting c. 1830–1865* (Washington and London, 1991); Stephen Daniels, *Fields of Vision: Landscape Imagery and National Identity in England and the United States* (Cambridge, 1993); Richard Thomson, ed., *Framing France: The Representation of Landscape in France 1870–1914* (Manchester, 1998). Two recent exhibitions have offered magnificent perspectives on how differing views of nationhood were contested in French and English landscape art of the eighteenth and nineteenth centuries. *Glorious Nature: British Landscape Painting 1750–1850*, Denver Art Museum (London, 1993); *Landscapes of France: Impressionism and Its Rivals* (London, 1995).

9. See Christopher Ely, "Critics in the Native Soil: Landscape and Conflicting Ideals of Nationality in Imperial Russia," *Ecumene* 7, no. 3 (2000), 253–70; John McCannon, "In Search of Primeval Russia: Stylistic Evolution in the Landscapes of Nicholas Roerich, 1897–1914," *Ecumene* 7, no. 3 (2000), 271–98; Abbott Gleason, "*Russkii Inok*: The Spiritual Landscape of Mikhail Nesterov," *Ecumene* 7, no. 3 (2000), 299–312.

10. For general studies, see Alfred Schmidt, *The Concept of Nature in Marx* (London, 1971); Wolfdietrich Schmied-Kowarzik, *Das dialektische Verhältnis des Menschen zur Natur. Philosophiegeschichtliche Studien zur Naturproblematik bei Karl Marx* (Freiburg/Munich, 1984); Schmied-Kowarzik and Hans Immler, *Marx und die Naturfrage. Ein Wissenschaftsstreit* (Hamburg, 1984); Jean-Pierre Lefebvre, "Marx et la 'Nature'," *La Pensée* 198 (March–April 1978), 51–62; J.-L. Cachon, "Nature," *Dictionnaire Critique du Marxisme* (Paris, 1982), 797–801; Casimir N. Koblernicz, "Philosophy of Nature in Marxism," *Marxism, Communism, and Western Society: A Comparative Encyclopedia*, 5 vols. (New York, 1973), vi, 92–97; Mark Bassin, "Nature, Geopolitics, and Marxism: Ecological Contestations in the Weimar Republic," *Transactions of the Institute of British Geographers* 21, no. 2 (1996), 315–41; Bassin, "Geographical Determinism in Fin-de-Siècle Marxism: Georgii Plekhanov and the Environmental Basis of Russian History," *Annals of the Association of American Geographers* 82, no. 1 (1992), 3–22.

11. Mark Bassin, "Nature as Culprit in Russian Cultural History," paper delivered at the Association of American Geographers national convention, Atlanta, April, 1993; Bassin, "Turner, Solov'ev, and the 'Frontier Hypothesis': The Nationalist Signification of Open Spaces," *Journal of Modern History* 65 (September 1993), 473–511, *passim*.

12. *Tridtsat' let sovetskogo izobrazitel'nogo isskustva* (Moscow, 1947), 119, quoted in Golomstock, *Totalitarian Art*, 262.

13. A. A. Fedorov-Davydov, *Sovetskii Peizazh* (Moscow, 1958), 18.

14. Igor Golomstock, *Totalitarian Art in the Soviet Union, the Third Reich, Fascist Italy, and the People's Republic of China* (London, 1990), text under plate 17 (no page number).

15. Groys, *The Total Art of Stalinism*, 20–21.

16. Kazimir Malevich, "From Cubism and Futurism to Suprematism: The New Painterly Realism," in John E. Bowlt, ed., *Russian Art of the Avant-Garde*, 2d ed. (London, 1988), 119, 133.

17. *Bespredmetnoe tvorchestvo i suprematizm (X Gosudarstvennaia Vystavka)* (Moscow, 1919), quoted in Bowlt, *Russian Art of the Avant-Garde*, 143.

18. V. V. Maiakovskii, "Kak delat' stikhi," *Sochineniia v trekh tomakh* (Moscow: Khudozhestvennaia Literatura, 1978), vol. 2, pp. 465–500, here 472. On the continuity of the avant-garde and socialist realism in regard to the principle of service to Soviet state, see Groys, *The Total Art of Stalinism*, 14–32; Golomstock, *Totalitarian Art*, 21–23; Flaker, "Presuppositions of Socialist Realism," 99–100.

19. Bown, *Art under Stalin*, 32–33.

20. A. Zhdanov, *Sovetskaia literatura—samaia ideinaia, samaia peredovaia literatura v mire* (Moscow, 1953). This passage was then adopted nearly verbatim in the founding Charter of the Union of Soviet Writers. Bowlt, *Russian Art of the Avant-Garde*, 297.

21. Zhdanov, *Sovetskaia literatura*, 9.

22. Groys, *The Total Art of Stalinism*, 51, 55–56.

23. Richard Stites, *Revolutionary Dreams: Utopian Vision and Experimental Life in the Russian Revolution* (New York, 1989); Victor Margolin, *The Struggle for Utopia: Rodchenko, Lissitzky, Moholy-Nagy 1917–1946* (Chicago, 1997); *The Great Utopia: The Russian and Soviet Avant-Garde*, exhibition catalog, Guggenheim Museum (New York, 1992); *The Great Russian Utopia* (Art and Design Magazine 29 (London, 1993).

24. Stites, *Revolutionary Dreams*, 266; Stites, "Stalinism and the Restructuring of Revolutionary Utopianism," in Hans Günther, ed., *The Culture of the Stalin Period* (Basingstoke, 1990), 78–94, here 80.

25. Stites, *Revolutionary Dreams*, 226.

26. Aleksandr Bogdanov, *Engineer Menni*, in his *Red Star: The First Bolshevik Utopia*, trans. Charles Rougle (Bloomington, Ind., 1984), 141–233, here 204; Stites, *Revolutionary Dreams*, 252.

27. Zhdanov, *Sovetskaia literatura*, 3 (emphasis in original).

28. Lars Erik Blomqvist, "Some Utopian Elements in Stalinist Art," *Russian History/Histoire Russe* 11, nos. 2–3 (Summer-Fall 1984), 298–305, here 298 (emphasis in original).

29. Flaker, "Presuppositions of Socialist Realism," pp. 99–101. Stalin himself is reputed to have first uttered the phrase at a meeting of writers at Gorkii's flat

in October 1932. Elliott, "Engineers of the Human Soul," 5.

30. Aleksandr Kamenskii, "Art in the Twilight of Totalitarianism," in Matthew C. Bown and Brandon Taylor, eds., *Art of the Soviets: Painting, Sculpture, and Architecture in a One-Party State, 1917–1992* (Manchester, 1993), 154–60, here 155.

31. *Voprosy teorii sovetskogo izobrazitel'nogo iskusstva* (Moscow, 1950), quoted in Golomstock, "Problems in the Study of Stalinist Culture," 113.

32. Northrop Frye, "Varieties of Literary Utopias," in Frank E. Manuel, ed., *Utopias and Utopian Thought: A Timely Appraisal* (Boston, 1966), 25–49, here 31.

33. Blomqvist, "Some Utopian Elements in Stalinist Art," 299.

34. Zhdanov, *Sovetskaia literatura*, 10.

35. Groys, *The Total Art of Stalinism*, 72.

36. Bown, *Art under Stalin*, 92.

37. Groys, *The Total Art of Stalinism*, 42.

38. V. N. Pilipenko, *Peizazhnaia zhivopis'* (St. Petersburg, 1994).

39. Christopher Ely, "Russia Is a Country of Landscape: Nation and Nature in the Paintings of Ivan Shishkin," unpublished MS.

40. Katerina Clark, *The Soviet Novel: History as Ritual*, 2d ed. (Chicago, 1985), Chap. 4.

41. Clark, *The Soviet Novel*, 99.

42. Urban population expanded by at least 30 million people from 1926 to 1939. Moshe Lewin, "Society, State, and Ideology during the First Five-Year Plan," in Sheila Fitzpatrick, ed., *Cultural Revolution in Russia, 1928–1931* (Bloomington, Ind., 1978), 41–77, here 53.

43. Clark, *The Soviet Novel*, 106–11.

44. Quoted in Golomstock, *Totalitarian Art*, 265.

45. For an enthusiastic contemporary appreciation of this point, see N. Nikolaev, "Kontraktatsiia khudozhnikov 1935 goda," *Tvorchestvo* 7 (1936), 6–19, 19.

46. Katerina Clark, "Utopian Anthropology as a Context for Stalinist Literature," in Robert C. Tucker, ed., *Stalinism. Essays in Historical Interpretation* (New York, 1977), 180–99, here 189.

47. Igor Golomstock, "Problems in the Study of Stalinist Culture," in Günther, *The Culture of the Stalin Period*, here 117–18.

48. Papernyi, *Kul'tura dva* (Ann Arbor, 1985), 135.

49. Wolfgang Holz, "Allegory and Iconography in Socialist-Realist Painting," in Bown and Taylor, *Art of the Soviets*, 73–85, here 75.

50. Peter Adam, *Art of the Third Reich* (New York, 1992), 177.

51. Bown, *Art under Stalin*, 114.

52. David Elliott, *New Worlds: Russian Art and Society, 1900–1937* (London, 1986), 128. For an insightful overview, see Barbara Keys, "Totalitarian Corporealities: Educating the Body under Nazism and Stalinism," paper delivered at the AAASS national convention, Boca Raton, September 1998.

53. Cf. "Physical Education and National Socialism," in George L. Mosse, ed., *Nazi Culture: Intellectual, Cultural, and Social Life in the Third Reich*, trans. S. Attanasioet al. (New York, 1966), 281–82.

54. Golomstock, *Totalitarian Art*, 264; Bown, *Art under Stalin*, 113. On a vist to occupied Kiev in the summer of 1942, Albert Speer was much impressed by Stalin's reversion to Greek and Roman models but was struck nonetheless at how the Soviet "statues of athletes in the fashion of classical antiquity" were not presented in all their naked glory but rather were all clad "touchingly" in bathing suits. *Inside the Third Reich*, trans. R. and C. Winston (New York, 1970), 314.

55. Bown, *Art under Stalin*, 116.

56. Bown, *Art under Stalin*, 154–55.

57. Pictures such as Isaak Brodskii's *Maksim Gorkii* (1937) or Arkadii Rylov's *Lenin in Razliv* (1937) set their subjects against turbulent skies and stormy waters in order to accentuate the drama of their protagonists' thoughts (and perhaps as a veiled allusion to the purges that were raging at that moment). Depictions of Stalin, however, such as Iraklii Toidze's *Stalin at Rioges* or Fyodor Shurpin's celebrated *Morning of our Fatherland* (1948) consistently opted for the sun, to emphasize the radiant glory of the Great Leader.

Chapter 12 *The Rise and Fall of Stalinist Architecture*

1. The works on which I focus here are Vladimir Papernyi, *Kul'tura dva* (Ann Arbor, Mich., 1985); Alexei Tarkhanov and Sergei Kavtaradze, trans. Robin Whitby, Joan Whitby, and James Paber, *Stalinist Architecture* (London,1992), especially 82–92; Igor Golomstock, trans. Robert Chandler, *Totalitarian Art* (New York, 1990), 266–301; and Peter Noever, ed., *Tyrannei des Schönen: Arkhitektur der Stalin-Zeit* (Munich, 1994), especially Noever, "Arkhitektur zwischen 'Tyrannei der Unterdrückung' und 'Tyrannei des Schönen,'" 9–13.

2. Tarkhanov and Kavtaradze point out that a number of the era's films depict architects as "sybarites and gentleman of leisure"; they imply that this portrayal was accurate.

3. See, for example, Papernyi's (*Kul'tura dva*, 17) and Golomstock's (*Totalitarian Art*, 273) assertions to this effect.

4. See, for example, Papernyi, *Kul'tura dva*, 135; and Golomstock, *Totalitarian Art*, 281.

5. The terms are Golomstock's, Tarkhanov and Kavtaradze's, and Papernyi's, respectively.

6. Golomstock (*Totalitarian Art*, 278) maintains that whenever Stalin said anything about architecture, "what spoke through [his] lips was the soul of totalitarian culture."

7. A. Chuianov, *Stalingrad vozrozhdaetsia* (Moscow, Gospolitizdat, 1944), 6.

8. State Archive of the Russian Federation, RSFSR branch (hereafter GARF RSFSR) f. A-314, op. 1, d. 7873, l. 81–87.

9. RGAE f. 9432, op. 1, d. 17, l. 24.

10. See especially K.S. Alabian, "Kontury budushchego Stalingrada," *Literatura i iskusstvo* (July 24, 1943), reprinted in *Iz istorii sovetskoi arkhitektury 1941–45 gg.* (Moscow, 1978), 78.

11. On this, see S. Frederick Starr, "Visionary Town Planning During the Cultural Revolution," in Sheila Fitzpatrick, ed., *Cultural Revolution in Russia, 1928–1931* (Bloomington, Ind., 1978), 207–240; Anatole Kopp, trans. Thomas E. Burton, *Town and Revolution: Soviet Architecture and City Planning, 1917–1935* (New York, 1970); S. O. Khan-Magomedov, trans. Alexander Lieven, *Pioneers of Soviet Architecture: The Search for New Solutions in the 1920s and 1930s* (New York, 1987), Part 2, Chap. 1; and Stephen Kotkin, *Magnitogorsk: Stalinism as a Civilization* (Berkeley, 1995), Chap. 3.

12. On this, see my "Building Socialism: The Politics of the Soviet Cityscape in the Stalin Era" (Ph.D. diss., Columbia University, 1998), Chap. 2.

13. In his 1930 draft plan for Moscow, Le Corbusier proposed tearing down most of the city's existing buildings and filling its central district with residential and administrative superblocks surrounded by parkland. He submitted this project to a city-planning competition conducted by the Moscow Section of the Communal Economy (a local-level affiliate of NKKKh); his and others' entries are reproduced and discussed in S.M. Gornyi, *Sotsialisticheskaia rekonstruktsiia Moskvy* (Moscow, 1931).

14. On VOPRA's attacks on scientist modernism, see Day, "Building Socialism," Chap. 1; and Hugh Hudson, *Blueprints and Blood: The Stalinization of Soviet Architecture, 1917–1937* (Princeton, 1994), Chap. 6.

15. Moscow Party chief Lazar Kaganovich outlined the regime's socialist reconstruction strategy in a speech to a July 1931 Central Committee plenum. L.M. Kaganovich, *The Socialist Reconstruction of Moscow and Other Cities in the USSR* (New York, 1934).

Urban-development specialists were quick to reconfigure their profession's basic practices to bring them into line with the principles outlined at the plenum. On this, see the proceedings of 1933's First All-Union Conference on Urban Planning and Construction, in Vsesoiuznyi sovet po delam kommunal'nogo khoziaistva pri TsIK SSSR, *Pervaia vsesoiuznaia konferentsiia po planirovke i stroitel'stvu gorodov* (Moscow, 1933).

16. The absence of Western-style private property did not mean that there were no landholders in the Soviet Union. Land-use rights were divided among a wide variety of institutions, each of which had a good deal of control over what it built on the parcels it controlled.

17. On the Stalin regime's obsession with the power of planning, see Day, "Building Socialism," Chap. 2; and Moshe Lewin, *Political Undercurrents in Soviet Economic Debates: From Bukharin to the Modern Reformers* (Princeton, 1974), 97–124.

18. On socialist reconstruction in practice, see Day, "Building Socialism," chaps. 2–3.

19. See, for example, the proceedings of two key plenary sessions of the Directorate of the Union of Soviet Architects (SSA): Soiuz sovetskikh arkhitektorov, *Planirovka i stroitel'stvo gorodov. Materialy III plenuma Pravleniia SSA SSSR* (Moscow, 1938); and Soiuz sovetskikh arkhitektorov, *Rekonstruktsiia Moskvy. Materialy VII plenuma Pravleniia SSA SSSR* (Moscow 1940).

20. As of January 1, 1939, basic general plans had been completed and approved for only seven of the RSFSR's twenty largest cities, and for only thirteen RSFSR cities in total. GARF RSFSR A-314, op. 1, d. 312, l. 43, and ibid., d. 7264, l. 1.

21. The example of Stalingrad is typical—the city was growing so fast that between the time Vladimir Semenov finished his general plan and the time it was approved, a number of areas he intended to be left undeveloped had already become bustling factory and residential districts. GARF RSFSR f. A-314, op.1, d. 7871, l. 41–59.

Between 1926 and 1939, as industrial employment exploded and material deprivation and political turbulence wracked rural areas, more than 30 million people moved to cities from the countryside; during this period, the share of the Soviet population living in urban areas rose from 18 to 33 percent. In Moshe Lewin, *The Making of the Soviet System: Essays in the Social History of Interwar Russia* (New York, 1985), 219.

22. See, for example, Soiuz sovetskikh arkhitektorov, *Planirovka i stroitel'stvo gorodov*, passim; *idem, Rekonstruktsiia Moskvy*, passim.

23. This is not the place to list and summarize historians' accounts of the various anti-enemies campaigns of the 1930s. Among the more interesting and influential recent works on this topic are Gabor T. Rittersporn, "The State Against Itself: Socialist Tensions and Political Conflicts in the USSR, 1936–1938," *Telos* 41 (Fall 1979), 87–104; Kotkin, *Magnetic Mountain*, Chap. 7; and Robert Thurston, *Life and Terror in Stalin's Russia, 1934–1941* (New Haven, 1996).

24. See, for example, materials on efforts to deal with supposed wrecking in Sverdlovsk, in GARF RSFSR f. A-314, op. 1, d. 7844–7851, and in various other Russian Republic cities, in ibid., d. 272, 286.

25. The most famous such ensemble consists of apartment houses designed by Arkadii Mordvinov for the southwest end of Moscow's Gor'kii Street (today, Tver' Street). On this project, see Greg Castillo, "Moscow: Gorki Street and the Design of the Stalin Revolution," in Zeynep Celik, Diane Favro, and Richard Ingersoll, eds., *Streets: Critical Perspectives on Public Space* (Berkeley, 1994).

26. Such facades were known as *nadstroiki* (over-constructions).

27. Quoted in Leonard Schapiro, *The Communist Party of the Soviet Union* (New York, 1971), 437.

28. On Stalingrad, see GARF RSFSR, f. A-314, op. 1, d. 7871, l. 50–59, and ibid., d. 7873, l. 65–70; on Sverdlovsk, see ibid., d. 7844, l. 5, and ibid., d. 7849, l. 70–74.

29. "O perestroike planirovochnogo i proektnogo dela Mossoveta" (Moscow City Council Presidium decree, July 27, 1939), *Stroitel'stvo Moskvy* 14 (1939), 3–4.

30. This proposal and various supporting materials are in GARF RSFSR f. A-314, op. 1, d. 7264.

31. See his speech to the 1943 plenum of the SSA Directorate, excerpted in *Iz istorii*, 79.

32. "Ob obrazovanii Komiteta po delam arkhitektury pri Sovnarkom SSSR" (USSR Council of People's Commissars decree, September 29, 1943), reprinted in *Iz istorii*, 95, 102. This decree largely followed recommendations contained in a report drawn up by Alabian and V. A. Shkvarikov, a leading Russian Republic urban-development official. In L. B. Karlik, *Karo Alabian* (Ereven, 1966), 31.

33. *Arkhitektura SSSR* sb. 6 (1944), 1.

34. "Ob obrazovanii Komiteta po delam arkhitektury."

35. In early 1944, the State Committee put Shchusev in charge of planning Novgorod, Georgii Gol'ts (a well-known disciple of the prominent neo-Classicist Ivan Zholtovskii) of Smolensk, Iofan of Novrossiisk, Nikolai Kolli (a onetime associate of Le Corbusier) of Kalinin, and Rudnev of Voronezh. Russian State Economic Archive (hereafter RGAE) f. 9432, op. 1, d. 9, l. 110–12.

36. On the city-center projects, and rebuilding in general, see Day, "Building Socialism," Chap. 4.

37. On this, see Matthew Gallagher, *The Soviet History of World War II: Myths, Memories, and Realities* (New York, 1963).

38. This consensus is reflected in various projects, drawings for which were displayed in several wartime exhibits. For more on these projects, see *Iz istorii sovetskoi arkhitektury 1941–45 gg.*, passim.

39. RGAE f. 293, op. 3, d. 95, l. 64.

40. RGAE f. 293, op. 3, d. 258, l. 142–44; RGAE f. 293, op. 3, d. 259, plates 48–51.

41. RGAE f. 9432, op. 1, d. 17, l. 6–12. In February of 1944, SNK approved Alabian's general plan for use in guiding reconstruction, "O general'nom plane g. Stalingrada (USSR Council of People's Commissars decree No. 110, February 6, 1944), in RGAE f. 9432, op. 1, d. 17, l. 24–25.

42. It is worth noting in this context that Alabian was one of the founders of VOPRA, whose members made a name for themselves, in the late 1920s and early 1930s, by accusing the constructivists of design-

ing buildings that were incapable of serving as symbols of the Soviet political order.

43. RGAE f. 293, op. 1, d. 95, l. 5.

44. RGAE f. 9432, op. 1, d. 17, l. 61.

45. RGAE f. 9432, op.1, d. 17, l. 128.

46. RGAE f. 9432, op.1, d. 249, l. 50–51. See also V. G. Gel'freikh, "O proektakh tsentra Stalingrada," *Arkhitektura i stroitel'stvo* 15/16 (1946), 6.

47. RGAE f. 9432, op. 1, d. 249, l. 26.

48. *Volgograd. Chetyre veka istorii* (Volgograd, 1989), 290.

49. RGAE f. 9432, op. 1, d. 249, l. 26.

50. RGAE f. 9432, op. 1, d. 46, l. 71.

51. Gel'freikh, "O proektakh," 6.

52. RGAE f. 9432, op. 1, d. 51, l. 3.

53. RGAE f. 9432, op. 1, d. 51, l. 17 ob.

54. RGAE f. 9432, op. 1, d. 51, l. 12 ob., and ibid., d. 249, l. 81–90.

55. RGAE f. 9432, op. 1, d. 17, l. 140–49.

56. RGAE f. 9432, op. 1, d. 247, l. 53–4.

57. On these projects, see Day, "Building Socialism," chaps. 2–3.

58. In the wake of the State Committee's approval of Alabian's center plan, this competition was conducted as a matter of course, as part of an effort to flesh out the plan's particulars.

59. Lev Rudnev, "Dom Sovetov v Stalingrade," *Arkhitektura i stroitel'stvo* 3 (1947), 9–14. The quotes are from p. 9 and p. 13, respectively.

60. RGAE f. 9432, op. 1, d. 17, l. 121.

61. RGAE f. 9432, op. 1, d. 340, l. 23–24, 31.

62. GARF RSFSR f. 250, op. 6. d. 4142, l. 75–76.

63. It would reach its apogee in 1948, when he received the commission to design the new Moscow State University complex.

64. In early 1949, for reasons I have been unable to ascertain, Alabian was removed from his position as president of the Academy of Architecture, after which he quickly fell from the ranks of the country's prominent architects.

65. RGALI f. 674, op. 3, d. 546, l. 19. The term *vysotnoe zdaniia*, which literally means "tall building," came into use around this time, in references to the seven tall buildings that were erected in Moscow beginning in 1947, and to others that looked like them. Colloquially, it was (and still is) abbreviated as *vysotka* (plural: *vysotky*). Most likely, the term *neboskreb* ("skyscraper") never caught on because it was associated with American buildings of similar or greater height. Outside the capital, proposals to build Moscow-style skyscrapers proliferated, but found scant substantive support, and in the end, *vysotka*-type buildings were erected only in Riga and Warsaw. City chief architects and local political leaders, it would seem, had plenty of incentive to draw up and publicize these projects: by doing so, they could show that they were hard at work devising bold-stroke solutions to the problem of moving socialist reconstruction forward.

But finding someone to pay to build a *vysotka* was a much more difficult enterprise, since patrons had limited funds and other, more pressing projects on which to spend them.

66. RGAE f. 9432, op. 1, d. 134, l. 31–33.

67. RGAE f. 9432, op. 1, d. 247, l. 185–86.

68. See "O merakh po vosstanovleniiu Stalingrada" (USSR Council of People's Commissars decree No. 2141, August 22, 1945), in RGAE f. 9432, op. 1, d. 17, l. 68–72; and "O vypolnenii postanovlenii SNK SSSR ot 22. avgusta 1945–ogo g. 'O merakh po vosstanovleniiu Stalingrada' " (RSFSR Council of People's Commissars decree No. 58, January 27, 1946), in GARF RSFSR f. 259, op. 6, d. 2837, l. 1–6.

69. See, for example, the minutes of the State Committee's December 17, 1946, meeting, in RGAE f. 9432, op. 1, d. 47, l. 139–43.

70. V. Simbirtsev, "Nereshennye voprosy stroitel'stva Stalingrada," *Arkhitektura i stroitel'stvo* 14 (1947), 4–5; "Vosstanovlenie i rekonstriuktsiia russkikh gorodov," *Arkhitektura i stroitel'stvo* 11 (1948), 24–25.

71. RSFSR Sovmin bore primary responsibility for tracking implementation of these decrees; various materials on its efforts to do so are in GARF RSFSR f. 259, op. 6, d. 4142, 5106, 5717.

72. *Volgograd. Chetyre veka istorii*, 286–87.

73. Simbirtsev and his colleague E. Levitan won a 1950 Stalin Prize for their design for one of these buildings, which housed the local Party School. "Stalinskie premii za 1950 god," *Arkhitektura SSSR* (1952), 14–18.

74. *Volgograd. Chetyre veka istorii*, 286–87.

75. On problems with these and other city-center projects, see Day, "Building Socialism," Chap. 4.

76. "Ukaz Prezidiuma Verkhovnogo Soveta SSSR. Ob obrazovanii obshchesoiuznogo Ministerstva gorodskogo stroitel'stva," *Arkhitektura i stroitel'stvo* 7 (1949), 1.

By the late 1940s, creating a Union-level ministry had become one of the regime's favorite tactics for tackling problems of all sorts. As of 1947, there were 59 such ministries, their sheer number a testament to its abiding faith in centralized administrative authority, to which it at times seem to have attributed near-magical powers. Jerry F. Hough and Merle Fainsod, *How the Soviet Union Is Governed* (Cambridge, Mass., 1979), 384.

77. On this, see my "Home Is Where the Heart Is: Housing Construction and the Birth of the Soviet Welfare State, 1943–1953" (Paper delivered at the University of Chicago, February 16, 2000).

78. RGAE f. 9510, op. 1, d. 131, l. 27–31.

79. These reviews were conducted by the State Committee on Construction (Goskomstroi) and its Union republic-level affiliates, which the regime set up in 1951 to regulate construction of all sorts. See, for example, materials on Goskomstroi's review of projects for Tallinn, Leningrad, and Saratov, in RGAE f. 339, op. 1, d. 637.

80. RGAE f. 9510, op. 1, d. 141, l. 130.

81. The buildings were completed in time to serve as the backdrop for the city's 1950 May Day celebration. RGALI f. 674, op. 3, d. 546, l. 16; V. Simbirtsev, "Vtoroe rozhdenie Stalingrada," *Zhilishchno-grazhdanskoe stroitel'stvo* 5 (1951), 25.

82. GARF RSFSR f. 471, op. 8, d. 44, l. 1–6; and GARF RSFSR f. 471, op. 8, d. 49, l. 1–32; V. Masliaev, "Arkhitektura Stalingrada," *Literaturnyi Stalingrad* kn. 8 (1954), 257.

In 1945, Gel'freikh had argued against plans to line the Alley with apartment houses, which, he contended, were inherently mundane structures, and thus inadequate to the task of making this pedestrian street grand enough to "depict the heroism of the Fatherland War." Gel'freikh, "O proektakh," 9.

83. RGAE f. 9510, op. 1, d. 141, l. 130.

84. V. Simbirtsev, "Vtoroe rozhdenie," 25–26.

85. See, for example, the comments of several architects at a 1952 plenary session of the SSA Directorate: "XIV plenum Pravleniia Soiuza Sovetskikh Arkhitektorov," *Arkhitektura SSSR* 7 (1952), 31–33.

86. See, for example, V. Shkvarikov, "Neustanno povyshat' kachestvo zastroiki gorodov," *Arkhitektura SSSR* 3 (1952), 4–15; and O. Shvidkovskii, "Problemy arkhitekturnogo ansamblia tsentra Stalingrada," *Arkhitektura SSSR* 8 (1952), 15–20.

87. RGAE f. 9510, op. 1, d. 204, l. 11–32.

88. Masliaev, "Arkhitektura Stalingrada," 256.

89. See, for example, the minutes of a 1951 meeting of the local SSA branch, in RGALI f. 674, op. 3, d. 546, l. 28.

90. See, for example, "Khronika. XIV plenum pravlennia Soiuza Sovetskikh Arkhitektorov," *Arkhitektura SSSR* 7 (1952), 32.

91. V. Simbirtsev, "Vosstanovlennyi Stalingrad," *Sovetskaia arkhitektura* 11 (1959), 56.

92. On this campaign, see, for example, various articles on the May 1953 plenum of the SSA Directorate, in *Arkhitektura SSSR* 6 (1953), and on an August 1953 conference on standardized design and construction, in *Arkhitektura SSSR* 9 (1953). See also the summary of debates at a 1954 Academy of Architecture conference in "Protiv formalizma v arkhitekturnoi praktike i nauke," *Arkhitektura SSSR* 10 (1954), 37–40. See also various pieces on the 1954 and 1955 All-Union conferences of architects, planners, and construction professionals, including "Vsesoiuznoe soveshchanie stroitelei, arkhitektorov, rabotnikov promyshlennosti stroitel'nykh materialov, stroitel'nogo i dorozhnogo mashinostroeniia, proektnykh i nauchno-issledovatel'skikh organizatsii, sozvannogo TsK KPSS i Sovetom Ministrov SSSR," *Arkhitektura SSSR* 12 (1954), front cover overleaf; "Obrashchenie uchastnikov Vsesoiuznogo soveshchaniia stroitelei, arkhitektorov, rabotnikov promyshlennosti stroitel'nykh materialov, stroitel'nogo i dorozhnogo mashinostroeniia, proektnykh i nauchno-issledovatel'skikh organizatsii, sozvannogo TsK KPSS i Sovetom Ministrov SSSR, ko vsem rabotnikam stroitel'noi industrii," *Arkhitektura SSSR* 1 (1955), 4; and "Tsentral'nomu Komitetu Kommunisticheskoi Partii Sovetskogo Soiuza i Sovetu Ministrov Soiuza SSR," *Arkhitektura SSSR* 1 (1956), 2–3.

Chapter 13 Conflict over Designing a Monument to Stalin's Victims

1. Yevgeny Yevtushenko, "Monuments Still Not Built," trans. Albert C. Todd, in *The Collected Poems, 1952–1990*, ed. Albert C. Todd with Yevgeny Yevtushenko and James Regan (New York, 1991), 619–20.

2. Avner Ben-Amos, "Monuments and Memory in French Nationalism," *Memory and History* 5, no. 2 (1993), 53.

3. As James Young observes, monuments once built can "take on lives of their own" that diverge from the "original intentions" of the governments or interest groups that sponsored them. *The Texture of Memory: Holocaust Memorials and Meaning* (New Haven, 1993), 3.

4. W. J. T. Mitchell, "Introduction," in *Art in the Public Sphere*, ed. W. J. T. Mitchell (Chicago, 1992), 3.

5. See Lenin's April 1918 "Dekret o pamiatnikakh respubliki," in *Serdtsem slushaia revoliutsiiu: iskusstvo pervykh let oktiabria*, comp. Mikhail German (Leningrad, 1985), 8.

6. John E. Bowlt, "Russian Sculpture and Lenin's Plan of Monumental Propaganda," in *Art and Architecture in the Service of Politics*, ed. Henry A. Millon and Linda Nuchlin (Cambridge, Mass., 1978), 185–88, Sergei Konenkov cited on p. 186.

7. Nina Tumarkin, *The Living and the Dead: The Rise and Fall of the Cult of World War II in Russia* (New York, 1994), p. 47.

8. For their study of dissident artists Renee and Matthew Baigell interviewed forty-seven nonconformist artists of whom only eight were sculptors and five of the eight had emigrated before Gorbachev came to power. Renee Baigell and Matthew Baigell, *Soviet Dissident Artists: Interviews after Perestroika* (New Brunswick, N.J., 1995). For examples of kinetic sculptural works see V. F. Koleichuk, *Kinetizm* (Moscow, 1994).

9. Craig R. Whitney, "Sculptor to Honor Siberia's Victims," *New York Times*, April 17, 1990, A6.

10. For a detailed account of Memorial's formation and activity, see Kathleen E. Smith, *Remembering Stalin's Victims: Popular Memory and the End of the USSR* (Ithaca, 1996).

11. Kirk Savage, "The Politics of Memory: Black Emancipation and the Civil War Monument," in *Commemorations: The Politics of National Identity*, ed. John Gillis (Princeton, 1994), 130–31.

12. Ibid.

13. Evgenii Ass in the roundtable "Memorial zhert-

vam stalinskikh repressii," *Dekorativnoe iskusstvo* 3 (1989), 14.

14. See Young, *The Texture of Memory*; and Jan C. Scruggs and Joel L. Swerdlow, *To Heal a Nation: The Vietnam Veterans Memorial* (New York, 1985), esp. pp. 80–85.

15. Letter from Aleksandr Sheremet'ev to Memorial, no. 535, Interregional Memorial Society Archive [IMSA], Moscow; Nina Braginskaia, "Slava besslav'ia," *Znanie—sila* (January 1991), 14–15; "Vo vsem vinovat . . ." (interview with architect and camp survivor N. M. Shestopal), *Arkhitektura i stroitel'stvo Moskvy* 5 (1989).

16. Letter from I. S. Alyshev to Memorial, no. 410 and letter from V. Makhonin to Memorial, no. 3211, in IMSA. *Dekorativnoe Iskusstvo* 3 (1989), 14; see also, *Dekorativnoe iskusstvo* 4 (1989), 3.

17. He adds on all sorts of relics of Soviet misrule—remnants of a destroyed church, a falling-down peasant hut, an ICBM shell, a tree from Chernobyl, and a scarred armored personnel carrier from Afghanistan! Letter from A. T. Sinitsin to Memorial, no. 901, IMSA.

18. On the interaction of anti-Stalinism and ethnic identity, see Smith, *Remembering*, 112–17.

19. Letter from Georgii Trubetskoi to Memorial, no. 133, IMSA.

20. *Dekorativnoe iskusstvo* 4 (1989), 2; letter from Aleksandr Vasilevskii to Memorial, no. 3135, IMSA.

21. Letter from Andrei Shishkov to Memorial, no. 518, IMSA; letter from Sergei S. Sen'kin to Memorial, no. 2463, IMSA.

22. Letter from I. F. Lizareva to Memorial, no. 1164A, IMSA; *Dekorativnoe iskusstvo* 3 (1989), 13; M. I. Kantor to Memorial, no. 1758, IMSA. On the Tomb of the Unknown Soldier, see Tumarkin, *The Living and the Dead*, 127–28.

23. Aleksandr Rubtsov, "Mezhdu dvumia konkursami," *Dekorativnoe iskusstvo* 3 (1989), 13–14.

24. Braginskaia, "Slava besslav'ia," 14.

25. Letter from N. V. Sokolovskii to Memorial, no. 8696, IMSA.

26. Letter from N. A. Krenke and O. A. Murashko to Memorial, no. 299, IMSA.

27. Letters to Memorial from M. N. Voinova, no. 2268; N. S. Poleshchuk, no. 4698; and Boris V. Loznevoi, no. 8175, all in IMSA.

28. Young, *Texture of Memory*, 32.

29. See for instance, "Pamiatnik zhertvam repressii 'kotlovan,'" *Arkhitektura i stroitel'stvo Moskvy*, no. 3 (1989), 19.

30. Letter from Vladimir Kosulin to Memorial, no. 2225, IMSA.

31. Arsenii Chanyshev, "Ochishchenie cherez vozmedie," *Dekorativnoe iskusstvo* 4 (1989), 2; A. Melik-Pashaev, "Dolgo budet rodina bol'na," ibid., 5–7; "Zakliuchenie obshchestvennoi ekspertizy obshchestva 'Memorial' po pervomu turu konkursa na luchshii proekt pamiatnika ZHERTVAM REPRES-SII," n.d., IMSA.

32. *Dekorativnoe iskusstvo* 3 (1989), 14.

33. "Zakliuchenie."

34. Smith, *Remembering Stalin's Victims*, 174–88.

35. Photographs of Klykov's recent works can be found in the journal *Derzhava*, which he founded in 1994. *Derzhava*, no. 2 (1995) and no. 1 (1996).

36. The monument to Nicholas II ended up in the village of Tainskoe north of Moscow, where the Tsar rested on his journey to his coronation in Moscow. It was later destroyed by a self-proclaimed revolutionary group. Ella Maksimova, "Kamennoe nashestvie tsarei na Moskvu," *Izvestiia*, April 17, 1996, 6; Jose Alaniz, "Monument to Nicholas II Unveiled," *Moscow Tribune*, May 28, 1996, 1, 2. Valeria Korchagina, "Mystery Explosion Dethrones Nicholas," *Moscow Times*, April 2, 1997, 1, 2. On the Zhukov monument, see Irina Panova, "Krasnaia ploshchad' marshala Pobedy," *Pravda*, February 14, 1995, 4.

37. A cluster of military monuments to "forgotten wars" can be found on the grounds of the Church of All Saints in Moscow near the Sokol Metro station and in the adjacent park. The civic council in charge of the ensemble has recently added a monument to Russian military personnel killed in Chechnya. Tat'iana Morozova, "Eto nuzhno zhivym," *Pravda*, June 4, 1996, 4.

38. Irina Bazileva, "Dossier Moscow," *Sculpture* 14, no. 4 (July-August 1995), 12–14; on Luzhkov's efforts to restore parts of Moscow's historic visage, see Kathleen E. Smith, *Mythmaking in the New Russia: Politics and Memory during the Yeltsin Era* (Ithaca, 2002).

39. One of their suggestions was "to supplement the statue of Felix Dzerzhinsky . . . with bronze figures of the courageous individuals who climbed onto its shoulders and wrapped a noose around its neck [on the day that the August coup attempt was defeated]." Vitaly Komar and Alexander Melamid, "Monumental Propaganda," in *Envisioning Eastern Europe: Postcommunist Cultural Studies*, ed. Michael D. Kennedy (Ann Arbor, 1994), 66–72.

40. Kira Dolinina, "Tsar i Chizhik—novye figury v peterburgskom panteone," *Kommersant-DAILY*, July 6, 1996, 16.

41. Savelii Feodorov, "Nevy derzhavnoe techen'e i sfinksov molchalivyi vzgliad," *Smena*, April 29, 1995, 1.

42. Nadezhda Kozhevnikova, "Novye pamiatniki v starom Peterburge," *Nevskoe Vremia*, April 29, 1989, 2.

43. Veniamin Iofe, "Kogda vlast' stavit pamiatniki, ona vospevaet sama sebia," *Nevskoe vremia*, May 16, 1995; letter from E. M. Proshina to Iu. A. Kravtsov, President of the St. Petersburg legislature, n.d. and letter from V. V. Iofe, R. L. Tkachev, and L. P. Beliakov, to Mayor Anatolii Sobchak, n. d., both in St. Petersburg Memorial Society Archives, St. Petersburg.

44. Irina Borotan, "'Maska skorbi' na magadan-skoi sopke," *Segodnia*, June 8, 1996, 12.

45. Zh. Vasil'eva, "Iskusstvo i vlast' nes-ovmestny? . . ." (interview with Ernst Neizvestny), *Literaturnaia gazeta*, August 24, 1994, 7.

46. Whitney, "Sculptor to Honor"; Vasil'eva, "Iskusstvo i vlast'"; Chris Bird, "Mask of Sorrow un-veiled in east," *Moscow Tribune*, June 13, 1996, 5; Irina Shcherbakova, "Stolitsa Kolymskogo kraia," *Itogi*, June 30, 1996, 36.

47. Individuals, local Memorial chapters, and even factories have commemorated their losses in small ways.

48. Iofe, "Kogda vlast' stavit pamiatniki."

Chapter 14 Architecture, Urban Space, and Post-Soviet Russian Identity

1. Kevin Lynch, *The Image of the City* (Cambridge, Mass., 1959), 2.

2. Jonathan Raban, *Soft City* (London, 1988), 242.

3. For further information on Yaroslavl's "typical" economy at the close of the Soviet era, see Andrei Treivish, "Tipichnyi krizis v tipichnom regione," *Vash vybor* (1993), no. 1, 12–13; and Andrei Kuzlmichev and Igor' Shapkin, "Delovoi Iaroslavl'," *Vash vybor* (1993), no. 1, 18–21.

4. The survey, designed by Susan Goodrich Lehmann of Columbia University and the author, was adminis-tered in late 1993 by Tatiana Pavlovna Rumiantseva of the Mayor's Office of Public Opinion Research to a sample of residents of 1400 apartments drawn from the Yaroslavl Housing Registry office. A more complete analysis of the results of this survey may be found in Susan Goodrich Lehmann and Blair A. Ruble, "From 'Soviet' to 'European' Yaroslavl: Changing Neighbor-hood Structure in Post-Soviet Russian Cities," *Urban Studies* 34, no. 7 (1997), 1085–107.

5. Among them being Yaroslavl's award-winning restoration architect, Corresponding-Member of the International Academy of Architects Ivan Borisovich Purishev (I. Vaganova, "Bor'ba za pamiatniki byla nachalom politicheskikh strastei," *Zolotoe kol'tso* (August 15, 1992), 4).

6. I. Bolotseva, "Il'ya Prorok: sud'ba i vremiia," *Severnyi rabochii* (July 25, 1990), 3. *Severnyi rabochii* ceased publication following its enthusiastic support of the failed August 1991 Putsch, only to return later as *Severyni krai*.

7. See, for example, Alla Sevast'ianova, "Nuzhna pravovaia osnova," *Severnyi rabochii* (August 9, 1990), 3; L. Karaseva, "Liudi vo chto-to veriat . . . ," *Severnyi rabochii* (August 9, 1990), 3.

8. Comment during seminar with author, Yaroslavl State University Archeographic Laboratory, April 28, 1992.

9. Sergei Safronov, "V kogo veriat Iaroslavtsy," *Vash vybor* (1993), no. 2, 28–29.

10. I.P. Bolotsova, "Ch'i na rusi ikony?," *Vash vybor* (1993), no. 1, 43.

11. For an account of the city's founding myth, see V. Khrapchenko, "Stranitsy istorii: vstrecha so 'skazaniem o postroenii grada Iaroslavlia,'" *Severnyi krai* (October 23, 1993), 1.

12. Craig R. Whitney, "Yeltsin Appears in Public to Honor a Hero of the Past," *New York Times*, October 24, 1993, 12; "Segodnia—otkrytie pamiatnika Iaroslavu Mudromu," *Severnyi krai* (October 23, 1993), 1.

13. Viacheslav Kozliakov, "Vozvrashchaias' k napechatnomu. Novye demonstratsii ne nuzhny!" *Iunost'* (Yaroslavl) (June 16, 1987), 3.

14. This discussion is based on conversations with Moscow architect Iurii Bocharov in Moscow on June 26, 1997. Mr. Bocharov was a consultant on the chapel's design.

15. Richard S. Wortman, *Scenarios of Power: Myth and Ceremony in Russian monarchy. Volume One: From Peter the Great to the Death of Nicholas I* (Princeton, 1995), 4.

Contributors

MARK BASSIN is a reader in cultural and political geography in the Department of Geography at University College London.

GREG CASTILLO is assistant professor at the University of Miami School of Architecture.

JAMES CRACRAFT is professor of history and University Scholar at the University of Illinois at Chicago.

ROBERT D. CREWS is assistant professor of history at Stanford University.

ANDREW DAY is an independent scholar.

CHRISTOPHER ELY is assistant professor of history at the Harriet L. Wilkes Honors College of Florida Atlantic University.

MICHAEL S. FLIER is Oleksandr Potebnja Professor of Ukrainian Philology and chair of the Department of Slavic Languages and Literatures at Harvard University.

LAUREN M. O'CONNELL is associate professor and chair of the Department of Art History at Ithaca College.

PRISCILLA ROOSEVELT is a research fellow at the Institute for European, Russian, and Eurasian Studies at George Washington University

DANIEL ROWLAND is associate professor of history and director of the Gaines Center for the Humanities at the University of Kentucky.

BLAIR A. RUBLE is director of the Kennan Institute and co-director of Comparative Urban Studies at the Woodrow Wilson Center.

DIMITRI SHVIDKOVSKY is a member of the Russian Academy of Fine Arts, senior research fellow at the Institute of Theory and History of Fine Arts, and professor and head of the Department of History at the Moscow Institute of Architecture.

KATHLEEN E. SMITH is adjunct professor of government at Georgetown University.

RICHARD WORTMAN is Bryce Professor of History at Columbia University.

Index